4/06

The Voyage of the CSS *Shenandoah*

The Voyage of the CSS *Shenandoah*

A Memorable Cruise

WILLIAM C. WHITTLE Jr.

Introduction and annotations by D. Alan Harris and Anne B. Harris

THE UNIVERSITY OF ALABAMA PRESS
Tuscaloosa

Typeface: Minion and Goudy Sans

∞

The paper on which this book is printed meets the minimum requirements of
American National Standard for Information Science—Permanence of Paper for
Printed Library Materials, ANSI Z39.48-1984.

Library of Congress Cataloging-in-Publication Data

Whittle, William C. (William Conway), 1840-1920.
    The voyage of the CSS Shenandoah : a memorable cruise / William C. Whittle, Jr. ;
introduction and annotations by D. Alan Harris and Anne B. Harris.
        p. cm.
    Includes bibliographical references and index.
    ISBN 0-8173-1451-2 (cloth : alk. paper)
    1. Shenandoah (Cruiser) 2. Whittle, William C. (William Conway), 1840-1920—
Diaries. 3. Sailors—Confederate States of America—Diaries. 4. United States—History—
Civil War, 1861-1865—Personal narratives, Confederate. 5. Ocean travel—History—
19th century. 6. Seafaring life—History—19th century. 7. United States—History—Civil
War, 1861-1865—Naval operations, Confederate. I. Harris, D. Alan (David Alan), 1929-
II. Harris, Anne B. (Anne Barber), 1932- III. Title.
    E599.S5W64 2004
    973.7'57—dc22
                                                                      2004019341

To Nell Serpell Whittle and the late B. Randolph Whittle, whose generosity made this work possible.

Contents

Preface   ix

Introduction   1

Prologue: The Cruise of the *Shenandoah*   45

1. Never did a ship go to sea so miserably prepared   53
2. I wish we could catch another Yankee   71
3. This is indeed a Merry Christmas   89
4. The Victorian Government treated us very badly   108
5. Oh, the terrible, terrible monotony   114
6. What an April fool for the poor Yanks   136
7. The news is bad, very bad   152
8. The darkest day of my life   174
9. In the name of honor . . . let us support the Captain   196

Epilogue   212

Appendix. List of Prizes Taken by the CSS *Shenandoah*   215

Notes   217

Bibliographical Essay   243

Index   251

Photographs follow page 131

Preface

The journal kept by William C. Whittle, Jr., on board the Confederate States Steamer *Shenandoah*, resurfaced in the Whittle family in the 1980s when Mary Whittle Chapman was cleaning out her late grandmother's attic. Her parents, B. Randolph Whittle and Nell Serpell Whittle, asked the editors if they wished to edit the journal, and the rest of the family agreed to let us edit it.

William C. Whittle kept the journal in a ledger purchased from "Philip, Son, & Nephew, Manufacturing and Mercantile Stationers, Liverpool," identified from a label inside the volume. This label is the same as one in the Charles E. Lining journal, also kept on board the *Shenandoah*, which is located in the Eleanor Brockenbrough Library of the Museum of the Confederacy in Richmond. The two ledgers were probably purchased just prior to the beginning of the journey in October 1864. The Whittle family donated the Whittle journal to the Museum of the Confederacy, where it joined Lining's journal and the journal of John Thomson Mason, who was a midshipman on the *Shenandoah*.

Whittle's journal consists of 300 pages of daily entries, plus 5 pages on which are written prayers, one by a woman from Baltimore and the other written by Whittle on July 22, 1865. Whittle's daily entries covered almost the entire voyage of the *Shenandoah*. Some pages at the beginning of the ledger were removed, to furnish instructions to the carpenter and others on changes necessary to convert the *Sea King* to the cruiser *Shenandoah*. Another section, covering the period when the *Shenandoah* was in Melbourne, Australia, was removed either at the end of the voyage or later. Whittle also blotted out individual passages, or portions of them. Where it is possible to determine a word or phrase beneath the blot, we have included the words. At times, words or phrases that were obvious from the context have been added in brackets.

We have left the language of the journal as close as possible to the original. We corrected spelling errors by bracketed letters where possible, to avoid the excessive use of the intrusive [*sic*]. Whittle, writing rapidly, sometimes used short words sounding the same as a longer word, such as "threw" in place of "through." These have not been marked, nor have abbreviations whose meanings were clear.

The journal mentions names of crewmen who concealed their identities. For instance, Ernest Mugguffeney, Third Assistant Engineer on the *Shenandoah*, served on the *Alabama* as Fireman Frank Curran. We have endeavored to ascertain the correct names of these individuals, but in many instances this has proved to be impossible.

The family relationships of some of the officers deserve explanation. Sidney Smith Lee, Jr., was the son of Robert E. Lee's brother, Sidney Smith Lee, who served in both the U.S. and Confederate navies. James D. Bullock and Irvine S. Bulloch were half-uncle and uncle to Theodore Roosevelt. The Lee connections might be apparent to readers but not the Bulloch and Roosevelt connection. James T. Mason was related to the Mason family of Virginia and a cousin of Smith Lee.

The editors thank numerous individuals for their assistance in the editing of Whittle's journal. The late Mary Beverley Dabney of Norfolk and the late Professor William M. Dabney of the University of New Mexico allowed us to use family papers in their possession. At the Museum of the Confederacy, Guy Swanson and John M. Coski gave us invaluable assistance. Margaret Cook, Ellen Strong, and Susan Riggs, in the manuscripts section of the Earl Gregg Swem Library at the College of William and Mary, graciously helped in searching the large number of Whittle papers deposited there. At the Southern Historical Collection at the University of North Carolina at Chapel Hill, Carolyn Wallace, David Moltke-Hansen, and the staff were helpful in researching the Whittle and Grimball materials. Peggy Haile McPhillips, now the Norfolk City Historian, assisted us in using the William C. Whittle, Jr., Papers located in the Sargeant Room at the Kirn Memorial Library in Norfolk. Ervin L. Jordan, Jr., helped in the research in the Whittle materials in the Library of the University of Virginia. The staffs of the Duke University Library, the Chicago Historical Association, the South Carolina Historical Association, the Virginia Historical Society, and the North Carolina Department of Archives and History were generous in aiding us in our search for sometimes fugitive material. Undoubtedly we have left out someone who should have been thanked. We apologize and blame it on the number of years the research has taken.

It is also necessary to thank several colleagues at Old Dominion University for their assistance, especially Chandra DeSilva, chair of the Department of History, for generously allowing retirees to use the facilities of the department, and Cynthia Duncan and the staff of the Perry Library. D. B. Hanna, Planetarium Director, helped interpret faded writing by telling us just what navigational stars and constellations Whittle was looking at in the South Pacific. Two oceanographers, Ronald Johnson and Gregg Cutter, generously answered questions asked by the editors. Tommy Crew and Gregg Cino, at the Mariners' Museum in Newport News, tracked down obscure references in the museum library. The anonymous reviewers selected by the University of Alabama Press, who first evaluated the manuscript, deserve our thanks for their suggestions. The manuscript was formatted by Elaine Dawson of Old Dominion University. We must add, however, that any errors or omissions are our responsibility.

The Voyage of the CSS *Shenandoah*

Introduction

During the Civil War Centennial, Philip Van Doren Stern examined the literature of the war and found it wanting. "Thousands of volumes of Civil War literature deal with land battles," he complained, "whereas all the books about its naval affairs—including a complete set of *Official Records*—can easily be shelved against the wall of a small room."[1] It is not surprising that historians neglected the navies. For most Americans the Civil War was a land war. Armies outnumbered navies by hundreds of thousands of men, and generals and their brigades were more visible than captains and their crews, whose ships often were at sea, sometimes on the other side of the world.

The first histories and memoirs published after 1865 reflected the American public's perception of the war. Their authors, more of whom had served in the armies than the navies, gave naval affairs short shrift. Only a few of their successors have tried to remedy the disparity that Stern deplored.

Stern was one of the historians who set out to redress the balance. His research convinced him that the navies played a major role in determining the outcome of the Civil War. The records of the Confederate navy, which he considered "a miracle of improvisation" and therefore "far more interesting than . . . its Northern rival," also convinced him of the need to rescue the Confederacy's naval statesmen and officers from undeserved obscurity. James Dunwody Bulloch, the South's chief naval agent and head of its secret service in Europe, was, in Stern's estimation, "worth far more to the Confederacy than most of its best-known generals, but . . . has never been given enough credit for what he did." He declared that Bulloch and his fellow officers should not be forgotten for serving a lost cause—rather, they should be remembered for their ingenuity and resourcefulness in promoting its interests.[2]

One of the most successful products of Bulloch's ability and imagination was the Confederate cruiser *Shenandoah*. The last of a group of commerce raiders that he procured and deployed to prey on American merchant ships, the *Shenandoah* was ordered to the Pacific to "greatly damage and disperse" the Yankee whaling fleet that frequented those waters.[3] Her epic and successful pursuit of her quarry, which compared favorably with the exploits of the more celebrated *Alabama* and *Florida,* was not as familiar to Americans because it coincided with the war's end and the Confederacy's downfall. It was, however, one of the best documented naval expeditions of the Civil War.

The official records of the Civil War contain excerpts from the ship's log and her captain's notes on the cruise, a list of her prizes, and correspondence of Confederate, Union, and British officials and diplomats pertaining to her voyage. Newspapers and pictorial journals around the world reported the *Shenandoah*'s depredations. Volumes of testimony concerning the cruiser's activities appeared in the cases of the British and American governments presented to the international court that arbitrated the "*Alabama* claims" at Geneva in 1872. Some of these records reflect their authors' biases, some contain inaccuracies, and thus they tell us only part of the cruiser's story. The rest of the story comes from the journals some of her officers kept. It is their descriptions of their experiences on board the *Shenandoah* that make the voyage come alive.

A number of the *Shenandoah*'s officers kept copies of the ship's log and at least five of them—Passed Midshipman John Thomson Mason, Lieutenants William Conway Whittle, Jr., Francis Thornton Chew, and John Grimball, and Surgeon Charles Edward Lining—also kept detailed journals of the entire voyage. The journals reflect the ingenuity and resourcefulness that Stern admired and that enabled them to convert an inadequately supplied, shorthanded merchant vessel into an efficient and successful warship. From the beginning of the voyage they worked side by side with the crew so the cruiser could get on with its mission of destroying Yankee ships.

The *Shenandoah*'s officers had few scruples about preying on their enemy's unarmed merchantmen and whalers. "It is to me a painful sight to see a fine vessel wantonly destroyed," William Whittle confided to his journal, "but I hope to witness an immense number of painful sights of the same kind." And, "I have rarely seen anything which is more beautifully grand than a ship burning at sea," he wrote after he had helped fire the whaler *Edward* in the South Atlantic. "Oh, it's a grand sight."[4] The pens of Whittle and his fellow officers transformed their prizes from statistics to real ships that represented victories for their cause and furnished them the additional crewmen and supplies they needed to carry on their war.

If the *Shenandoah*'s young officers complained that the intervals between prizes were monotonous, their journals indicate that the daily routine aboard a Confederate warship kept them busy. Whittle, who was the executive officer, was responsible for directing the crew's work and maintaining discipline on the ship. Lining commented on his duties as the ship's doctor. The cruiser's stops in Australia and at Ascension Island (today known as Ponape) introduced them to new people and exotic places. However, for most of their thirteen months at sea they had to create their own diversions, which they recorded in their journals as a part of their descriptions of shipboard life. Theirs was, William Whittle declared, "a memorable cruise," and no one told the story of the *Shenandoah* and her men better than he did.

William Conway Whittle, Jr., was a member of the American naval aristocracy.[5] The great-grandson of James Whittle, "an Irish gentleman of fortune," and Colonel William Davies, aide to George Washington during the American Revolution, he could also count among his forebears Pocahontas and the Reverend Samuel Davies, president of Princeton College from 1759 to 1761. His grandfather, Fortescue Whittle, a young Irish nationalist involved in the Rebellion of 1798, emigrated to Virginia soon after the British suppressed the uprising. He went into business with his older brother Conway in Norfolk, Virginia, and there he married Mary Ann Davies.

By the time William Whittle was born in Norfolk on 16 January 1840, Norfolk was "the center of naval society" in the United States, and his family had become part of the American naval establishment. His father, William Conway Whittle, Sr., had begun his career as a naval officer in 1820. His father's cousin, Conway Whittle, served as a midshipman for a time, and Conway's two sisters married naval officers. His uncle, John Samuel Whittle, a surgeon in the United States Navy, died of yellow fever off the coast of Brazil in 1850. Elizabeth Beverley Sinclair, his mother, was the daughter of Commodore Arthur Sinclair, and her brothers Arthur, William, and George served in the United States Navy and later in the Confederate navy, as did Whittle's father.[6]

We know little about Whittle's life before he entered the Naval Academy. His family seems to have spent as much time in his father's country place, "Woodstock," in Mecklenburg County, Virginia, as in Norfolk, and he and his brothers and sisters were educated at home.[7] His father, whose assignments took him away for months at a time, served on various ships, including the ship-of-the-line *Ohio* off Tuxpan during the Mexican War and the sloop *Decatur* on the Newfoundland Banks. He was on the sloop *Dale* off the coast of Africa when his son William received his appointment to Annapolis in 1854.[8]

By the time Whittle became an acting midshipman in the fall of 1854, the nine-year-old Naval School at Annapolis had become the United States Naval Academy. A series of dedicated superintendents, especially Commanders

Cornelius K. Stribling and Louis Malesherbes Goldsborough, had quadrupled the size of the former nine-acre army post. During Stribling's term the academy got a new mess hall, recitation hall, laboratory-armory, chapel, observatory, and dormitories; Goldsborough's tenure provided the dormitories with amenities such as steam heat and gas lamps. Stribling presided over the school's 1851 academic reorganization, which created a four-year course of study with summer cruises. The academic reorganization, along with the act of 1852 which gave Congress—the House of Representatives—control of appointing midshipmen, ultimately made Annapolis the principal source of officers for the navy.[9]

Whittle's classmate George Dewey recalled that appointments to the Naval Academy "were due entirely to the political favor of representatives in Congress," but family connections also helped. William C. Whittle, Jr., had both. He was one of the "one in every ten" appointees whose father was a naval officer, and his father's cousin, Conway Whittle, was a prominent Norfolk lawyer and collector of customs in that city for years.[10]

An appointment to Annapolis, however, did not guarantee anyone a diploma and a midshipman's warrant, or even admission to the school. The high attrition rate in Whittle's class was typical of that of other classes in the 1850s. Of the eighty-nine young men who received appointments to Annapolis in 1854, fifty-seven passed the entrance examinations.[11] According to the academy's Board of Examiners, the appointees' failures were due not to the difficulty of the entrance examinations but to their youth and educational deficiencies. The board repeatedly asked the secretary of the Navy to raise the minimum age for admission to fifteen and recommended raising academic requirements for entrance.[12]

While academic failure accounted for most student departures, dismissals for violating academy regulations and resignations for other reasons, such as illness, also took their toll of cadets. The graduates of the 1850s did not consider the academy's course of study difficult, but some agreed with George Dewey's complaint that rote learning made their education "an endless grind." Of the thirty-five members of Whittle's class who survived their plebe year, fifteen graduated in 1858.[13]

Whittle, despite a bout with whooping cough during his plebe year and the deaths of his mother and elder brother Arthur during Norfolk's yellow fever epidemic in the summer of 1855, maintained satisfactory grades in his courses and "the sincere respect and good wishes of every Officer and Professor." In 1858, at the end of his course of study—which included English, mathematics, French, Spanish, history, and philosophy as well as naval science and tactics and two summer cruises—he graduated in a ceremony in the academy chapel. Superintendent George S. Blake described him as "a most promising young officer."[14]

The navy required Whittle and his classmates to spend two years at sea after graduating from the academy. The Board of Examiners then evaluated each midshipman's seamanship, added that score to his academic average, and determined his order of rank—his position on the promotion list and in the naval hierarchy—in the Navy Register.[15] Whittle served on the *Colorado*, a first-class steam frigate, in the Caribbean; on the *Roanoke*, flagship of the Home Squadron, off Colombia; and on the sloop-of-war *Preble* in the Gulf Blockading Squadron off Mexico.[16]

Whittle's performance at sea justified Blake's expectations. His service on the *Roanoke* earned him a commendation "for handsome service to our merchant vessels in distress during an unprecedented 'Norther' at Aspinwall" (present-day Colón, Panama). His duty aboard the *Preble*, the former academy training ship on which he had made both of his summer cruises, was more eventful. It enabled him to take part in his "first fight" in March 1860, in which the *Preble*, the *Savannah*, and the *Saratoga* intercepted two Cuban ships bringing supplies to rebels who were attempting to overthrow Mexican president Benito Juarez. For his part in the action he received more commendations from his superiors.[17] After the *Preble* escorted her Cuban prizes to New Orleans, she sailed for the Navy yard at Warrington, Florida, near Pensacola. There "Willie" Whittle served his remaining sea duty in a congenial society that included Lieutenants John McIntosh Kell, Robert Dabney Minor, and John Newland Maffit, who became his lifelong friends.[18]

Whittle returned to Annapolis for his final examination in December 1860. He received the highest grade in his class in seamanship. As George Dewey's biographer noted, Whittle's grade kept the future admiral from being "at the head of all midshipmen" in his class, and it raised Whittle's ranking from tenth to ninth. He was warranted a passed midshipman on 28 January 1861 and a master in line of promotion on 28 February 1861. Less than two months later Virginia's secession cost the United States Navy a promising line officer.[19]

After the Navy accepted his resignation in May 1861, Whittle served briefly as a lieutenant in the Virginia navy. He became an acting master in the Confederate navy in June 1861 and lieutenant in February 1862. In October 1861, he left the York River batteries for duty aboard the CSS *Nashville*, the first Confederate warship to visit England.[20]

The *Nashville*'s four-month cruise showed the Confederate flag abroad and indicated that the Union blockade was deficient. The *Trent* affair—the seizure of Confederate commissioners James Mason and John Slidell from the British steamer *Trent* by Union Navy Captain Charles Wilkes of the USS *San Jacinto*—which occurred during the *Nashville's* visit to England, increased British pro-Southern opinion. British authorities accorded the *Nashville* every courtesy, and when she left Southampton they enforced the queen's neutrality proclamation and international law so as to prevent the USS *Tuscarora* from capturing the Confederate ship. Having seized and burned two Yankee merchantmen on her way home, the *Nashville* masqueraded as a U.S. mail steamer to get past the blockaders off Beaufort and into Morehead City, North Carolina. Captain Robert B. Pegram, learning that the Confederate government had sold the ship to John Fraser & Company, removed all Confederate property from her and left Third Lieutenant Whittle with a skeleton crew to take her to her new owners in Charleston.

Whittle, aware that General Ambrose Burnside's forces were closing in on Morehead City, decided to run the blockade. Shortly after sunset on 17 March 1862, he got up full steam and ran toward the Union vessels guarding the narrow channel at the bar. Aiming the *Nashville* at the side of one of the enemy ships, whose captain gave him the right of way, he cleared the bar and escaped without damage from the blockaders' guns. A sizeable Union squadron off Charleston prompted him to go on to Georgetown, where he found that the blockaders usually stationed there had moved up the coast. After he took the ship into Georgetown, he returned by train to Richmond to confer with the secretary of the navy. Mallory sent him back to Charleston to transfer the *Nashville* to her new owners, who got her out of Georgetown before the blockaders returned. Northern newspapers demanded that Lincoln fire Secretary of the Navy Gideon Welles for his "notorious incompetence," and a Currier and Ives cartoon depicted the blockading ships as inept tubs in the *Nashville's* wake. Small wonder that the Union's assistant secretary of the navy, Gustavus Vasa Fox, described the cruiser's exploits as "a Bull Run to the Navy."[21]

Within a month after he left the *Nashville,* Whittle was ordered to New Orleans where his father, Commodore William C. Whittle, was commandant of the naval station. When the lieutenant went aboard the ironclad *Louisiana*, the Confederate forces were preparing to meet Flag Officer David G. Farragut's attack on New Orleans. As the Union squadrons moved upriver, the *Louisiana* was still unfinished: her propeller machinery was not completed, her railroad iron plating was not all laid, and her guns were not mounted. A flaw in the ship's design—two "miserably conceived" paddle wheels, placed one behind the other in a well in the middle of the ship—made it impossible to steer the vessel. The *Louisiana* had to be towed downriver to a position above Fort St. Philip and tied to the east bank to act as a floating battery.[22]

After the battle began, mechanics continued to work on the ship's machinery and mounted her guns. Whittle, third lieutenant in charge of the bow guns, noted that the poorly made portholes did not permit his crew to train the guns laterally or elevate or depress them. Nevertheless, the *Louisiana* "used her guns against all of the Federal fleet as they passed, and every man fought bravely and well," Whittle recalled.[23] But bravery did not compensate for defective gun ports, and the immobile ironclad did not sink any of Farragut's ships.

Although her armor plate enabled the *Louisiana* to survive the battle, Commodore John K. Mitchell, commander of the Confederate naval defenses at New Orleans, did not want the ship to fall into enemy hands. The divided Confederate command at New Orleans made the army and navy independent of each other. Since Mitchell was not bound by General Johnson K. Duncan's decision to surrender the forts, the commodore and the *Louisiana*'s officers decided to burn her.

After Mitchell transferred the crew to the tenders *Landis* and *W. Burton,* he had five of the officers, including Whittle, fire the ironclad. Because Mitchell was not certain how effectively they had drowned the charges in the guns and magazine, and because he knew that the ropes that secured the ship to the banks might burn, leaving her free to float out among the Union ships, he sent Whittle to inform Union Commodore David Dixon Porter that they had fired her. As Whittle's boat approached Porter's ship, the fire reached the 10,000 pounds of powder in the *Louisiana*'s magazine and she exploded, pieces of her railroad iron armament flying through the air like arrows. Whittle delivered Mitchell's message to Porter and then returned to the *Landis,* which surrendered to Porter. Whittle and the other officers on the tender were sent on the USS *Rhode Island* to Fort Warren in Boston, where they were held until they were exchanged at Aiken's Landing, Virginia, on 5 August 1862.[24]

Less than a month after he was exchanged, Whittle found himself on another Southern river assigned to another unfinished ship that became a floating gun platform. Unlike his duty on the *Louisiana,* however, which put him in the thick of the fighting, service on the *Chattahoochee* took him to an isolated boat landing 175 miles south of Columbus, Georgia.[25] At Saffold he joined an experienced and able group of officers commanded by Lieutenant Catesby ap Roger Jones, who had won renown as ordnance and executive officer on the *Virginia* in her duel with the *Monitor.* Aware that the steam gunboat was designed for blockade running as well as river defense, Jones and his men were anxious to see her completed. But manpower shortages, design flaws, and problems created by the Confederacy's divided command thwarted their efforts to get her afloat.

Work on the *Chattahoochee* was more than six months in arrears when Whittle got to Saffold.[26] In a letter to Robert Minor, who was in the Bureau of Ordnance in Richmond, he described her as "a pretty vessel," but her deck design made him doubt that she would be fast enough to run the blockade. He was more concerned about the crew's health; most of them were down with malaria. "This will never do," he wrote, "for before the ship will be ready sailor work has to be done, and sailor work can only be done by Jack." He concluded that "she will not be ready for a long time."[27]

A chronic manpower shortage and the Confederacy's inefficient supply system, both of which slowed work on the *Chattahoochee,* were recurring themes in Whittle's letters to Minor during the fall of 1862. Despite the captain's repeated applications to Richmond, the ship did not have enough officers or sailors. As more men got "the shakes," he complained to Minor that Richmond's failure to send the ship a surgeon was "outrageous, when so many Surgeons are doing nothing," and he begged Minor to get one sent.[28] By the time Dr. Marcellus Ford reported for duty in October 1862, only two sailors and three officers—Whittle, Jones, and Engineer John W. Tynan—were fit to work.[29] Whittle also felt that Richmond was ignoring Jones's requisitions for supplies. He and the captain repeatedly asked Minor to intercede with Commodore French Forrest, head of the Office of Orders and Detail, and other officials who might expedite shipments of things they needed, such as a gunner's quadrant, ammunition for the ship's guns, coal, and the whiskey in which they mixed Peruvian bark as a remedy for malaria.[30]

Whittle's letters to Minor also reflected his frustration at being stuck in an isolated duty station. Despite infrequent mails he managed to keep up with some of their friends. He reported that he had visited the family of John Kell, the *Alabama*'s executive officer, and that he had heard about John Maffitt's getting command of the *Florida.* That he bombarded Minor with questions about other friends, his place on the promotion list, the status of the Court of Inquiry on the *Louisiana,* where Lee's army was, and the location of the Union's South Atlantic squadron indicated that he felt cut off from Richmond and left out of the war.[31]

As Christmas neared, the *Chattahoochee* still was not finished. The people in the river valley, and the 100,000 bales of cotton they had stored there, had no defense against the Yankee blockaders on the Gulf coast. Their appeal to the secretary of war for help resulted in a new plan for defending the river valley: the army and Confederate engineers began to build obstructions in the river and fortifications to protect them above Apalachicola. In January 1863, the *Chattahoochee* was ordered downriver to guard the army's project. On the day before she left, her engines failed and she had to be towed south. Two hours after she left Saffold she ran aground, smashed her rudder and developed a serious leak. When she arrived at Chattahoochee, her officers realized they were stuck on a floating battery.[32] A number of them, including Whittle, applied for transfers. By March 1863, Whittle was on his way to Europe.[33]

When Whittle arrived in England in April 1863, detailed by Secretary Mallory for duty on one of the Confederate ironclads under construction there, he was assigned to serve under Commander James D. Bulloch, the Confederacy's senior naval officer in Europe. Bulloch, who had met Whittle when the *Nashville* stopped in Bermuda on her way to England in 1861, and who had been trying ever since to get the lieutenant appointed to his staff, employed him as a courier in England and France. On 10 July the commander sent him back to Richmond by way of Halifax and Bermuda with dispatches for Mallory and Secretary of State Judah P. Benjamin. Although concern that Whittle might "be forced to destroy the dispatches" en route prompted Bulloch and John Slidell, Confederate commissioner to France, to entrust the lieutenant with verbal as well as written messages, Whittle got to Richmond without incident and delivered the dispatches on 20 August.[34]

Two weeks later Whittle and Captain Samuel Barron, whom Mallory ordered to Europe to take command of the ironclads when they were ready for sea, left Wilmington for Bermuda on the British steamer *Cornubia*.[35] During a ten-day layover in St. George's, Whittle renewed acquaintances from his *Nashville* days and, like many fellow officers who visited neutral ports, busied himself shopping for blockaded family and friends. He noted in his diary that when the *Cornubia* returned to Wilmington, she carried a box containing hard-to-get items: four pairs of gloves and four pairs of gaiters for his "sweet little cousin Matoaka," a dozen toothbrushes, a sponge and six cakes of soap for two Whittle aunts, a pair of shoes for a Dr. Skipwith, and 28 pounds of shot and 49 yards of calico for a Dr. Harrison.[36] The *Cornubia* also took back letters to his father and his uncle, Captain Arthur Sinclair, both of whom were at home "awaiting orders," and to his "dear little Pattie K——," a young lady with whom, although he had seen her only once, he declared he was in love.[37]

Whittle was an inveterate letter writer. A number of the entries in his small diary were drafts of letters to younger brothers and sisters at "The Anchorage," his father's place near Buchanan in Botetourt County, Virginia.[38] Some described his passage to England on the British steamer *Florida*. The stormy voyage did not bother him, but he wrote to his sister Jennie that the "amiable" and "agreeable" Barron suffered from "chills" for most of the trip. A letter to his brother Stafford from Liverpool described a shopping expedition. "After breakfast . . . the first thing [we did] was to put ourselves in tall black hats. . . . Can you imagine a red headed brother in a 'bull teaser'?" he asked the fourteen-year-old. "He looks much better than you can realize." He also purchased for his Uncle Arthur "a set of lace and buttons" and for his Uncle William Sinclair "a set of buttons and a . . . syringe for the subcutaneous injection of morphine [that] . . . may save the life of my dear Aunt Lucy."[39]

From Liverpool, Whittle and Barron went to Glasgow to deliver despatches from Mallory to Lieutenant James H. North and Whittle's uncle, Commander George Terry Sinclair, and then to Paris. After the British government's decision to seize the ironclads that Barron was supposed to command, he became the Confederacy's flag officer in Europe, commander-in-chief of the officers and men awaiting assignment to ships, and Whittle was ordered to his staff. Barron set up headquarters in Paris at 172 Rue de Rivoli, where Whittle and several other officers, including Surgeon Charles E. Lining, also had rooms,[40] and the commodore and his flag lieutenant became part of the sizeable Confederate colony in France and England.

Whittle seems to have enjoyed Paris. The families of European supporters of the Confederacy—such as English financier James Spence and German-born banker Emile Erlanger—and expatriate Southerners like Virginia-born James T. Soutter, as well as those of Confederate officers and agents who belonged to the colony, opened their homes to the newcomers and directed their sightseeing. Whittle's last entry in his 1863 diary described an excursion to Versailles in the company of Spence and his three daughters, two of Soutter's daughters, Barron, Bulloch, and Lining. Louis XIV's palace did not impress Whittle as much as the charms of Louisa Spence. She had "the gentleness of a dove and the beauty of an angel," he wrote. "Where is my heart? If I do not fall in love with this sweet creature, I shall think it gone." Fellow Virginian Douglas French Forrest, paymaster of the *Rappahannock,* observing "Miss Lou" at a party they both attended at the Soutters' home, agreed with Whittle that she was "a beauty."[41]

By the summer of 1864, the pleasures of Paris had begun to pall for Whittle, Forrest, and most of the other Confederate officers who were there "awaiting orders" to ships. In June, Whittle and Lieutenant John Grimball, an Annapolis classmate who had been in France for a year, went to Cherbourg on learning that Semmes, who had brought the *Alabama* in for repairs, had challenged the USS *Kearsarge.* When French police and Yankee spies prevented their going aboard the Confederate cruiser, Whittle sent a note volunteering their services to his old friend John Kell, the *Alabama's* first lieutenant. Kell replied that they should not try to come aboard, and they returned to Paris.[42]

The forced sale of the *Georgia* in May, the loss of the *Alabama* on 19 June, and Bulloch's difficulties in procuring ships were disheartening. The would-be cruiser *Rappahannock* was a visible reminder of their plight. Sent into Calais for repairs immediately after she was purchased in November 1863, she had been sitting there ever since, her departure blocked by the French government and by the presence of U.S. warships in the English Channel. During June and July, as Whittle traveled back and forth between Paris and Calais with Barron, or with dispatches from Barron to the *Rappahannock's* captain, Charles M. Fauntleroy, the Confederacy's hopes of getting her afloat dwindled. After a conference with Fauntleroy and Bulloch on 1 August, Barron ordered the captain to pay off and discharge the crew preparatory to selling the ship.[43] On the same day, Lieutenant Francis Thornton Chew, who had spent a year "awaiting orders" and studying French in Lyon because living in Lyon was cheaper than living in Paris, wrote in his journal, "It seems that our mission in Europe is fruitless." He felt that his year of inactivity had not helped him to become a competent naval officer. "I am all theory and but very little practice," he concluded, and declared that it was "high time" he left France for home.[44]

Captain James Bulloch did not share Chew's conviction that it was time to pull out of Europe. After the Confederate government obtained control over all blockade runners earlier that year, Bulloch had begun to buy and build ships that could slip through the Union blockade. Once they had made a couple of trips carrying supplies to Southern ports, he planned to convert them to gunboats that could prey on Federal blockading squadrons. As soon as he learned that the *Alabama* had been sunk, he began looking for a replacement for her, so that the Confederate navy could continue its offensive against enemy merchantmen on the high seas. By August 1864, he had found the *Alabama*'s successor.

A year earlier Bulloch and Lieutenant Robert R. Carter had seen in Glasgow a magnificent merchant ship built to British government specifications for transporting troops.[45] The *Sea King*, about to make her maiden voyage to the Indian Ocean, was not for sale at that time, but Bulloch seems to have kept up with her; on 27 August 1864 he advised Barron that a ship he was "very anxious to get hold of" was about to return to England and he hoped to buy her.

When Bulloch had begun putting together a new Confederate fleet, he and Barron had decided to start sending officers home—they wanted it to appear to the United States, France, and Britain "that we have given up all intention of continuing naval operations on this side of the Atlantic." Once the purchase of a new cruiser was in the offing, however, Bulloch notified Barron that he would need several officers who "are willing to work, and who are capable of making much of small means." With money from the sale of the Laird rams and the assistance of an English friend, Richard Wright, who helped him deceive Union spies, he bought the *Sea King*.[46]

On the same day that Bulloch informed Mallory of his purchase, Barron noted in his diary that there were, besides Bulloch and himself, twenty-seven Confederate naval officers in Europe. He marked seven of the names to order to Bulloch's new ship. He agreed with Bulloch that Whittle, one of the seven, should be appointed executive officer of the new cruiser. The captain's name was not among the seven because Barron and Bulloch were still negotiating his selection. Bulloch wanted Lieutenant William R. Murdaugh, but the Department of Ordnance refused to release Murdaugh, and Barron instead sent Lieutenant James Iredell Waddell to Liverpool for "prospective duty." Bulloch, who was trying to assemble the cruiser's officers without attracting the enemy's attention, was annoyed and said so. "If you mean to detach Lt. W——for the command," he admonished Barron, "please order him specifically to report to me, and I will then take him entirely into my confidence." On 14 September, Barron ordered Lieutenants Waddell, Whittle, and John Grimball to report to Bulloch, and on 30 September he ordered other officers, including Lieutenants Chew and Dabney Scales, to Liverpool.[47]

By 3 October 1864, Bulloch had at hand his officers, his ship, and a tender, the *Laurel*—commanded by Lieutenant John F. Ramsay, Confederate naval officer and licensed British merchant captain—in which he could send the officers and crew to board the *Sea King*. On 6 October, Bulloch initiated intricate maneuvers resembling those he had devised to get the *Florida* and the *Alabama* to sea. He ordered Whittle to Wood's Hotel in London. There, in a manner worthy of a Victorian melodrama, the lieutenant registered as Mr. W. C. Brown and met Richard Wright, who introduced him to the *Sea King*'s captain, Peter Suther Corbett. On 8 October, "Mr. Brown" boarded the ship, which sailed down the Thames toward her rendezvous with the *Laurel* at Madeira.[48] Meanwhile, Waddell, the rest of his officers, and his crew, who were living under assumed names in hotels and boardinghouses in Liverpool, packed their trunks in boxes "so as to make them look like cases of goods." These boxes of merchandise and the guns and stores labeled "machinery" were loaded on the *Laurel* on 8 October; the officers and men went aboard the tender that evening and sailed for Madeira the next morning.[49]

After the *Laurel* arrived in Funchal on 14 October, she had to wait three days for the *Sea King* to appear. Bulloch, concerned that someone in Funchal might discover the "direction or intent" of their voyage and report it back to Europe, instructed Waddell to keep his officers and men on board. Only Ramsay, who had to deal with customs officials and with coaling the ship, and Waddell, who had to draw £1,000 on Fraser, Trenholm & Company, went on shore. The rest, like Chew, were forced to admire Funchal's "places and the mountains in the back ground" from the *Laurel*'s deck. When the *Sea King* appeared at the entrance to the harbor on the morning of 18 October, however, the secret was out: on sighting the *Sea King*, sailors in small boats around the *Laurel* began shouting, "Otro Alabama!" That afternoon the *Laurel* rendezvoused with the *Sea King* in the lee of Las Desertas, a rocky island a few miles from Funchal; the two ships anchored and the crews transferred the arms, ammunition, and supplies from the *Laurel* to the *Sea King*.[50]

In addition to supplies, Waddell needed sailors. Bulloch had sent out on the *Laurel* a group of experienced men—eight had enlisted before the ship left Liverpool, and at least six had served on the *Alabama*—to form the nucleus of the *Shenandoah's* crew. He also had instructed Corbett to ship young unmarried men who would be inclined to "a roving cruise." When Corbett and Ramsay mustered their men, however, and Waddell urged them to sign on the Confederate cruiser, the response was disappointing. Plying them with liquor, offering to double their wages and to pay each a £15 bounty, and setting a bucket of gold sovereigns on the deck to tempt them induced only twenty-three men to join the raider's crew. Ramsay and Corbett took the men who refused to enlist back to the *Laurel,* and, after Waddell had christened the cruiser *Shenandoah* and hoisted the Confederate flag, the two ships left the Madeiras.[51]

With but 46 officers and men on a ship that should have had a crew of 150, Waddell was reluctant to put to sea. Both Corbett and Ramsay had advised him to take the ship to Teneriffe and ask Bulloch to send more men to him there, but when Waddell suggested that plan to his executive officer, Whittle was appalled. Recalling the plight of the *Rappahannock,* he was sure that a similar fate would befall the *Shenandoah* in Teneriffe, and he begged the captain to consult the cruiser's other officers. With Whittle they voted to steer clear of ports and "take the ocean."[52]

They were, Whittle observed, "the youngest set of officers who ever went to sea." The captain, who was the oldest—forty-one during the voyage—had served in the United States Navy for twenty-one years before he resigned his commission in 1861. He was one of a group of midshipmen warranted in 1841, who were ordered to the newly established naval academy in 1847 for a year's instruction prior to taking their lieutenant's examination. While he passed the examination and received a certificate of graduation in 1848, the captain never considered himself an academy alumnus. Although he served briefly at the Washington Naval Observatory and taught a few navigation classes at the academy in the 1850s, he spent most of his career on ships in the United States Navy's Gulf, South Atlantic, Mediterranean, and Far Eastern Squadrons. His experience had convinced him that learning his profession "at sea, on shipboard, while a boy" was superior to learning seamanship from books. This conviction helps to explain his reluctance to embark on a cruise with young officers whom he did not consider "practical seamen."[53]

As one historian observed, Waddell's disapproval of the navy's new method of training officers created a generation gap between him and his officers, so that the captain "often underestimated the experience and intellectual capacity of his 20-year-olds."[54] Whittle and Grimball, both graduates of the academy's four-year course, also had completed the academy's required two years at sea, Whittle in the Gulf Squadron, Grimball in the Mediterranean. Whittle and Master Irvine S. Bulloch had served on the cruiser *Nashville* and Paymaster William Breedlove Smith on the cruiser *Sumter;* Bulloch, Smith, and Chief Engineer Matthew O'Brien on the *Alabama;* Sidney Smith Lee, Jr., who before the war had sailed on merchant ships, on the cruisers *Georgia* and *Rappahannock.* All of the officers had seen action in Southern harbors and rivers. Frank Chew was on the *Resolute* and Dabney Scales on the *Savannah* at the Battle of Port Royal, South Carolina. At the Battle of New Orleans, Chew and Lee were aboard the *Louisiana* with Whittle, and Grimball and Scales were on the ironclad *Arkansas* at Vicksburg. Grimball went from Vicksburg to Mobile, where he was on the ironclad *Baltic.* Whittle served on the steamer *Chattahoochee* in south Georgia, and Chew and Lee served respectively on the ironclad *Palmetto State* in Charleston and the ram *Atlanta* at Savannah. Midshipmen Orris A. Browne and John Thomson Mason were on the Confederate school ship *Patrick Henry,* which was part of the James River Squadron, as were the gunboats *Hampton* and *Nansemond,* on which Mason and Bulloch served. Dr. Charles E. Lining was also on the James River in 1862, where he watched the James River Squadron repulse the Federal fleet. Lining, who was a surgeon on the USS *Cyane* in the Gulf and the Pacific before 1861, had served on the upper Mississippi and on the steamers *New Orleans* and *Pontchartrain* before he was ordered to the Richmond Station and then to France. At thirty-one he was the oldest officer in the wardroom.

If the *Shenandoah's* officers were young and inexperienced, they were, as Bulloch had hoped, "willing to work, and . . . capable of making much of small means." From the time they began to transfer supplies to the cruiser, they toiled cheerfully alongside the crew. "I never worked so hard in all my life," Lining wrote, "& as for 'Smith Lee' he was a perfect team in himself." In contrast to the enlisted men, most of whom were not Americans, much less Southerners, and who signed on for the voyage because the Confederates promised them high pay, the commissioned officers were all Southerners and dedicated to the Confederate cause. Although some of their families owned slaves, their racial attitudes seem to have been like those of most American white Anglo-Saxon Protestants of their time. "The issue [of the war] was not the liberation of the slaves," John Grimball stated, "but the enforcement of a union, and only when the South proceeded to withdraw, and when the North insisted upon blocking the way, did the parties come to blows." They supported states' rights. Once the states had seceded, they could not, as Waddell had written in his resignation from the United States Navy, bear arms against the South or their people. They were professional line and staff officers, and they had waited a long time for orders to a ship that would enable them to strike a blow for the Confederacy.[55]

To these men Bulloch entrusted a ship in "good and sound condition" provided with "ample stores . . . for a voyage of fifteen months." Noting, however, that her equipment was "incomplete," his orders advised Waddell that they would have to "draw supplies as much as possible from the prizes" they took. The conduct of the cruise he left to "the judgment and discretion" of the *Shenandoah*'s captain.[56] Owing to Confederate naval usage, which followed United States naval tradition, much of the responsibility for organizing the ship and ordering the officers and crew devolved on his executive officer, William Whittle. Herman Melville had observed twenty-odd years earlier in *White-Jacket*, his autobiographical novel of life aboard an American man-of-war, that a ship was "a state in itself." The captain was "its king" and the executive officer was "by the captain . . . held responsible for every thing." Besides presiding over the officers' wardroom, the executive officer was "an excellent seaman, prompt, loud, and to the point . . . a good disciplinarian, and . . . an energetic man." At the captain's behest, he was "supposed to be omnipresent; down in the hold, and up aloft, at one and the same time."[57] Melville might have been describing the *Shenandoah*'s captain and executive officer.

Whittle was so busy the first week of the voyage that he had no time to write more than daily log entries—latitude, longitude, course, and wind direction—in his journal. It was up to him, as executive officer, to supervise the work of bringing order out of the *Shenandoah*'s "disordered condition." She had had such a short time to take on her supplies from the *Laurel* that when she left the Madeiras, her guns, gun carriages, ammunition, boxes of blankets, wearing apparel, boots, woolens, hardware, and provisions were scattered all over the spar deck, and the berth deck and hold were full of coal. The ship had no magazine or shell room; her supply of powder was stored under tarpaulins in Waddell's starboard cabin and in the after hold under the wardroom, and the shells, boxed up, were stowed forward. The wardroom and the officers' rooms were "nearly entirely void of furniture," Lining noted. His room had in it "a wash stand & a shelf, no bunk, drawers, no nothing," and like most of the *Shenandoah*'s men he spent several nights sleeping on a mattress on deck "not very comfortably." The captain's quarters were no better. Waddell's furnishings "consisted of a broken plush-velvet bottomed armchair . . . [and] a half-worn carpet, which smelt of dogs or something worse." Although the chaos bothered the captain, the officers and crew met the challenge cheerfully and energetically.[58]

At the end of a week at sea, Whittle had nothing but praise for the ship's officers and men. After they had cleared the main deck, mounted the guns, and begun cutting gun ports, the men began shifting coal into the bunkers so that they could sling their hammocks on the berth deck and restow the ship's supplies in the hold. Some of the officers were setting up a magazine in the after peak, and others, including Dr. Lining, were rigging and hoisting sails. Lining, who had been made caterer of the wardroom mess, alternated "hauling on ropes" with cleaning out the pantry and making out the ship's ration table. When the helmsman was needed to work elsewhere on the ship, the captain took the wheel. That the *Shenandoah* had steam as well as sails and self-reefing topsails helped to compensate for her lack of men. Cunningham's Patent Self-reefing Topsails, for which Whittle gave thanks, required only three men to close reef a topsail—they did not have to go aloft but slacked the halliards and hauled on the trace from the deck, and the sail rolled itself around the yard. Since there were only three firemen in the crew, Waddell put the ship under steam during the day and under sail at night.[59]

The shortage of sailors and the cruiser's lack of supplies, such as blocks for gun tackles, without which her battery was useless, continued to bother Waddell. Although Bulloch had advised the captain to wait thirty days before he took prizes so that Corbett would have time to return to England and cancel the ship's old register, the *Shenandoah*'s needs overrode the commander's advice. On 29 October she took her first prize, the *Alina*.[60]

Lieutenant Chew, who, like most of her officers, had never participated in capturing an enemy ship, described the procedure from the time the *Alina* ran up her flag—"the old gridiron"—to the end when she "reared up like a war horse and went down stern first." The prize court, held in the *Shenandoah*'s wardroom, was to Chew "a novel scene." Waddell acted as judge. Whittle and Captain Staples of the *Alina* sat on his left, and the rest of the *Shenandoah*'s officers sat on either side of the table. After Whittle put Staples on oath, they questioned him about the ownership, tonnage, and cargo of the *Alina*, then called in the mate and repeated the questions. Because the bill of lading "was not sworn to before a magistrate," and the shippers had warned Staples to avoid a Confederate cruiser, Waddell and his court ruled that the *Alina* was a prize. The cruiser was not permitted to take captured ships to neutral ports for adjudication; therefore they had to destroy her. They condemned and scuttled the *Alina*.

Before they scuttled the *Alina*, they took off the Yankee bark provisions and supplies that the cruiser needed: blocks for gun tackles, cotton canvas, manilla rope, canned meat, and the first of many chronometers the *Shenandoah* acquired on her voyage. The *Alina* also furnished her seven new crewmen. The officers and men also collected "manaverlings": articles such as basins, dishes, cutlery, and any kind of souvenirs that would make their shipboard existence more comfortable.[61]

By the time the *Shenandoah* passed south of the Cape of Good Hope into the Indian Ocean on 17 December—well ahead of the 1 January deadline Bulloch had set—she had captured five more enemy merchant ships and a whaler. These prizes provided her with twenty-two badly needed sailors, who increased the crew to forty-four, and with most of the furniture she needed, including sofas, bureaus, and "very nice light hickory chairs . . . for our Ward Room." The installation of a "splendid galley" on the berth deck while the ship was in Melbourne in February 1865, and the acquisition of a stove for the captain's quarters from the *Abigail,* which she captured in the Sea of Okhotsk the following May, completed her furnishings. The officers and men continued to pick up manaverlings. Chew "brought off from the *Pearl* [at Ascension Island] . . . shells . . . a curious spear . . . a large whale's tooth and some native beads," and he and some of the other officers took off the *Abigail* "some beautiful Japanese boxes, silk and some shells." The *Shenandoah* routinely took chronometers and sextants from the prizes she scuttled or burned.[62]

Maintaining and provisioning the *Shenandoah* were ongoing concerns. The ship replenished her supply of coal from the *John Fraser,* which the Liverpool branch of Fraser, Trenholm & Company had sent out to Melbourne, but most of the supplies for keeping her in good repair came from the ships she captured. The officers and men who boarded her prizes from the South Atlantic to the North Pacific took off manilla rope and canvas necessary for making or repairing sails and rigging, lumber, barrels of fish oil, barrels of sand for holystoning decks, whale line, soap, blocks and tackle, quantities of "slops"—work clothes for the crew—and infantry pants to be worn by the ship's Marine guard, and whale boats.[63]

The *Shenandoah*'s prizes also yielded a variety of provisions. From the whaler *Edward,* for example, she got 50 barrels of beef and 49 of pork, 6,000 pounds of bread, 46 barrels of flour, 600 pounds of coffee and 400 of butter, a barrel of hams and one of pickles, and several thousand pounds of ship's biscuit that Waddell pronounced "the best I have ever seen." Not all the cruiser's food was preserved or canned: like other ships of that era, the *Shenandoah* carried livestock—chickens, geese, pigs, sheep, goats—and the men sometimes caught fish for the mess; in addition to livestock they obtained fresh fruits and vegetables whenever they could. The provisions they took from the *Harvest* at Ascension Island included limes; the natives brought them pineapples and bananas, and before they left the island Dr. Lining picked thirty green coconuts to add to the ship's stores. When the ship went into the Bering Sea, where she captured twenty-four Yankee whalers in six days, most of her officers were so busy that they limited journal entries regarding provisions to "plenty of nice things to eat" and "water and provisions." Chew, however, noted that they took off the whalers meat, sugar, coffee, potatoes, hogs, and 10,000 gallons of fresh water. The water would, he explained, "save [our] coal in condensing; up to this time all our fresh water has been obtained in this way."[64]

Some of the whalers, Lining observed, "carried a crowd of liquor on board." From their stores the *Shenandoah* took spirits to resupply the wardroom mess and the ship's dispensary and for the enlisted men's daily grog ration. Unlike the United States Navy, which had abolished the grog ration for enlisted men in 1862, the Confederate navy still offered Jack a daily tot of one gill of spirits or a half-pint of wine. The daily tot was important to the Confederate cruisers; their men had few opportunities to enjoy liberty on shore, and, along with promises of high pay—in gold—and prize money, guarantees of generous grog rations helped the ships to enlist and keep a full crew.[65]

Capturing a crew—enlisting men from prizes—was a continuous process necessary to the success of the raider's voyage. Men from the *Delphine,* which the *Shenandoah* took in the Indian Ocean, increased her crew to 51, so that, including officers, she had 70 men aboard a ship whose complement should have been 150. When she put in to Melbourne for repairs, she lost twenty sailors. The U.S. consul, William Blanchard, and his "emissaries" offered sailors on liberty bribes of $100 and other inducements to desert; some accepted and never returned to the ship. A few men, like John Williams, the ship's cook, jumped ship and swam ashore. Williams, a free black from Boston, Massachusetts, had served on the USS *Congress* and the USS *Minnesota* until 1864. After he received his discharge from the navy, he signed on the bark *D. Godfrey;* when the *Shenandoah* captured her, he signed on the Confederate cruiser. On Whittle's recommendation, Williams became the ship's cook. He also became a troublemaker. Whittle had to discipline him for getting in fights, neglecting his duty in the galley, being insolent to an officer, and attempting to steal the wardroom steward's shirt. Whittle finally conceded, "I have no doubt [he] will leave us in the first port we enter."[66]

Williams was not the only deserter who complained to the consul of mistreatment by Waddell and his officers. But his charge that they were recruiting and concealing crewmen, including an English cook called "Charley," touched off a controversy between Blanchard and Waddell that threatened the cruiser's continued operation. Waddell needed men and Blanchard knew it. Enlisting British subjects on a belligerent ship was a violation of British neutrality. If Blanchard could prove that the Confederate officers were recruiting in Melbourne, he could end the *Shenandoah*'s cruise. The American consul, armed with affidavits from Williams and other deserters, fired off a series of protests to Victoria's governor, Sir Charles Henry Darling: he claimed that the *Shenandoah* was a pirate and that her captain was recruiting British subjects in violation of the Foreign Enlistment Act, and he demanded that Australian authorities seize the cruiser. Waddell countered Blanchard's charges with letters defending the *Shenandoah*'s status and rights as a belligerent ship of war, and he repeatedly denied that he or any of his officers had violated British neutrality in any way.[67]

Darling and his legal advisors rejected Blanchard's charge that the cruiser was a pirate. But evidence in affidavits and depositions that Blanchard collected from deserters and that appeared in the Melbourne newspapers indicated that her officers might be violating the Foreign Enlistment Act. Darling sent the Victoria police to the *Shenandoah* with a warrant to search for "Charley the Cook." Waddell refused to let the police search the ship. On 14 February, the day before she was to be launched, the governor ordered repairs on the *Shenandoah* suspended. That night Waddell ordered the ship's police to search her, and they found on board four "stowaways," including "Charley." As soon as they put the men off the ship, the harbor police arrested all four. The next day a ruling by the Crown Court—that the government did not have the authority to search or detain a foreign ship of war—enabled Darling to back down. The governor reprimanded Waddell for trying to evade the Foreign Enlistment Act, but he revoked the order of suspension. Waddell got the cruiser off the slip on schedule and left Melbourne three days later.[68]

Once the *Shenandoah* was outside Australia's territorial waters, forty-two "stowaways" climbed out of the ship's hollow bowsprit, empty water tanks, and coal bunkers onto the deck and joined her crew. Although Whittle and the other officers knew that men were trying to enlist from the time the cruiser anchored in Hobson's Bay, some of the officers expressed surprise when the newcomers appeared. None of them, except Waddell, ever admitted knowing anything about the stowaways before the ship left Melbourne, and none of them, including Waddell, ever conceded that they had violated British neutrality. The new recruits were a welcome addition. One of the Australians, J. C. Blacker, who had been an officer on the *Saxonia,* was "a first-class pilot for the Australian, India and China Seas." He joined the *Shenandoah* as sailing master and became Waddell's clerk. Waddell and Whittle were able to organize six of the new men into a Marine guard, which acted as "something of a police force," with George Canning, who had served in the Confederate army under General Leonidas Polk, as sergeant.[69]

From the four whalers the *Shenandoah* captured at Ascension Island, the cruiser shipped ten more men, and from the whalers she took in the Bering Sea thirty-one, ten of whom enlisted as Marines. Twenty-two of the men who had shipped in Madeira or from the early prizes enlisted for six months, but six of them deserted in Melbourne. Of the sixteen who remained on board after Melbourne, twelve reshipped.[70]

The *Shenandoah* recruited from her prizes and at Melbourne 110 men. Like the other Confederate cruisers procured in Europe, she had an international and multiracial crew. Before she reached Melbourne, Chew observed that she had crewmen from the "Confederacy, U. States, England, France, Holland, Denmark, Sweden, Norway, Russia, East India, Africa, Ireland, Scotland, Wales. What a medley!" In the Pacific she added men with Spanish names, Kanakas—natives of various South Pacific islands—and Yankees. Besides her recalcitrant black cook, John Williams, who deserted in Melbourne, she shipped three other free black sailors: "Charles Hopkins from the *Lizzie M. Stacy* in the South Atlantic, Joseph Stevenson from the *Pearl* at Ascension Island, and Edward Weeks from the whaler *Waverly* in the Arctic."[71]

Since the cruiser took a total of 1,053 prisoners from her prizes and only 68 of them shipped, Waddell had to find some means of disposing of the remaining 985. He persuaded the captain of the Danish brig *Anna Jane,* bound for Rio de Janeiro, to take the first lot of prisoners in exchange for a barrel of beef, one of biscuits, and a chronometer. Four days later the *Shenandoah* captured an American clipper, the *Kate Prince.* Instead of destroying her, the captain decided to bond the Brazil-bound clipper and transferred the rest of his prisoners to her. By the time the cruiser had collected 28 more prisoners, she was able to land them, with a month's rations, at the British settlement on Tristan da Cunha. Waddell released the prisoners from the *Delphine* at Melbourne. The native ruler at Ascension Island agreed to let the prisoners from the four whalers the *Shenandoah* captured in his harbor remain there in exchange for rations for them and a whale boat. The hundreds of prisoners from the *Abigail* and the twenty-four prizes she took in the Bering Sea were transferred to four of the whalers—the *Milo,* the *General Pike,* the *Nile,* and the *James Maury*—which Waddell bonded and sent to San Francisco.[72]

Having prisoners on board created extra work for Whittle. The captains of the prizes had to sign paroles "for the war until regularly exchanged." Once they were paroled they and any family members who accompanied them had the freedom of the ship, occupied officers' quarters, and dined with Waddell or in the wardroom. The Confederates treated their prisoners courteously but did not always like them. Whittle referred to Captain Everett Staples of the *Alina* as a "real down East Yankee," and Lining described him as "a black hearted rascal . . . who showed a mean spirit." Captain Samuel J. Gilman of the *Charter Oak* brought with him his wife, her sister Mrs. Gage, widow of a Union sergeant who had been killed at Harpers Ferry, and the latter's six-year-old son, Frank. Even though Whittle grumbled that he was "very sorry to have females onboard," he and the other officers treated the ladies "in the most queenlike manner" and made friends with Frank.[73]

Their next female prisoner made it difficult for some of them to be courteous hosts. Mrs. Nichols, wife of Captain William G. Nichols of the *Delphine,* was a handsome, cultured young woman who was also a termagant. Lieutenant Grimball commented that "if she had been in command the *Delphine* would have escaped—she said so." Waddell, comparing the "refractory lady" to her "melancholy" husband, concluded that "she will be the one for me to manage." Before the *Shenandoah* reached Melbourne Mrs. Nichols unbent, chatted with her captors, and played checkers and backgammon with them in the wardroom. Lining, amused and disgusted by the discovery that Captain Nichols was "infernally jealous of his wife, and never allows me to talk with her that he does not come poking around," vowed to continue chatting with the lady "to plague him." Mrs. Nichols was rude to her husband and the ship's officers about signing her parole, declaring that she did not consider herself bound by its terms and that she would give anybody any information they wanted about the ship, and she ended her tirade by asking Lieutenant Smith Lee sarcastically if there was anything he wanted her six-year-old son Phineas to sign. Whittle's habitual good manners enabled him to mask his dislike of the lady until the day she left the cruiser in Melbourne. The morning they went off the ship, she told her husband that if the *Delphine*'s sextants and chronometers were hers she'd make Waddell give them to her, and she demanded that all the books from the *Delphine* be returned to her. She did get the books, except *Uncle Tom's Cabin,* which Whittle threw overboard.[74]

After a frustrating encounter with Mrs. Nichols, during which she had conned Whittle into giving her a Confederate uniform cap, the *Shenandoah*'s executive officer admitted that often he didn't know how to deal with women, but he asserted "I . . . know how to deal with men." As executive officer—or first lieutenant—he was responsible for maintaining discipline on the ship. The Confederate navy followed disciplinary procedures outlined in the United States *Navy Regulations* and Articles of War. Because no man of the ship committed an offense serious enough to warrant a court-martial during her cruise—except for the deserters at Melbourne, who were safely in the hands of the U.S. consul—disciplinary procedures on the *Shenandoah* were subjudicial. Waddell meted out officers' punishments; he also presided over a few captain's masts at which he heard complaints against crewmen and passed sentence on them. Whittle, however, dealt with most of the recalcitrant crewmen and enlisted prisoners on the ship. When the executive officer received a report of an offense, he recommended a penalty for the offender to Waddell. The captain accepted or rejected the recommendation—usually the former—and Whittle administered the punishment.[75]

Although the *Shenandoah* later was accused of being a "hell ship," in fact her discipline was not harsh by the standards of the time. The United States *Navy Regulations*, which had been amended in 1850 to abolish flogging, called for punishing crewmen who committed petty offenses by tattooing or branding them, forcing them to wear signs, confining them in sweat boxes or in irons, and tricing them up by their wrists to the rigging. Officers guilty of minor offenses were to be reprimanded, confined to quarters, or suspended. Since the *Shenandoah* was at sea for most of her thirteen-month career, desertion was not a common offense on the cruiser as it was on many other Civil War ships. The offenses most frequently committed on the *Shenandoah*, and on all ships in the Civil War navies, came under the headings of disrespect, disobedience, and drunkenness. Whittle usually punished sailors guilty of the first two by confining them in irons or tricing them up. He often withheld the grog rations of sailors who got drunk.[76]

The first offender on the *Shenandoah* was George Sylvester, a fireman who had come out from England on the *Laurel*. When he refused to cook for the firemen's mess, Whittle decided that he had to make an example of Sylvester to prevent further trouble. He put the fireman in irons, triced him up, and, when Sylvester complained, gagged him. After an hour, Sylvester got the master at arms to tell Whittle "he would do anything if I would let him down." The outcome of Sylvester's punishment confirmed Whittle's conviction that the best way to maintain order on the ship was to follow a policy of "prompt and just punishment for all offenders." Whittle occasionally had to discipline petty officers, such as the ship's carpenter, John O'Shea, whom he had to reprimand for insolence to him, and the gunner's mate, William Crawford, for being insolent to the master's mate, John Minor. Whittle believed that Crawford, a veteran of the CSS *Alabama*, was simply an old hand trying to see how far he could go. He put the gunner's mate in irons and triced him up, remarking that most "old man-of-war's men will try these experiments . . . but if they are properly met they behave beautifully." Although Crawford was reported for insolence again, he reshipped after his six-month enlistment ran out and remained gunner's mate until the end of the cruise.[77]

Prisoners and captured crewmen added to Whittle's disciplinary problems. When the *Shenandoah* took a prize, the executive officer paroled the mates as well as the captain. If the mates were uncooperative, as were four mates from the *Alina* and the *Charter Oak* who refused to clean their quarters, he revoked their paroles and put them in irons. He confined sailors from prizes in the forecastle. Thinking that these men would rather work than be locked up, Whittle assigned them jobs on the ship. If they disobeyed his orders, as did two Yankees from the *Lizzie M. Stacy* who refused to shift coal, he punished them. After he triced up one of the men, the other elected to move coal, and the first subsequently "begged to be let down, as he desired to ship." Even prisoners who shipped and who got along well with the Confederates sometimes ran afoul of the executive officer. Midshipmen John Thomson Mason and Orris A. Browne made friends with Peter Raymond and Louis Rowe, French sailors who had shipped from the *Alina*. Mason and Browne employed the Frenchmen to look after their hammocks and wash their clothes, but more important to the midshipmen was the opportunity to converse with them in French. Being popular and skilled, however, did not prevent Rowe from being triced up for fighting with Thomas Hall or Raymond from being triced up for disobeying Master's Mate Minor. Whittle did not enjoy punishing men, but he concluded, "if you do not rule them they will rule you."[78]

Drunkenness, "the disciplinary plague" of the United States Navy, which continued to be a major problem on Union and Confederate ships, caused Whittle little trouble before the *Shenandoah* reached the North Pacific. The *Shenandoah*'s crew, like the crew of the *Alabama,* received a double spirit ration. When the captain or first lieutenant gave the order to "Splice the main brace" morning and afternoon, the crew gathered on the deck to receive their grog that Midshipman Mason brought up from the spirit locker. On special occasions, such as Neptune's visit when the ship first crossed the equator in the Atlantic, the captain ordered extra spirit rations for all hands. Only once before the cruiser reached Melbourne did Whittle have to discipline anyone for being drunk: Gunner John Guy and Carpenter John Lynch, who had "been saving their daily tots for a grand blow out Christmas," had a "spree" on Christmas Eve, and Whittle stopped their grog rations indefinitely.[79]

During the *Shenandoah*'s stay in Melbourne the ship's log listed few punishments for any reason. Five offenders who went ashore without permission or were late returning from liberty were suspended or confined to the ship, and one man was triced up for disobeying orders. That John Williams, the troublesome cook, was the only man disciplined for "drunkenness and disorderly conduct" is surprising. According to Mason, some of the petty officers on shore leave got drunk and got in fights, so that "they disgrace the ship, the uniform & . . . the whole of us." Assistant Surgeon McNulty, whom Mason called "a confirmed old drunkard," started a memorable fracas in the dining room of Scott's Hotel. As he and some fellow officers were "indulging in an occasional patriotic toast," a member of Melbourne's anti-Confederate faction accosted the doctor's party and insulted the Southern people and their government, and McNulty knocked him out. The ensuing fight, during which "glasses and decanters . . . turned into missiles, . . . knives were drawn, and one or two shots were fired," ended in victory for the Confederates, who then went on to the theater.[80]

Most of the ship's officers, conscious that they had foes as well as friends in Australia, were circumspect in their behavior. Lining, who had more free time than the line officers and engineers, enjoyed convivial gatherings at Scott's and a night out with Melbourne's "medical profession." While the first citizens of Victoria lionized the Southerners, Whittle, because of his duties as executive officer, was stuck on the ship. On one of the two or three occasions he was able to go on shore, the first lieutenant, much to Lining's surprise, got "exceedingly drunk." He and Lining went to dine with a Mr. Weymouth, who had known Whittle's uncle, Commander Arthur Sinclair, when Sinclair was a midshipman in the United States Navy's Pacific Squadron. When Lining realized, as they were returning to the ship, that Whittle was drunk, the doctor "*walked him around* until time . . . for the cars to start & thus got him to the ship safely . . . pretty well able to take care of himself" so that nobody would know "he had been taking too much." Lining noted in his journal that "our crowd especially behaved well" at the exclusive Melbourne Club's dinner honoring the *Shenandoah*'s officers, and after a lavish ball several of them attended in the gold mining city of Ballarat, he wrote, "although liquor flowed in profusion, I did not see a single case of uproarious drunkenness."[81]

Two weeks after the *Shenandoah* left Australia, Whittle and some of the other officers discovered that somebody in the crew had gone through the propeller tunnel, tapped a keg of rum, and removed over fifty gallons. Whittle was concerned about the crew's grog running out, but the thieves apparently stashed some of the rum—the first lieutenant had to confine Seaman George Flood for fighting and drunkenness a week later. When the ship was at Ascension Island the first week in April, the crew sampled the native *gorwa*, made of fermented roots, or, Master's Mate Hunt speculated, "they found a better beverage . . . that had been smuggled from one of the whalers" the *Shenandoah* captured there. During the next month and a half the first lieutenant meted out punishments for insolence and disobedience, but he had no more problems with drunkenness until the cruiser captured the whaler *Abigail* in the Sea of Okhotsk on 27 May 1865.[82]

By the last week in May, Mason observed that the *Shenandoah* was "much in want of grog." Ebenezer Nye, captain of the *Abigail*, also was a fur trader; he kept on his ship a large supply of liquor to exchange for pelts and he sold it to his crew. Lining, who went on the whaler after the Confederates condemned her, discovered that the crewmen who were transferring provisions to the *Shenandoah* had gotten into the liquor. Some of them had to be put in irons, and Lynch, the ship's carpenter, was triced up in the cruiser's propeller well. Thus began the so-called mutiny, which was, in fact, a three-day-long drunken brawl.[83]

The next day many of the men who were transferring provisions from the *Abigail* got drunk again. According to Chew, the liquor "was all over the ship, so we found it impossible to prevent our men from getting it." Seaman William Swanton, who was in Chew's work party, was so drunk that Chew had to take him back to the *Shenandoah*. After Swanton jumped out of the boat into the freezing water, Chew had him lashed down so that he couldn't jump in again. Whittle, who knew that some of the men were smuggling liquor onto the cruiser, was trying to find where they were hiding it when he was not busy putting drunk sailors in irons. "This has been a terrible day for me," he wrote in his journal late that night. "I never had such a time." The captain had to discipline several officers for drinking too much: Mugguffeney, Boatswain George Harwood, and Lynch, who not only was triced up but also was gagged—"an everlasting disgrace for an officer," commented Mason. It took Waddell and Whittle two more days to locate and confiscate private stores of spirits and restore "things . . . to their own old course" on the ship. "In brief," Cornelius Hunt concluded, "I think it was the most general and stupendous 'spree' I ever witnessed."[84]

There were no more "stupendous sprees" on the *Shenandoah*. Waddell, learning from the *Abigail*'s men that many Yankee whalers had shifted operations to the Arctic, "where the whales were more plentiful & less shy," left the Sea of Okhotsk for the North Pacific. After 22 June, when she caught up with her quarry in the Bering Sea, the officers were careful to supervise parties boarding the whalers and transferring provisions from them. Lining, who went on the first ship they captured to get medicine for his dispensary, stayed on the *William Thompson* for several hours "engaged . . . in trying to keep Lynch &c. from getting at the liquor." The following week was the busiest of the raider's entire voyage: capturing twenty-four prizes in six days kept her crew too busy to indulge in a spree. She left the North Pacific with her tanks full of fresh water, her hold filled with provisions, and six or seven hundred gallons of brandy, rum, and whiskey in the spirit locker.[85]

The cruiser's fresh water and supplies of provisions ran low before the voyage ended, but the liquor lasted until she dropped anchor at Liverpool. The *Shenandoah* was, Mason explained, "what sailors call a very 'wet ship.' . . . It means that there is always plenty of liquor knocking around." Besides all the drink under Mason's charge in the spirit locker, the captain had a small private stock in his cabin, including wines, such as the champagne he sent to the officers' mess to celebrate the *Shenandoah*'s circumnavigation of the globe on 29 August. The wardroom also had its supply of wines which the officers used for celebrating holidays and birthdays. Lining kept in his dispensary a supply of wine and whiskey for remedies such as the hot toddies he gave Waddell to relieve the captain's stiff neck, and on one occasion he furnished liquor for the wardroom's traditional Saturday evening toast to "Sweethearts and Wives." Despite the abundance of spirits on the ship, Whittle punished only one man for a liquor-related offense before 2 August, when the *Shenandoah*'s men learned that the war was over. Without the backing of a government or any authority for being at sea, the ship's officers wondered whether the crew would cause trouble. The crew, however, assured Waddell "that they would continue to obey them as they had always done," and Chew noted that the men's behavior was "more respectful and polite." The officers' journals indicate that members of the crew managed to get extra liquor somehow. When dry weather in the South Atlantic resulted in water rationing on the ship for almost two weeks, Mason served grog three times a day, "a kind of substitute for water." Whether they supplemented their grog ration legally or illegally, the sailors confined their drinking to their quarters; the black eyes that occasionally appeared on deck the morning after a brawl in the steerage did not interfere with their work on the ship. John Mason gave Whittle credit for the continued cooperation. The first lieutenant, he stated, "had from the start preserved the most admirable discipline on board at all times, and it was in a great measure due to his excellent management of the crew that no difficulty occurred." [86]

To Whittle, discipline was a means of ensuring the crew's and the ship's well-being. "If every man could do and say what he pleased the ship would soon go to the devil," he declared. "On a cruise of this kind particularly I consider discipline . . . absolutely necessary to our very existence." As the officer in charge of sailing an undermanned ship, Whittle had work aplenty for the crew; his ability to organize the men's work and his seamanship contributed to an ordered cruise. Whittle's journal attests to his skill as a sailor. In addition to recording the ship's noon location, course, distance covered, and wind direction, his daily entries often describe the canvas she carried. From them the reader can visualize the *Shenandoah* under all sail in the South Atlantic, "going steadily with her wings spread," and in the midst of a Pacific storm running "before a furious gale & terrific sea" under the main staysail and goosewinged foresail. Having steam was an advantage when she was chasing a Yankee, but Whittle thought her "much more comfortable under sail than steam." She tacked well, she was "like a duck on the water, steers beautifully," he wrote. "I never saw a vessel work better." Near the end of the voyage, although she had crumpled her copper sheathing in the Arctic ice and she was running low on coal and stores that had served as ballast, he observed that she "sails remarkably well under all circumstances."[87]

Whittle's journal and his Morning Order Book of daily work orders for the morning watch officer indicate that his job of directing the crew's work on the ship took him, like Melville's first lieutenant, "down in the hold, and up aloft, at one and the same time." He assigned men to stations at a gun, on the deck, in the sails. In addition to loosing, reefing, clewing, and furling sails, they continuously inspected and, when necessary, repaired or replaced the canvas and rigging. The *Shenandoah*'s spars—masts and yards—were steel. Her standing rigging—the stays and shrouds that supported the masts—was wire, and her running rigging—the gear that controlled the yards and sails— was rope. The cruiser did not lose any spars during the voyage, but gales and storms caused Whittle to splice wire stays and halliards, paint yards and masts, and replace sails. Hard use as well as salt air caused the running rigging to wear. Whittle periodically had the men "black down" the rope with a protective mixture of hot tar, Stockholm tar, and saltwater, but some of the gear, especially the ratlines in the shrouds on which the men climbed aloft, had to be replaced from time to time. The sailmaker, Henry Alcott, repaired damaged sails and made a supply of new sails he kept in reserve in the hold; as late as 27 September 1865, Whittle noted that they had "bent and ready . . . 38 sails. This is tremendous, is it not?"[88]

Responsibility for maintaining the *Shenandoah*'s engines, boilers, and propeller belonged to the ship's chief engineer, Matthew O'Brien, and his two assistants. Whittle occasionally had to take crews "down in the hold" to shift coal into the bunkers or to restow provisions and supplies. He considered the former, which also included scrubbing the berth deck, "dirty work," and when he restowed the after hold for the seventh time, he noted that "fresh installments of provisions from every prize made keeping the holds in order impossible." Most of the chores he directed were topside. Scrubbing hatches, white paintwork, and decks, holystoning the spar deck if the ship had a supply of sand, wiping up the poop deck and waterways, and cleaning and polishing the brass, or "brightwork," were daily chores on the cruiser. Less frequently Whittle had the men oil the teak waterways, chicken coops, and deck rails, clean the boats and their covers, and black the ironwork. He had them paint the ship's sides three times: shortly before she got to Melbourne, after she left the North Pacific, and about three weeks before she returned to Liverpool. The men worked from stages rigged on both sides of the ship and painted from her copper sheathing up to but not including the bulwarks. Whittle's orders to the watch officer reminded him to attach two seven-fathoms-long knotted lines to the main brace bumpkin and to have the ship's dinghy ready to launch "in case a man falls overboard." During the last part of the voyage, Whittle also had the men paint the ship's port and starboard cabins, berth deck, and hold. The week before she reached England he used the small store of sand he had hoarded to holystone the decks, and Mason observed that everything looked "as nice as a new pin."[89]

Whittle expected the crew to keep themselves, as well as the *Shenandoah*, shipshape. The entries in his Morning Order Book often began "Scrub and wash clothes," and sometimes he added other instructions, such as "put the white clothes on the upper line, grey next & black or blue next." Early in the voyage, the officers participated in wash days. It was "a new sight to see officers so employed," Whittle commented; "I laughed heartily at Jack Grimball and Dr. Lining." Lining admitted that he "had to give them at last to one of the sailors to finish for me," and Mason and Browne employed sailors Peter Raymond and Louis Rowe to wash their clothes. Whittle tried to designate certain days as wash days, but in fact wash day often occurred after a rain storm supplied extra water. Prolonged dry weather, and Waddell's reluctance to use his dwindling supply of coal for condensing, caused him to ration water on the *Shenandoah* the first two weeks in October. Mason noted that the crew rigged "all sorts of purchases" on deck in anticipation of catching "every drop of water that may come on board." When a "fine shower" broke the drought, Mason, who was dispensing the evening grog, was not able to catch any water, but one of the crew later gave him a bucketful, which he considered "a most valuable present, almost worth its weight in gold."[90]

"Jack" not only saved the rainwater for washing clothes and taking a bath but also again "had enough water to wash down salthorse, beans &c" that made up his diet during the last three months of the cruise. For most of their voyage the *Shenandoah*'s men ate well. The officers' journals indicate that they got fresh meat and vegetables in addition to canned, dried, and salted provisions from their prizes. At Christmas the crew dined on "the largest pig in the [ship's] pen," and the wardroom had goose as well as pork, "nice corned beef, fresh potatoes &c., Mince pies &c." For the captain's birthday dinner on 13 July, "fresh meats and vegetables, great luxuries at sea," appeared on the table covered with the ship's last white cloth. On 20 August, however, Whittle wrote that the officers celebrated Paymaster Breedlove Smith's twenty-fourth birthday "without any extra show, as saltbeef is all the go." Mason, the wardroom's caterer for September, used his position as "Master's Mate of the hold" to "ransack" the supplies so that he could put on a few "knobby" dinners. He killed the ship's last hog at the beginning of the month, and on his last day as caterer he got the cook to serve the officers "a respectable array of dishes," including mutton and clam pies, tongue, salt meat, canned potatoes, puddings, nuts, port, and sherry. "For a ship more than seven months out of port," he wrote, "this was a magnificent repast." By the end of October, Chew, who described the wardroom's stock of food as "scanty," noted that the officers' mess had only a week's supply of sugar and coffee left. Although Mason declared he didn't "attach much importance to such matters," he confessed, "I never before longed so much for something nice to eat."[91]

The steady diet of salt horse and salt pork, besides being monotonous, contributed to the appearance of three cases of scurvy among the crew during the last month of the voyage. Up to that time there had been little illness on the *Shenandoah*. Dr. Lining, like Whittle, considered discipline necessary to the ship's well-being. Early in the cruise, when Carpenter John O'Shea didn't want to follow Whittle's orders and asked the surgeon to put him on the sick list, Lining refused. Noting that O'Shea "has been a politician in some Navy Yard in the U.S. & accustomed to have all about him do just as he wanted them to do," the doctor continued to ignore the chronic "growler" whenever he was "in a pet" and maintained a policy of refusing to put men on the sick list without good reason. References to colds, accompanied by coughs, sore throats, and inflamed eyes, appear in Lining's and the other officers' journals. Lining noted that Dabney Scales had neuralgia, Irvine Bulloch had rheumatism in his knee, the captain had headaches and a stiff neck, but ailments such as these seldom kept men from their duties on the ship. More serious was Jack Grimball's fever—unidentified—which put the lieutenant on the sick list for two weeks, and, when it recurred, for two weeks more, and the surgeon had to order Bulloch relieved from his duties as navigator because taking sun sights had injured his eyes. Lining reported few injuries: Grimball cut his thumb badly while he was unloading provisions from a prize; a Kanaka sailor jammed his hand in the main halliard block; and two sailors aloft got rope burns as they tried to keep the fore royal yard from falling to the deck.[92]

Since the *Shenandoah* was never engaged with enemy warships, none of her men was killed or wounded in combat. The two men she lost—Seaman William Bill, a Kanaka who shipped from the *Abigail,* and Marine Sergeant George Canning, one of the Melbourne stowaways—died of diseases they contracted before they joined the ship's crew. According to Lining, William Bill "had been suffering from Venerial [*sic*] for a long time & was covered with ulcers ... [and] had all the symptoms of Sub-acute inflammation of the brain and chest." Canning, an Englishman who had served on General Leonidas Polk's staff until he was wounded at Shiloh, had returned to Europe in 1863. From there he went to stay with a brother in Australia and, wanting to return to the Confederacy, had managed to get aboard the *Shenandoah* before she left Hobson's Bay. His wound never healed, and Lining attributed his death to "'Phithisis' [pulmonary tuberculosis] brought on by a gun shot wound through the right lung." Chew and Mason, neither of whom had witnessed the death of a shipmate at sea, described the last rites for the two men. In each case, the body, with two eight-inch shot, "was sewn up in a canvas and was laid out on the poop wrapped in the Confederate flag," with a watch put over it until the next morning. After inspection, the flag was half-masted, the burial service was read—by Waddell from the Episcopal prayer book for William Bill, by McNulty from the Roman Catholic missal for Canning—and "the body went down to its watery grave; a mournful splash . . . and he disappeared forever." The burials of the two men, only four days apart, made Whittle feel melancholy. Mason, however, remarked that he was "rather astonished at my own insensibility." After William Bill was buried, he "spent the morning working in the hold & the usual routine went on as if nothing had happened."[93]

The two burials were the only religious services held on board the *Shenandoah.* She did not have a chaplain—the Confederate Navy Department included chaplains in the list of officers, specified their duties and pay, and described their uniforms, but never appointed any—and Waddell never read a Sunday service during the voyage. Chew deplored the omission. "I wish it were otherwise," he wrote, "for I think nothing more beautiful than the Episcopal service." While the cruiser was at Melbourne, several of the officers, including Mason and Scales, attended Anglican churches in the city, but when she was at sea, observing the Sabbath was left up to the individual. Whittle spent time in his room on Sunday, "reading the service" in the Book of Common Prayer, as did Mason, and Chew mentioned that "a few of the officers collect in the evening & sing hymns &c."[94]

Although Waddell never mustered the officers and men for a church service, he did follow the tradition of holding inspection on Sunday morning. Barring the appearance of a prize or a storm, between ten and eleven o'clock the captain inspected the crew at quarters—stations assigned the men on deck or aloft—and then the ship. On the first Sunday of the month there was also a general muster, at which the captain or first lieutenant read the Articles of War. All of the men wore their "Sunday best." The officers wore traditional whites in the summer, but Waddell ordered them to wear grey uniforms, or a grey jacket with blue or black pants. Whittle and Lining, along with many other Confederate naval officers, did not like grey uniforms. Whittle, who had a brand-new grey uniform, complained that after a month on the ship "it looks as though I had been wearing it for a year. Oh! no the old blue was the best." Lining, one of the officers who had managed to continue wearing the "old blue" until he came on the *Shenandoah,* had to draw "some flannel from the ship . . . to make . . . a [grey] wool jacket" before the next inspection. After the *Shenandoah*'s men learned that the war had ended, there were no more Sunday musters. However, "for the sake of discipline," Lining noted, "we have daily inspection." "Sunday now differs little from the other days," he observed, "except in most persons putting on their 'Sunday Go to Meeting' to give them an airing."[95]

The *Shenandoah*, like other Confederate ships, followed a naval tradition that decreed Sunday a day of rest. After morning inspection, officers and men not on watch could do as they wished. Evenings during the week also provided those not on duty free time for rest and recreation. Singing was a popular pastime on the *Shenandoah*. The officers occasionally sang together on deck after supper, and the sailors entertained the officers with dancing as well as singing. Lieutenant Lee on one occasion "got all the dancers among the men by the main hatch & by a little whiskey set them dancing until after nine o'clock." Lining liked the Kanakas' singing but not their dancing. Mason thought the Kanakas were "beautiful dancers" and noted that there were other "very accomplished dancers on board," one of whom had been on the stage in San Francisco. He did not appreciate the accordionist who sometimes accompanied the sailors: the man was, he wrote, "an amateur," and his accordion was an "unmusical" and "detestable" instrument whose inventor should be hanged "for murder in the first degree."[96]

The officers also enjoyed listening to the older sailors' tales of their experiences. They discovered that some of the old-timers were superstitious. During a Pacific gale that caught them by surprise, somebody reported that the cat was overboard, and Lining noted that "all the old sailors shook their heads and said that [the cat's loss] was the Cause of it." When Whittle declared that losing the cat wouldn't upset him, the sailors accused him of being the Jonah. Much to the crew's relief the cat turned up.[97]

"Pussy" was the ship's cat, but the dog on board, brought off the prize *Susan*, became Smith Lee's pet. The cruiser's livestock sometimes provided diversions for the officers. When James Martin, the officers' cook, couldn't get the geese to eat, Lining taught James how to feed them by "stuffing them, which seemed to delight him." Mason was amused by the raider's "good Confederate pigs," who objected to sharing their pen with pigs taken off the *Delphine*. They "kept up a tremendous noise," he wrote, until the mid-watch, when "he went forward & noticed them lying apart in the pen, the Confederates on one side & the Yanks on the other." With the exception of a penguin some of the officers brought back from an excursion to St. Paul in the Indian Ocean, the *Shenandoah*'s men had no exotic animals like the parrots and monkeys that Captain Rafael Semmes allowed his men to keep on the *Alabama*, but some of the officers' journals described unfamiliar creatures they observed from the cruiser's deck as she made her way around the world. Lining saw for the first time Portuguese men-of-war and a big sunfish, which he thought looked "more like a turtle than a fish," and he watched some of the sailors catch a small shark that they planned to feast on. Chew described in detail the Cape pigeons that followed the ship around the Horn and often landed on the deck, "picking up crumbs of bread from the men's meals." The whales that played around the ship in the North Pacific and the walruses and seals from islands in the Behring Sea entertained officers and men as they searched for their elusive quarry.[98]

Making their quarters more comfortable and keeping their clothes in order consumed some of the officers' free time. Chew devoted an afternoon to packing the shells he had collected for his sister, putting up clothes hooks, and nailing canvas to the bulkhead to keep out air that came in between the planks. Lining had to install the shelves in his dispensary because the ship's carpenters all were busy caulking. Cold weather in the North Pacific prompted the officers to put up a stove in the wardroom, and it helped to warm and dry out their quarters. Dampness caused them problems no matter what the temperature. As Whittle noted, the *Shenandoah* was "a wet ship." In storms that produced high winds and heavy seas, the cruiser shipped water that flooded the wardroom and adjacent officers' quarters as well as parts of the berth deck and hold, soaking everything on the floor and even the bunks. Persistent damp weather forced Whittle to air all his clothes on deck because they were moldy. The officers darned socks and mended clothes, and when articles of clothing wore out they made replacements. Mason, who became adept at making pants, agreed to make Chew a pair if Chew would polish walrus tusks for him. During the last two months of the voyage Lining observed that sewing had become "a mania," so that "if any one should enter our ward room he might think himself in a tailor's shop. I counted five officers who were making pantaloons & I am engaged in a night shirt." Anticipating the end of the cruise, they also made bags to hold their bedding, "so that they may carry it ashore with them."[99]

Games—chess, backgammon, dominoes, whist—were a favorite pastime in the wardroom. After "a chess mania came over the mess" and threatened to keep backgammon enthusiasts from using the ship's only game board, Lining made a second board. Having two boards enabled the officers to play a kind of duplicate chess. Although they had only one set of chess pieces, the second player announced his move to a third officer, who recorded the moves of both contestants, while other officers gathered in the wardroom to watch the game. The Confederate navy, unlike the Union navy, did not frown on card playing on warships, and the *Shenandoah*'s officers occasionally played whist in the evening. Whittle apparently enjoyed whist, and Lining reported in his journal that he and Whittle had beaten Waddell and McNulty "very badly—three straight games." In the late spring of 1865 some of the officers decided that they needed exercise, and Lining noted that "*dumb bells & gymnastics* have taken the place of chess," but their interest in "good hard exercise" didn't last. Games and making up puzzles for each other to solve continued to be favorite off-duty pastimes for them to the end of the voyage. And they read.[100]

The *Shenandoah* did not have a library, except for some works on navigation and Phillimore's *Laws of Nations*. Several of her officers, however, brought with them books they had purchased in Bermuda and Europe, and some of the cruiser's prizes added their collections. These volumes, which they shared, included works on French and English history, such as Thiers' account of the French Revolution, which Lining admired, D'Aubigne's study of the Reformation, and a new history of France by Durny, her current minister of public instruction, which Mason thought was "tiresome" and abandoned for Hume's *History of England*. Chew and Mason, both of whom continued studying French grammar, read Jean-Jacques Rousseau's *Confessions* and *La Nouvelle Heloise,* Victor Hugo's *Les Miserables,* and Mme de Stael's *Corinne, ou l'Italie*. Mason admired *Corinne* for the author's style—"her language and expressions"—as much as for her story, both of which made him "cry over the most touching passages." Lining particularly liked the Duc de Saint-Simon's *Memoirs* of life at Louis XIV's court; he also praised a book on travels through Madeira, Portugal, and Andalusia as "one of the most readable . . . which ever fell into my hands." Matthew Fontaine Maury's *Physical Geography of the Sea* inspired the doctor to study navigation, "for," he wrote in his journal, "who does not know that I may not need it one of these days?" The officers also enjoyed novels by Edward Bulwer-Lytton, Charles Dickens, and William Makepeace Thackeray, although Mason took exception to Dickens's "abuse of American customs & institutions" in *Martin Chuzzlewit*. While Whittle's duties as executive officer gave him less free time than the other officers, he spent a number of evenings in the wardroom reading Thackeray's *Adventures of Phillip* and *The Newcomes*.[101]

The wardroom, besides being the officers' mess, was also their recreation room. Their journals indicate that they observed the navy's traditional amenities in the mess, but at other times life in the wardroom was quite informal. The *Shenandoah's* officers were a congenial group. Whittle discovered that *The Newcomes* couldn't compete with Lining's and Grimball's discussion of all their mutual acquaintances "from Savannah to Charleston." Fascinated by their conversation, he quit reading because, he told Lining, he was confusing their friends and relatives with the characters in the novel, and "Ethel Newcome" was about to marry "Thomas Rhett." Although Lining complained when Bulloch and Lee interrupted his reading—"D——m these fellows! . . . Old Bulloch has slung his old Rheumatic leg across Smith Lee's lap, giving my book a kick"—the doctor usually was amused by his fellow officers' tomfoolery. Describing the evening when Lee, the wardroom's clown, "went to work & danced all his clothes off," he declared, "I don't know when I have laughed as much as I did, comme il est drole." He was not above joining in the roughhousing: "I had a great sky-lark with Bulloch this morning," he reported, "rolling over each other around the Ward Room."[102]

Early in the voyage Lining noted that "we are all good friends, have no quarrelling—but good jokes are going around all the time & good spirits prevailing." As the ship made its way around the world, however, her officers had to work at maintaining morale. In the intervals between prizes, which lengthened after the *Shenandoah* left Melbourne, the officers found the cruiser's daily routine monotonous. They were homesick. Their journals contained frequent references to rereading letters they had brought with them and earlier journals. They missed their families and friends at home and in Europe and worried because they did not know how the former were faring in the midst of a war.[103]

In addition to boredom, homesickness, and no news from home, differences in the officers' training and experience sometimes caused friction among them. Two of the four lieutenants who were watch officers, Dabney Scales and Frank Chew, had completed only a year and a half at Annapolis when the war began; after they went South, they both served on Confederate ships on the Mississippi and Savannah Rivers and at Charleston and Mobile, but neither had been to sea. It was up to Whittle, the *Shenandoah*'s first lieutenant, to see that they went by the book in following naval regulations and carrying out their duties with the dignity befitting their rank. His Morning Order Book indicates that he was not amused when Scales, as morning watch officer, apparently made some inappropriate remarks about the directions to "wipe up the poop." For the benefit of Lieutenant Scales and other watch officers, Whittle's instructions the next day included "wipe up the poop (*I mean by the latter expression, that each mizzen topman, except the captain, is to take a wet swab and apply it where he may find any spots of dirt in the poop*)."[104]

Chew, who readily admitted that he was "all theory and [had] but very little practice" as a line officer, was a willing student. His journal of the *Shenandoah*'s voyage is a recital of lessons learned, not only in seamanship but also about all aspects of the cruise, from taking and destroying prizes and burying the dead at sea to disarming and surrendering a warship. He was also a hapless young man whose misadventures alternately amused and annoyed the other officers and led Whittle and Lining to nickname him "Chew the Unfortunate." The surgeon, on discovering that Chew's slop tub had "capsized" in his cabin and "made a perfect wreck of it," declared, "if anything happens it is sure to be in his room." When Chew was airing clothes on deck, his trunk overturned and a number of his letters went into the water; two days later he slid on deck and his uniform cap went overboard. On another occasion Whittle, who was enjoying a sunny morning on deck, commented that as soon as "Chew the unfortunate" came on watch, "it clouded up and . . . commenced to rain in torrents."[105]

While Chew's haplessness amused Whittle and Lining, it seems to have confirmed Waddell's conviction that a naval officer could not learn practical seamanship from books. Furthermore, Chew and Scales had almost no experience at sea. When the *Shenandoah* ran into a severe gale in the Indian Ocean, the captain decided that neither Chew nor Scales was competent to keep the mid- and morning watches by themselves, but he refused Whittle's offer to keep watch with Chew. He ordered the first lieutenant to relieve Chew of the mid-watch and replaced Chew with Master's Mate John Minor. Minor, who was not warranted but had only an appointment from Waddell, was ranked by Midshipmen Mason and Browne as well as Lieutenant Chew. They and the rest of the officers on the cruiser considered Waddell's action a breach of naval law and custom, and Whittle predicted that "there will be a row in consequence of it."[106]

When Chew protested Waddell's decision the next day, the captain refused to reconsider his order, declaring that he considered Chew incompetent and therefore would not respect him or his commission. Chew then asked to be relieved of duty and permitted to leave the ship at the next port she reached, and Waddell agreed. Whittle, concerned that the captain's "arbitrary and unwarrantable acts of authority" would destroy the esprit de corps on the cruiser, decided that he would have to "have a long talk with him," even though he had promised Mrs. Waddell "to keep out of all quarrels" with her husband. The first lieutenant defended Chew for wanting to leave a ship whose captain did not respect an officer's commission or person and repeated his offer to stand watch with Chew. He urged the captain to restore Chew to duty and predicted, "You are going to have an unhappy ship if you do not." When Waddell defended his action by accusing Whittle of not volunteering to supervise Chew "with the right spirit," Whittle reminded the captain that he had refused his offer to keep watch with Chew by saying " 'I have not a friend in the ship.' 'You are all against me!' " The subsequent "extraordinary & plain conversation" between the captain and first lieutenant ultimately resulted in Waddell's apologizing to Whittle and restoring Chew to watch under Whittle's supervision. But the incident, which seemed to confirm the officers' earlier questions about Waddell's seamanship and his disregard for naval law and custom, brought into the open their concern with his command.[107]

The *Shenandoah* was Waddell's first command. Because he was on the USS *Saginaw* in the Pacific when the war began, he did not resign from the United States Navy until December 1861, and he entered the Confederate navy on 17 March 1962, almost a year later than most of his officers. He was commissioned in time to take part in the action at New Orleans aboard the CSS *Mississippi*, but the remainder of his duty in the Confederacy, on the James River and at Charleston, earned him little mention; his duty in France, from the spring of 1863 to September 1864, earned him even less. His fellow officers in Europe seldom mentioned him in their letters and diaries. Waddell was at times, by his own admission, "unsocial," and the editor of his memoirs noted that he "was not a warm man," "aloof" in his relations with other officers and crewmen. Bulloch and Barron never employed him to carry dispatches between England and France or to Richmond or sent him on odd jobs, such as procuring cargoes for blockade runners, that they entrusted to other officers under their command. One historian noted that no officer of his rank in Europe "receives less mention in the dispatches of the European agents to Richmond than Lieutenant Waddell." After "apathetically awaiting orders" in Paris for over a year, Waddell's "conspicuous inactivity" finally ended when Barron appointed him a lieutenant commandant and sent him to Liverpool to report to Bulloch for a ship.[108]

While Waddell was not Bulloch's first choice for captain of the *Shenandoah*, Bulloch knew that Waddell was willing to destroy unarmed enemy merchant ships and that he was an experienced sailor. He also knew that Waddell, like most of his fellow officers, had never "joined a ship . . . except when she was fully manned and in apple-pie order for a cruise, or at a government dockyard, with ample force of men and abundant supplies to fit her out." To aid Waddell in coping with equipping an undermanned ship in the middle of the ocean for "a cruise to the distant Pacific," Bulloch provided him with a longer, more explicit letter of instructions than he had given to any other cruiser captain. After expressing confidence in Waddell and encouraging him to use his initiative, Bulloch devoted over 3,500 words to spelling out the objectives of the cruise, the procedure for transferring equipment and supplies at Madeira, the routes that Waddell might follow "to catch the whalers," and locations of possible coaling stations, and he included advice on a variety of matters, such as international law, places from which he might communicate with Liverpool, and suggestions as to where and how he might dispose of the ship at the end of the voyage. More important, Bulloch provided Waddell with a group of young, able officers. His letters to Barron indicate that he accepted Waddell as captain of the *Shenandoah* because Barron had let him choose the cruiser's other officers, especially the commodore's aide, Whittle, who became the ship's executive officer.[109]

Whittle and Lining knew that Waddell had not been Bulloch's first choice for captain of the *Shenandoah*. His reluctance at Las Desertas to go to sea troubled them. During the first weeks of the voyage, while the ship's officers worked willingly with the crew to stow supplies and mount guns, the captain wandered the deck and worried about calamities that might occur. What if they met an enemy ship? They couldn't fire the guns because they had no tackles. And what if the enemy attacked and a shell hit the powder stored in Waddell's starboard cabin? Lining discovered that the captain was afraid of encountering a squall that might capsize the ship. "Whenever *night* comes on," the doctor wrote, "the skipper begins to get uneasy, can't sleep, gets fidgety & then takes in sail."[110]

Whittle became concerned about Waddell's "uncalled for and unnecessary interference" with his duties. On one December morning, when Whittle ordered the boatswain to fit sail "in a particular way," he complained that Waddell "without my knowledge, and though told that it was my order, . . . had all undone and fitted another way." Whittle did not question the captain's right to change his orders, but he noted that Waddell had "promised that all his orders to my subordinates should go through me." Whittle declared that "if my orders are to be changed this way in trifling matters, I may as well take a watch and give him the Executive duties, for both of us cannot be the Executive officer," and added, "I will not quarrel with him [because] . . . it would injure the service, and . . . his little wife . . . begged me to keep out of all quarrels on the cruize."[111]

When Waddell attempted to take Chew off watch, however, Whittle did object. After standing watch with Chew for several days, he noted that both Chew and Scales "are gaining in experience and . . . before long . . . it may not be necessary for anyone to keep watch with them." Two weeks later Waddell appointed Chew ordnance officer, gave him charge of all nautical instruments taken from prizes, and relieved him "of all duty pertaining to a watch officer." When the captain then put Master's Mate J. F. Minor on watch, Orris Browne and John Thomson Mason, who outranked Minor, protested and created what Lining called "another small sized row."[112]

Chew's journal never mentions Waddell's initial attempt to take him off watch. He accepted his appointment as ordnance officer, but he was not happy. He noted that he had left Liverpool only three months earlier, "but it seems to me six; I take no pleasure in destroying; my companions do not suit me. I sometimes wish to leave the ship, but when I think of the advantages of the cruise, it passes off."[113]

After Waddell took Chew off watch, the captain had to relieve Irvine Bulloch of his duty as master, or navigator, because Bulloch's eyes were badly injured from taking sights. The captain then appointed Chew master and put Bulloch on watch in Minor's place. "This relieves us of a dilemma," Whittle noted, and added that Minor "should have never been given the deck over Mr. Mason & Mr. Browne."[114] Chew was pleased with his opportunity to do "my first real navigating . . . there [is] much difference between working a supposed altitude of the sun and taking that altitude and working for the position of the ship." After two weeks of taking sights, Chew made a perfect landfall at Cape Otway, near the entrance to Melbourne's harbor, and noted that the captain "complimented me for it."[115]

Two months later Bulloch was able to resume his duties as master, and

Waddell assigned Chew to keep the forenoon watch every day. As Chew gained experience, Waddell also ordered him to keep Dabney Scales's watches when Scales developed neuralgia and again when the captain suspended Scales for bringing whiskey off the *Abigail*. After Chew protested to Waddell that he "was making a *convenience* of me," the captain told Chew to turn over all the nautical instruments to Bulloch and gave him back his regular watch, to Chew's "great satisfaction."[116]

A week after the *Shenandoah* left Melbourne, Whittle complained that Waddell was again "meddling" with his duties on the deck and with the work of the other lieutenants. The next day he wrote that the captain was "still in the dumps" and would not speak to any of the officers "except on duty." As Waddell's "dumps" continued, Whittle noted, "He has gone so far with me that now all his orders . . . are written," and he added that the captain "has come out in new colors and has spoken to all but me."[117]

Whittle was mainly concerned about the effect Waddell's attitude would have on the crew, whether it would undermine the discipline the executive officer had worked so hard to maintain. "I am fearful that his conduct to me will not go unnoticed by the crew, upon whom it could have no other than a bad effect," he wrote. "I am fearful that the efficiency of the ship will suffer." Whittle resolved to "do all I can with proper maintenance of self-respect to bring about reconcilliation." When Waddell complained that having to supervise both Chew and Scales on their watches "was beginning to tell on his health . . . and he would not last the cruise," Whittle "volunteered to keep all Scales' watches with him in addition to my duties as Executive Officer." He concluded that being on deck "from seven in the morning until 8 at night" and then keeping a watch "will tell on me, but if one is to break down it had better be me than him."[118]

Fortunately for Whittle, Waddell's "dumps" disappeared two weeks later when the *Shenandoah* found and destroyed four Yankee whalers at Ascension Island. From Ascension the cruiser proceeded to the Sea of Okhotsk and then to the Bering Sea, where the Confederates captured 25 whalers, of which they burned 21 and bonded 4 to carry the crews back to San Francisco. The newspapers they got from the whalers told them that Savannah, Charleston, Wilmington, and Richmond had fallen, that Lee had surrendered to Grant, and that Lincoln had been assassinated. The papers also reported that Jefferson Davis had removed the Confederate government to Danville and urged Southerners to carry on the war "with renewed vigor." Although the news reports worried Waddell, he followed Davis's orders and kept burning whalers.[119]

When the *Shenandoah* left the Arctic, Waddell considered raiding San Francisco or cruising farther south where he could intercept merchant steamers operating between Panama and San Francisco. Deciding on the latter, he began looking for a ship that would have recent news of the war. On 2 August the British bark *Baracouta,* thirteen days out of San Francisco, provided the Confederates with newspapers that reported their country was "a thing of the past." All her armies had surrendered, Jefferson Davis and other officers, civil and military, had been imprisoned, much of the South was occupied by Union troops, and "all vessels at sea under the Confederate Flag [were] declared pirates."[120]

The first question Waddell had to consider was the disposition to be made of the ship. Should he surrender the cruiser or destroy it? If he surrendered it, into which port should he take it? When he suggested to Whittle that they return to San Francisco, Whittle told him "that he would continue to support him . . . in anything except going to a U.S. port, where all would be hung certainly. That he must ask the Captain in case of such a decision to give him his chance on a board in the open Pacific." The majority of the officers favored going to Australia, and the captain finally agreed and set the ship's course for Sydney. The next morning, however, Waddell changed his mind and altered the course for Cape Horn. Most of the men were English, and rather than abandon them in Australia he promised to take them to the "nearest English port."[121]

Waddell ordered Whittle to disarm the ship. Whittle had the men dismount the deck guns, and they "fired off all the pistols and muskets . . . boxed them up," and "struck them below." John Thomson Mason observed that "our old ship is now as harmless as a woman *without finger nails or teeth*," but removing the guns made "the deck . . . beautifully clear for working ship. ('It's an ill wind that blows nobody good.')"[122]

More disturbing to Whittle than defeat was its consequences for his father and brothers and sisters. Captain Whittle had been at home in Buchanan, Virginia, "awaiting orders" since the fall of New Orleans, and he was "excluded from the amnesty proclamation." His brother Beverley was in the Confederate army, and his sister Jennie, who was twenty-one, was a teacher. His four younger brothers and two sisters were with his father, and he had no idea how the war had affected Buchanan. The entries in his journal for the month of August each contain a sentence or two about the weather and the ship's sails and expressions of concern about his family. The last day of August he wrote, "Looking at what I have gone threw with during this month, I will always recall it as the most trying time of my life." Lining considered "his situation was the most to be pitied of any on board on account of his family."[123]

After the *Shenandoah* rounded Cape Horn, her officers and crew became interested in the ship's direction—was the captain taking her to "Liverpool, or Capetown?" Some of the men wanted to go to Cape Town, others favored

Liverpool. Waddell left the decision to the five lieutenants. Whittle favored Cape Town but did not vote; as the executive officer he was obligated to support Waddell. Chew voted for Cape Town; Grimball, Scales, and Lee voted for England. The decision to go to England satisfied the crew, most of whom were English, and who assured the captain that they "were willing & ready to go wherever he thought proper." Lining noted that there was considerable "coldness" between the "Capetown" and "Liverpool" officers, but it wore off after a few days.[124]

As the *Shenandoah* sailed toward England, Whittle was busy readying the cruiser to go into port, painting the ship inside and out, breaking out and restowing the hold, and holystoning the deck. He was also challenged to a duel by the ship's assistant surgeon, Dr. Frederick McNulty, who got drunk and "got into a row with [J. C.] Blacker, calling him an English-Irish-Orangeman . . . an insult," Lining noted, "that no Irishman can stand, as it brings in Religion, Politics, and a deadly feud." When Waddell ordered Whittle to confine McNulty to his room, the doctor got out his pistol, which Whittle took away from him.[125]

The next day the doctor told Waddell "that he had *not* been drunk . . . that he had only drawn the pistol *to show it to Whittle*," and that he had quarreled with Blacker because "Blacker began abusing the Captain." Whittle learned from other officers that McNulty had been drunk, that "the quarrel . . . [with] Blacker originated in . . . [McNulty's] own abusive language, and that Mr. B—— said nothing of the Captain." Whittle subsequently questioned McNulty in Scales's presence, and McNulty again denied that he was drunk and insisted that he had taken out the pistol to show it to the executive officer. When Whittle told McNulty that he was certain the doctor had not pulled the pistol simply to show it to him, McNulty challenged Whittle to a duel. Smith Lee, who was McNulty's second, and Lining, who was Whittle's second, decided that a duel could not take place on the ship and "must come off when we get onshore." McNulty agreed to postpone the duel, and it was never mentioned again by anybody.[126]

Whittle had mixed feelings about returning to Liverpool. He was "impatient to get where I can hear from my dear ones, and relieve their uneasiness about us," but he did not "look forward to our arrival at an English port with as much hope and good cheer as the rest." He was afraid that "if the Yankees were to declare . . . [England's] refusal to give up our persons a just cause for war and England's interests were opposed to a war, the English . . . would . . . sacrifice . . . honor to interest."[127]

Whittle need not have worried. After a pilot took the cruiser up the River Mersey, he anchored her next to the British guardship *Donegal*, and Waddell surrendered her "by letter to Earl [John] Russell . . . through Captain [J. C.]

Paynter, R.N., commanding H.M.S. *Donegal*." Charles Francis Adams, the U.S. minister to England, requested that the Earl of Clarendon, British secretary of state for foreign affairs, deliver the *Shenandoah* to the United States and her officers to American authorities to be tried for piracy.[128]

While the law officers of the crown deliberated Adams's request for three days, the *Shenandoah*'s officers and men were confined to the ship. But, as Orris Browne recalled, "in the meantime we had some fun going on . . . a little convention . . . in the ward room . . . and . . . a jubilee in the stearage." They enjoyed looking at "civilization" from the deck and eating fresh food the cook brought from the market, even raw onions, "the big strong kind," that "were grabbed by officers and men alike and eaten as though they were the finest apples." At the end of the third day, the law officers of the crown ordered the *Shenandoah* "delivered up" to Adams, but they ruled that they found "no case for any prosecution on the ground of piracy." Captain Paynter, ignoring the fact that some of the crew members were English, allowed all officers and men to land. Whittle and Lining got their bags in a cab and "finally got into the 'Clifton Hotel.'" They dressed, ate supper, and "went to the Queen's [Theater] to see 'Colin McKenzie.'"[129]

The next day Whittle, "still not feeling any confidence in the British government," went to Paris, where he stayed with friends for several weeks. His letters from home relieved his concern about his family, but they advised him "not to dream of returning" to Virginia. When Orris Browne's father, Dr. Peter Browne, who had served in the Confederate army, went to Washington to try to get pardons for his son and Lee, Mason, and Whittle, "the President and many leading men" told Browne that the *Shenandoah*'s officers "were pirates . . . who can never come back." After investigating possibilities for employment in England, France, Mexico, and Argentina, the four young men decided that Argentina offered them the best prospects. They "left Liverpool on the 23rd of January and arrived in Buenos Ayres on the 9th of March [1866]."[130]

As soon as they arrived in Argentina, Lee and Browne got jobs on John Page's sheep ranch on the Uruguay River. John's father, Captain Thomas Jefferson Page, like the other Confederate officers in Europe who could not return to the United States, was also on the ship, going to stay with his son, who had settled in Argentina before the war. Whittle and Mason went to Rosario, a city on the Parana River northwest of Buenos Aires. From there Whittle made a tour of the province of Cordoba and decided that Rosario was the place to settle. The second largest city in Argentina, it was becoming a major port: an ex-Confederate colonel had a beef packing plant there; an ex-Confederate naval officer was establishing an English line of steamers; a railroad from Rosario to the interior of the country was almost completed; and land in the area was increasing in value. He and Mason bought "fifty acres of superior land" with "two nice and one ordinary house[s]." There they planned to raise chickens and cows, cultivate a large garden, and sell vegetables, fruit, eggs, and butter. His friends in Rosario told him he was "bound to make money," since there were no truck farms in the area and the population there was increasing rapidly.[131]

Meanwhile, Dr. Browne kept working to obtain pardons for his son, Mason, Lee, and Whittle; with the assistance of three senators, a congressman, and a number of prominent Virginians, he succeeded in September 1866. Mason and Browne left Rosario in May 1867, and Whittle and Lee remained to dispose of their property. It took Whittle longer than he expected to "make arrangements for leasing reliably," and his funds "got very low," so that he had to work "on a river steamer to raise money to defray my expenses." He and Lee finally left Rosario in October 1868 and arrived in Brooklyn in December. After he stopped in Baltimore to get the documents pertaining to his pardon from Browne's older brother, he finally arrived at his father's house in Buchanan on Christmas Eve.[132]

Whittle immediately started to look for work. As he wrote to Robert Dabney Minor, "I cannot wait long as I have not the means." In their correspondence, Minor asked if Whittle had seen Waddell in Baltimore. Whittle replied that Waddell had been on the train from Baltimore, and he saw him briefly when he was changing cars at Annapolis Junction. Whittle told Minor that Waddell's "greeting was warm, very."[133] Not long afterward, however, Whittle saw a letter from Waddell that had appeared in the Petersburg *Daily Press* and several other American papers. In the letter Waddell stated that the officers of the *Shenandoah,* at the time when they learned from the *Baracouta* that the war had ended, had "set a bad example to the crew," and "their conduct was nothing less than mutiny." Although Waddell "denied publicly the offensive portions of the letter," Whittle and his fellow officers subsequently had little contact with him. Waddell went to work for the Pacific Mail Line in California, as captain of the company's steamships, for a number of years, and then returned to Annapolis, where he died in 1886.[134]

Whittle found a position with the Old Bay Line in Norfolk, Virginia, in 1868. He was captain of several of the company's passenger steamers that ran between Norfolk and Baltimore until 1890. From 1890 to 1901 he was superintendent of the Norfolk and Western Railroad's floating equipment. After the railroad sold the fleet, he became one of the founders of the Virginia Bank and Trust Company in Norfolk and was a vice-president and director of the bank until he retired in 1917.[135] Whittle also was an active member of the Confederate Veterans. He was elected Grand Commander of the Grand

Camp, Department of Virginia, in 1910, and presided over the state meeting in 1911.[136]

His membership in the Confederate Veterans enabled Whittle to keep up with some of the officers who had served with him on the *Shenandoah*. Shortly after John Thomson Mason died, in 1904, Whittle wrote a tribute to Mason which was read by Dabney Scales at a reunion of Confederate navy veterans in Nashville, Tennessee.[137] Scales, after a brief, unsuccessful attempt to establish a plantation in Mexico with Frank Chew and John Grimball, settled in Memphis. There he practiced law, was a member of the Tennessee legislature, and was a lieutenant in the United States Navy during the Spanish-American War. Chew, who disliked Mexico and had been ill for some time, also left Cordova in 1866. He went home to Missouri, where he had a job waiting for him.[138]

Grimball, who admitted that their "Mexican enterprise was a failure," returned to Charleston on 20 January 1867, in time to escort his sisters Gabriella and Charlotte to the St. Cecilia Ball. His father wrote in his diary that "John was invited on account of his conduct and services during the war." He studied law in Charleston, moved to New York City where he practiced law for sixteen years, then returned to South Carolina and became a rice planter. After he retired from planting, he moved back to Charleston where he was active in the Confederate Veterans and the Graduate Association of the United States Naval Academy.[139]

Charles Lining, who had gone to Argentina from England in 1865, was appointed government surgeon at Santiago del Estero, where he remained until 1874. When he returned to the United States, he went to Kentucky, where his brother was living, and practiced medicine in Paducah until his death in 1897.[140] Sidney Smith Lee, who returned from Argentina with Whittle in 1868, settled on his farm in Stafford County, Virginia. For a time he was the captain of the steamer *Ironsides,* which ran between Acquia Creek and Washington, D.C. He died on 14 April 1888 and was buried in Alexandria, Virginia, in the Lee family plot at Christ Church.[141]

After John Thomson Mason came back from Argentina, he studied law at the University of Virginia and practiced law in Baltimore. According to Whittle, who saw him often, he was "brilliantly successful." Orris Browne, who had returned from Rosario with Mason, went home to Cape Charles on Virginia's Eastern Shore. There he became the owner of Hollywood Place, which, according to his stationery's elaborate letterhead, was "The largest truck farm in Virginia."[142]

Whittle was unable to attend a dinner at Mason's home in 1893, and Browne wrote to Whittle to say that they had missed him. They had looked through Mason's log book and reminisced about the *Shenandoah*'s cruise and their experiences in Argentina after the war. Browne wrote, "you were during the cruise of the ship the real commander of her in many tight places and at times . . . you were the only man . . . who could have directed Waddell," and he reminded Whittle that "You are now the senior officer of the crew."[143]

Whittle outlived all of the *Shenandoah*'s officers except Scales, who died on 26 May 1920, and Grimball, who died on 25 December 1923. When Whittle died on 5 January 1920, the *Virginian-Pilot and Norfolk Landmark* proclaimed that "no other son of Norfolk made such a record in the war between the states as did Captain Whittle." Whittle's Civil War journal and letters, and those of his fellow officers, indicate that they all agreed with Whittle that the voyage of the *Shenandoah* was a "memorable cruise."[144]

Prologue

The Cruise of the *Shenandoah*[1]

[Lt. Whittle wrote the following for a speech to the Stonewall Chapter of the United Confederate Veterans. It was later printed in the *Southern Historical Society Papers* as "The Cruise of the Shenandoah."[1] This portion of the published account is reprinted here as an introduction to the actual journal—*Ed.*]

From time immemorial, one of the most effective and damaging means resorted to in wars between nations and peoples has been an attack upon the commercial marine of an adversary. It was a mode of warfare legitimatized by being resorted to all through the ages. It was adopted by our colonial cruisers during the revolutionary war, and during the war of 1812, 1813, and 1814, seventy-four British merchant vessels were captured by the United States Navy, under direct orders from their Navy Department and President Madison. Such depredations only became "piratical," in the minds of the Federal Government, when their own interests were jeopardized during our late war. Situated and conditioned as we were when that war began and during its continuance, such means of warfare were peculiarly alluring and suggestive of many and great results. The Southern Confederacy had no commerce, and was at war with the United States, which had a large commercial marine. To attack it was not only to inflict heavy pecuniary loss from vessels destroyed, but to force upon them great expense in insuring against these ravages and marine war risks.

Nor was this all. The United States had a formidable Navy with every facility to increase it; utilized most disastrously to the South by blockading its ports and closing the doors through which to receive from the outside world, materials and munitions of war, so greatly needed, and, too, in attacking its sea-board cities and towns. Every cruiser put on the ocean must, and did, have the effect to divert a force to protect as far as might be their threatened commerce.

But the South had no vessels of war, nor such as could be converted into cruisers. The quickest, best, and well-nigh only way to procure them was by purchase abroad, from the proceeds of sale of their cotton. Early in the beginning of the war this was seen, and the course adopted. To manage this difficult and important work a man of professional ability, clear business capacity, wise judgement and discretion in selecting and dealing with men, a knowledge of maritime and international law, calm equanimity, and great sagacity, was needed. To find such a man meant such a measure of success as all the difficulties and counteracting efforts would admit of. To select the wrong man meant foreign entanglements, prejudice of cause, and failure.

For this work the Confederate Government selected Captain James D. Bulloch, formerly an officer in the United States Navy, from Georgia, who, when the war began, commanded a merchant steamer running between New York and a Southern port. They might have searched the world over and would have failed to find another combining all the qualifications needed, as pre-eminently as he did. His heart was thoroughly in the cause, and he threw his whole body and soul into his work. To his judgment, sagacity, energy, and tact were due the possession and fitting out of the *Alabama, Georgia, Florida, Rappahannock, Stonewall, Shenandoah,* and the building of the ironclad rams at Liverpool, and the vessels in France.

Such of these vessels as took the sea, took it, not as privateers, as they were called by some, not as pirates, as our enemies opprobriously spoke of us, but as armed Government vessels of war, commanded and officered by men born in the South and holding commissions in the Confederate States Navy, of a Government whose belligerent rights were acknowledged by the kingdoms of the earth—commissions as valid as those held in the United States Navy.

The Confederate States had, as I said, no naval vessels, and none, or very few, that could be converted into cruisers. They had, however, a fine, loyal, able, and true personnel, composed of officers educated and commissioned in the United States Navy before the war. They were Southern-born men, who represented their respective states in the United States Navy, just as their representatives in Congress, and other Governmental branches, represented them in their respective spheres. The expense of educating and qualifying them for their positions was borne from the general fund collected from all the states, their respective states bearing their just proportion for the qualifying of their quota. These men were not politicians, but when the war clouds gathered felt bound by every sense of duty, love, and devotion, many of them against their judgment as to the judiciousness of disruption, and all of them against their professional hopes, aspirations, and pecuniary interests, when their mother states withdrew, to rally to their standard, resigned and tendered their services. They were accepted, and given commissions properly signed by the executive, and confirmed by the Congress of the Confederate States. No more loyal men lived on earth. Let no slanderous tongues or libelous pens impugn their motives. Let not their reputation for purity of purpose, as they saw their duty be handed down to posterity with any stain, but let their children have perpetuated in their minds and hearts the fact that their fathers were neither knaves, fools, cowards, nor traitors. These men were ready and anxious to serve their country in her hour of peril in any honorable field that they might be called to by her. These men officered the cruisers of the Confederate States.

The Confederate States Steamers *Sumter, Alabama, Florida, Tallahassee, Nashville, Georgia,* and others, had gone out and done damaging service against the United States merchant marine. There was, however, one branch of that marine, a large and remunerative interest, prolific with gain and profit, against which no special expedition had been sent. That interest was the whaling fleet of the United States.

The conception of the judiciousness of such a special expedition came, I think, primarily from Lieutenants John Mercer Brooke and the late Robert R. Carter, two distinguished officers of the United States Navy, who, upon the secession of their native State, Virginia, had resigned and joined her cause. Captain Brooke is now, and has been for years, a professor at the Virginia Military Institute at Lexington. They had, as members of a scientific expedition fitted out by the United States, become acquainted with the extent and cruising grounds of the whaling fleet. Lieutenant Carter, afterwards associated with Captain Bulloch, talked the matter over with him, and to him it was due, from his knowledge of the field, that a comprehensive letter and general plan was formulated for such a cruise.

Of course it could only be an outline of an expedition which constant and unavoidable emergencies and exigencies must qualify, shape, and control. But the sequel to its general observance by Commander Waddell, of the *Shenandoah,* proves with what masterly hand it was drawn up. Captain Bulloch also procured from the distinguished Commodore Matthew F. Maury, "the pathfinder on the ocean," who had likewise followed the standard of Virginia, a full set of "whaling charts." This expedition was to be the work of another vessel. It was to operate in distant and extensive fields and against vessels whose voyages were not finished until they were filled with oil. For such work, remote from every source of supply of coal or other stores, a cruiser of peculiar construction, etc., was needed. She must have good sail power and sailing qualities to economize coal, and she must have auxiliary steam power to carry her through the calms of the tropics and to get her out of any peril in which

Arctic ice might place her. She must have a propeller that could be, when not in use, detached and hoisted out of water, so as not to impede her headway under sail. She must have a means of condensing steam into fresh water, for drinking purposes. She must have comfortable and healthy quarters for her crew and strength of construction to carry her battery.

The very vigilant professional eyes of Captain Bulloch and Lieutenant R. R. Carter, who was associated with him at that time, fell upon the trim new British steamship *Sea King,* when just on the eve of sailing from the Clyde for the East Indies on her first voyage. They, as far as circumstances permitted, possessed themselves of thorough knowledge of her. She was built for an East Indian trader, with capacity, etc., to carry government troops, if desired. They were greatly impressed by her fine lines, sailpower, deck capacity, arrangement of machinery, her hoisting propeller, etc., and Captain Bulloch saw in her the very vessel he wanted to convert into a cruiser against the whaling fleet. He kept track of her, laid his plans for purchase, and quietly awaited her return to carry them out, making, ad interim, all arrangements to speedily equip and dispatch her.[2]

This and all his work required great caution, tact and judgment, for a sharp system of espionage surrounded him all the time.

The *Sea King* was a composite built vessel. That is, had iron frame and teakwood planking about six inches thick. She was 220 feet long, 35 feet breadth of beam and was of about 1,160 tons. She had a single, detachable, and hoisting propeller. Direct acting engines; two cylinders of 47 inch diameter and of two feet nine inch stroke; of 850 indicated horse power. She had three masts, the lower masts and bowsprit being of iron and hollow. She was a full rigged ship, of full sail power with royals, rolling, self-reefing topsails and royal topgallant, top-mast and lower studding sails, with all proper fore and aft sails.[3]

By October 6, 1864, the officers of the Confederate Navy who were to go on her had been quietly collected at Liverpool, Eng., by Commodore Samuel Barron, commanding Confederate Navy officer abroad, to hold themselves in readiness, without a clear knowledge of for what, but simply at Captain Bulloch's call.[4] On October 6, 1864, I was ordered by Captain Bulloch to take the 5 P.M. train from Liverpool for London, and on arrival to register at Wood's Hotel, Furnival Inn, High Holborn, as Mr. W. C. Brown. I was to appear the next morning for breakfast in the restaurant of the hotel, and while reading a morning paper to have a napkin passed through a button hole of my coat. So seated, I would be approached by a stranger with, "Is this Mr. Brown?" to which I was to reply, "Is this Mr. [Wright]?"[5] Upon an affirmative reply I was to say "Yes," and Mr. [Wright] and I, after finishing breakfast, were to retire to my room.

All this was done, and on October 7, A.M., Mr. [Wright] and I were in my room arranging for my getting on board the *Sea King,* which was then in port ready to sail. I went with Mr. [Wright], and at an unsuspicious distance viewed the ship, and later at a safe rendezvous, was introduced to her captain, Corbett. The ship was loaded with coal and cleared for Bombay by the captain, who had been given a power of attorney to sell her, at any time after leaving London, should a suitable offer be made for her. As I had been selected to be her executive officer after her transfer, naturally much, in every way, would devolve upon me, in the transformation of the vessel and her equipment. It was deemed expedient that I should observe her qualities, see her interior arrangements of space, etc., and formulate and devise for a utilization and adaptation of all the room in her. Captain Bulloch wisely deemed it best that I should thus have all opportunity of familiarizing myself with her, and hit on the plan of letting me join her in London.[6]

On the early morn of October 8, 1864, I crawled over her side, at the forerigging, and the ship in a few moments left the dock and went down the Thames. To everybody on board except Captain Corbett, who was in our confidence, I was Mr. Brown, a super-cargo, representing the owners of the coal with which she was laden. We were fully instructed to proceed to Madeira, where we were to call, a fact only known on board to Captain Corbett and myself, and not to exchange signals with passing vessels en route. On the voyage, with judicious caution and Captain Corbett's assistance, I possessed myself of much information that served a good purpose afterwards.[7] No one on board suspected anything out of the usual course.

By preconcerted arrangement, on the same October 8, 1864,[8] the propeller steamer *Laurel,* J. F. Ramsay, Confederate States Navy,[9] commanding, sailed from Liverpool for Havana, with passengers and general cargo. The *Laurel* was to call also at Madeira and get there sufficiently ahead of the *Sea King* to enable her to coal up. The *Laurel* arrived at Madeira on October 15 and coaled all ready for moving, upon the appearance of the *Sea King.* The "general cargo" of the *Laurel* consisted, as [was] afterwards found, of the guns, carriages, ammunition, etc., and stores for the future cruiser, and her passengers were the commander, officers, and small nucleus for her crew. On the early morn of October 18, the *Sea King* arrived off Funchal, Madeira, and running in sight of the harbor, displayed a private preconcerted signal. This was answered by her little consort and the two moved off successively to the Desertas, a rocky, uninhabited island not far from Madeira. There the *Sea King* anchored and her consort was secured alongside. It was perfectly smooth and a sequestered place, where there was little chance of observation or interruption. A rapid transfer of everything from the hold of the *Laurel* to the deck and hold of the *Sea King* was made on October 19.

[Whittle listed the officers at this point.]

List of the Officers of the CSS *Shenandoah*

[Lt. Whittle first listed the officers of the *Shenandoah* who were on board at the Madeiras; the list of officers published in the *ORN* is printed here because it is more complete,[10] including officers who joined in Australia and in the Arctic—*Ed.*]

James I. Waddell, lieutenant, commanding, C. S. Navy.
William C. Whittle, Jr., first lieutenant and executive officer, C. S. Navy.
John Grimball, first lieutenant, C. S. Navy.
Sidney Smith Lee, Jr., first lieutenant, C. S. Navy.
F. T. Chew, first lieutenant, C. S. Navy.
D. M. Scales, second lieutenant, C. S. Navy.
Irvine S. Bulloch, acting master, C. S. Navy.
Charles E. Lining, passed assistant surgeon, C. S. Navy.
W. B. Smith, acting assistant paymaster, C. S. Navy.
Matthew O'Brien, acting chief engineer, C. S. Navy.
F. J. McNulty, acting assistant surgeon, C. S. Navy.
O. A. Browne, acting passed midshipman, C. S. Navy.
J. T. Mason, acting passed midshipman, C. S. Navy.
W. H. Codd, acting first assistant engineer, C. S. Navy.
John Hutchinson, acting second assistant engineer, C. S. Navy.
Ernest Mugguffeney, acting third assistant engineer, C. S. Navy.
J. F. Minor, acting master's mate, C. S. Navy.
C. E. Hunt, acting master's mate, C. S. Navy.
Lodge Colton, acting master's mate, C. S. Navy.
George Harwood, acting boatswain, C. S. Navy.
John L. Guy, acting gunner, C. S. Navy.
Henry Alcott, acting sailmaker, C. S. Navy.
John O'Shea, (resigned), acting carpenter, C. S. Navy.
John Lynch, acting second carpenter, C. S. Navy.
Thomas S. Manning, acting master's mate, C. S. Navy.*
J. C. Blacker, captain's clerk, C. S. Navy.*
*Blacker was recruited in Melbourne; Manning in the Arctic Ocean.

. . . These twenty-three men were the officers who were transferred to the *Sea King;* all except myself and two engineers[11] who joined from the *Sea King*, went out on the *Laurel.*

Captain Waddell read his commission and addressed both crews, calling for volunteers. Only nineteen men,[12] including the small nucleus from the *Laurel,* volunteered, making, with the twenty-three officers, forty-two in all. Captain Waddell had the Confederate flag hoisted at the peak, received a bill of sale, and christened the *Sea King* the CSS *Shenandoah.* I do not know why the name *Shenandoah* was chosen, unless because of the constantly recurring conflicts, retreats, and advances through the Shenandoah Valley in Virginia, where the brave Stonewall Jackson always so discomforted the enemy, causing, it is said, one of the distinguished Federal generals to say of that valley that it must be made such a waste that a crow to fly over it would have to take its rations. The burning there of homes over defenseless women and children made the selection of the name not inappropriate for a cruiser, which was to lead a torchlight procession around the world and into every ocean.

Guns, carriages and their fittings, ammunition, of powder, shot, and shell; stores of all kinds, all in boxes, were transferred from the *Laurel* to the *Sea King.* All was confusion and chaos. Everything had to be unpacked and stored for safety. No gun mounted, no breeching or tackle bolts driven, no portholes cut, no magazine for powder, or shell room for shell provided. All was hurriedly transferred and in a lumbering, confused mass was on board. Every particle of work, of bringing order out of chaos and providing for efficiently putting everything in a condition for service, and of converting this ship into an armed cruiser at sea, amidst wind and storm, if encountered, stared us in the face.

The entertained and expressed hopes, that from the two crews a sufficient force would be induced to volunteer, were disappointed. Only nineteen men volunteered, which, with the twenty-three officers, made forty-two men for this stupendous work, and to man and care for a ship whose crew, with her battery, etc., as a cruiser, should be at least 150 men.

Captain Waddell, though brave and courageous, accustomed as a naval officer, to step on the deck of a man-of-war fully fitted and equipped at a navy-yard, where every facility aided to make everything perfect, was naturally discomforted and appalled. He conferred with Captain Corbett, late commander, and Lieutenant Ramsay, Confederate States Navy, who told me that they both said they considered his taking the ocean in such a condition, and so shorthanded, impracticable. As his executive officer, he naturally consulted me, saying that it was his judgment that he should take the ship to Teneriffe, communicate with Captain Bulloch, and have a crew sent to him. I knew every one of the regular officers personally. They were all "to the manner born."

With the fate of the CSS *Rappahannock* (which about a year before had gone into Calais, France, for some such object, had been held there inactive ever since) before me, and a positive conviction that our fate would be the same and result in ignominious failure, I strenuously advised against it. I said, "Don't confer, sir, with parties who are not going with us. Call your young officers together and learn from their assurances what they can and will do." They were called together; there was but one unanimous sentiment from each and every one, "take the ocean," and so it was, be it ever said with credit to them, and to the zeal and courage of the now lamented Waddell, we did take the ocean, as we were, and steered clear of Teneriffe and every other port not in our cruise. Let those who hear the sequel judge of the wisdom of the decision.

The battery consisted of four eight-inch smooth bore guns of 55 cwt., two rifled Whitworth 32-pounder guns, and the two 12-pounder signal guns belonging to her as a merchant ship. The two vessels parted company at 6 P.M., October 20, 1864,[13] and left the Desertas, we on our southerly course and the *Laurel* for Teneriffe, to report progress. Every officer and man "pulled off his jacket and rolled up his sleeves," and with the motto "do or die" went to work at anything and everything. The captain took the wheel frequently in steering to give one more pair of hands for the work to be done. We worked systematically and intelligently, doing what was most imperatively necessary first.

In twenty-four hours we had mounted and secured for sea, two eight-inch guns and two Whitworths, and the next day the other half of the battery was similarly mounted and secured. We cleared the holds and stored and secured everything below, and in eight days, after leaving the Desertas, had all portholes cut and guns secured therein.[14] Under our instructions we had to allow sufficient time for Captain Corbett to communicate with England and have the custom house papers cancelled and all necessary legal steps taken before any overt act.[15]

[The week after the *Shenandoah* left Desertas found Lt. Whittle too busy to begin entries in his journal. As executive officer his responsibilities included directing the work of the crew and sailing the ship. His account published in the *Southern Historical Society Papers,* his journal, and the journal of Dr. Charles Lining, Surgeon on the *Shenandoah,* agree that officers and crew, few though they were, toiled extremely long hours putting the ship, fittings, and cargo in some semblance of order. Lt. Whittle did not begin narrative entries in his journal until 26 October, a lengthy entry relating what had occurred during the past week. From this point on, his entries were quite regular. The Whittle journal begins below. Entries from 21 October 1864 through 25 October 1864 included only the date, the noon location, course, distance covered, and wind direction—Ed.]

1
Never did a ship go to sea so miserably prepared . . .

October 21–November 14, 1864

At Sea, Friday Oct. 21st, 1864
Lat: 29°52′N   Course South   85 miles
Long: 17°55′W   Winds Westward.

At Sea, Saturday Oct. 22d, 1864
Lat: 29°22′N.   Course WSW   60 miles
Long: 19°00′W.   Winds Westward.

At Sea, Sunday Oct. 23d 1864
Lat: 27°54′30″N.   Course SW by S1/2S   100 miles.
Long: 19°52′W.   Winds Westward

At Sea, Monday October 24th 1864
Lat: 26°49′30″N.   Course SW1/2 W   110 m.
Long: 21°27′W   Winds Nd & Wd.

At Sea, Tuesday October 25th 1864
Lat: 24°17′N.   Course SW by S   185 m.
Long: 23°16′30″W   Winds. Nd & Wd and Nd.

C. S. Steamer *Shenandoah*
At Sea. Wednesday Oct: 26th 1864
Latitude 22°33′00″N.   Longitude 24°34′W.
Dist 125 m.   Course SW3/4 S.   Wind NE.

What a very busy day these twenty four hours have been. Thank God we have a fine set of men and officers, and although we have an immense deal to contend with, all are industrious and alive to the emergency. When we look back and remember what the ship was when our gallant little band [commissioned her] and contrast her then disordered condition to what she now is—we have every reason to be proud of what we have done. The men were employed today in shifting coal from hold to the bunkers. This will clear to some extent our Berth deck. In the latter part I cleared up the deck so that all could sling their hammocks, after which I gave all the men clean mattresses and they will now sleep in the berth deck—which [is] one of the finest decks I ever saw. The officers were employed in clearing out the after Peak to receive our powder. All these shiftings are tremendous jobs as everything is upside down without any care or order. Never I suppose, did a ship go to sea so miserably prepared. The Gunner is fitting breechings for his rifle guns. Mr. O'Shea our carpenter hurt his foot very much today, but I trust he will not lay up for it, as the heaviest of our work now comes in his department. We are getting along wonderfully. Never did I see a set of officers and men work harder or more cheerfully than our noble band. When we set out who could have imagined that in so short a time, with 22 men and 24 officers[1] and every disadvantage under the Sun to contend with, we should have accomplished so much. The holy devotion to the cause has been handed by the officers to the men, and the work is not only done but cheerfully done. This afternoon made our first chase. She was a full rigged ship to leeward but we had not the daylight to catch her. All very well, and with one exception all very cheerful. I trust we may soon get a prize from which we may get some men. Imagine my anxiety to have more when I say that one more man would do an immense amount of good. Think of a ship of this size having only four men in a watch. Never mind we are enough to take care of the ship, and we must trust in God's aid. It is so much better than it would have been to go to some port and run the risk of being in the same position that the *Rappahannock* has for months been—besides what advantage would it have been to us to go into port? We could not have gotten men, we could not fit our ship, and we would have had a Yankee fleet awaiting us at the entrance of the harbor, and our position would have been most humiliating.

No indeed I never shall regret the advice I gave, which advice, I flatter myself kept us at sea.[2]

At Sea. Thursday Oct: 27th 1864
Latitude 21°05′N.   Longitude 25° 43′ W.
Course SW by S   Wind NE.   Distance 113

We have been hard at work all day. I got up at daylight feeling better but still have a severe pain in my side. I cannot account for it but thank God I am much better. Men employed all day in shifting coal from the Main Hold to the Bunkers. Officers busy in rigging and sending up Royal Yards. Carpenters busy fixing ports for our rifle guns. Gunner & gang arranging ammunition and Sailmaker fitting Hatch hoods. Altogether there is not an idle man in the Ship. Oh that we only had more men. We have a fine ship and the nucleus of a fine crew, but we want men of all things. The truth is, we will have to capture our crew, and win their affections by firmness & kindness. We have been distilling water all day. Saw a ship from aloft at sunrise, made sail and gained on her. Got up steam, and came up with her, and fired a blank 12 pd. cartridge and hove him to. A clear case of a Yankee built vessel, but a legal transfer. Lowered a boat and boarded her, Act. Master Bullock & Asst. Paymaster Smith the Boarding Officers & Masters Mate Hunt in charge of the boat. She proved to be the ship *Mogul* from London to Point de Galle, Ceylon. Her papers all right. Hoisted the propeller & made sail to Royals. This time we were sold by the *Mogul,* but better luck next time.

Friday, Oct: 28th 1864
Latitude 18°58′30″N.   Long. 26°10′90″N [W]
Distance 130 miles   [Course] S 3/4 W.   Wind NE to East.

Got up as usual at daylight. Saw from the deck the ship *Mogul* which we boarded on yesterday. We soon left her out of sight although she had all studding sails set on one side. Our ship must be fast as we were under topgallant sails and beat her easily. In the afternoon we made a Barque ahead under all sail. We commenced chase and at dusk were only about seven miles off and rapidly gaining on him. I am certain that he is a Yankee or a transfer. After dark we clewed up Royals to prevent running away from him during the night. Fortunately he suspects nothing or he would give us the slip—as it is very dark. As it is I am sure we will catch him bright and early. We have been hard at work all day, arranging parts, shifting coal and water and storing our temporary magazine. We have done an immense deal, but are so short handed and have so very much to do that our little makes but a small show. All hands are well and seem to be happy. In our young officers the Confederacy has a parcel of men of which any country would feel proud. We have done wonders. Notwithstanding my being so busy, I have time to feel blue, as I can't get my usual letters from my own dear ones. Oh! how much would I give to know how they are. I leave they [*sic*] and all to God. We have so much to be thankful for. We have fine weather and are preparing for bad.

At Sea, Saturday Oct. 29th 1864
Latitude 16°47′N.   Longitude 26°43′W.
Dist. 135 miles.   Course S by W.   Wind E & ESE

This morning to our surprise we found that the Barque which was right ahead last night had worked way to windwards of us. She still had every appearance of being a Yankee and we hauled up for her. We sailed much faster than the chase and rapidly gained on him. At 11:30 we lowered the propeller, got up steam and stood for him. Took in Royals & Top Gallant sails as we approached. We hoisted the English flag, and he, to our great joy, hoisted the hateful Yankee flag. We then ran up our flag and hove him to with a blank cartridge. We lowered and armed a boat and crew, and sent Act.: Master Bulloch, Pd Mid J. T. Mason, & M. Mate Hunt to board her. Very soon we had the extreme satisfaction of seeing the flag which is now the emblem of tyranny hauled down. Captain Everett Staples and Mate Peterson were sent onboard with papers. They were each sworn and examined separately before the Captain, myself Paymaster & Surgeon, and the Barque *Alina* of Searsport, Maine, 573 tons, laden with rail road iron from New Port, Wales to Buenos Ayres, was condemned a prize to the Confederate States. We stripped her of everything we wanted, which well may be imagined was an immense deal particularly as she was our first prize. As she had a fine sinking cargo we had [her] scuttled. The Barque and cargo were estimated at $90,000 in gold. At 4.45 P.M. she went down stern first under all plain sail and the sight was grand and awful. You might go to sea for many a day and would not see a vessel sink. She had been gradually sinking for some time and had gotten to the water's edge. She was in this position a man going down for the first time and struggling to prevent it. Finally at 4.45 a sea swept over her, she settled aft, her stern sank very rapidly, and her bow went straight into the air, and she turned a regular summersault. As she went down, the yards being square and the sails sheeted home, they had to yield and we could distinctly hear the cracking and tearing of the spars & sails. And as her bow went under a beautiful jet of water was thrown up high in the air. This is our first prize, and a good day's work we have had. The *Alina* was a bran[d] new barque having made but one trip from Searsport to New Port. She was a beautiful vessel and I am told by all on board that she was as clean as a new pin. God grant that we may have many just such prizes. There were on this vessel twelve souls. The Captain, two mates, a steward and eight hands. One of the men shipped at once as Coal Heaver,[3] and all of the rest except the officers were confined. I ordered the mate to lend a hand at something and he refused. I confined him for a short time and he came to his senses. All the crew except the steward and one man are German, and can speak very little English. I wish every one of them would ship except the Yankee. I would not have him. The Steward is from East India Madras. I trust we may get them all. One thing they will learn, that they will be in irons the whole time. We have done an immense quantity of work, and I ordered the "Main brace" to be spliced. As long as my men behave as they did today I shall be content. All went on well, notwithstanding the demoralizing tendency of the work. Many, many things which we wanted we succeeded in getting from her. You might see one officer come to me with a basin, another with a soap dish, and every imaginable thing and ask if they might have it for their issue. Of course it would have to be thrown overboard or given to those who needed it, and of course I pursued the latter course. This vessel might at first seem not to be a good prize, as she was an enemy's vessel it is true, but she was from a neutral port, bound to a neutral port and having what might be a neutral cargo. There was one flaw which spoiled all, that was that the owner of the cargo did not let it appear on his bill of lading that he had sworn before a notary that it was his property and that he was an Englishman—to this paper, to be in form, must have the signature & seal of the Notary. This Captain had a paper signed by the owner as to its being his cargo, but it was wanting in not having the Notary's signature. The Captain, Staples is a real down East Yankee, and "calculates" & "guesses." Oh how I do hate the whole race—and still, I can't help from treating them kindly. After we got threw with this fellow we made chase for another vessel, but found him to be a foreigner.

At Sea. Sunday Oct. 30th 1864
Latitude 15°25′N   Long: 26°44′W
Course S 1/4 W   Distance 90 miles.   Wind East to E by S.
This is a day of rest. We have done nothing all day, and unless it is absolutely necessary we will always observe the Sabbath. Capt. Staples and his two mates Peterson & Staples signed their paroles for the war or until regularly exchanged. The other eight I confined in the forecastle. Today to my great joy six out of the eight, ie. two [F]renchmen and four [D]utchmen shipped as seamen.[4]

These make seven out of twelve which, I think is doing very well. It will be a very great accession to us. We now have fifty three souls attached to the ship, of whom twenty four are officers. I trust that at this rate we may soon increase our crew from our prizes to sixty exclusive of the officers. This would make us eighty four all told. Even now we have enough to take care of her. This prize has given us a tremendous lift as we got from her, men, rope, blocks and every imaginable thing. Our men and officers are all well and cheerful, and no set of men ever had more or greater blessings to thank their God for than the crew of the *Shenandoah*. We have a fine ship and all will be well. We can run as fast as any can pursue. A vessel was in sight tonight and I trust that tomorrow may give us a prize. My prisoners thank me for my kindnesses to them. What a contrast with the treatment of our noble veterans by their side. Really when today I was sitting looking at Capt. Staples who is as free as anyone onboard, I could but think what a difference this treatment presented with that meted to us, and I felt at the same time, when I thought of the insults heaped by the Yankees upon our women, an amount of hatred which strongly tempted me to say here, Master-at-arms, take this old scamp and trice him up, gag & buck him. Oh, no, this must not be.

At Sea. Monday Oct: 31st 1864
Latitude 13°34′20″N   Longitude 27°18′30″
Course S by W 1/2 W   Distance 112 miles
Wind E N E to E by S.

Today I have had a hard day's work and still I do not see that I have done much. The fact is that where there is so much to be done and so few to do it, the little which is by great toil gotten through with seems small. We all have the satisfaction of knowing that we have in the aggregate done an immense amount and under unprecedented difficulties—and we can all say that no man onboard has been idle, or who has not shown the greatest zeal in doing every thing possible. I can now say that my gun gear is all fitted and I only want the ports cut in order to fight the guns. I have the chains unbent and the anchor is secured on the forecastle; the decks are all clear, and we have every reason to be thankful. An Executive Officer under such trying circumstances has an immense deal to do. I thank God that I have the health, strength and will to accomplish all. Today the prisoner Captain & his Mates came to me and said that they were very kindly treated and that they would never forget me for it. I simply replied that I treated them well for humanity's sake, and begged them not to think that my feeling was for them any other than that of hatred and this hatred of the most intense kind. And I told the Captain that I hated them as I did the "old boy" himself. Notwithstanding I will treat them kindly as long as they will allow me to do so, and when they do not conduct themselves properly they will find me as severe as I am now kind. At about 3.00 P.M. we made a large ship ahead standing to the Nd & Wd. We made sail in pursuit, lowered our propeller and got up steam. We were at dusk about two miles off when by the darkness she was almost hidden from view. We got within a mile and she hoisted the English flag, when a squall separated us a little and the night was so dark that we did not like to risk our boat, as beside the darkness there was some sea. The Captain concluded to leave her. I am strongly of the opinion that she was a Yankee, from her actions and appearance, and I am pretty sure that we left a fine prize when we gave her up. She was a very fast, full rigged, six topsail yard ship. She was so fast that we were going 11 1/2 knots under half steam and top gallant sails, and we had as much as we could do to catch her. All day we have had passing rain squalls, and tonight the weather looks a little threatening. The change of latitude begins to tell as it is now very warm. Capt: Staples is a thorough specimen of a low Yankee—a regular down Easter.

At Sea, Tuesday Nov: 1st 1864
Latitude 12°22′N   Longitude 27°51′W
Course SSW   Distance 85 miles
Wind NE to East–generally East

Hard at work all day, in fitting gun breechings and tackles. Shifting coal, un-bending chains, securing anchors and commenced overhauling running rig-ging aloft. Towards evening it commenced a series of rain squalls with some wind. We are under topsails, Fore Sail & Fore topmast Staysail. It has rained in torrents and sometimes the wind has been very fresh. It looks as though we might have an ugly night. The movements of the ship are much easier than I thought a ship of her size could be. All seem contented with her. "Spliced the Main Brace."

At Sea, Wednesday Nov: 2nd 1864
Latitude 10°36′N   Longitude 27°57′W
Course S 1/4 W   Wind from NE to SE by S   Distance 100 miles

This morning at 4.30 I was startled by a very heavy squall. I went on deck and found it blowing very hard and told Lieut: Lee he had better reef down to it. He got two reefs in without damage being done. What a blessing it is that we have Cunningham's Self-reefing topsails. Without them I am sure that short handed as we are we would be under reefed topsails the whole time—for the men we have would soon be worn out by continual reefing and turning out reefs. As we now are, all we have to do is to haul on the weather topsail brace & downhaul tackle, and slack the starboard halliards. The sail will in com-ing down roll itself snugly on and around the yard. It has been squally all day, rain & wind. I took a close reef in the topsails and a single reef in the foresail—these made the ship very comfortable indeed. It rained in torrents and the officers & men availed themselves of the fresh water to wash their clothes. It was to one a new sight to see officers so employed but they can and will do anything to get along. I laughed heartily at Jack Grimball and Dr. Lin-ing. I filled my water casks with nice water. I released the two mates and a man named Stinson from confinement. I can't help being kind to the rascals, and I often wonder at myself.

At Sea, Thursday Nov: 3d 1864
Latitude 9°50′N.   Distance 56 miles   Long. 28°20′W.
Course SW by S 1/2 S   Wind SSW & South

Today commenced and continued overcast and rainy with very little wind. We got up steam at 7.30 and steamed easily until 6 P.M. when we made sail and stopped the engines. Hard at work all day breaking out the sail room and holystoning the decks. We have an immense deal to do, and never I am sure did men labor under such great and so many disadvantages. I was very sorry today to have it reported to me that Silvester,[5] one of our firemen refused to cook for his mess. I sent for him and he positively refused. This is the first piece of insubordination or anything approaching trouble, and I shall punish the offender severely and make an example of him. I had him put in irons & triced up, and as he commenced to complain I had him gagged. In about an hour he sent the master at arms to me to say he would do anything if I would let him down. I sent for him and told him that he was the first person I had had to say a cross word [to], or take a harsh step [with], and that this ought to make him feel ashamed of himself. I do not think I will have any more trouble with him. I am sure that by this prompt dealing a lesson has been taught to all. I shall adopt prompt & just punishment to all offenders. Our men are a fine set of fellows and I only wish I had more of them.

> At Sea. Friday Nov. 4th 1864
> Latitude 8°23′N   Course SE E1/2 E   Longitude 27°54′W
> Distance 90 miles   Wind Variable N

I got up very early and found a nice little breeze blowing. The order was to get up steam at 4 o'clock but in consequence of this little breeze we triced up our propeller and made all sail. She spread a great deal of canvas in her plain sails. The ship is very much more comfortable under sail than steam, and I am always glad to see her going steadily with her wings spread. I have been very busy all day. My hands are full, and every one comes to me for everything. I rove today new fore braces, new main topsail halliards, and one new main brace. All those were from prize rope, and as that is all out I will have to wait for another prize. We are employed besides reeving braces in fitting guns and holystoning decks. A very disagreeable thing took place today. Mr. O'Shea, our carpenter had a quarrel with Mr. Lynch his assistant and when spoken to, being clearly in the wrong, he was very insubordinate. He was clearly in the wrong and I reprimanded him very severely indeed, and had much trouble in bringing him to his bearings. I find that for a time I will have to rule with an iron hand, and by checking in the bud all offences I will get all straight. In the afternoon we reduced sail to Royals. The wind is very variable, with passing squalls of rain & wind.

> At Sea. Saturday Nov: 5th 1864
> Lat 7°38′N   Long 27°49′W.
> Course S 3/4 E   55 miles   Distance   Wind—Variable

Today has been a great one with us. Saturday a week ago we destroyed by sinking our first prize and today we destroyed by burning our second, the

Schooner *Charter Oak* from Boston to San Francisco and valued at about $25,000. Last night this vessel was in sight but at so great a distance off that we could not make anything out with regard to her—and we simply steered such a course as would place us nearer today. During the night there was very little wind and this morning it was no better but we saw our friend the schooner quite near us. At daylight we ran for him under steam, and of course rapidly overhauled him. We hoisted the English flag but as usual he paid no attention to us. At 7.30 we fired a blank cartridge when to our great joy he hoisted the hateful Yankee flag, and hove to. We ran up our flag and sent a boat to send off the papers & officers. Very soon her Captain, Gilman & Mate Burgess came off with their papers. We put the Captain on oath, found the stranger to be the Sch. *Charter Oak* 168 tons from Boston to San Francisco, and a good prize. Now came the trouble. He had his wife, and a female passenger with one child. The Captain left it to me as to whether we should burn her and be burthened with two females and a child, or simply bond her & let all go. I concluded that whatever be the difficulties we should burn her—and this was decided upon. The Schooner had a cargo of about 100 tons of coal and the rest in sofas, ploughs and chairs and bureaux; as we are very much in need of furniture we will make the best of this chance. On one of the first boats came Capt. Gilman, his wife, his sister in law Mrs. Gage and her little son Frank. They all came onboard and brought their personal effects. When we took the deposition of the Captain he was on oath and I asked if he had any money plate or specie of any kind either private or public—he very candidly said that he had about $200. While he was onboard his vessel Capt. Waddell said that he thought of taking his money from him, and asked me what I thought of it. I told him that if I were in his place I would not take it from him, and reminded him that it might be all he had. He then said he had made up his mind to order Gilman to give it to him—and then he would in the presence of an officer give it to his wife. I thought the plan excellent. When the Master came onboard the Captain ordered him to give up his money—this he did at once, and Capt. Waddell in the presence of Passed Midshipman Mason gave it all to Mrs. Gilman. They all seemed to be thunderstruck and she was very grateful. We put the Captain, the two females and the little boy in the Starboard cabin, where they will be so much more comfortable than they have been in the Schooner that I think they will like it. We laid alongside of her until we had gotten from her all we wanted among which were upwards of 2000 lbs. of canned tomatoes and 600 lbs. of canned lobster. The former will come in very nicely. Having gotten from her all we wanted I sent all the men onboard our vessel and fired her. I started her aft, Mr. Bulloch forward and Mr. Mason amidships. When this war ends I am sure that we will all know how to make good fires. After firing her we lay in our little boat not very far off. It is an awfully grand sight to see a vessel on fire at sea. I could but think how very horrible it would be if any person had been onboard of her. It is wonderful how quickly the fire spreads and how rapidly the whole vessel seems to be enveloped in flames, and still it takes a vessel a very long time to burn. It is to me a painful sight to see a fine vessel wantonly destroyed but I hope to witness an immense number of painful sights of the same kind, and I trust that the *Shenandoah* may be able to continue her present work until our foolish and inhuman foes sue for peace. God knows I pray that their deluded minds may soon be enlightened but until they are I think that our present occupation will greatly tend to bring about the desired result. Today while onboard the prize Jack Grimball cut his left thumb to the bone right under the nail. It was painful but I trust he will soon get well. While we were shifting things from the prize she drifted too far from us, and I commenced to back down. I stopped the engine when about three hundred yards from her, and noticed one of her boats rowed by two of her crew coming off to us with a load of articles. I called out to them that we had sternboard on and cautioned them to keep well clear. Just then something called my attention somewhere else—and in a few minutes there was a great excitement onboard. The two foolish fellows had attempted to cross our stern and their boat had been capsized. We threw them life buoys and succeeded in saving both of them, but we lost the boat load. This was altogether their own fault but still an officer does not like to have a thing of the kind occur. The two men were from the Western Islands and were Portugueese [*sic*] and maybe did not understand what I said. One of our *lady* prisoners was Mrs. Gage, the sister of the Captain's wife. Her husband was in Grant's Army in Virginia and was killed. She does not seem to hate us as we would think she ought to. I am very sorry to have females onboard but I will do all I can to make them comfortable. I was very busy in the cabin and with the Master at Arms made & arranged their beds with my own hands—having finished it I sent for the Captain and asked him if he thought he could make out. I never saw a fellow express such pleasure & gratitude, and I believe he was sincere. He said, "Well, Sir, I cannot for the life of me see how you can be so kind." I do not wonder at their being surprised for I am astonished at myself, when I consider how stud[i]edly cruel they are to our dear women. Now the noble act of Waddell today in giving the money to Mrs. Gilman, does any one suppose that it was appreciated or that we will not be abused just as much as if we had kept the money. I paroled the Captain and Mates and confined the crew. There were ten souls. Two women, one child, Captain, two mates and four men—three of these were Portuguese. Our prize and cargo was valued at [$15,000]. Our prisoners seem rather pleased than otherwise especially the women. Poor things they must have been very uncomfortable in that small affair. After hoisting up boats & propeller we made all plain sail. The burning wreck is astern looking very pretty. I saw both of her masts go by the boards.

At Sea, Sunday Nov: 6th 1864
Latitude 7°27'15"N   Longitude 27°13"W
Course E 3/4 S   Distance 40 miles   Wind S W.

Another glorious day of rest. We did none but necessary work. At 10.30 mustered our crew and read "the Articles of War." The men all looked very well, and the ship quite well, but there is an immense amount to be done yet. Today at dinner I did a thing which has rendered me very unhappy in as much as it is very dangerous. In eating a piece of rhubarb pie I swallowed a piece of the glass bottle in which the fruit was preserved. I found out that the cook instead of drawing the cork had broken the neck off the bottle. I took three strong emetics and I trust I got clear of it, as the emetics were very strong & active. I feel very anxious, but I know that my life is in God's hands. This morning the four mates ie. of the *Alina* & *Charter Oak,* were ordered to clean out the place where they and the rest of the prisoners were kept, but positively refused. I withdrew their paroles and put them all in irons and now will keep them there. Our men are conducting themselves very well—there is no complaining. All are well.

At Sea. Monday Nov. 7th 1864
Latitude 6°28'30"N   Longitude 27°06'W
Course S 1/2 E.   Distance 65 miles   Wind S W.

Hard at work all day long getting things in order. I find it uphill work but I find my work getting easier each day as things are being put in a little better order. After 12 it was almost dead calm when we made a barque ahead, got up steam, lowered propeller and made chase. Came up with her in an hour, ran up the English flag, and to our joy she ran up the Yankee. We then ran up our flag and hove him to with a blank cartridge. Sent an officer to board him and send off his papers. The Captain, S. W. Hallett and mate came off. We assembled our usual board of Examiners, put the Captain on oath and took his deposition. Found our prize to be the American Barque *D. Godfrey* 30 days from Boston and bound to Valparaiso. She was an old vessel but had a valuable assorted cargo. We found that all of the cargo was under a large quantity of pine lumber and concluded that it would take us too long. We took a good deal of the lumber and some very nice rope. At 6 P.M. we fired our prize and stood on under sail. This is our third prize in less than ten days. On board of our prize there were ten souls, all told, Viz. Captain, 2 Mates, 6 Seamen and a negro Steward. To my great joy 5 seamen and the Steward shipped.[6] They are all good, young men and the darky is the very man I want for Ship's Cook.[7]

We now have on board sixty souls including the Steward of the Barque *Alina* whom I shipped tonight, and will make him Ward Room Steward.[8] Our men and officers all behave so very well when we take a prize, it makes me feel proud. Beyond all doubt this is the most demoralizing work any set of men were ever engaged in and the strictest and most constant discipline will alone answer, more particularly when we are actually capturing our crew. When in the world's history was a parallel ever known. We are really high up in the world in the way of getting a crew. Of the six we shipped today three were English, two Yankee and 1 from New Brunswick (St John's). Today I knocked away a portion of the house forward, which will give us a fine place to work our two forward 8 in guns. I hope we may never have occasion to use them for with the crew which we have gotten under unprecedented circumstances we could not do much. It is really amazing to see our female prisoners, they really are so much more comfortable here than when we found them that they are quite in love with the ship and really seems [*sic*] to enjoy a capture as much as we do. As to the little boy, he gives three cheers for Jeff Davis every day. All prisoners except the Captains are in irons.

> At Sea, Tuesday Nov: 8th 1864
> Latitude 4°42′N.   Longitude 28°24′W.
> Course SW 3/4 S   Distance 130 miles   Winds. Easterly

Today we have done a great deal. We have never done more work in one day. Now all our guns are in their positions and if necessary we can fight, but I trust it may not be necessary. I ran up much of our running gear and regulated all the officers' messes. Tomorrow I think we will catch a Yankee. I trust I may be correct, for nothing gives me more pleasure than to do as much harm as I can in a legitimate way to our inhuman foes. Really it would appear from their acts of brutality and barbarity that any thing would be legitimate, but I mean things which are legitimate between two civilized nations at war— which I do not at all grant to be the case here. But how often do I think of my dear home and country. Oh how they are all suffering. Oh how often I think of my own dear ones [here Lt. Whittle scratched out "Pattie" and replaced it with "ones."—*Ed.*], and wish that I could see them. Will we ever meet again? God grant that we may, and in the mean time I invoke the protection of God on [them]. [Lt. Whittle has scratched out a word and replaced it with an indecipherable word; "them" fits the context and grammar. Three full lines are then blotted out.—*Ed.*]

> At Sea. Wednesday Nov: 9th 1864.

[Until this point in the manuscript Lt. Whittle had inserted the noon position, course, speed, and weather information at the bottom of the entry.

This information is inserted after the date in the remainder of the manuscript. This seems to have occurred in conjunction with the change from sea time to civil time in keeping the log which occurred on 8 November 1864.—*Ed.*]

Longitude 26°52'W   Latitude 4°43'N
Course East.   Distance 95 miles   Wind. Var. S W

We have been hard at work all day. We are gradually getting things in order, but very slowly: however every one does his whole duty and we can do no more. At an early hour we made a full rigged Brig to leeward and ran for her. She proved to be the Danish Brig *Anna Jane* from New York bound for Rio [de] Janeiro. Got him to heave to and sent Lieut. Scales to ask him if he would take some of our prisoners off our hands. He very kindly consented and we sent Capt. Staples, Mates Peterson & Staples and Seaman Hinson of the late bark *Alina* and Capt. H. W. Hallett, Mates Taylor & Brown & Seaman Iameo of the late barque *D. Godfrey*, on board as passengers, sending a barrel of beef & bread for their use, and sent also a chronometer for the Captain who thus kindly relieved us of these eight Yankees. Our female prisoners asked if we were going to let them go, and when we said no, she [*sic*] did not seem at all disappointed, but the fact is they are treated with more consideration than ever before in their lives, and they are more than contented. It is a perfect farce to call them prisoners. This evening when Staples & family left, they showed the regular Yankee character, and although we were by his own account very kind to him, he did not thank anyone of us or did not say good bye to any one of us. What a miserable set of villains our enemies are. I hate them more than ever the more I see of them. We saw a large ship to windward and stood for him. We soon came up with him and we exchanged English colors to him. We went so close to her and found her name on the stern to be the *Royal Saxon* from New Sydney. I thought she was a Yankee built vessel as she had long mast heads, and looked like a Yankee vessel. I expect she was built in St. Johns, New Brunswick. All vessels built there look very much like American vessels. I am very much disappointed as I expected to capture a Yankee today. I was opposed to the prisoners today being sent away as their release will certainly let all the Yankees know that we are near.[9] I trust however that I may be wrong. Today I rated as Captains of Tops William West, John Davey, Louis Rowe and Peter Raymond; and Mich'l Moran, C. Hold, also John Griffiths, Coxswain. All four of these men rated Captains of the Top are men whom we have shipped from the crews of our prizes.

At Sea, Thursday Nov: 10th 1864
Latitude 4°20'30"N   Longitude 26°39'W
Course SE by S 1/2 S   Distance 28 miles   Wind S by E & S

Another glorious day in our legitimate calling. At an early time I was awak-[en]ed by Mr. Browne who was officer of the forecastle coming down and reporting to the Captain that "She was the Brig *Susan* from New York." I had no idea that any vessel was anywhere near us. I jumped out of bed and going out on deck found that Jack Grimball had a nice looking Brigantine close on our weather bow. Grimball reported that she had been made during the Mid-watch, and that we had gained steadily upon her. She had every appearance of being a Yankee, having long poles, square sails and cotton canvas and her build being Yankee "sans doute." We ran up the English flag and she to our great delight hoisted the detestable Yankee rag. We hoisted our true colors and fired a blank cartridge. She showed no signs of heaving to and we gave him another, which threw his headyards all aback. Lieut Chew of Jack Grimball's watch went onboard, and soon we saw the emblem of tyran[n]y come down. The Captain Hansen and Mate came onboard with all papers. The Captain was put on oath and his deposition taken. We found his vessel to be the Her. Brig *Susan* of New York with a cargo of coal from Cardiff, Wales, to Rio Grande do Sul, Brazil. After due examination, the bill of lading not being sworn to before a Notary as English property, the Captain was told that his vessel was a prize, and he was sent off to get his things onboard. She was valued at $5,443. This is our fourth prize and the first to catch [for] which we have had no steam [up]. There were seven souls onboard of which number three came up at once and desired to ship. These three were all [E]nglish-men.[10] We have been extremely lucky in getting men. I expect another tomorrow. As soon as we got all useful articles from our prize, which we generally call "Manaverlings,"[11] we scuttled her, and she went down bow first, her stern raising straight up into the air. Oh! how much I wish she had been a fine clipper ship. It is rarely the case that a vessel will go down bow first; it is generally the reverse. Today we tacked ship three times and each time the ship went round beautifully. I never saw a vessel work better. With even our few men we can tack her very easily and have enough to man our guns. I want just about sixty more good men. I had today a fine opportunity to holystone the decks and gladly availed myself of it. I also rove off new topsail braces and topgallant gear. I am always very tired at night but manage to sleep very well. Tonight I divided the prisoners in two watches, as they prefer to keep watch to being in irons.

At Sea, Friday Nov: 11th 1864
Latitude 3°18'N   Longitude 27°35'30"W
Course SW.   Distance 85   Winds Ss/Es/Ss/Ws

Today we have been busy all the time—in fact I should like to know when we were not busy. The weather has been boisterous with passing heavy wind and rain squalls from the Sd. This morning we saw the same ship to leeward which was yesterday to windward but during the day we lost him astern. Employed during the day in reeving new gear and shifting coal from the "Tween" decks to the main hold. We will soon have our berth deck clear. Today the Captain disrated Geo: Silvester from fireman to Coal Passer. This poor fellow is I really think little better than half idiot, being very deficient. He is something of a knave as well and I made him a steady cook to the fireman's mess. This afternoon we saw a large ship to windward and clewed up everything and steered such a course as would bring us together. At midnight nearly all of us were on the look out even the two female prisoners. They say that they hope she may be a Yankee, as they want us to catch a big one when they are with us.

At Sea, Saturday Nov 12th 1864
Latitude 1°45'N   Longitude 29°22'W
Course SW   Distance 150 miles   Wind S by W

At a very little past midnight we saw the sail in chase of which we were last night and stood right for her. We passed very close to her and fired a gun and hail[ed] her. She replied by heaving to and giving her name which we did not understand. It was a very rainy disagreeable night but we sent a boat on board in charge of Lieut. Lee. Very soon the Captain and mates came onboard, and we were congratulating ourselves upon having a fine prize, when examination of the papers put us in a stew. We swore the Captain and took his deposition, found his vessel to be the ship *Kate Prince* which belonged in Yankee land and was clearly a Yankee ship but she had an English cargo of coal bound to Bahia, Brazil. All of her papers as to the ownership of the cargo were clear and in form, as the owner had sworn before a Notary as the owner and that he was an English subject. The owners were Hett, Lane & Co. of Liverpool, and the case was apparently the same as in the case of the Brig *Susan* but the notarial oath in the latter's case was missing—and this was necessary to show that the cargo was neutral. But here was a case where the coal from Cardiff was when compared to the vessel, of very little value, and to inflict heavy loss on our Enemies, the owners of the ship, we might have destroyed ship and cargo and afterward paid the owners of the coal its value, but the Captain concluded to bond him and make him take all the prisoners. We therefore bonded him for $40,000 and sent all our passengers paroled onboard. The two females and little boy were of course not included in the parole. They were all exceedingly grateful for our kindness particularly the women, who I am quite certain would have preferred to have staid. Therein we differ for I am very glad to get clear of them and I hope never to have a female prisoner onboard again. These two were treated in the most queenlike manner by all hands. The little boy

(Frank) did not want to go, and said he liked the Rebels. We were working until 5 A.M. and I was in charge of the deck the whole time and as it was raining in torrents, I was heartily tired of it. The Captain was a man named Libby and was as plaus[i]ble a Yankee as I ever saw. He sent us as a present two barrels of [I]rish potatoes. We have been hard at work all day. We overhauled another vessel which hoisted English colors and she really looked so English that we did not board her. Very soon afterward we saw a clean nice looking Bark and made chase. We overhauled her about 12 o'clock, and hoisted the flag and fired a gun. She hove to and ran up the flag of Buenos Ayres, but he looked so very much like a Baltimore vessel that we boarded her. Jack Grimball was the boarding officer, and he very soon came back, and said to the Captain, "Well Sir it requires a better lawyer than I am to condemn this vessel but I have brought off all the papers, but did not feel authorized to take the Captain from under his flag." She proved, as we thought, to be a Baltimore built Barque and bound from Baltimore to Rio [de] Janeiro. The Captain contended, the Register & clearance set forth, that she had been a Baltimore vessel but that she was sold to parties in Buenos Ayres—but still she had no bill of sale onboard. Her cargo was flour and was shipped by Messrs. Phipps & Bros. of New York, and everything was so mysterious that we decided to get the master on board and examine himself and his Mate. They came on board and the Captain James P. Williams of Matthews County, Virginia was sworn. He testified that the sale was a good one and that the vessel was a regular Buenos Ayres vessel, but the cargo was owned apparently by Phipps Bros. N.Y. it having been shipped by them by Pendergrast of Baltimore. This latter gentleman was the former owner of the vessel, but the Captain had no bill of sale and this was deemed necessary. There was something very singular in the manner and bearing of the Captain, and we called in the Mate sending the Capt. on deck. Mr. Smith from Baltimore was Mate and we put him on oath, and he testified that in his opinion the sale was a mock one intended to prevent the Federal Authorities from seizing the vessel which was the property of Mr. Pendergrast an earnest and warm Southerner in Baltimore who has two sons in the Army. He said that he believed that Pendergrast was the real owner. The case was very much mixed up and there was evidently foul play somewhere. We concluded that Mr. Pendergrast was the real owner of the vessel, but the Capt. said that if Mr. P—— was no better a Southerner than to ship a Yankee's goods as the flour appeared to be, his property could have no protection from us. We sent for the Captain and told him that we were going to burn him. He was very much excited and said "Well Sir, Mr. Pendergrast will lose the whole value of the vessel, for she is not insured for a single cent." I caught him up at once and said how is it Sir, that to save the vessel you said you knew the sale was a good sale and that she was a Buenos Ayres vessel, and swore to this, and now that you are told that we are going to burn her, you say that Mr. Pendergrast will lose the whole. I put him on oath and he testified that P—— would lose the whole value as she was not insured and said that it would break his heart as she was named for his wife. Thus the Captain perjured himself before all of us, and when I asked him how his two depositions could be so utterly and entirely incompatible he had not a word to say—and the poor wretch stood before us a renegade Virginian and a perjured man. We stuck to our determination to burn her and just as we sent the Captain off to pack his traps, he went to the Captain [Waddell] and begged him not to burn her as he was a young man just married and all his little savings were invested in her—this was so disgusting that I could scarcely keep my hands off the perjurer. We removed from him seven Spanish Brazilian prisoners and were busily engaged in shifting everything we needed from him when Dr. Lining came off with the letter bag. One of these was from Phipps Bros. N.Y. to the Consignee at Rio, telling him that the Cargo was sent in their name but that the money must be remitted to Pendergrast. This letter threw open the mystery. It was evident that the name of Phipps Bros. was used to save the cargo which really belonged to Mr. Pendergrast. It was very late and much damage had been done but we could not burn the property of our friends and our only course was to undo what we had done and return everything to the vessel. This we did but great damage had been done as the preparations for firing, as made by us, to not leave any portion of the cabin whole. I am truly sorry the thing occur[r]ed and attribute the whole to the want of truth on the part of the Captain, or to the fact that he was not allowed in the secret. We did all we could to repair the damage, and have the satisfaction of knowing that the vessel is perfectly sea worthy. For fear the fact that his vessel was let off might cause a confiscation of Mr. Pendergrast's property by the Yankees, we concluded to consider the sale good, and to bond the cargo. If ever I have a chance I will explain this to Mr. Pendergrast. I wrote a few lines to my own dear Pattie and sent it by this opportunity enclosing it in one from Waddell to his wife. There is no telling how long it will be before she gets it, but I am pretty certain that it will be received some day or other. Oh! how much would I not give just to know that my darlings were well. My thoughts are constantly of them I console myself very often by reading over and over again their letters to me, letters full of affection and love. [Five and a half lines are scratched out.—Ed.]

At Sea, Sunday Nov 13th 1864
Latitude 1°40′North   Longitude 28°24′W
Course E 1/4 S   Distance, 62   Wind Sd/Ed(light)

This day of rest is most acceptable to us after the very hard work of yesterday and the night before. At 10.30 we had muster. All of our little band came out in uniform. We did nothing until about 3 P.M. when we made a schooner standing toward us. Very soon she tacked and stood a little higher than we. We got up steam and stood in chase. I soon concluded that she was a Yankee schooner. We rapidly overhauled her—and hove her too [*sic*] and to our great delight she ran up the Yankee rag. We boarded her and had her Captain and Mate sent onboard. I put the Capt. Archer on oath and taking his deposition and examining her papers we found her to be the Schooner *Lizzie M. Stacey* from Boston to Honolulu with an assorted cargo. The case was clear, and as soon as we got everything from her we burnt her. She had seven souls all told and was 143 tons. She was a fine little vessel and would make a fine cruiser, and if we had the men I would have applied for her. I trust we may get three men from her. She has a Baltimore negro steward—and a sailor named Cook lately discharged from the U.S.S. *Brandywine*. She was valued at $15000. This is a nice piece of Sunday's work. Put the Mate & crew in irons. Made Sail & triced propeller.

2

I wish we could catch another Yankee . . .

November 15–December 12, 1864

At Sea, Monday Nov: 14th 1864
Latitude 1°39′20″N.   Distance 218 m.   Long: 28°01′W.
Course E 1/4 S   Wind Sd/Ed(light)

We have been busy all day clearing all the coal off the Berth deck; this we are doing to promote the comfort of our crew, and when we finish I am certain that we will have as nice a Berth deck as ever was seen. This morning the Baltimore darky Chas. Hopkins shipped as O. Sea. and I handed him over to the tender mercies of the forward Officers' mess. One of the Seamen, a Scotchman named [James] Strachen, from our last prize shipped as coal passer. During the day I sent the prisoners to work at the coal with our men, supposing that they would prefer it to confinement. Two of them who were Yankees positively refused, but as I had given the order it must be obeyed, so I determined to punish them. I may not have been right in giving them the order although for their good; but as I had given it there was but one course to pursue and that was to punish the parties who refused to obey it. I triced one fellow up and the other said he would prefer going to work to being similarly dealt with. The tricing up had a most wonderful effect—in two hours the man begged to be let down, as he desired to ship. We shipped him as Seaman.[1] Very soon the fourth Seaman, a Swede named [Jacob] Hansen came aft and shipped. Thus we have gotten four out of the seven—and that I consider doing wonderfully. We now have 43 men and 24 officers which makes in all 67 souls. By this it will be seen that our original number of men has been doubled. We now have men enough to take care of the ship, but there is one thing which gives me great concern and it is that so many of our crew are enlisted for only six months instead of for the cruise. These when the time comes will all leave us as they will have a sufficient amount due them to get drunk and have a spree onshore. After they have spent all their money I have no doubt but all would reship, but suppose we can't remain where we discharge them. Why then our condition will be really worse than when we first came out. However, I shall use my best endeavor to have no more six months' men. We have indeed been most wonderfully blest and have a immense deal to thank a good God for. . . . [Six lines are scratched out.—*Ed.*] In the mean time all I pray for is success in our holy cause.

> At Sea, Tuesday Nov: 15th 1864
> Latitude 0°02′30″S.   Longitude 29°31′W.
> Course SW 1/4 S   Distance 135
> Wind—S, S by W & S & Ed.

Today hard at work again, but now it does not come so hard to the men as I work watch and watch in the day time as well as at night, instead of all hands all day. We came up with and easily passed a large English ship. We crossed the Equator at about 11.30 A.M. and there are a great many officers and men who had never done so, I among the number. At about 7.30 P.M. there was a great hailing forward and then a brilliant light was over the bow—and every one was informed that Neptune was coming. I did not know of the preparation, but very soon was convinced by hearing the ship hailed and permission to come onboard demanded—this was granted and such a noise you never heard—then came a very tall figure aft with a very long harpoon in one hand and a large chafing mat as a hat, and asked permission to look for "his boy"— excused himself for being so late for he had been on the English ship. Very soon the ship was in an uproar caused by the "Police" [who] collected all the poor devils who had not "crossed the Line." I think the first was Chew (Lieut) who resisted at first but then took it in good part. They first asked "where are you from" and woe be to the man who replies for as he opens his mouth it is filled with soap, grease and molasses—if you do not answer the[y] lather your face with this same stuff, and go threw the form of shaving you, with a large wooden razor. After this they start the pump and nearly drown you by filling your eyes & mouth and wetting you threw and threw.

Grimball came on watch at 8 and thought that he would get off, being the officer of the deck, but his horror was great when Chew came and said, "Grimball I'll relieve you," and at the same time two policemen Lee and Bullock collared him. After he was through when I was congratulating myself upon my escape, he (Jack) came up and walked me up—I pulled off to an undershirt and took it well and thoroughly. Boatswain's Mate Warren was Neptune. Master at Arms Reid was his wife, or Mrs. Neptune, and Mr. Guy, Gunner, was his barber. The shaving soap which they used on me was a most wonderful mixture of soap, grease, molasses and stewed apples. All went on very well, and all took it very well except Mr. Codd one of the Engineers who got mad. And Dr. McNulty who when the Barber asked him where he was from, was not smart enough and replied very politely and had his mouth filled with the shaving soap. This his Irish blood could not stand and he struck the barber and knocked him sprawling full length on deck. It was rare sport—but I am very glad that it comes but once. There was but one Lieut. (Lee) out of five who escaped.[2]

At Sea. Wednesday Nov: 16th 1864
Latitude 2°45′S   Longitude 30°17′W
Course S by W.   Distance. 167 miles
Wind. SE.

This morning we could scarcely see the Englishman whom we beat so shamefully on yesterday. All day hard at work getting the ship in order. It is very up-hill work I can assure you. No one knows how much I go threw with and I am sure what we have done will never be appreciated, but I have but one aim in this cruise and that is to do my duty to the greatest advancement of my Country's Cause. I care neither for reputation or anything of the kind.

At Sea. Thursday Nov 17th 1864
Latitude 5°39′S.   Distance 180 m.   Longitude 30°50′W.
Course S by W.   Wind from SE to ESE.

Hard at work all day in clearing the Berth Deck and in fitting a bulkhead athwart-ships over the middle of the main hatch. We made a Brig, but upon coming up with her, in reply to our English flag she hoisted the Prussian flag. Today we have steady SE trade winds and hope we may hold on to them for some time to come. Our ship sails very well for the sail we have had set as we have generally been under short canvass [sic]. We ran by the Prussian today very rapidly, having made him in the morning ahead and lost him astern by sunset. Today I have felt wretchedly and am very uneasy for fear the piece of glass may have something to do with it. The doctors say it has been too long since it was swallowed for it not to have shown itself long since. It is either glass or tobacco and I am not certain which. If the former I will not long be in doubt for it will prove fatal by day after tomorrow. I trust that I may be better tomorrow, for the anxiety makes me miserable.

At Sea, Friday Nov: 18th 1864
Latitude 8°36′30″S.   Dist: 172 m.   Longitude 31°13′W.
Course S 3/4 W.   Wind from ESE to SE.

All day have had the regular SE trades and more or less fresh—towards evening the breezes freshened and they shortened Sail to Top gallant sails. Had our regular evening quarters. I feel today very much better and came to the conclusion that it was the excessive use of tobacco which was injuring me, and I determined to stop both chewing and smoking. I took all my tobacco and gave it to my mess mates, and am going to do my best to break the chains of slavery to a habit which has done me so much damage. I may not have the power to quit it, but I am going to make all the effort that I am capable of—God give me strength. This is by no means the first time that I have tried to rid myself of this habit, but heretofore I have made the attempt when I had little to occupy my time, and I was therefore more tempted to recommence.[3]

At Sea, Saturday Nov: 19th 1864
Lat: 11°45'   Dist: 192 m.   Long: 31°23'W
Course S 1/4 W   Wind. ESE

Today we had a general cleaning up, and really I was surprised to see the deck look so very well. The whole day was spent in holystoning the Spar deck, and really I am still so short handed that I did not finish on deck. I am eternally busy and will be for some time, but after awhile when I get things in good working order, I will have comparatively so little to do that I fear I may become lazy. We have now been within one day of a week without catching a Yankee and it is becoming monotonous. This too should be our lucky day. We were just one month old yesterday as I count the vessel's becoming Confederate as soon as we commenced to get into her our munitions of war. It is a little singular that this ship I may say was born on the birth day of my own dear Pattie. This will give me good luck I am sure, and nothing is good luck to me which is not good luck to all onboard. Oh what would I not give to see my darlings, or to receive one of their dear letters. And, how much would I not give to hear from home. I place all dear to me in God's hands, and only say "Thy Will be done."

At Sea, Sunday Nov: 20th 1864
Latitude 14°50'S   Distance 190 m.   Long: 31°33'W
Course. S 1/4 W.   Wind SE by E.

At 10 A.M. we had a regular inspection and mustering of our crew. The men were all dressed in uniform and looked very well but grey will never stand the sea air. I have a suit which I never had on until I came onboard and now it looks as though I had been wearing it for a year. Oh! no the old blue was the best, and I think the only colour which will stand. Made chase for a Brigantine, soon came up with and lost her. She was an English vessel. Also saw a bark and found, upon overhauling her that she too was an English vessel. The trades are now very regular.

At Sea, Monday Nov: 21st 1864
Latitude 16°36'S   Dist: 100 m.   Long: 31°58'W.
Course S by W 1/4 W   Wind E SE to SE

Hard at work cleaning up the Berth deck and reefing off new running rigging. We now have changed nearly all of our running gear from old hemp to new manilla, all of which we have captured in our various prizes. We passed during the day a great many vessels but all showed a foreign flag and all looked foreign. Today I was a little amused by our Captain of the hold, an [I]rishman named Moran, coming aft and saying to me "Mr Whittle, Sir, I wish, Sir, that you would take me on deck, Sir. I am not much of a scholar, Sir, and Mr. Smith, Sir, expects me to recollect where every package is, Sir, and what is in it, Sir, and I can't do it Sir." He is a hard working, quiet man and I put him there because he would get more pay. I explained this to him and he said he would rather not stay. I rated Walter Madden (Sea) Captain of the Hold in his place. We are getting along quietly and remarkably well, the only fear that I have is that when our six months men's times expire they will not re-enlist. I trust however that the neucleus [sic] will stay and we can get another crew.

At Sea, Tuesday Nov. 22nd 1864
Latitude 18°36'S   Dist: 120   Long: 31°51'W
Course S 1/2 E   Wind. ESE & SE by E.

Today we have done a great deal, but really there remains so much undone that to see what has been done is rather difficult. We are now having very unsettled weather and we have passing squalls which are sometimes very fresh. This morning before we made sail a large English ship crawled up on our lee quarter, but when we set our royals and top-gallant sails we dropped them very rapidly. He telegraphed his name as the English Ship *Harwich* bound to Sidney New South Wales. We telegraphed ours as the British Gunboat *Hesper* bound on a cruize. He no doubt knew that such was not the case as the *Hesper* is a very small craft. We tell any number of fibs, but all is fair in love and war.

At Sea, Wednesday Nov 23rd 1864
Latitude 21°25'30"S   Dist: 168   Long: 32°02'W.
Course S 1/2 W   Wind ESE & E by S.

Our work is progressing slowly but surely. Today I am at work at our rigging and battery. All these are heavy jobs, but thank God, the heaviest of our work is over. Still we want more men. I want men enough to be able to see, when an order to take in a sail or sails, is given, every rope manned, and every thing go in together. These things cannot be until we have more men, but when I consider that when we started we had five (5) men, including two quartermasters in each watch, and now we have twelve besides the Quarter Masters, I say that if ever a set of men had cause to thank God, we are those men. We have enough to take care of the ship in heavy weather, and we will get more in the course of time.

> At Sea, Thursday Nov: 24th 1864
> Latitude 24°41′S   Dist: 200 m.   Longitude 31°28′W
> Course S 3/4 E   Wind. E by S. hauled to E.

Today we have had a nice breeze all the time and the ship has been running splendidly. We have been hard at work all day at the after hold and rigging. This evening we made a fine looking five topsail yard ship and stood for her. I would have sworn that she was a Yankee as she had the appearance of one, in every particular. We soon came up with her and to our disgust she hoisted the Norweigen [sic] flag, and I suppose she is one of the many transfers in consequence of the war. We did not board her. Today I am sorry to record the second trouble with our men. While we were running for the above referred to ship, two men Hall (2d Mt) and Raymond (C. Top) got to quarrelling in consequence of a discussion as to her character—and from words they got to blows. I came up in the early part of the skirmish. It now became my painful duty to punish them, which I did in a novel way, by putting them in single irons *each one embracing the other,* around an iron stanchion, and then taking their hands to a beam. The first impulse on their part was to laugh at the joke, but they soon concluded that it was all on one side, and sen[t] me word "please to let them down." I did so after they had been long enough their [sic] to make an example of them.

> At Sea. Friday 25th Nov. 1864
> Latitude 27°38′S   Dist: 195 m.   Longitude 30°12′W.
> Course SSE.   Wind. East hauled to NNE

We have been engaged all day in overhauling our rigging. At daylight made a bark on the lee beam and stood for her. We soon came up with her and she hoisted the English colors. She proved to be an English Bark from London to Algon Bay. We hauled up to our course and stood on. Today one of our 1st class petty officers, the Gunner's Mate William Crawford, was reported by Master's Mate Minor, for insolence to him while in the execution of his duty. The conduct was willfull and I am inclined to the opinion that he was only trying an experiment to see how far he could go under the cover of being an old Petty Officer. The pretty little experiment succeeded perfectly as he found out that he had gotten to the end of his line—which was proved by my putting him in irons and tricing him well up. I let him stay there until I thought he had enough to last him a year when I let him down, telling him I would at any time repeat the dose when it was necessary. I hate to punish men but if you do not rule them they will rule you. Nearly all old man-of-war's men try these experiments and if not punished will go on—but if they are met properly they behave beautifully.

At Sea, Saturday Nov: 26th 1864
Latitude 28°54'S.   Dist. good 106.   Long: 28°48'00"W.
Course. SE.   Wind 1st part N NW   last part S by W.

At a very early hour this morning in the Midwatch I was aroused by a great noise on deck, and rushed out in my slippers and when I got forward I found we were close to a bark on the opposite tack. I gave the order hard-a-port, and we passed right under her stern. If we had not kept away we would have been into her. Scales who was in charge of the deck, tho' without much experience is very watchfull and attentive and will make an excellent officer. Today we hauled fires and blew the water out of the boilers to enable Mr. O'Brien to scale them. They no doubt need it very badly, as I doubt very much if they have even been overhauled since the ship was built. At 3 p.m. the wind came out suddenly, with a squall from the Sd & Wd, and we ran off before it, but when we reefed down we hauled up again by the wind. Latter part of the day has been squally and rainy. We have I venture to say as comfortable a ship as there is any where to be found. I am certain that the men of no ship have as fine a berth deck. It is a treat to go down there in the bad weather, as they are always dry, singing and as happy as they can be. I am certain our gallant little crew is happy, and if I had twenty more I would be satisfied.

At Sea, Sunday Nov: 27th 1864
Lat: 29°03'S   Dist. good 120 m.   Long: 26°36'W
Course E 1/4 S.   Wind S by E to SE.

This another day of rest. The weather is good but the wind is not very favorable. We came and tacked as the wind would haul aft or forward. Today I was again forced to punish one of the men. I caught Hall (2d Mt) being guilty of a piece of scandalous conduct and I confined him by tricing him up.[4] He was afterward very abusive and I gagged him and triced him up higher. I kept him in this way until he said he would behave himself, when I took him down and by my recommendation he was disrated by the Captain and Hansen the last man we shipped, who is a steady old Swede was rated in his stead. This punishment will I think last Hall for a few days at the end of which time I think he will try his hand again—when, if I repeat the dose with a gradual increase he will be made as good a man as any to be found. He is active, smart, energetic and all he wants to make him as good a man as you might want is that he should be ruled into subjection. Never had I to deal with a man the nature of whose case was more plainly understood by me than it is in this. And I will bet that the day is not far off when he will be as good a man as any of the ship. Today he was disrated, not for his first offence but for his abusive language. We had inspection at quarters at 11.30 when all the men were required to be in uniform, and after that the Captain inspected the ship. Mr. Minor who is the Master's Mate of the deck (berth) has gotten the deck to look quite well—and as for comfort, I am sure no men had more than ours. Yes, the[y] have it and they shall continue to have it as long as I can let them. The ship can be made a happy one and I shall do all I can to bring about this state, but rely upon it the first thing to be done is to show that you are to rule and govern, and not be ruled and governed. Discipline is more necessary to the happiness of men than anything else. By discipline I do not mean tyranny but a thorough governing. You must thoroughly examine all reports, give the accused the advantage of any doubt, but finding him guilty punish him well. Let the man see that you are ruled by Justice, and he is ruled by you. This day I spent in reading my [B]ible and reading the letters from my darling Pattie and from my dear ones at home. Reading letters from those I love always has a good effect on me—it is like reading some good book, in as much as it makes me think of God, and be grateful for his manifold and great mercies.

>At Sea. Monday Nov: 28th 1864
>Lat: 30°44′S   Dist 104   Long: 26°40′W.
>Course S 1/4 W.   Wind from ENE to ESE.

The weather through the day has been squally, and we have been making and reducing sail as was deemed prudent. Today I found that our head casings had sagged down very much and I set the Boatswain to work getting them up in the yard. We are blest in our topsails. We have Cunningham's Patent Self-reefing topsails, by which three men can close reef a topsail, simply by slacking the halliards and hauling on the trace. I do not know what we should have done, short handed as we have been had it not been for this rig. We can at any time in a very short time and without risking the safety of the men by sending them aloft, reef down to almost no sail—and the sail rolls itself tightly around the yard. We have been greatly blessed in every way, and if ever a set of men had cause to be thankful to God, we are those men.

>At Sea, Tuesday Nov 29th 1864
>Lat: 32°34′30″S.   Course SE by S 1/4 S.   Long: 25°11′W.
>Distance made good 130 m.   Wind. from E to NE by E.

The whole day we have had a fresh breeze with occasional heavy squalls—this together with an overcast sky and a rain squall now and then makes the weather unsettled and disagreeable. We were towards night put under short safe sail, so that the men would be as little called upon as possible during the night. At an early hour we saw a large sail standing to the Sd, but she had every appearance of being an English vessel. Between the rain squalls our men have been employed in overhauling the rigging. We are gradually getting things in what may be called a safe condition but can boast of very little neatness. I would like to have everything as I am accustomed to seeing them in excellent order, but when with the few men we have worked with so much [h]as been done we can only feel proud of the miracles which have been accomplished. Indeed we have every reason to thank God, who has mercifully given us good weather, and his blessing in everything. I wish we could catch another Yankee. The work becomes a little dull, unless broken in upon by an occasional capture.

At Sea, Wednesday Nov. 30th 1864
Lat: 34°21′S.   Course SE by S.   Long: 23°43′W.
Distance made good 130 m.   Wind E to ENE.

Last night Dabney Scales was a little unwell, and Bulloch was ordered to take his night watch. Our mess has been very regular at meals and this is the first indication of any one of them not being well. This is however a temporary, slight affair. The strong wind moderated to a good Royal breeze and we made sail to Royals and flying Jib. The weather looks very much like that of the Banks of New Foundland as it is very foggy and damp. We saw today rather a favorable sign, in passing a great deal of what is called "Whale food." This indicates that there are whales about here, and generally you may look for a whaler in the well known whale ground. This "Whale food" is a very singular thing. It is observable in spots and streaks in the water, and when it is thick the water is turned to a perfectly red color. I had a great desire to see what it was and caught some in a bucket. I found the water alive with little red insects looking in form very much like lobster or shrimp. The water is more or less red, as it contains more or less of these insects. They say that the whales eat this, but some say that they do not, anyhow it is a good sign of whaling grounds.[5]

At Sea, Thursday Dec. 1st 1864
Lat. 35°53′30″S.   Course SE   Long: 21°50′W.
Dist. made good 132 m.   Wind. from NE to East.

Today I can say very little as nothing of any moment has occurred. We have a light breeze from the NthEst and are jogging along. The sky is overcast and we have not seen much of the Sun. I have had the men employed again with the Boatswain in overhauling our standing and running rigging. I find that while we are far better off in men than we ever were before still we ought to have a great many more. Only think of a Man-of-War only having twelve men in a watch—but when we remember that when we came out we had but four this is a great increase, and we can only realize our having [been] blessed by comparing the past with the present. I was not as busy today as usual. Oh what would I not give to receive a letter from my darlings. I miss their letters more than I can express. God grant that we may soon meet and then what a jolly time we will have chatting together. Whenever I am a little downcast I have but to think of the happiness in store for me if I get home and any little melancholly is at once changed to joy. God hasten our Freedom. [A line and a half blotted out.—*Ed.*]

At Sea, Friday Dec. 2d 1864
Lat: 37°22′40″S.   Course SE 1/4 E.   Long: 19°33′W.
Distance made good 113.5 m.   Wind ENE to NNE

This has been as beautiful a day as I ever saw in my whole life. All day we have had a nice warm sun with a fine royal breeze. At first the wind was from such a direction that we could not head on course but the wind veered afterward and we came up to our course which if we keep for 300 miles we will strike in sight the Island of Tristan D'Acunha. At, around and about this Island is a great whaling ground and the Island is their great resort, and I am a little disappointed that we have not caught a whaler or so—however I suppose our time will come ere long. Today I was forced to punish one of our men very severely. Two of them Louis Rowe (CMT) and Thos. Hall (Sea) were brought aft for fighting. Hall has given more trouble than any man in the ship. He has been punished severely and disrated for bad conduct. Fighting is an offense generally for which both parties should be punished—but here was a peculiar case where one (Hall) used such language to the other that if I had heard it and the man had not resented it at once by knocking him down I would have punished him very severely. I therefore triced Hall up and let Louis Rowe go. Hall being an Englishman and Louis Rowe a [F]renchman. punishing the former, might with our English crew, produce a bad effect at first, but what I do in this way I do with decision and if they have any sense, they will acknowledge that I am right; however it makes very little difference whether they do or not. In about two hours I cut Hall down and had him brought to the mast with the intention of releasing him but I found that the devil had not left him and I had him triced up. I was determined to conquer him, and I kept him up eight hours more and I found him as subdued as a lamb. He gave me his word that I would never have any more trouble with him. I hate to punish men but it must be done. You must either rule them or they will rule you. On a cruise of this kind particularly I consider discipline not only desireable but absolutely necessary to our very existence. And when the men once see you determined and firm they will be better, happier and better contented. I had also to report Mr. Hunt Master's Mate for neglect of duty. He has given me an immense deal of trouble in this way: he is either very careless or utterly worthless. I put him on extra watch, and when he thinks he can attend to his duty I will try him. Mr. O'Brien today finished scaling his boilers. They were very foul and were very much in want of overhauling. I am very glad that they are finished for I like at all times to be ready to run well.

At Sea, Saturday Dec. 3d 1864
Lat: 38°07'S.   Course E by S 1/4 S   Long. 15°29'W.
Dist. made good 198 m.   Wind Nd & Ed, N. & NNW.

Today our men were employed finishing our Top Gallant rigging, and I can now with great joy say, that we are ready for heavy weather as everything has been well overhauled. I have been greatly annoyed for fear that with our very small crew, bad weather might overtake us before we had made those preparations about the rigging which are always necessary. I am now greatly relieved. I have been longing all day for a Yankee but so far have been disappointed. We are now in the midst of a busy whaling ground, and I shall be very much disgusted if tomorrow we have not better luck. Mr. Minor today reported Silvester for insolence to him, upon examination I found the report correct and I triced the offender up, and kept him there until he swore that he would never be guilty of the offence again. I dislike to punish men, but I can't help it, and it is only by punishing that I will ever cease to punish. If every man could do and say what he pleased the ship would soon go to the devil.

This being Saturday, a party of us drank about 9 o'clock "Sweethearts & Wi[v]es"—Lining furnished the liquor. Whenever this toast is proposed, I think how dear she is to me, and I always invoke God's blessing on my own dear Pattie. Oh how much do I want to see her. God speed our meeting.

At Sea, Sunday Dec. 4th 1864
Lat: 37°47'S.   Course E 3/4 S   Long: 12°30'30"W
Dist: made good 140 m.   Wind NNW & S by E

The day commenced and continued foggy and overcast and we could not see very far. At an early hour we saw a large double topsail yard ship standing as we were, but very much ahead of us and under all sail. We rapidly gained upon him under topgallant sails and hove too [sic] under his lee quarter, but we saw her name on the quarter which was the *Dia del Mario,* showing the Sardinian flag. She looked so much like a Yankee that we boarded him. We found her to be the Sardinian ship *Dia del Mario,* from Genoa to Rangoon in the Bay of Bengal. She had been a Yankee but was transferred. We filled away as soon as our boat was hoisted and found that there were two more vessels insight [*sic*], one astern coming up and the other to leeward. The one astern looked very much as though she might be a Yankee, but it was so misty that we could not tell certainly. The one to leeward was the nearest and the Captain concluded to make chase for her first. We kept away and made all plain sail, but we came up with her very rapidly and regarded her very closely. She looked so suspicious that we decided not to go any nearer. This was a very wise conclusion for if she was not a steam gunboat under sail, I never saw one—and she looked to me exactly like a Yankee steamer of war. We did not go so close as to endanger our safety even had she chased us, for we had a splendid breeze and a smooth sea and it would have taken a wonderful vessel to catch us. At 10 we had a muster of the crew and read the "Articles of War." The men in the grey looked as well as is possible with the color but I can't say much in its favor. The breeze after muster was a little fresher and the ship was as close as she would lie, so that we had a fine chance to judge of our speed when by the wind, we were close to the wind with Royals set and she went hour after hour ten knots. I think that this is doing remarkably well, and I never was in a vessel, which could compare to her. We pass everything which comes near us and that too generally under reduced sail. At 11 A.M. we made Inaccess[i]ble Islands on the port beam and very soon after we saw the island of Tristan d'Acunha which is very high, also Nightingale Island which is to the Westward of Tristan d'Acunha. We passed them and stood on by the wind. It came on quite misty, but about 5 o'c. the man at the wheel saw a sail on our lee (Stbd) beam, and we kept away for her. We soon made her out to be a Bark under single reefed topsails, and we concluded that she was a whaler— and if a whaler, a Yankee. At 5.45 we came down upon the sail and all doubt was removed as we found her hove too [*sic*] under double reefed topsails and actually engaged [in] "trying out" as they call it, that is boiling out the oil. We ran up the English flag, and after some little delay she ran up the Yankee flag. This gave us great joy as it is just three weeks since our last. We sent a boat onboard which very soon returned with the Captain and Mate. We held our meeting and I put Captain Charles Worth on oath, and we took his deposition and found his vessel to be the Bark *Edward* of New Bedford on a whaling cruise. He had on yesterday caught a whale, and they had just finished cutting him up and commenced trying. His vessel is very old but she is a good prize as we will lay by her and get all her beef, pork and bread. We of course condemned her and sent the Captain & Mate back to bring off their personal effects. We made all preparations to stay by her all night. Placed Mr. Bulloch and Mr. Minor with a prize crew to take charge of her. We brought onboard Capt. Worth, three mates and twenty two sailors as prisoners. These with our three from the *Stacey* make twenty nine. This is too many to have at one time. We paroled the Captain and confined the others for safety. The Captain is the most manly looking Yankee I have ever seen. Tonight we have heavy rain and fog, but Bulloch has such directions about lights that there is no danger of his getting out of sight.

At Sea Monday. Dec. 5th 1864
Latitude 37°55'40 S   Course E 1/2 S   Long. 10°44'W.
Dist. made good 81 m.   Wind. NNW & WNW.

At daylight we found our vessel a good way from our prize and we stood for her. We got our large boat and commenced at once at shifting her beef & pork to our vessel. She had five nice whale boats which together with our two large boats will soon do the work. I never saw two prettier boats than are two of hers. They are, of course, whale boats and are perfectly new. I shall induce the Captain to keep both of them as they will be excellent for boarding in heavy weather. We have been very busy all day in shifting beef, pork, bread and flour. I employ the prisoners as they must lend a hand to get provisions for them to eat onboard. At night we found it not half done and we decided to remain by her again. Bulloch & Minor in charge. We are under steam tonight and will find it very easy to lay near her. Today I shipped Francis Tuft as Landsman and rated him Cooper. He was in the Bark and is an Englishman and will be a great man for us.

At Sea, Tuesday Dec. 6th 1864
Lat. 37°45'S   Course NW 3/4 N   Long. 10°34'W
Distance 20 m.   Wind Variable

Commenced at an early hour to get the cargo from our prize. We could not have finer weather for our work as it is perfectly smooth and so misty that a vessel would pass quite near us without seeing anything. While we were thus briskly employed it lightened up and we saw to windward of us a large five topsail yard ship. We left our prize and made chase, but she was shut in by the fog and we were some time in finding her. We ran up the Yankee flag, and to our disappointment she hoisted the English, and we ran back to our prize. We found that Bulloch had all the boats loaded and was far advanced in breaking out, so that we soon got through. It may be well for me to mention here how valuable a store ship this vessel has been—we have gotten from her two new whale boats, 50 barrels of beef, 49 of pork, 46 of flour, 6000 lbs. of bread, 1200 of soap, 600 of coffee, 400 of butter, 1 barrel of hams, 1 of pickles, a very large quantity of manilla rope, 2 barrels of black fish oil, two half barrels of sand. Now anyone who would not be content with this is very unreasonable. We have more than enough provisions to last us our cruize. I went onboard when everything was said to be out and got in the water all the whale boats, two of these we will keep and three we will keep for what reason, tomorrow will develop. We send all the men aboard except enough to pull us back—and Bulloch, Mr. Minor, Mr. Harwood and I set her on fire fore and aft. She was so old that we were careful to do our work well, and I am sure she will never go on another trip. She will burn well when well warmed up. I went onboard twisted up all boats and stood off toward the Island of Tristan d'Acunha. All the prisoners with one or two exceptions are Portugueese [sic] and they are so cowardly that you could not induce them to ship. I had all hands except the Captain and one mate put in irons. We now have twenty eight prisoners and that number is entirely to[o] large to permit to run loose about the deck, more particularly as we have captured the majority of our crew. I wonder when in the annals of history such a thing ever took place before. I venture to say, never. Indeed we would be a miserable set if we did not feel grateful to the God who has thus visited his kindness upon us. Our burning prize was distinctly in sight and I have rarely seen anything which is more beautifully grand than a ship burning at sea. To see the rigging onfire after it has burnt in two and the burning ends swinging as the vessel rolls. Oh it's a grand sight.

At Sea, Wednesday Dec. 7th 1864
Tristan d'Acunha
Lat: Course   Long:
Distance   Wind.

At an early hour this morning we made very high land ahead, and made a most beautiful land fall from the Sth. We stood towards it steering about NNW in order to clear the NW end; having cleared this we saw the small collection of houses on the N.W. side and stood for them. This is rather a remarkable island, and is called Tristan d'Acunha for its discover[er] a Portugueese [sic]. It is now owned by the British and when Bonaparte was a prisoner at St Helena they had a naval station here. The island is about 7 miles each way and is very high. A large portion of it is so high as to be inaccess[i]ble, but the remainder which is on the NW. side is very productive, and from a ship seems to be covered with cattle. There are but thirty five people on the island, and these are divided into seven families. The women are more numerous than the men. The island is said to be very productive but flour and clothing are very scarce and the people live from one year's end to another dependent upon their own exertions, and for clothing dependent upon any vessel which may from time to time call there. The vessels which generally stop here are Yankee whalers and they only come in to get a beef or mutton, for which they exchange clothing and flour. We came in with the intention of landing all our prisoners and we sent the whole twenty eight with their luggage in the whale boats which we towed and they pushed off. I must say I pitied the poor devils going as they did to an island at least 1000 miles from any land, and with no chance of getting off until some vessel stops there—and this chance may be so remote that they may be here a year.[6] However if I come here ten years hence I shall confidently expect to find some of them here. Just as they shoved off from the port side a shore boat came on the starboard side and a man came onboard and wanted to know if we wanted to buy anything, telling us that they had cattle, chickens, milk, butter, eggs, sheep &c in great quantities. We tried to arrange the prices but he said he could not do it, that it was not his turn. It seems as he told us, that there are seven families on the island and they take regular turns in selling and trading, but he said he would go off and bring off the man whose turn it was. We told him that we would exchange flour at $8.00 per barrel for beef at 18 cts [per pound]. This is paying dearly for our whistle, but that makes little matter. This fellow told me that he was from Connecticut from New London, and had been there 15 years. He is the only Yankee here. Whoever ever went anywhere that any people were that a Yankee was not there. One would very naturally suppose that if there was any place in the world where a Yankee would not be found it would be such a place as this. I would willingly bet that this fellow not only has more money than any of the rest and that he is a leading man among them. He is a fine hearty looking man, and has evidently had enough to eat. All of us forgot to ask his name. This individual had been gone a long time when I saw them launching the whale boat which we gave to the prisoners to bring off what they had. They came alongside and we found a new party headed by a man named Peter Green, a Dutchman from Holland who has been here about twenty five years, he seems to be a kind of leading man among them, and on this occasion acted as spokesman, and said to the Captain in the way of a protest that there was not provision enough upon the island to last the prisoners we landed until a vessel would probably take them off—and urged the absolute propriety of either taking them back or sending provisions to serve them. We asked him how long they would probably be here and he said that we ought to leave provision enough to last them until the 15th of January (next month). We saw the propriety of doing as he said and left a full ration for twenty eight men until the latter part of February. I asked the Yank who was Governor; he replied, no one, but that each one ruled his own family, and if anyone did any thing outraging the public, there was a meeting and he was denounced as a "dog." They were very anxious to get clothes, and [Paymaster] Smith sold them prize clothing to the amount of $40. There are only some ten houses onshore and those are made of stone, and are very much scattered. When we first got around the point they hoisted right in the middle of their settlement a very large English ensign, and we ran up the Confederate. It is wonderful that even here, in this remote island, away entirely from our country, the people feel the effects of the war in our country. This proves to us our importance. In time of Peace as many as seventy Yankee whalers have been insight [sic] at once off the island, and now we had a hard time in finding one single one. It was a hard matter to get rid of these land sharks for by charging exorbitantly for every thing they prove that they are great thie[ve]s. However I can readily understand that to see new faces is such a treat that they hate to see the chance go. Just think sometimes they go a year without having a vessel call. They finally left us, the Yank of course going last, and we put the ship under sail, triced up the propeller, and shaped our course to the Ed. It is a great relief to get clear of prisoners, as I do not like to have strangers among our men—it is demoralizing. Old Peter Green said to me, well sir, I see you are poorly off for men. No, said I, not at all, we work with quarter watches—this is a fib, but is a fib in the cause. Any vessel coming near here had better call in and get fresh grub. There is plenty of water close in but the "kelp" a kind of sea grass growing up from the bottom would probably prevent a vessel from going too close in.

At Sea, Thursday Dec. 8th 1864
Lat: 37°05'S   Course E 1/2 S   Long: 10°02'W.
Distance 99 miles   Wind WNW to NW

This morning bright and early we discovered a crack in our propeller, which if it had not been seen might have proved fatal to us. To get the propeller up so that it could be worked at was now the trouble. To do this we had to take the top off of our Pilot House. We then got the propeller well up and found that the brass bearing of the couppling [sic] was cracked. It is an old break and has been done for a long time, as we saw where the screws had been put in to repair it. As our propeller is to us our life we stopped all work to have it fixed. The only means by which I could hoist this great weight higher than by the regular apparatus . . . [was] by means of the Spanker boom, by having it well supported by a prop of wood and tackles from the Mizzen mast head— and this by tackles at preventer stays. John Williams (colored) ship's cook and Geo. Flood were brought to the mast for fighting. I found that the former had called the latter a violent and outrageous name and I justified Flood and triced up Williams. Here was a negro against a Yankee. I had trouble in bringing him to his bearings but he finally came down.

At Sea, Friday Dec: 9th 1864
Lat: 37°30'S.   Course E by S   Long: 7°07'W.
Distance 140 miles   Wind Wd, Sd & W. & Sd &Ed

The weather today is disagreeable in the extreme. It reminds me very much of the weather off the Banks of Newfoundland in as much as it is cloudy, overcast, foggy, damp and cold. A Yankee might be within six miles of us and he would be as safe as if he were a hundred. I wish it would clear off for I am very, very anxious to catch another fellow. I am always glad to catch them and very glad to get rid of them, the truth is that I hate them so much that I find it hard to have my wants gratified, the more we catch the happier will I be. This afternoon our Chief Engineer finished the work on the propeller and we lowered it in its place and unrigged all our purchases and commenced re-fitting the pilot house. I am delighted to know that we are again in running order. We were engaged all day in scrubbing the paint work on the Spar deck. We are getting along very nicely in everything.

At Sea, Dec. 10th, Friday [Saturday], 1864
Lat: 37°35′S.   Course E 1/2 S.   Long: 5°38′W
Distance 69 miles   Winds. Calm, Var, & NW.

Today we had our first exercise at quarters, Jack Grimball giving them a good long drill. The guns work very hard as the whole weight of the piece comes on the four dumb trucks. These I hope will soon wear up to their proper places. I do wish that our ports were in proper order but as yet all we can boast of is that there is a round hole through which the muzzles of the guns point. If however we were to get into a fight all "ginger bread work" would come down, and we would do our best, however poor that might be—but I trust that we may have no fighting to do as we would fare badly. I am very anxious to catch Yanks, but when Yanks are Tartars I want to let them alone.

At Sea, Sunday Dec 11th 1864
Lat. 38°35′S   Course ESE.   Long: 2°30′W.
Distance 153 m.   Wind. SW.

Another day of rest. Oh, how rapidly does time fly. Sunday seems to have just gone and here it is again. I have been somewhat disappointed today as I had hoped that we would have caught a [Y]ankee, as Sunday seems to be our lucky day. A nice breeze sprung up today and we very easily glided along at 11 knots per hour. Had inspection of men and ship at ten o'clock. The men looked quite well and so did the ship. Mr. Minor reported Louis Rowe for refusing to obey his orders, and I had him triced up. At first, with the usual excitability of a [F]renchman he became very angry and commenced to use some very improper language when I had him gagged. He was very determined not to be subdued, but I brought him down by tricing him a little higher each time, and when I took him down he was like a lamb. I have spent the day in reading the service and re-reading some of my letters from my own Pattie. Oh how much would I give to hear from [her] if but to know that my darling is well. I read these letters as next to later ones they are most dear. No wonder I should love her so profoundly. She has been at all times so devotedly attached to me. God grant her health and happiness.

> At Sea, Monday Dec. 12th 1864
> Lat. 39°20'S.   Course E by S 1/2 S   Long: 0°15'30 East.
> Distance 142 m.   Winds. Sd & Wd & WNW

Today I had a fine day for my rigging and I set all hands to rattling down and reeving our topgallant and royal gear. We now have every piece of running gear with one or two exceptions, of manilla rope, and this too, all captured from our prizes. Grimball exercised his men at the guns; they will soon learn the drill. I sincerely wish that we had our ports fixed as they ought to be but I fear it will be a long long time before I can so congratulate myself. We have had very little breeze today and what there has been was aft, which with a heavy sea abeam makes the ship roll very heavily, and of all vessels for rolling I think the *Shenandoah* goes ahead. She however rolls very easily.

3
This is indeed a Merry Christmas

December 13, 1864–January 23, 1865

At Sea, Tuesday Dec. 13th 1864
Lat: 40°17′S.   Course ESE   Long: 3°37′E
Distance 165 m.   Wind. NW.

Today the ship has been very uneasy, rolling very deeply. All this is in consequence of the wind being right aft, so that the sail does not steady her. The sea is on the starb'd quarter, but if the wind continues where it is the sea must follow it and will come aft; in this position of the sea, the ship's condition would be very much more comfortable. She now rolls the muzzles of her guns under nearly every time, but her rolls are very regular. We have been employed today in reeving some new running rigging it being rather too cold to get to work at the standing rigging, for when rattlings [ratlines] are put in in cold weather they have to be altered afterwards as they get too long when you get in a warmer climate. I was very much provoked today by the uncalled for and unnecessary interference of the Captain with my duties. I ordered the Boatswain to fit the Mizen Topgallant sheets in a particular way, and after it was done, without my knowledge, and 'though told that it was my order he had all undone and fitted another way. Now he has the power to give any order he chooses and to revoke any order of mine, but he should do it through me— if my orders are to be changed in this way in trifling matters, I may as well take a watch and give him the Executive duties; for both of us cannot be the Executive officer. I showed by my manner that I did not like it and I hope he saw and will profit by it. I did not speak to him because I have once requested and he has promised that all his orders to my subordinates should go through me, and I regard him a very unreasonable man in most things. It is a piece of conceit to suppose that because he is the Commanding officer he can perform the Executive duties and the duties of all his officers better than they can. If he does his own duty he will, as a general thing do well. I will not quarrel with him for two reasons: one is that it would injure the service, and the other is that when I last walked with his little wife she begged me to keep out of all quarrels on the cruize.

At Sea, Wednesday Dec. 14th 1864
Lat: 40°55'S   Course E by S.   Long: 7°48'E
Distance 194 miles   Wind. NW & NW by N.

Today we have had a fresh wind from nearly astern W.N.W. and a very heavy sea, although not as heavy as last night; still her guns go under nearly every time. One thing gives me some anxiety and that is a jarring about the rudder, and I fear that some of the pintles may be loose. The Carpenter & Boatswain say no, but I am very much afraid of it. The Carpenter is at work at the Bulwarks.

At Sea, Thursday Dec: 15th 1864
Lat 41°35'S   Course E by S.   Long 12°26'
Dist: 213 miles   Winds NW, WSW & SW

The wind has been on the increase since my last was written, commencing with a strong breeze, then a half gale, and now it is blowing a whole gale, like blue lightning. This comes in puffs, some of which are as fresh as one would like to see. The ship is under close reefed fore & main topsails, single reefed foresail and fore topmast staysail, and behaves very admirably, but the rudder makes a great noise and I am anxious about it. We shipped a good deal of water. She is decidedly a wet ship.

At Sea, Friday Dec. 16th 1864
Lat: 41°35'   Course East.   Long: 17°09'E
Distance 213 miles   Wind. WSW & NW by W

Today it has been blowing a whole gale of wind and a very heavy sea. The ship behaves very well except that she ships an immense amount of water. At midnight she shipped a very large sea and was a long time in clearing. The noise of the rudder continues and I cannot form any plan to cancel it. Tonight a thing was done by the Captain which seems to me can produce no good, but an immense amount of evil. Lieut. Lee had the watch from 8 to 12, being relieved at Midnight by Lieut. Chew, and he in his turn by Lieut. Scales at 4 o'clock. The Captain sent for me and commenced to talk of what a bad night we were going to have, and remarked that such weather required the best seamanship on deck, and that he would have to be up all the mid watch and all the morning, as he did not consider Lieuts. Chew & Scales competent to take care of the ship in such weather. He is a regular self made martyr and thinks that the troubles, privations and toils of no man can be compared to his. I said, no, Captain if you will keep Mr. Chew's watch with him I will do the same with Mr. Scales, or vice versa. To this he replied, "No, you have enough to do in being on deck the whole day." I told him that I would much prefer keeping one of the watches. He said, no. I could do no more and went below. Chew had turned in for the Mid-watch. I had been below but a short time when I was told that the Captain wanted to see me. I went on deck, and he said, "I want you to send for Mr. Minor and tell him to keep the Mid-watch." Here was a Master's Mate not warranted with only an appointment from a commander of a Confederate vessel, to be ordered to take the watch of a 1st Lieut. in the Navy, so appointed by the President of the Confederate States, "by and with the advice and consent of the Senate." Is this right? This too, done without one word being said to the Lieut. who was on his bed preparing to keep his watch. I saw at once that it was wrong, ruinously wrong, and said to the Captain that I would infinitely [prefer to] keep the watch myself. His reply was, "No, you have enough to do." I urged no more; what more could I urge. I sent for Mr. Minor & gave him the order as coming from the Captain—and then with the heavy heart of a man who s[aw] evil ahead started below, when the Captain said, "if Mr. Chew is not asleep you can tell him that I relieve him of his watch tonight." I told Chew and he said "all right." Now if Chew takes of this matter the same view that I do, why, there will be a row in consequence of it. I shall try and keep my skirts clear, but I know that everything like an esprit du [sic] corps will be destroyed by such arbitrary and unwarrantable acts of authority.

At Sea, Saturday Dec 17th 1864
Lat: 41°39'S.   Course East   Long. 22°34'East.
Wind Sd & Wd & WNW & Calm   Distance. 243 miles

The weather has greatly moderated and the sea has gone down. I trust that tomorrow will bring us good weather and a smooth sea. The thing which I mentioned yesterday which [might] produce trouble has turned out as I said. Lt. Chew feeling himself most improperly treated went to the Captain and told him that he could not stand it, whereupon the Captain said that he did not consider him competent and said furthermore that under such circumstances he would respect neither person or commission. Oh how it grieved me to learn that this was his ground. It was no excuse for so high-handed an act in as much as I offered to keep the watch with Chew. Upon being told this, bad matters with Chew were made worse, and he could stand it no longer. He made a request to be relieved from duty altogether and send him from the first port. The communication was sent through me and I forwarded it by handing it to the Captain. Upon reading it, I was told to inform Mr. Chew that his request was granted and I was to put him off duty, and "*put the officers in three* watches." I saw that I must have a long talk with him and try the part of a good friend. Having told Chew, I went on deck and commenced to talk with the Captain and told him that if I were Chew I would not only do what he had done in protesting but that I would report it to the Secretary of the Navy—and said that I considered that by his act a young man of fine spirit and sense was forced out of the ship. He said that what he had done was only at the request of Mr. Chew. My reply was that any man of spirit would pursue a similar course to get clear of a ship the Captain of which had told him that he intended neither to respect commissions or persons. And then I asked him what right he had to say that Mr. Chew was not to be trusted with the deck, when the wording of Mr. Chew's commission was identically the same as his own, and besides this even if you consider him incompetent, I have volunteered to take the watch with him and your relieving him proves that you have no confidence in me. He said, "You did not volunteer with the right spirit, you did not mean what you said; you have not done as I had hoped or expected on repeated occasions when I have been on deck with these two inexperienced young officers i.e. come up and say Captain go below; I will look out." I was astonished, but replied, ["]You Sir did not hear me, or else have a very poor memory and as you replied to me I must think it due to a bad memory. You not only knew that I volunteered in proper spirit, but replied to my desire to keep the watches of Mr. Chew by saying I had enough to do.["] I then said, ["]my volunteering was in earnest and I must say I think you thought so at the time. As to your second charge that I had disappointed you, I have to say that you have no right to be disappointed, as when I urged upon you the propriety of giving the Lieutenants their watches I told you that I would agree to be on the look out at all times. And this I have been and you knew perfectly well that at any time I was ready. And you furthermore know that besides my duties as Executive officer, there is not an officer on the vessel who has done as much watching as I have.["] He said, "Well everyone is opposed to me." I marked well the remark. He said several days ago that we were all his enemies. He then said, ["]Well, Sir, what do you want.["] I said, ["]Sir, I want to advise you to restore Chew to duty. I will look out with him. You are going to have an unhappy ship if you do not.["] "Well," said he, "if that is all that Mr. Chew wants I will agree if he will withdraw his application." I must say I was very much disgusted at the conversation, but determined to do all I could to bring matters straight. I went to Chew, and he said he would not withdraw his application unless the Captain promised him the deck, and that he should not be interfered with in future. I said no more, but after supper the Captain sent for me. His manner was very much changed and in a very pompous way he said, "Well Sir, what has Mr. Chew decided?" I said I did not know. "Well, Sir, I saw you holding a *consultation* with him; what did he say?" I said that I thought that he very properly, I thought, decided not to withdraw his application unless you promised not to interfere with him. "Well, Sir, I have not a friend in the ship." "You are all against me." Then I opened my mouth to speak fairly what I felt. I said ["]now, Sir, you have said that repeatedly and I want to know what you mean by it.["] He said, "Whittle, be careful, you are speaking to me." ["]Yes, Sir, I am speaking when there is no such thing as silence. I demand to know what you mean.["] I can't write any more of this extraordinary & plain conversation but the result was that Chew was sent for, was restored to watch, and I was begged by Waddell to forget what had happened. I told him my promise to his little wife, and said that I had kept it as long as I could. I trust now, that there will never be another disturbance, but I shall do all I can to keep all straight. He makes one very great mistake in thinking that when I go to him in these matters it is with the view of finding fault with him, whereas I go only to preserve peace in the ship when that peace is being broken up by some unwarrantable act of his. My mission is always that of a friend, but he is so weak as to regard me in the light of an enemy. God knows I want peace for the good of the service.

At Sea, Sunday Dec. 18th 1864
Lat: 42°00′S   Course E 3/4 S   Long: 25°53′E.
Distance 150.   Wind E. ENE & NNE

Another day of rest, and we have done no work but such as was absolutely necessary. We have a nice breeze on the port beam and are slipping along splendidly. I was very much surprised this morning upon getting up to find the sea very nearly smooth, and the wind nearly in the opposite direction to what it had been. I dare say that this breeze is cause[d] by the wind coming through the Mozambique Channel and it therefore will not hold very long. Tonight I sent for Thomas Hall and told him that I would re-rate him Quarter Master, but that if he behaved badly I would break him again. He was very grateful and said that I would never have cause to punish him again. He has had the old boy taken out of him. Had our usual inspection at Quarters.

At Sea, Monday Dec 19th 1864
Lat: 42°12′S.   Course E 1/4 S.   Long: 30°25′E.
Winds NNE to North   Distance 200 miles.

Today we have been going along very nicely the ship going 11 1/2 knots with the Fore and Main Top gallant sails set. Later it came on squally and they took in the Top gallant sails and single reefed the Topsails.

At Sea, Tuesday Dec 20th 1864
Lat. 42°10′S   Course made good East.   Long: 34°44′E
Winds to 4 NNE after that North then NNW & finally WNW
     Distance 190 miles.

The day commenced with light airs & breezes and made sail to Royals. The spectacle of the lee Main Topsail clew carried away, but we got the sail up without splitting it. Unbent it and sent up the spare Main Topsail. Today Mr. O'Shea commenced the construction of the Magazine, and I hope he will get ahead rapidly and let us take our powder from its present exposed position. We have had all day rain at intervals. The Barometer is very low being 29.45 but I think it only indicates SW wind.

At Sea, Wednesday Dec 21st 1864
Lat. 42°05′30″S   Course E 1/4 N.   Long: 38°19′30″E.
Wind NW by W. West & SW.   Distance 160

Today we have had a leading breeze the whole time and have been under all plain sail. I have been busy today in trying to get the battery in order, making a Magazine and fitting studding sail gear. With so few men I find every job a long one, but when I contrast our present numerical strength with what it used to be I have reason only to be thankful. I am getting heartily tired of not catching another Yankee. This is too much sailing without a prize. I gave the Berth deck a good holystoning.

At Sea, Thursday Dec. 22nd 1864
Lat: 42°00′S.   Course E 2°N   Long: 41°34′E
Winds. Sd & Wd, Sd & Sd & Ed   Distance. 145.

Today I gave the spar deck a thorough holystoning. Employed variously during the day. The Gunner's gang firing up the guns, Boatswain's at work preparing the studding sail booms for going aloft, Carpenter's hard at work at the Magazine, and the Sailmaker at work on the Main Topsail. We got up the topmast studding sail booms but not the topgallant, as it looks as if we are going to have bad weather.

At Sea, Friday Dec. 23d 1864
Lat: 42°26′S   Course E by S.   Long: 44°04′E
Winds ESE, SE, E & NE by E   Distance 115.

This day commenced finely but we know not what a day may bring forth as towards the latter part it commenced to rain and blow. And tonight, taken all in all is as disagreeable an eve as I ever saw anywhere. It is blowing a whole gale of wind and raining in torrents—the rain being a kind of sleet and as cold as hail. When you attempt to face the wind your breath is fairly taken away and your face feels as if you had a number of prickers sticking in it. Chew had the first watch and I in consequence had to remain on deck the whole time. Both he and Scales are gaining in experience and I hope before long that it may not be necessary for anyone to keep watch with them. Such a night as this makes the poor mariner regret the day on which his destinies were linked with the sea. Oh, how much would I not give now to be on shore, with our dear country at peace, and a certain little angel sitting by me as my wife. I would certainly be the happiest man in the world. I may say that the first trouble which we have had with any officer occurred today, while the ship was rolling very heavily I found the chocking quoins of the guns were not in their places under the trucks and I asked Mr. Guy the Gunner the reason, he replied in a most unsatisfactory manner, and was then so very insolent and insubordinate in his manner and language, that I ordered him to be silent, and sent him on the Quarter deck and reported him to the Captain, who saw him and ordered me to put him off duty. I am very sorry the thing happened for he is a good man, but I will break these parties in or I will break their necks in the attempt. Today I told the men that I had selected the largest pig in the pen for their Christmas dinner, and all they had to do was to kill it. They were very much delighted.

At Sea, Saturday Dec. 24th 1864
Lat: 43°29′S   Course E.S.E.   Long: 47°37′E.
Winds N by E, NW, W, WNW & West.   Distance 164 m.

The day commenced and continued with a very fresh gale, increasing as the day advanced. At night the wind and sea were very high, and we are shipping a great deal of water. She is a very peculiar ship: aft and forward she is very dry, and amidships she is flooded. I have seen her today do a most extraordinary thing i.e. take in the top of the same sea on both sides. She is now under close reefed Fore & Main Topsails, Single reefed foresail and fore topmast staysail, and is running very nearly before the wind and sea. Poor Mr. O'Shea came to me today and reported Mr. Guy and Mr. Lynch for being drunk on the berth deck and abusing him. I at once sent for Mr. Guy and he said he was coming. He did not make his appearance for some time and I went to the Main hatch and called him. Still he did not come. I then sent Mr. Mason to order him up. He replied that he had been put under arrest by the Captain and would only come by his order. I sent Mr. Mason to tell him that I, the Executive officer ordered him to come on deck. He positively refused, and then I reported the matter to the Captain and sent Lieut. Grimball with orders to bring him on deck, and to use any force necessary, but hearing that he was too drunk to know what he was about the order was revoked, but Mr. Guy came up very soon afterwards. The officer of the deck ordered him forward but he stood arguing. I then ordered him, but it had no effect. I repeated the order several times but as he showed no signs of obeying, I got down on the ladder and shoved him forward. He fell on deck and I picked him up and started again when he caught a rope and held fast. Mr. Browne & Mr. Minor now came to my assistance and we landed him on the berth deck. I was never so tempted in my life to pitch in and thrash him well. I next sent for Lynch and found him slightly tight. Just enough to make him look like a fool. The question now was where did they get their liquor, and I conclude that they have been saving up their daily tots for a grand blow out Christmas. It is the last spree the worthies will have as I have ordered their grog stopped from toujours [sic]. The crew are preparing their pig for Christmas. It weighs 120 lbs—I am anxious to see them enjoy Christmas, and would rather have a dull day myself than see them do so. This evening, as the weather is exceedingly bad, and promises to be worse, I got up the preventer braces on the starboard side and "spliced the main brace." I retired early as I have the midwatch with Chew. Two very large seas came aboard this afternoon but fortunately did not get to the Magazine, although they flooded everything. She is a very wet ship. I think this due to her having amidships all her battery and heavy weights, such as machinery & coal. This is certainly a very miserable Christmas eve. And it is a night upon which each one and all of us know that at our far distant homes our dear ones are wondering where we, the absent Spirits, are. God grant that they are all well, and give them all his blessing and guid[ance]. I am sure that my own dear Pattie has thought of me more than once tonight. Most sincerely do I on the eve of the birth of Christ, invoke God's blessing and protection on my dear, dear Country and all my dear ones. God bless them all.

At Sea, Sunday Dec: 25th 1865 [1864] (Christmas)
Lat: 42°57′S.   Long: 53°25′E.   Bar: 29.57–.65–.70
Course E 1/2 N.   Dist: 254 m.   Ther. 41°
    Wind: W.S.W & SW by W

This is indeed a merry Christmas. During the whole mid watch which I kept with Chew the gale and sea was on the increase—shipped several seas. I went on deck about 6 A.M. Just as I got up the Captain kept the ship off before the wind and sea, & close reefed the Main topsail. Battened down the hatches. At 7 a heavy sea came over at the starb'd main chains and she rolled to port and took it over the port side. It was so heavy as to fill our spar deck so that some of the men swam to catch over a rope to save themselves. The guns were actually covered entirely up. I never saw a sea come onboard half as heavy. It rolled aft and went threw the wardroom filling several rooms, wetting several officers in their upper bunks. I was on the quarter deck and managed to knock out the after port allowing her to clear. The men were frightened but they soon recovered and worked hard with water waist deep—it was very cold but I sang out Merry Christmas, and indeed it looked very little like it for I never saw much worse weather. A thing occurred today which I suppose would not take place once in a thousand times. When we shipped the two seas Wm. West, the Capt. of the Main top, was in the main hatch—the sea swept him overboard on the port side and the sea which came over to port washed him inboard again. When the second sea took him he was well clear of the ship on the port side.[1] Toward night the gale moderated but still a fresh gale is blowing with a tremendous sea. Saw a sail in the port quarter steering to the Ed, but it is too bad weather to think of capturing anything. We had a fine Christmas dinner, but the weather was so bad that we could not enjoy it much. We drank success to our dear ones, and noble cause. Restored the Gunner to duty.

At Sea, Monday December 26th 1864
Lat: 41°55′S.   Long: 57°05E.   Bar: 29.70–.80–.84
Course ENE.   Dist 178 m.   Wind. Sd & Wd.   Ther. 44° to 50°.
In the mid watch a sea struck her on the starb'd side abreast the fore rigging & swept away our starb'd swinging boom. The weather much more moderate, and sea tho' still high is smoother. The brig seen yesterday on our port quarter, kept off to our course, steering East. Weather cloudy & cold.

At Sea, Tuesday Dec. 27th 1864
Lat 41°41′S.   Course E 1/2N   Ther 50° to 58°   Bar. 29.7 to .80
Long: 60°47′E.   Dist: 166 m.   Wind W, NW, SW.
Pleasant weather; made sail to Royals, Flying Jib & staysails, but toward night we had showers with a fresh breeze, when we reduced sail to Top Gallant Sails. Afterwards reefed down to about double fore & main & close mizen topsl.

At Sea, Wednesday Dec. 28th 1864
Lat 41°30′S   Course E1/4N   Dist. 225   Ther. 47° to 52°
Long 65°50′E   Wind Wd & Sd & W   Bar. 29.70–.64–.92
Blowing fresh & very heavy sea. Close reefed the fore main topsails & furled the Miz. topsail. At 4.15 a pretty fresh gale with a heavy sea from Sd. ran the ship off before the sea. At midnight both wind & sea moderated.

At Sea, Thursday Dec. 29th 1864
Lat: 39°13′S.   Course NE 1/4N.   Bar. 29.95 to 30.26
Long: 68°33′E   Dist: 185 m.   Wind S, SSE, S, S by W   Ther. 58
Hauled by the winds under double reefed topsails & foresail. Saw a bark astern coming up with us and waited for her to come up. She did so on our weather quarter. All hands thought that she was a Frenchman. We ran up the English

flag & she, to our great surprise, hoisted the Yankee colors. She ran across our stern. We fired a cartridge, hoisted at the same time our own colors. She hove to and we sent a boat onboard. She proved to be the American Bark *Delphine* Capt. Nichols—in ballast from London to Akyab [Present day Sittwe, west Burmese port.—*Ed.*]. She was a good prize, but the Capt. said that his wife was onboard and that to move her in such a sea might prove fatal. It was decided to leave the matter to the decision of our surgeon, who took the Captain aside and upon hearing what Mrs. Nichols's complaint was, considered that there would be no danger in making the transfer. Accordingly she was brought off and hoisted up in a chair without any trouble. We also brought off the Capt., two mates & 11 men as prisoners of war & the Steward, Stewardess & Mrs. Nichols's little son Phineas. The Starboard cabin was fitted up for the Capt. & his wife & stewardess. All their baggage was brought off & the vessel set fire to. We filled away. Shipped six of her crew and put the remaining six in single irons.[2] The Capt & his mates signed their paroles. The prize's value was estimated at $25,000. Mrs. Nichols really looks like anything but an invalid being a large fine looking person, rather pretty. At first she is a little frightened but we can soon drive fear away by proving by kindness that we are gentlemen. They are from Searsport, Maine, the same place that Capt. Staples of the *Alina* was from.

At Sea, Friday Dec: 30th 1864
Lat: 38°41′S.   Course. E b. N 3/4 N. 89 m.   Bar. 30.27 to 30.39
Long: 70°19′E.   Wind S by W SSE & Varble.   Ther. 53° to 57°
Lost sight of our burning prize at 3 o'clock. This day has been very pleasant and we have had nice breezes. Mrs. Nichols is becoming quite sociable, and converses quite freely. We made sail to Royals and staysails.

At Sea, Saturday Dec. 31st 1864
Lat 38°37′S   Course E 2°N.   120 m.   Bar. 30.35 to 30.40
Long: 72°50′E   Wind SW. & W.S.W.   Ther. 54° to 61°
This has been a lovely day. We have been under all plain sail with a light breeze, nearly aft. Our lady passenger's becoming more sociable, and really seems to think that we are not all a parcel of piratical barbarians. This is the last of the year. I shall sit up, bid it adieu, and welcome the new one in. Oh! may the incoming one be happy. God grant us freedom & peace, I humbly pray. Oh! how many many changes may take place in the time which will intervene between this . . . [and] the last of next year. Oh! God grant us thy blessing upon our dear ones at home; upon my afflicted country. How much would I not give to see the dear ones at home again, and my own darling Pattie. God protect them I pray.

At Sea, Sunday, January 1st 1865
Lat: 38°24′S.   Course E 1/2 N. 105 m.   Bar: 30.30 to 30.38.
Long: 75°02′E.   Wind WSW(light.)   Ther. 57° to 61°.

This is the first day & Sunday in the year; the first day and Sunday in the month. At 8. we hoisted the Confederate flag & kept it up all day to welcome in the new year. And made all sail, with studding sails on both sides. It is the first time we have ever had all sail set at one time. Mrs. N. is very cheerful. We had a nice dinner.[3] This is a day upon which all persons however separated think of their absent dear ones more than on any other. Oh! how my heart feels for my dear ones. My darling Pattie, Father, brothers & sisters and my dear Country. Oh! how earnestly I invoke God's blessing upon you all. May we all be better & happier in the incoming than [we were] in the outgoing year. God grant it. My constant prayer is that a merciful God will guard, protect and cherish our dear country. That he will open the eyes of our enemies to the cruelty of the war they are waging against us, and that he may teach them that they are wrong.

At Sea, Monday, January 2d 1865
Lat: 38°39′S.   Course E 1/2 S 118 miles   Ther: 58° to 64°
Long: 77°33′E   Wind W.N.W.   Bar. 30.27 to 30.17

This has been a very pleasant day, being neither too warm nor too cold. I never saw more beautiful weather than we are now having. At 8.20 A.M. we made the Island of St. Paul's, distant about 30 miles, Amsterdam bearing about NE 1/4 N distant about 50 miles. At noon a party of officers desiring to go to St. Paul's Island to explore we lowered a boat & let them go, Lieut. Grimball in charge, the officers pulling themselves. At 4.15 they returned thoroughly tired out from pulling. We had supposed the island uninhabited but when they pulled to the beach in the little harbor (on[ly] navigable for small craft) they saw two houses, and two white men approached them. They conversed freely in [F]rench and found out that the two [F]renchmen belonged to a [F]rench fishing smack which had gone to the island of Bourbon. They were the only people on the island. They said that there was one vessel which came there during the fishing season to fish & when it was over, left two of their number to look out for their property. They are sometimes here six & eight months without seeing a soul, as vessels generally only sight it. They have a plenty of a fish not unlike the cod, which is dried & very nice. They have chickens, eggs, hogs, vegetables &c. enough for some two or three persons for a year. The island is almost inaccess[i]ble from the little harbor, but before you get to the high cliff there is a table land which enables them to have a garden. There were the greatest quantity of penguins sitting in every direction about the little harbor, which were so gentle that they could be caught without trouble in the hand. These birds in their erect position looked like soldiers. The two [F]renchmen were then expecting their schooner. Our officers brought off a penguin & some eggs & one chicken. At 4.30 made a sail standing to the Nd & Ed. Made sail in chase. She hoisted [D]utch colors & we squared away on our course. At 7.40 St. Paul's bore West per compass about 15 miles distant.

At Sea, Tuesday January 3rd 1865
Lat: 38°52'S.   Course E 1/2 S 112 miles   Ther. 58° to 62°
Long: 80°07'E.   Wind Nd & Wd   Bar. 30.12 to 29.89

All day we have been getting along comfortably at the rate of from 6 to 11.5 knots per hour, with a nice breeze nearly aft, with all plain sail set.

At Sea, Wednesday January 4th 1865
Lat: 39°00'S.   Course E 2°S   240 miles   Ther. 58° to 56°
Long: 85°13'E.   Wind NW, NNE & SW   Bar. 29.83 to 29.77

Today we have had very variable wind. The wind from the Nd & Sd was fresh and we reduced sail to double reefed topsails during the squalls. Between noon yesterday and noon today we have made a good run of 240 miles, being an average of ten knots per hour.

At Sea, Thursday January 5th 1865.
Lat: 38°58'35"S.   Course East   145 miles.   Ther. 52° to 57°
Long: 88°19'15"E.   Wind SE to South   Bar. 29.60 to 29.90

Made sail to Royals & Flying Jib. During the whole day we have had very pleasant weather. Had our usual exercise at quarters.

At Sea, Friday, January 6th 1865.
Lat: 38°21'S.   Course NE by E 3/4 E   87 m.   Ther. 56° to 58°
Long: 89°59'E.   Wind Var'ble, E, Nd & Ed   Bar. 29.90 to 29.94

Clear and pleasant. Commenced to condense fresh water. Towards night, as the weather looked squally, reefed down to double reefed topsails. Had our usual drill at quarters.

At Sea, Saturday January 7th 1865.
Lat: 39°08'S.   Course E by S 1/2 E   168 m.   Ther. 57° to 60°
Long: 93°22'E.   Wind Nd & Ed.   Bar. 29.95 to 29.99

Clear and pleasant weather. Made sail to Top gallant Sails. Today I triced up John Williams (Ship's Cook) (colored) for neglect of duty. Kept him up until he was as docile as a black sheep, when I let him down.

[At this point Whittle began an entry for January 8, 1865, but crossed

much of it out and began the entry again on the following page. This appears
to have occurred when he copied the noon location for 7 January 1865 from
the log.—*Ed.*]

At Sea, Sunday, January 8th 1865
Lat. 39°48′S.   Course E 10°S   Long. 98°12′E.
Distance 224   Ther. 56° to 60°.   Wind, NNE   Bar. 29.99

All hail another day of rest! Three months ago I sailed from England (London) in the *Sea King* and here I am thousands and thousands [of miles] away,
no one knowing outside of the ship where we are—or where we will probably be at any time. This is the 50th anniversary also of the Battle of New
Orleans. The day commenced with a nice topgallant breeze and misty disagreeable weather. So much so that the Captain told me to dispense with the
usual inspection. I, however, inspected the decks, and am rejoiced to find
that Mr. Colton has made a fine commencement as the Berth deck looks better than I have ever seen it. I am sorry to say that our wardroom steward
Wm. Bruce is very ill, and he being a very feeble man I fear he may die. Oh!
how very much I would right such a thing. I spent the day in reading the service in my room. I had today to punish our Ship's cook, John Williams (colored) for impertinence to the Master at Arms. He is a sullen fellow and I have
no doubt will leave us in the first port we enter.

At Sea, Monday Jany, 9th 1865
Lat: 39°48′S.   Course East.   Long: 102°51′E.
Distance 213 1/2   Ther 59 to 62.   Wind, North & West
   Bar 29.95 to 30.12

We are now having damp, foggy weather which I suppose is indicative of our
approximation to land. Only think that here we are from our homes distant
half the circumference of the Earth. Last night about 11 o'clock we passed the
half way mark and now we are getting nearer and nearer home in distance
each day. The wind has been very light and variable all day and the ship has
been under studding sails. I commenced early this forenoon to shift the coal
from the foreholds to the athwartship bunkers preparatory to fitting up our
shellroom. The steward of the last vessel we destroyed [Barque *Delphine*]
came to me today and asked me please to put him "on parole" as he did not
want to be put in the Federal army when he got back. He is from Missouri and
I told him that he was a southern man and I had no parole for him as I considered him nothing but a traitor. I dare say he thinks he will be hung in consequence. He claims to be a southerner in all his sympathies and would join
us if his wife was not with him. He is not much loss anyhow as he is worthless. He was, he says with Capt. Bulloch in the *Black Warrior.* Today for curi-

osity sake I got weighed. My weight astonishes me beyond measure. It is 140 pounds and two months ago when I stopped the use of tobacco I weighed only 118 pounds. I have thus gained twenty two pounds in two months. This is one of the proofs of how ruinous tobacco was to me. I do not think I will ever re-commence its use.

> At Sea, Tuesday Jany: 10th 1865.
> Lat: 39°54'S.   Course E 1/2 S   Long. 104°25'E.
> Distance 72 m.   Bar. 30.00 to 30.10.   Wind S by E to Var'ble
>   Ther. 57° to 64°.

Today it has been blowing almost "Paddy's hurricane" the whole day, and the sea almost smooth. We commenced early at shifting the coal. This is onboard any ship a dirty job, and I care not how soon we may finish it. The Captain asked me if I would let him have a boat to take a run around the ship. I had the gig cleared away, lowered, and manned, and had him piped over the side. This is the first time the ceremony of piping over has ever been done in the *Shenandoah*—it sounded very natural. He came back very much pleased with her outside appearance. Bulloch today with my advice went to the Surgeon and got him to recommend his being relieved of the duty of Master in consequence of his eyes. This relieves us of a dilemma in my opinion—as Chew was ordered to do Master's duty and Bulloch took the watch thus relieving Mr. Minor, who in my opinion should never have been given the deck over Mr. Mason & Mr. Browne.[4] I have put Mr. Minor as Master's Mate of the Fore Castle where he properly belongs. I trust that this, or similar difficulties, will be avoided in future. I am sorry for Bulloch but he will soon get well now. His eyes have been very much injured by taking sights. Tonight the Captain & Dr. McNulty and Bulloch & I, played four games of Whist. B. & I beat three out of four.

> At Sea, Wednesday Jan'y: 11th 1865
> Lat: 40°10'12"S.   Course E 1/2 S.   Long: 107°11'30"E.
> Distance 140 m.   Winds, Nd & Ed.   Bar 29.95   Ther. 60 to 64

Very little worthy of noting occur[r]ed to day. The whole time has been occupied in shifting coal from the fore holds to the Bunkers. Tonight the Captain, Dr. McNulty, Lee & I, played three games of whist. Lee and I beat the rubber.

> At Sea, Thursday Jan'y: 12th 1865
> Lat 39°59'   Course E 4°S.   Long. 111°09'E.
> Distance 172 m.   Bar. 29.75 to 30.   Winds. Var'ble
>   Ther. 60° to 64°

This morning early we commence[d] to break out the coal from our spare propeller, and having done so, and hoisting it up, found everything in its place. We leveled the coal around it and commenced to stow the beef and pork. Thank goodness we are nearly done [with] this dirty job and I trust it is the last dirty work we will have to do. We have had a head sea nearly the whole day, and the wind has been fine for carrying out a plan which I suggested to the Captain as being advisable, but he says he cannot consider it. I consider that by taking the trip we would take at least four or five prizes before getting into port.

I today with the permission of the Captain rated Mich: Moran & Alphonso Robeson Captains of the forecastle. The latter is a Yank, but a good man. Today I caught the ship's cook, John Williams (colored) in a piece of rascality, i.e. stealing the wardroom steward's shirts. I have stopped his grog until further orders and trice him up when he is not at work. I fear he is a great scamp.

Today I, Grimball, Lining, Bulloch, Smith & McNulty were appointed by the Captain a Board to survey the ship's galley. All considered that it was too small for our ship's company and recommend getting a larger one.

At Sea, Friday Jany: 13th 1865
Lat: 38°58'S.   Course NE by E 1/2 E.   Long: 113°38'E
Dist: 140 m.   Ther. 64°.   Wind, Sd. & Ed.   Bar. 29.97

All day have we been hard at work at stowing the forehold in some sort of order—this is a very dirty job but I am in hopes that we will get through with it tomorrow. This evening at 5 O'c. P.M. I triced up John Williams (ship's cook) for the offence of stealing in which I detected him on yesterday. Commenced a long letter to Commodore Barron which I shall send as soon as we get into port. I shall, in this letter, give the dear old gentleman an insight to our condition past and present. I am certain that when he reads the account of what we have done he will be proud of us.

At Sea, Saturday, Jany: 14th 1865
Lat: 38°11'11"S.   Course NE.   Long: 114°52'   Ther. 66°
Dist 75 m.   Winds. East, E by N.   Bar. 29.90 to 30.00

The whole of today we have been busy stowing the Forehold. We did not finish but will be able to complete our work on Monday. This will give us a berth deck entirely clear of shell boxes, etc., and will make all things much more comfortable.

I punished John Williams, ship's cook, as before, for the same offence.

At Sea, Sunday, Jan'y: 15th 1865
Lat: 39°34'S.   Course SE by E 1/2 E   Long: 118°03'E.

Dist: 168 m.   Ther 65°   Wind. NE by E, NNE.
Bar. 30.00 to 29.86

Another day of rest. As the day was damp and disagreeable the Captain had no inspection. I simply inspected the decks.

At Sea, Monday, Jany: 16 1865
Lat: 39°57′S.   Course E by S.   Long: 119°38′E.
Dist: 80 m.   Ther. 63°   Wind. NNE & ENE.   Bar. 29.80 to 29.70

This day is my 25th birthday. It has only been celebrated by the Captain's giving me a nice book marker, [and] Lining trying to give me twenty-five knocks, and my writing to my dearest Pattie. She wrote to me on my last birthday, and I will write to her now. We had a head wind and got up steam and lowered our propeller. The ship is not near as comfortable as under sail. Today I finished stowing the forehold and I consider this a great job finished. God in his mercy grant me many, many returns of this day. I can scarcely realize that I am twenty five. I am getting right ancient. This evening we sent down Royal yards, to lessen the opposition to going ahead, this is the first time, and the fore & mizen did very well, but the main did badly. Louis Rowe, the Capt. of the Top, was so much provoked at being beat that, [F]renchman like, he actually cried. The Captain & McNulty beat Lining and myself three out of five games of whist.

At Sea, Tuesday Jan'y: 17th 1865
Lat: 39°40′17″S.   Course E by N.   Long: 122°17′E.
Dist. 160.   Ther. 63°   Wind ENE and calm.   Bar. 29.75

This morning at an early hour I heard Louis (Rowe) one of our [F]renchmen, sing out, "Sail ho!" and I heard Jack Grimball ask, "Where away[?]" I went on deck, and we soon made the vessel out to be a large ship with double topsail yards except the Mizen. As we were under steam with a very light head wind we soon came up with her. We hove her too and Chew went onboard. She showed the English flag. The boarding officer had orders, that if he saw anything suspicious to *ask* the Captain to come onboard. Chew soon sent the boat back with Capt: Finlayter of the British ship *Nimrod*. His papers appeared all right, but he had no bill of sale, and his vessel had been the Yankee ship *Cinco Panza* [*Sancho Panza*].[5] Her register & papers were now all in form. The Captain said she was bonafide transfer[r]ed property. We asked him if he had any objection to being put on oath—he said, "no"—I swore him, and from his answers concluded that she was really British property. The Captain was a jolly old Englishman. He said that his "wife and sympathies were southern," as the former was from New Orleans. The valve to the air pump gave way and we stopped the engine for repairs. Let the steam go down and triced up the propeller. I forgot to say that Capt. Finla[y]ter sent us 1/2 doz. [bottles of] Brandy as a present.

At Sea, Wednesday Jan'y: 18th 1865
Lat: 39°24′S.   Course E 1/2 N.   Long: 124°51′E
Ther. 64°   Bar 29.86   Distance 125 miles.
Wind from NE by E to NE by N.

At five oclock this morning the Chief Engineer Mr. O'Brien reported the work on the air pump valve finished. Upon tricing up our propeller we found that all the bolts which we had put on the c[o]upling strap had broken and that it was as bad as ever. Mr. O'Brien got to work at it and I hope will soon have it in fine order. We want a new strap for this has been drilled so often as to weaken it.

This morning in the forenoon watch the Jib stay carried away and of course the halliard went also. We soon got the sail in and spliced the stay and halliard. Both were of wire. The stay carried away in consequence of its being wire and having in its lead such a short nip.

At Sea, Thursday Jany: 19th 1865.
Lat: 38°23′S.   Course NE by N.   Long: 125°44′E.
Ther. 65°   Bar. 29.70 to 30.00
Dist. 75 miles.   Wind. N by E & variable.

Today I have had nothing to occur worthy of note. All the forenoon I was occupied in having the Berth deck holystoned. After shifting coal it was very dirty. It is not clean now but at least one coat is taken off. The Capt. has a good joke on me about today. This morning I was standing by the wardroom door and Mrs. Nichols came up and commenced talking to me. She said, ["]Well Mr. Whittle, I trust that we may soon have peace.["] I concurred in the hope. She then said, "Do you think we can ever be friends?["] Said I, "No, Madam, never." "But Mr. Whittle, if after the Peace was made you were to meet me, would you speak to me." "Certainly, Madam, I would speak at any time to a female." "But would you not speak to my husband?" I simply said, "I might do so as he has never served against us." She was admiring the uniform cap of our men, and wondered if she could make one. I replied, No, as it was woven. She said she would like of all things to have one. She said this in such a way that I was forced to yield, and said that I thought I could get one for her. She thanked me a little, but when she gets it she will thank me more. The truth is I can at all times know how to deal with men but not always with women. If proper I can always say no, to a man, but not so with a woman. Now I contend that before one of our southern women would have done such a thing as this she would have cut her hands off. Such is the marked difference. If I had given her a cap I have no doubt she would have handed it over to her husband, and he would probably [have] sold it, and considered his wife what they call "a smart one." Waddell was told all about it by Jack Grimball who overheard the conversation from his room, and tells it as a very good joke on me, because I told him he was to[o] yielding and asked him to refer all prisoners to me when he did not grant them a thing. He says he will tell all in Annapolis how I flirt with the Yankee prisoners, and says that he would advise me to write to my sweetheart and make a clean acknowledgement as she will certainly hear of it. I contend that with any woman who has so little delicacy as to place a gentleman in the fix I am, he has the perfect right to consider the promise as not made and on this principle I will let the cap alone.

> At Sea, Friday Jany: 20th 1865
> Lat. 38°34′S   Course NNE   Long: 126°37′45″E
> Ther. 66°   Bar. 29.95
> Distance 120 m.   Wind: Nd & Ed & Sd & Ed.

The greater part of the day was pleasant; but we had very light and adverse winds. We have made very little, as purposely we have been under easy sail. I had enough black paint mixed to paint ship, and will commence tomorrow morning if the weather will allow me. This evening I did a thing which I have been longing to have finished. I got all the powder securely stowed in the Magazine which we constructed ourselves. This to me is a great relief, as it is now well clear of all danger and out of harms way. Today John Williams (ship's cook) reported Wm. Jones the Steerage Steward for calling him "a black scamp." I had an idea of telling him that I agreed with Jones; but upon examination by questioning witnesses I found that Williams had called him by some outrageous epithet, and not being able to tell who was most wrong I by the rule of "evenhanded justice" punished both of the worthies. Williams is a great villain.

> At Sea, Saturday, Jan'y: 21st 1865
> Lat: 38°22′S.   Course E by N   Long. 128°10′E
> Ther. 62°   Bar. 29.95
> Distance 75 m.   Wind. Sd & Wd and Sd and Ed

I did not commence painting as early as I desired because it looked like rain. I commenced and painted aft and as low down as I could without the waters washing up over it. It has been a good day and we have had a nice breeze. As long as we have to go to port, I do not care how soon we get there, but I had much rather not go at all. Except to hear some news, ports have no attraction for me, as there is no chance of my hearing from my darling or from home. Oh! how much joy it would afford us all to hear that Peace had been made.

We would then take our noble ship into port in Dixie. Then where would I go? I would strike a "bee line" for her whom I love. She knows who.

At Sea, Sunday Jan'y: 22nd 1865
Lat: 37°06'S.   Course ESE 3/4 E   Long: 131°03'E
Ther. 64°   Bar. 29.97
Distance 140 m.   Wind. South & SW.

Another day of rest although really the men have had a great deal to do, as right after breakfast having gotten up steam and lowered the propeller we took in all but the fore and aft sails. We had inspection at quarters. We saw three sails this morning of which two were English and one Swede. I commenced a long letter to my dear father so as to have it in readiness to send as soon as we get to Melbourne. I sincerely wish that we were not going there for I think that our cruise will be greatly injured by it, as from that place there are little vessels carrying regular mails to different fishing depots, at which the Yankee whalers congregate, and as soon as they hear that we are in the neighborhood they will all run into port, and we will catch very few.[6] Waddell has his mind bent upon getting a mail, and that settles the matter.

At Sea, Monday January 23rd 1865
Lat: 37°58'S.   Course ESE 3/4 E.   220 m.   Ther. 66° to 54°
Long: 135°21'E.   Wind. Sd & Wd.   Bar. 29.90 to 29.80

Stopped the engine for a half hour in order to repair valves and set all fore and aft sails. Saw four sails—one of them a six topsail yard ship* which I took to be a yankee ship, but the Captain did not make chase as he thought it the *Nimrod,* already boarded. The weather is beautiful.

*This vessel was the *David Brown,* bound to Adelaide, which was commanded and in great part owned by Mr. Nichols' Brother. I learned this by the arrival of that ship at Adelaide about that time. Capt. Nichols, when he saw the arrival said that she was the ship we passed at this time, and that he was certain of it at the time and was very uneasy for fear we would give chase. [Asterisk and insert in original MS.—*Ed.*]

4

The Victorian Government treated us very badly . . .

January 24–February 19, 1865

At Sea, Tuesday January 24th 1865.
Lat: 38°30′S.   Course E 3/4 S 220 m.   Bar 29.88 to 29.90
Long: 140°02′E   Wind Variable.   Ther. 58° to 64°

Under steam and sail. Very pleasant weather. Passed an English Hermaphrodite Brig. Employed painting ship outside preparatory to going into port.

At Sea. Wednesday January 25th 1865.
Position—entering the Port of Melbourne, Australia.

Clear weather, & moderate breeze. At 3.30 A.M. made a large sail on the lee beam; made chase; she proved to be an English ship. Ship under steam. At 5 A.M. saw Cape Otway, a point on the port bow, beautiful land fall. Stood along the coast for Port St. Phillip with the land all on our port beam. Several sails in sight. All hands getting the anchor ready for letting go. Furled all sail at 11:30 A.M. At 1:45 P.M. stopped the engine and took onboard Mr. Nicholsen, Pilot, and proceeded up the bay, stopping off the fort to be overhauled by the port surgeon. Passed on with our flag flying, numerous steamers, tugs and sailing craft saluted by dipping their Ensigns to us—and in some instances cheering. All these greetings were cheering, and were returned cheerfully. At 6:45 let go the st'b'd anchor off Sandridge, veering to 45 fathoms. The pilot brought us a great deal of news, which after being out nearly four months, during such a war, was most interesting to all parties. Lee had gained a great victory near Petersburg; some other small victories in Virginia; the *Florida* disgracefully seized in the port of Bahia, Brasil. Lincoln re-elected President and Andrew Johnson of Tennessee Vice President. This all looks like no end to the war. God alone can tell when or how it will end. Lieut. Grimball was sent to take a communication to the Governor Sir (Somebody) Darling [Sir Charles H. Darling], stating the object of our visit, and asking permission to undergo certain necessary repairs, reprovision, and land prisoners. Neither feeling authorized to hold our prisoners in a neutral port or send them ashore without permission, we simply gave them to understand in so many words that there were a plenty of boats along side, that they could remain until we got permission to land them, or avail themselves of the shoreboats. They decided (sensibly) as it was late to remain all night. If we can judge from outward signs, we are likely to find a good deal of sympathy here among the people. It is the first time that these people have ever seen our flag or any of our people, and as we have, as it were, the reputation of the Confederacy to make & maintain, it is very incumbent that every man an[d] officer should be circumspect. Lt: Grimball returned; the Governor will give an answer tomorrow.

At Anchor, Hobson's Bay, Melbourne, Thursday Jan: 26 [1865]

Early this morning Paymaster Smith went onshore with our letter bag for England. It contained, of mine, one to Commodore Barron giving him in detail a full account of our cruize [and] one to my dear father, enclosed in a short note to Mr. Moses R[obertson] and one to my darling Pattie. I trust they may all reach their destination to relieve the anxiety produced by the report of the wreck of the ship; and to let them know, under how many trials we have done our duty. The Steamer Ship *Bombay* bound, (I think) to London left the port.[1] As soon as the permission requested was granted by the Governor, the steam tugs commenced to come alongside filled to overflowing with visitors. Before the permission was given we had to warn a great many off. I never saw anything like the rush; the anxiety to see the ship & crew. The[y] look at us with apparent surprise that we have not tails. If this is what we are to expect, the sooner we get to sea the less chance I will incur of going deranged. Invitation after invitation has been already extended to us, and the hospitality of the people is, apparently, only surpassed by their immeasurable curiosity. Having so few men we employed George Nickells in the *Modesty* as our boatman to take the officers & men onshore, and run errands for the vessel.

Mrs. Nichols on leaving the ship said that she was very much obliged for our kindness but hoped that we would sink at sea in six months. She said she liked all the officers except Dr. Lining & myself. I thought I was a kind of chicken of hers—anyhow I was very kind to her. [The above paragraph was inserted at the extreme top of the next page, as if Whittle had penned it in later, after hearing from someone else what Mrs. Nichols had said.—*Ed.*]

Hobson's Bay, Friday January 27th 1865

Received fresh provisions. Oh! how I did enjoy my first fresh meal. I am an epicure, but that is not necessary to make one, after four months at sea, enjoy something fresh. Commenced painting Ship. Caulkers, commenced their work on our upper deck. The Captain paid an official visit to the Governor but did not see him. The ship crowded with visitors. They were so thick that the Caulkers had to give their mallets a good sweep as the only means of getting on with their work. These crowds are composed of all sorts, men, women, children, halt, lame and deaf, all bound to see the ship. The labor of showing them around is becoming very boring. If I have said once that "this is a 32 pdr of 57 cwt," "this is a sight," "this is a rifle gun," I have said it 50 times. I am polite to all, but as often as possible I excuse myself from showing them around, as the Capt is onshore, and I feel more the responsibility of my position. Throughout the whole day there were never less than 1,000 persons onboard and these would come & go as fast as the steamers and sailboats could go & return. The rush is tremendous and still there is no way to prevent it. The steamers had their signs up, "1 shilling to the *Shenandoah* and back." I had to tell the Captains that if they did not take off one party as the[y] brought another I would have to stop them. Each officer who went onshore came off a little "how come you so."

Hobson's Bay, Saturday January 28th 1865.

During the whole day the ship has been thronged with visitors, of all ages, sexes, and conditions of life. The ship is entirely in their possession as they roam all over, in and about her. I am thoroughly disgusted and tired, and wish we were out of the place. I thought the crowding could not continue without some accident. Today a boat with three men and one woman in it capsized. They were all fished out, with no damage except a good cold ducking. I never saw anything like the sensation which our ship has created. People have come from points at various distances from one mile to 300 miles in the country to see the ship. All these people have the same questions to ask and receive the same answers—and when I told several that I did not expect to see so many visitors they consoled (?) me by saying, "this is nothing to what you may expect tomorrow." Little did they know how miserable their consoling words made me—Sunday being the day when the working class are at liberty. A good many of our men came back from liberty but some remained.[2] The Yankee sympathisers & consul are "on dit" using every inducement to strip us of men. The highest rewards are offered to any and all who will desert.[3] The general underhanded rascality which characterizes them as a nation is showing itself here in the individuals who reside here and who come from the U.S. The Consul is now said to have some of our men at boarding houses defraying all their expenses. We could get here five thousand men, as there is not a day which passes that we have not application after application. We will not & cannot violate the neutrality of the port—and the same answer, i.e. that we can't ship them, is given to all. A very singular thing occured today. An old gentleman, a Mr. Waymouth, [Weymouth?] came up and said to me, "I should very much like to ask you about a friend of mine who was in the U.S. Navy, and ask which side he is on." I told him I would give him any information in my power. He said, "His name was Arthur Sinclair and I think he was from Virginia." It was strange that he should have hit on me to ask about my own Uncle. When I told him that I was his nephew, he most warmly grasped my hand. He said that when he knew my uncle he was a *midshipman* on the Pacific Station 34 years ago—that they were about the same age and that the greatest friendship sprung up, and that he has never seen him since. He gave me the warmest invitation to his house, and appointed a day for me to take a family dinner with him.[4] He is one of the most perfect old gentlemen I ever met. He tells me to make his house my home. He is here in the General post office and has been here some thirteen years. Tonight I went onshore for the first time. Staid some hour or two & returned. Lining went with me.

Hobson's Bay, Sunday January 29th 1865
All that I can say today is that I have been harrassed almost to death. The ship has been a perfect mass of human beings, the rail, rigging & masts have been crowded & filled. There were so many that steamer load after steamer load had to shove off as they could not find an inch to land on. I really feared that the ship would burst. I learned that two of our men were onshore in jail for debt, and sent Mr. Alcott with a note to the Chief of Police asking for their release & a bill for their debts. We found that the report was false. The Captain is out of the ship and has been all day. Everything falls on me and the officers whose duties keep them here. Oh how I wish we were once more at sea. We have received warning that the Yanks are determined to destroy our ship by some means. There may be idle and boastful threats but they are of such a dangerous nature that we are on the alert.

Hobson's Bay, Monday, January 30th 1865
Thank goodness no more visitors will be allowed to come onboard the ship until our work is finished. Several of our men are still onshore and every inducement is held out to the others. The Caulkers & Mechanics recommenced their work onboard. We have had application after application to join the ship, but give the same reply to all.
[At this point twenty-eight pages (fourteen leaves) were cut out of the journal; six cut pages (three leaves) were left in the journal. The entries end on

30 January 1865, in Hobson's Bay, and resume on 20 February 1865, at sea. The material Whittle removed probably dealt with the recruitment of seamen in Australia, which would have been a violation of Queen Victoria's proclamation of neutrality and the foreign enlistment act. Since forty-two men stowed away as the ship left Melbourne someone on board had to have been in charge of seeing that these men were hidden. That task probably was undertaken by a petty officer. However, it is unlikely that a good executive officer would be totally ignorant of what was going on, although he would necessarily want to remain in ignorance of the exact location of the stowaways. The editors believe Whittle was a bit indiscreet in the journal and cut the pages out before the ship entered Liverpool in November 1865. From the condition of the pages, and the rust from the pins which once attached the three remaining sheets to the journal, it seems the pages had been removed many years ago. There are other possible explanations, but this seems the most logical. Whittle's article, "The Cruise of the Shenandoah," included the following account of the ship's visit to Australia.—*Ed.*][5]

January 25, 1865, arrived at Melbourne, Australia, and our prisoners, after being paroled, went ashore in shore boats with their effects. Mrs. Nichols' last words were to express a hope that we would come to grief. I cannot blame her much. The Shenandoah needed caulking and docking to repair the shaft bearings. We were given permission to do the work necessary for safety at sea. The population were generally kind and hospitable and treated us with marked courtesy. They came on board by thousands. Soon, however, enemies attempted to draw our men from us, but generally failed.

We had myriads of applications to enlist, but we had had notice given us not to violate the Queen's proclamation of neutrality, forbidding shipping men, and we refused all. Men of their own volition, or, as we were persuaded at the time, in many cases were secreted on board, to entrap us into some violation of neutral laws and get us into difficulty with the local government. We hauled out on the marine railway or slip, and at one time our enemies so far succeeded, despite our constant efforts to keep all men not belonging to the ship from getting on board, that one man was reported as on board and the authorities demanded to search the ship.[6] This was positively and firmly refused, we saying that as a vessel of war we would not allow it, but would search her ourselves and send anyone, not on the vessel when we came in, ashore. This did not satisfy them, and pending reference to the law officer, the slip or railway was embargoed and all of her majesty's subjects forbidden to launch or work on the vessel.

A formal demand, in the name of our government, for the removal of the embargo was being drawn up when the law officer decided in our favor and our work continued. She was repaired and launched, and notice as requested given of when we would sail. At request of the authorities I was ordered to have her thoroughly searched for any stowaways. I selected several of the best officers, who made a conscientious search, and reported that they had examined carefully and could find no one not on the vessel when she came. In the meantime, however, when we gave our men liberty, the American consul or his emissaries persuaded several of our crew to desert.[7] Application for assistance to arrest them was made to the authorities, but denied. Thus it is clear that the Victorian Government treated us badly.

We got some 250 tons of coal,[8] and on February 18, A.M., sailed. We had received an intimation of a suggested plot among some Americans to go on board, go to sea and capture the vessel, but we were on the alert and never saw anything to cause us to think that they did more than to talk of this desperate attempt. We were numerically weak, but it would have been fatal for all who had entered into any such plot.

Getting well to sea, outside the jurisdiction, after discharging the pilot, forty-two men, who had stowed themselves away, some in the hollow bowsprit and some in the coal, all where the officers of the ship could not find them, came on deck and wanted to enlist. We wanted men after our losses in Melbourne, but we were suspicious, after the intimated plot. The men were black with dirt. We drew them up in a line, took their names and nationality.[9] Thirty-four claimed to be Americans and the other eight of various nationalities. We shipped them all, but watched them closely. They turned out to be good, faithful men. These gave us seventy-two men on deck. Some were from New England. One, George P. Canning, said he had been aide-de-camp to General (Bishop) Leonidas Polk, C.S.A., who had been discharged as an invalid. With him as sergeant, a marine guard was organized.[10]

[The journal entries resumed on 20 February 1865.—*Ed.*]

5
Oh, the terrible, terrible monotony . . .

February 20–March 31, 1865

At Sea, Monday Febry: 20th 1865
Lat: 38°15′S   Course ENE.   Long: 149°37′E
Wind SW by S. Calm & Nd & Ed   Ther. 60°   Dist: 100 m.
    Bar. 30.05

Today we have all been very busy relieving the ship of a great nuisance. We have had all the time a most unsightly and useless house on our Spar deck forward and it has always looked very unlike a man-of-war. While in Melbourne we provided ourselves with a splendid galley and had it put up in the berth deck leaving it alone for us to remove this house and cut the hole for the pipe. All this we did today commencing early and working all the time. About mid-day we saw the land near Cape Herve, which latter with the wind from its present quarter we will have a hard time weathering and I reckon we will be working about a great deal in the neighborhood. I trust that the dull monotony of beating to windward will be occasionally relieved by catching a yank. Oh! how anxious I am to pick up some more. Our crew, greater than at any former period, seems to be a good set of men, but they have been stowed away so long that it is hard to give them enough to eat. After we get them well filled up we will be all right.

At Sea, Tuesday Febry: 21st 1865
Lat: 38°06′S.   Ther 64°   Dist: 40 m.   Long: 150°23′E.
Course E by N.   Wind NE by E & ENE.   Bar. 30.10 to 29.94

Today we have been hard at work clearing away the remains of [the] house. The improvement is very great as now we have a clear deck from our poop to the forecastle, and a fair open deck. There are still a good many complaints about enough to eat. It seems to be the hardest thing in the world to fill them up. We got the anchors in, secured them and unbent the chains.

[For some unknown reason Whittle made changes in the dates of several entries. Comparison of the journal with copies of the log indicates that the original dating was correct. The correct dates have been used, with Whittle's corrections placed in brackets.—Ed.]

At Sea, Wednesday Febry: 22d 1865
Lat: 38°32′S.   Ther. 66°   Dist: 90 m.   Long: 152°15′30″E.
Course E by S 1/2 S.   Wind Nd & Ed Nd & Nd & Ed   Bar. 29.90

This is the 130th anniversary of the birth of Our Washington, Virginia's Washington. And I'm sad a[t] the thought that the very spot where 130 years ago this "father of his country" was born is now flooded with blood of his countrymen fighting against the hordes of the North for principles and rights, for the protection of which he is this day hailed by these very hordes as the "father of his country," and his birth day celebrated as no doubt that of Old Abe will be if the Vandals are successful. These miserable Yankees are fighting against the very rights which they thought so sacred in the Revolution. Nothing but a desire to gain wealth induces them to do it. They will sacrifice everything for money, principle, life and honor. I regard them collectively & individually a pack of scoundrels consummated in every society to rascality. The day is another great national one, in as much as our dear President was inaugurated on the 22d of Febry: 1862. I can only celebrate it by drinking a glass of sherry, doing my duty and praying for the triumph of the Cause which our noble Jefferson Davis represents. The day is also one of private importance as it is the birthday of my dear [sister] Jennie who is on this day 21 years of age. I can scarcely realize that such is the case. Only a short time since and I thought & looked upon her as a little child. God grant me many happy returns of this the anniversary of our first father's birth, and of the inauguration of our first President & second father. I have been busy all day in getting up Royal yards & cleaning up the Spar deck. I was forced to punish a man very severely this evening. It was James Marlow, our Wardroom Cook who has been with us from the start. He got too much grog in him and this brought a slight touch of the "old boy" to show itself, and then came neglect of duty; and then, o! dear, to his great surprise the severest punishment he ever heard of. I punish myself when I punish one of the men who I know would stand by me at any time—but I must rule or he—both cannot—and I take the shortest, severest & surest way of proving to him that I and not he must govern.

At Sea, Thursday Febry: 23rd 1865 [Whittle corrected date to
   Wednesday Febry: 22nd 1865]
Lat. 38°14′S.   Ther 67°   Dist: 170 m.   Long. 155°49′E.
Course E 1/2 N.   Wind NNW & NW by N.   Bar. 29.90

Today I stationed the men for sending up Royal yards and had not the slight-est difficulty in walking them all up together. We have a fine crew which when well broken in would do credit to any ship. Oh how very much I would rejoice to catch a great big Yankee. The monotony is very great. I trust however that our time will soon come. Our deck looks pretty well, but all my sand is out and I will have to wait for a Yankee Whaler before we can have a regular holy-stoning.

At Sea, Friday Febry: 24th 1865 [Whittle corrected date to Thursday
   Febry: 23rd 1865]
Lat: 36°51′S.   Ther 68°   Dist: 225 m.   Long 160°17′E.
Course ENE   Bar. 29.95   Wind. NW by W & NW.

I have been busy all day. I do not at all like the way in which things are being conducted. Of all men I ever saw, Waddell has the most provoking way of meddling. I do not know half the time what is being done in the ship, as he gives orders which should either em[a]nate from or pass threw me. This way of doing business does not suit me and it must be stopped. I will not allow myself to be treated as though I was a boy. I am no boy, and claim that I am quite as qualified to perform my duty as he is to perform his. Nothing but my remembrance of his sweet little wife's last request has prevented my having had an open rupture with him. I know his good points as well as his bad and I know that few persons can understand him better than I. He is impulsive, weak and vacillating, going always by extremes. I will wait and try to let him come too [sic] without a break. I feel the importance of our being on perfectly good terms, but if he throws up the gauntlet what can I do? I humbly pray that he may see his error.

[Lt. Whittle entered the correct day of the week beginning with the following entry.—Ed.]
At Sea, Saturday Febry: 25th 1865
Lat: 35°19′S.   Ther 68°   Dist: 240 [miles]   Long: 164°54′
Course ENE.   Bar. 30.05   Wind. NW by W & NW.

The cloud which yesterday I represented as hanging over the harmony of the ship still remains. The Captain all day has had the appearance of a man who had lost all his friends and was all day as dignified as weak men become when dignity ceases to be a good quality. Poor W[addell] I pity him with all my heart but I will never feel the same kindly friendship for him which he knows

I have felt. He has treated me in a manner which he knows is unworthy of him, and he knows it, but he has not the moral force to come to or send for me and say Whittle I have been wrong. I am very, very sorry for "with all his faults, I love him still." My last promise to his wife is first in my memory and I am a great sufferer, but with him is the fault and *with him the cure*—I trust he will come to his better self. What makes me feel more for him is the fact that all the Lieutenants have become estranged from him by his impulsive steps. I trust he will relent—for this state of things does the ship's discipline great harm.

> At Sea, Sunday Febry: 26th 1865.
> Lat: 34°23′S.   Ther. 69°   Dist: 122 m.   Long: 167°15′E.
> Course ENE.   Bar. 30.00   Wind. NW., SW, SE & Calm

This has been as lovely a day as I ever beheld. The middle portion was terribly hot—so much so that the pitch boiled out of our deck. At 10 we inspected our crew and at 10.30 had a general muster. We have a fine crew, all able bodied men and good seamen. We now muster stronger than even before even including prisoners. We have now onboard ninety-six men, and we feel that we can take care of the ship in all weather. There is a dark cloud which over-hangs us and she is not the happy ship she ought to be. Our C[aptain] is still in the dumps. His conversation unless absolutely on duty is with his clerk.[1] Why what is the matter with him? Alas! I fear it is natural. I did not know him before. I regret simply on account of his wife whom I regard with the affection of a brother. God knows the fault is not mine and I am willing to meet him, when he consents to treat me with the respect due my position, instead of with a heartless, selfish, indifference. There is not an officer to whom he speaks except on duty except his clerk. I trust he will undergo a change. Today I spent in reading over the letters of my own dear Pattie. Oh! how sincerely do I long for the time when I make her mine. God bless her. As long as the war lasts, I wish to be afloat, and will put up with anything and will sacrifice everything to my country's cause. My great fear is that W[ad-dell]'s foolishness will impair the service of the ship.

> At Sea, Monday Febry: 27th 1865
> Lat: 34°00′S   Ther. 70°   Dist: 39 m.   Long: 167°58′E.
> Course NE by E.   Wind Calm & E by W.   Bar. 30.11 to 30.05

Today I have been as busy as ever a man was—engaged in breaking out the forehold and transfe[r]ing many articles to the after hold. I never saw any ship stowed as badly as this one was at Melbourne. The things were simply dumped in without any kind of care. In addition to other misfortunes we found that the greater portion of our rum had leaked out. This I consider attributable to the bad handling of the barrels. There is nothing which conduces more to contentment of the crew than the ration of grog. I am very tired. We have not seen a single sail since we have been out, and it is becoming very dull. How anxious I am to catch a Yankee. W[addell] is still in the dumps. He is the weakest man I ever saw in my life. I begin to think that he is under the foolish impression that in order to retain the respect of the officers he must cease to have anything to say to them except absolutely on duty. He has gone so far with me that now all his orders even are written. This is childish foolishness that a boy of ten would be ashamed of.

> At Sea, Tuesday Febry: 28th 1865.
> Lat: 32°21′S.   Ther. 70°   Dist: 120 m.   Long 169°18′E.
> Course NE by N.   Wind. Variable from Ed.   Bar. 30.04 to 30.00

Up to four oclock I have been very busy at restowing the forehold, and I now have it in some kind of order. Never did I see two holds stowed as badly as ours were, and If I go to Melbourne again I will take very good care that John Collins (Stevedore) has nothing to do with the ship I may be in. Now, everything is where we can get at it. W's dumps continue. I am entirely at a loss to understand this man, who I once thought I knew. I will not put my two opinions on paper, but his conduct proves to me that he is one of two things. What these things are, I withhold. I am fearful that his conduct to me will not go unnoticed by the crew, upon whom it could have no other than a bad effect. I trust it will; for I consider that it is more incumbent on the Captain & 1st Lt. to keep upon good terms than everyone else. These two as a nucleus is all, but without them we will, I fear, be adrift. The Captain now not only does not *speak* to me privately but does not *even* speak to me officially. I am fearful that the efficiency of the ship will suffer. For my country's sake I trust not.

> At Sea, Wednesday March 1st 1865
> Lat: 30°52′S.   Ther. 72°   Dist: 130 m.   Long 170°50′E.
> Course NE   Wind Eastward   Bar. 30.00 to 29.93

We are still jogging along in what is said to be the track of Yankee whalers and we have not seen a single sail. I think it looks very much as though we were out of the regular track. One thing is certain either we are out of the track or they are.[2]

I am getting tired of so much sailing to no purpose, but I feel that tomorrow we will make our first prize. I would like it to be a fast bark of about 400 tons with double topsail yards and I would make application to take charge of her. A vessel of that description fitted out here would do quite as much damage as the *Shenandoah*—and the probability of capture would be very remote, as we could pass right through a Yankee fleet without creating any suspicion. Oh how I would glory in such a chance. I think I would either call her the *Dixie*, the *Norfolk* or the *Tudor*. God grant me this blessing. Lee, Scales & Bulloch are all applicants for any vessel that I am placed in command of—in fact I could take any of them as all would like to go. The Captain has come out in new colors and has spoken to all but me. I am now the only one. I should have been first but I suppose he will try me next. His treatment of me has been very outrageous and he has lost in me as good a friend as he ever had or will have. This afternoon we fired for the first time our two rifle guns—they behaved splendidly. I finished the storage of the forehold, a very long job well done. Today I had rated Louis Rowe (C. Top) Geo. Flood (C. Hold) Wm Smith (Ship's Cook)

At Sea, Thursday March 2nd 1865
Lat: 28°13′S.   Ther. 73°   Course N 1/2 E   Long: 171°04′E.
Dist: 180 m.   Bar. 29.90 29.80   Wind East

Today I have been having the portion of the spar deck which was under the house caulked and pitched. This afternoon it was discovered that one of our 3d Asst. Engineers & Rawlinson a fireman were intoxicated. The question was, where did they get their liquor? Mr. O'Brien searched and soon came up from the Propeller alley with a tin bucket with about a pint of *rum* in it. Upon examination we found that the bulkhead of the stuffing-box had been forced back, and the head of the rum cask in the hold came right over the break. Through this they had bored a hole in the cask and had a regular spile. I am certain that Rawlinson was at the bottom of it all. This is the rum which we all considered had leaked out. Wm Crawford (G.M.) was insolent to me and I triced him up. After two hours I sent for him and asked if he thought that he could keep a civil tongue in his mouth—to which he very sullenly said he did not know. And I triced him up for five more hours—when he gave in and was as polite as you please. I dislike of all things to punish any man but there are some who force you to it.

At Sea, Friday March 3rd 1865
Lat 25°50′S.   Ther. 75°   Dist 140 m.   Long 171°12′E.
Course N 1/2 E.   Bar. 29.45   Wind E−. NE by E.

Today nothing stirring has occurred. We have not seen a sail since we got out. I can't tell why, but I do not like it. W's dumps continue. I do not understand them. I hope I have not been deceived in the man. I shall do all I can with proper maintenance of self-respect to bring about reconcilliation. God knows I will hail it with welcome. I have been quite sick all day.

At Sea, Saturday March 4th 1865
Lat: 25°08'S.   Course N by W 170 m.   Bar. 29.72 to 29.55
Long. 170°43'E   Wind NE by E. E by N. NE.   Ther. 78°

The weather today commenced with overcast sky and squally weather. At 11 A.M. commenced steaming but at 12.30 as the weather was threatening we hoisted the propeller & continued condensing. At 12.45 expecting a gale from the Nd & Ed we wore around on the port tack and shortened sail to close reefed Fore & Main topsails & Fore storm staysail & reefed Fore Sail. By night it was blowing a moderate gale from the Nd & Ed. Well this is the day on which President Lincoln will be inaugurated. Surely we ought to expect a gale on that day, but I think that thus far we have been so much blessed that we might conclude that Father Neptune was on our side. I think that we will have a heavy gale out of this fellow.

At Sea, Sunday March 5th 1865
Lat: 24°10'S.   Course S by E 1/2 E.   70 m.
Bar. 29.48-.45-.43-.34. 29.12-29.30-29.20-29.30
Long: 171°20'E   Wind (gale) ENE–E by N & ENE   Ther. 73° to 76°

Blowing a fresh gale from ENE with a heavy sea, took in the foresail and lay to under fore & main topsail close reefed & fore storm staysail. The Fore Storm staysail blew away. Got a tarpaulin in the weather fore rigging, and bent another staysail. Shipped a sea abreast the Wᵉ Fore rigging which carried away or rather stove in some of our bulwark & capsized one of our 12 p. guns.[3] Towards night the gale was very heavy, with very heavy squalls, and high sea.

At Sea, Monday March 6th 1865
Lat: 25°29'51"S.   Course S by E 75 m.   Ther. 70° to 79°
Long: 171°38'E.   Wind NE   Bar. 29.30 gradually to 29.59

Commenced with continuation of a very heavy gale and high sea. As the day advanced the Barometer gradually went up and the gale moderated very considerably. Made sail to double reefed fore & main & close reefed Mizen topsails. The weather towards night being threatening we reefed down again and furled the Mizen topsail.

At Sea, Tuesday March 7th 1865
Lat: 26°43'S.   Course SE 3/4 E 90 m.   Ther. 74° to 76°
Long: 172°32'E.   Wind NE.   Bar. varying from 29.55 to 29.60

All day it has been blowing a moderate gale with a heavy sea, with passing heavy squalls of wind and rain. Towards night both wind and sea moderated; the squalls becoming less frequent and severe.

At Sea, Wednesday March 8th 1865
Lat: 27°05'S.   Course S 1/2 E 215 m.   Bar. 29.54, 29.40, 29.50
Long: 172°26'E.   Wind NNE to Nd & Wd   Ther. 77°

Sea & wind going down. Bent a new main topsail and repaired the Fore Top-sail. Wore ship to the Nd & Ed, and made moderate sail.

At Sea, Thursday March 9th 1865
Lat: 26°25'S.   Course NE by E 74 m.   Bar. 29.45 to 29.75
Long: 173°46'E.   Wind NW & NW by W   Ther. 75° to 81°

A beautiful day. Made all plain sail and had a thorough drying up. Oh what a joyous thing is a pleasant day after a heavy gale. Truly it is one of those pleasures which cannot be estimated except by experience. "Little does the landsman know the hardships of the tar."[4]

Oh how much I would give to hear from my darlings. God protect them, I pray.

At Sea, Friday March 10th 1865
Lat: 25°23'S.   Ther. 76 to 86   Long: 174°34'E.
Course NE 3/4 N. 77 m.   Wind. NW & calm.   Bar. 29.75 to .86

This morning I got up rather late and found it a beautiful day. And as calm as possible. We had the remains of our old sea, and just after quarters at 9 A.M. I called all hands to shorten sail, took the deck and clewed up all sails, furling the Royals & Topgallant sails. We had up steam, and have been steaming all day, at an average rate of eight knots per hour. The heat of today has been terrible, and the pitch from our seams would scarcely allow you to walk on deck. Oh! how I wish we could catch a Yankee. I am tired of this idling—and still we are doing all we can. I trust that we may have some luck soon. We have today been repairing the damages of the late gale—our bulwarks, & rigging & sails. After such weather it is fair to expect a good [deal] of repairing to be necessary. This has been one of the warmest days I ever felt in all my life. I found all my clothes mouldy from dampness, and took them up to give them an airing. All hands in fine spirits, but I longing for my little Bark.

At Sea, Saturday March 11th 1865
Lat: 23°15'S.   Ther: 79 to 82°   Long: 173°43'E.
Course NNW 139 miles   Wind. Nd & Ed & Sd & Ed   Bar. 29.88

I have rarely seen a warmer day at sea than this has been. The height of the thermometer was 85 in the coolest part of the ship, showing that we are gradually getting up to the Equator. The monotony is becoming terrible, only awaiting the capture of a Yankee to show us that our efforts are not altogether without effect. We have been busily employed repairing damages from the late gale. I commenced filling shells and find that nearly all the fuze holes have to be reamed out afresh. Never had a first Lieut. . . . so much to contend with. We are in good spirits, and are as happy as can be. I am quite in love with the chances of getting a little vessel on my own hook. I do not care how soon my time comes for I am very anxious to have a second craft in these seas. I care not for distinction or anything except such as is to be won by doing my duty in my country's call. I am sure that with one gun a vessel, such as I desire could do fine work, before her existence was known. As soon as it became at all likely that a Yankee cruiser was informed of my approximate whereabouts, I would take a long cruize to distant parts.

> At Sea, Sunday March 12th 1865.
> Lat. 21°23′S.   Ther 76° to 82°   Long: 173°08′E.
> Course N by W1/2W.   Wind. Var. & Nd & Ed.   Bar. 29.85.

This, another day of rest has been very warm, and we have done nothing but what was absolutely necessary. We had inspection at quarters at ten o'clock, and at five bells (10.30) we called "all hands to muster." Just as we were in the midst of reading the "Articles of War" a rain squall came up and we had to suddenly wind up. The whole day we have had passing rain, with a tolerably nice breeze, our old ship going ahead about 7 knots per hour. Oh how anxious I am to capture a Yank. I would prefer a smart little Bark of about 600 or 500 tons, as the Captain has promised to give me the command of any vessel which would suit. If I get such a command I shall be very circumspect. I will form all my plans and will confide in none but my Executive officer. This would be not because I would not trust them but people will talk & speculate among themselves and as soon as they talk among themselves they will be less & less cautious and any prisoners we might have would get hold of information as to our movements, and we would find a Yankee cruiser on the "qui vive." I will do my best.

> At Sea, Monday March 13th 1865.
> Lat: 18°56′S.   Bar. 29.78 to 29.89.   Long: 173°30′30″E.
> Course N3/4E 149m.   Wind. East & E by N.   Ther. 81° to 84°

Today I have been busy all the time in restowing the fore and after holds. In the late gales a great many things broke adrift. I have also filled a good many shells. I never knew what work was until I came on this ship. When I consider how much devolves on me, and how unsatisfactory to myself my best endeavors are, I feel blue, but with the steady stern resolve to do my best, I drive ahead and it is only when I look back and see how much I have done that I feel at all content. God knows that no effort on my part has been spared to complete a work which seems almost interminable, i.e. getting the ship in efficient condition. I have worked as hard and as continuously as ever any man worked in the world. To be the First Lieut. of a vessel, regularly equipped as a vessel of war with a plenty of men, is one thing and a similar position on an impromptu vessel with about 1/3 of a crew is something altogether different. However I will do all I can. I have made up my mind to one thing and that is, that if the war ends when this cruize does, I will never go to sea again in a man-of-war. While the war lasts my whole effort, my life and all I have shall be my country's and after it closes, my whole effort shall be to make myself worthy of her whom I live for more than life. Oh! how happy I should feel to be able tomorrow to make her my own. I am as certain as that I am here that no change will take place until we meet, but I continually feel how much will be her disappointment in finding me so different from what fancy has painted. Our love has been most extraordinary. I dare say that there never was a similar case before, but I believe it to be as devout, pure and lasting as ever love way, for all the singularty of it. She has shown a confidence & confiding confidence which will rarely ever be known. All this is between us alone and with none other, and while away here, separated by tens of thousands of miles my constant hope is that a Merciful God will protect her. We have had a nice breeze the whole day and our gallant old ship has been slipping along beautifully.

At Sea, Tuesday March 14th 1865.
Lat: 15°33′S.   Bar: 29.75   Long: 174°07′E.
Course NE by E 208 m.   Wind East.   Ther. 82°

I have been hard at work all day at restowing the after hold. A most unusual thing took place in the performance of this work. The Captain of the hold [George Flood] and one of the men got drunk and the former got into a fight. I will have him disrated and will have the grog of both stopped.[5] I never saw a better set of men. They have had both at sea and in port the most tempting opportunities to get tight and this is I think only the second case of the kind. At Melbourne I made a rule to depart from the usual practice of having the men & boats searched, and this is the result. If you treat sailors as men, instead of rascals all will go on well, taking good care to punish all violators of discipline. Some of our old men are shipped for six months only, in fact about 16 out of 21. Their terms expire the 18th of next month and I fear that nearly all of them will want their discharges.[6] Goodness knows they will be great fools for desiring such a thing away out here, when by sticking to the ship they get better pay, grub & treatment than they ever did before, but sailors are singular animals. Such a decision would cut our 96 down to about 80 of whom 25 are officers, leaving about 55 men or about three times our original number. It will of course give the rest more to do, but thanks to the "Stowaways" we will be independent. The only thing is that the ones who would leave are our petty officers. I may say that we are almost out of the world. The Fiji Islands are near us and we are twisting and turning among the neighboring groups. Oh! if we could take a prize, it would revive us all. The monotony is very great. We have not seen a single sail since we lost sight of Australia, and since then we have gone some 2000 miles right in the usual track—this is disgustingly remarkable. Oh if I could have but the three words "I am well" from my darling Pattie how happy I would be. God protect her I pray and hasten the time when I can call her mine own. Jack Grimball is sick with inflamed eyes. The heat of the weather is almost overpowering and is beginning to tell on the health of the crew. Our sick list is larger than it has ever been.

At Sea, Wednesday March 15th [1865]
Lat: 13°37′S.   Ther. 80°   Bar. 29.65 to .78   Long: 175°06′E.
Course NNE 1/4 E 130 m.   Wind Nd & Ed & Variable.

Today has passed without any but the usual ship labors to relieve the monotony which is indeed becoming terribly great. Oh! if we could only catch a Yankee. It would so revive and encourage us all. It does seem to me that we are out of the world for since we lost sight of the Australian coast we have not seen a single sail. Even the sight of a [D]utchman would cheer us up, but I think that if we can't catch a Yank we had better not see anything as then we can't be reported. The day has been terribly hot, with frequent rain squalls. The thermometer was 92° in my room. I had a long chat with Waddell. He has had the blues all day. He gives way too much in trouble to sail such service. He told me that he felt that his having to be on deck so much was beginning to tell on his health and he felt himself breaking. He takes an exag[g]erated view of his troubles w[h]ich are far fewer than others'. He has not sufficient confidence in the ability of his officers, in which he is wrong, for I never saw a better set, and one who learned so rapidly. He complained that with S[cales] he had to be on deck all the time, and he would not last the cruise if it lasted. He was so blue & melancholy that I pitied him, and told him that he was very much mistaken as to S's qualifications and that I considered his being on deck unnecessary. He insisted the contrary and I volunteered to keep all Scales watches with him in addition to my duties as Executive Officer, which God knows are far more trying than those of any man I ever saw. My legitimate duties keep me on deck from seven in the morning until 8 at night, and then to keep one of *three* watches, (for Jack Grimball is sick) is very trying, & will tell on me, but if one is to break down it had better be me than him, and I shall stand it as long as I can walk. I never saw any man feel it necessary to remain on deck so much. He complains of never getting sleep enough, and really it seems to me that he gets more sleep than any man in the ship, but in his own opinion he is a perfect martyr. Tonight S[cales] has the first watch, and I am very tired but I shall be up until twelve. Surrounded as we are by rocks, islands and doubtful shoals the navigation is intricate. There is in this connection another thought not at all consoling, i.e. if by misfortune we should run ashore and be wrecked we would probably be thrown on the Fijies, or New Hebrides, and we might be eaten by cannibals—this would be a terrible fate. We are in the Coral Sea and we really do not know what those little insects have been doing since the last survey. I am decided that in such a case I would cover myself all over with coal tar, curl my hair and I might pass as an uneatable niger. With this dark bright idea I will say "bon soir," bad luck to the Yanks.

At Sea, Thursday March 16th 1865 [Lt. Whittle changed Wednesday to Thursday, which is correct.]
Lat: 12°53′S.   Bar. 29.73   Long: 173°57′E.
Course NW by W   80 m.   Wind. Nd & Wd, Nd & NNEd.
Ther. 80°

Another day of damp monotony, for with the monotony we have had a great deal of rain. Oh! for a cot in some vast wilderness. I am very tired but have five good sleeping hours, i.e. from 11 to 4 when I will have [to] "turnout" to keep the morning watch with S[cales]. Grimball & Lining are still laid up with sore eyes, the former much better, but the latter in great pain. This morning I felt as tho we were going to capture a [Y]ank but I have been disappointed, and will be satisfied if we get one tomorrow. Today we had a short drill, the men did very well. They are a good set.

At Sea, Friday March 17th 1865 [Lt. Whittle changed Thursday to Friday, which is correct.]
Lat: 12°40′S.   Ther. 78° to 82°.   Long: 174°27′E.
Course ENE   32 miles.   Winds. Nd & Ed.   Bar. 29.75

Monotony. Oh! Monotony. No Yanks in sight! No sails in sight!! No anything in sight!!! Except the heaviest kinds of rain squalls. I never saw more rain. I was up during the whole of the forenoon watch and it rained in torrents, and blew very fresh. We are making very little progress as we have mainly a head-wind and a strong current. Grimball came off the [sick] list today, and this puts S[cales] in again for the morning watch, so that I will have to be up as I was this morning.

At Sea, Saturday March 18th 1865
Lat: 11°18′S.   Bar: 29.70   Long: 173°36′E.

Course NW by N   96 m.   Wind. Variable.   Ther. 76° to 83°
water two degrees higher

This morning I got up at 4 O'c to keep the morning watch again with S[cales].
I must say that I did feel very tired, but after a nice cup of coffee, I felt very
much refreshed. The day commenced as clear as a bell and I felt sure that we
were done with rain, but with the watch of Chew the unfortunate it clouded
up and very soon commenced to rain in torrents as usual. Oh! the dull monotony of being at sea on such a cruise and not see a sail. When I first got up
I, the prophet's scholar, said we would have one today but the same unbroken
monotony reigns.

At Sea, Sunday March 19th 1865
Lat. 11°05'S.   Ther. 82° to 86°   Long. 172°28'E.
Course W by N   68 m.   Winds. Nd.   Bar. 29.70 to 29.77.

Another day of rest, differing very materially from the last few by our not
having any rain. All feel better, cheerfully passing the time. No sails. Had inspection at quarters. Had to trice up Jas: Fegan (o.s.) for refusing to obey the
Master at Arms. This is his first offence, and I will nip it in the bud, a[s] I
think he is trying the sailor's well known experiment, 'to see how far he *can*
go[']. I had a pleasant time in my room reading the letters of my dear Pattie.
Oh! how I long to see her. If I could only know that she was well, I would be
very happy. God in his mercy guard, guide & protect her prays the one who
loves her more than life.

At Sea, Monday March 20th 1865
Lat: 10°26'S.   Ther. 84°   Bar: 29.80   Long: 171°58'E.
Course SW 3/4 N.   49 m.   Winds North & Variable

The same weather lasts. Light variable airs with frequent and heavy rain
squalls. After the 1st watch of last night and my day's duty, together with the
mid-watch tonight in anticipation, I feel badly but I will soon rally. I am convinced that no 1st Lieut: ever had so hard a time. N'importe—all would be
well if I could be cheered by the capture of a Yankee. Tonight we are getting
up steam to try and steam out of our position. Tonight the sky is as clear as
a bell and we see what is rarely seen, i.e. the "Southern Cross" and the "Dip-
per." All is beautiful.

At Sea, Tuesday March 21st, 1865
Lat: 8°36'S.   Ther. 82 to 86°   Bar: 29.70 to .82   Long: 172°57'E
Course NE by N 1/2 N   125 m.   Winds. Calm, NNE & N by W.

Under steam quietly slipping along at the rate of 8 knots an hour. This has
been one of the warmest days I ever saw at sea, the thermometer rising to 100°

in the shade. I felt very much jaded after last night's mid-watch, but I was very much refreshed by a sly nap. Oh! to be able to catch a Yank. We have not seen a single sail of any kind since this day last month. Today I was forced to trice up one of the firemen [William Brice][7] for insolence to the Master at Arms. This is his first & I trust, by prompt action it will be his last offence. Oh! if I could know that all was well with those dear to me. In God's hands I leave them.

At Sea, Wednesday March 22d 1865
Lat: 5°43′S.   Ther 83° to 89°   Bar: 29.80   Long: 173°40′E.
Course. N by E 1/2 E   182 m.   Wind N by W & Calm

Like the case of the Sailor's last gale, so it is with me and the weather, each day being considered the warmest. Today the thermometer stood at 118° in the sun. We are still under steam with light airs from the Nd. After the morning watch I felt tired until between 12 and 1, while the men were at dinner, I took a sly nap. S[cales] protested with the Captain against my keeping watch with him but it was productive of no change by which I may expect to keep for an indefinite time one of four watches at night besides being up all day attending to my duties as the Executive officer, which are, in themselves, harder than those of any Executive officer I ever saw. It is hard, but as long as a merciful God gives me the health, I will do all I can. Monotony is unbroken and terrible. If we could take a prize it would give us new life. All will yet be well for I am sure we have good luck ahead. We are now standing for "Drummond" Island which is not far off, and then we may catch one, two or three. McNulty has been quite sick, and is still so. He looks very much reduced. He is a high minded, noble fellow, and has, that I know of, but one fault & that is an infirmity, by which he can't help from occasionally imbibing too freely. He is now on a stool of repent[a]nce and I trust his good sense will take *him clear of all temptation.*

At Sea, Thursday March 23d 1865
Lat: 2°30′S.   Ther 85°   Bar: 29.80   Long: 174°03′E.
Course N 3/4 E   194 m.   Wind N by W, NNE & Calm

Terribly hot with passing, heavy showers. We were under steam the whole day steering for one of the Gilbert group, which we expected to make before dark, but found that there was a strong westerly current. At 7 P.M. we calculated that we were about twenty miles from the reef, and as very little is known of its extent since the last survey, we determined to lay quiet all night. It is as nearly calm as is possible. I have the first watch. I trust we may be repaid for the recent monotony by finding several unsuspecting Yanks hovering around.

At Sea, Friday March 24th 1865
Lat. 1°21′S.   Ther. 80°   Bar: 29.84   Long: 174°22′E.
Course Ne by E 1/4 E.   73 m.   Wind. Calm & NE

This morning at 4 started the Engine, and at 8 saw land right ahead. This is the island for which we have been running. It is Drummond island one of the Bishop group of the Gilbert Archipelago. The native name for it is "Taputeouea" [Tabiteuea]. It is the largest of the Archipelago being about 30 miles long and 4 wide at the widest point. We did not deem it safe to approach within less than six or eight miles. The land is low and at the distance seems to be thickly wooded with cocoanut trees. There is no harbor, port or light. We soon saw several boats coming off under sail, and waited for one hoping to get some information of value. The boat was a canoe with three natives in it. They were the most miserable looking set. They were perfectly naked and heads bare. They had straight, coarse black hair, were of a dark copper color, and looked very like the American [I]ndian—except that in the face they had few signs of intelligence. They had in their boat nothing but a few fish, some of which we bought giving them tobacco. Our Sail Maker's Mate (Glover) who spoke the gibberish tried his best to get them to come onboard but they were too much afraid, and said they would come when the other boats got alongside. Their language is peculiar to them, being like that of no one else. They said they had not seen a ship for a long time and none had been near the island. They were very much frightened [by] the guns. Their boat was a peculiar canoe, made after their style. The whole ribs and frame was of a small bush twisted into the proper shape, and the outside was of bark. They had paddles and a small "leg-of-mutton" sail. One very peculiar thing they had was an outrigger on the weather side some seven feet long, which from its weight kept the boat, when under sail from capsizing.

"a.a." is a slight frame of bamboo or cane, between the slats of which was secured the piece of light wood "b" which is sharp at both ends like the boat—the whole rests in the water and is always on the weather side as she sails either end first, thereby preventing the necessity of shifting it over. [In the journal this sentence is indented, and Whittle drew a small diagram of an outrigger canoe in the space.—Ed.]

They sat in the boat exactly like a tailor on this [sic] table or bench except that the knees were up. We soon got clear of them and, without waiting for any other boats stood off under all sail, letting the steam go down & hoisting our propeller, and soon left the island out of sight. Imagine our disappointment at not seeing or hearing of a single Yankee. Oh the terrible, terrible monotony!!! N'importe—"let us live with a hope"—for our time will come. I am as certain that a merciful God has our holy cause in his own hands as that I am here—and I must devoutly say "Thy will, Oh Lord, not mine, be done."

At Sea, Saturday March 25th 1865
Lat: 00°23'00"S.   Ther. 81°   Long: 173°05'E.
Course NW 3/4 W   97 m.   Winds. Nd & Ed
   Bar. 29.70 to 29.83

A repetition of all the days since we have been in these low latitudes, except that we have a 4 1/2 knot breeze. Not a thing insight. Today our Gunner's Mate, Wm Crawford one of the Alabama's crew was guilty of insolent conduct at the Mast, and the Captain disrated him to seaman.[8] He is one of those whose term expires on the 7th and no doubt the short trip of his time influenced him. I wish he was out of the ship. I think all these men will leave, but thank God we can be independent as we have enough without them. I would like some to stay, but the importance of their so doing is not great. They will have a nice time in getting home. This evening about 8 P.M. we crossed the Equator or "the line," for the second time and are now again in the Northern Hemisphere.

At Sea, Sunday March 26th 1865
Lat: 0°09'30"N.   Ther: 80° to 84°   Long: 170°55'E.
Course W by N 1/4 N.   134 m.   Wind. Var. Nd & Ed & Nd & W.
   Bar. 29.80 to 29.85

Another day of rest. We had inspection at quarters, and afterwards we gave the day as one of rest. The same monotony still remains unbroken, and God alone knows how long it will continue. We have a light, baffling breeze from the Nd, not allowing us to steer our course. We also have passing showers and hot, hot weather. I spent the day quietly, reading the service for the day. Sunday always takes my thoughts home and to those I love. Oh! how much would I not give to hear from them and from my darling Pattie. She seems dearer and dearer every day. God protect her & them I pray.

At Sea, Monday March 27th 1865.
Lat: 1°18'N.   Ther. 76° to 82°.   Bar. 29.78   Long: 170°57'E.
Course North   69 m.   Wind. Sd & Wd, Wd, Nd & W, Nd & Ed.

Early this morning I was awak[en]ed by Smith Lee's startling voice reefing topsails. I went to the door and found it raining heavily and blowing very freshly. Smith was exercising his peculiar voice to its uttermost to reef down. I was not long in dressing, getting on my "great boots" and storm hat, and went on deck. It had every appearance of a terrific gale, and we soon got her under close reefed topsails to prepare for the worst. The wind was about East. It blew & rained heavily for a short time when the wind suddenly "chopped" around to the Nd & Ed, taking us flat aback. We "brought by" on the other tack, and very soon to our great delight we found that instead of being a gale, our weather was but the forerunner of the "N.E. trades," and now we are on our course with a steady free wind and going about 9 knots. We were all much excited and elated this evening by the report of "sail! ho!" but found it only to be a cloud. The Captain rated Chas: Cobby as Quarter Gunner, to take the place of Wm. Crawford.[9] No sails in sight. Oh! the monotony!!

At Sea, Tuesday March 28th 1865
Lat: 2°37′N.   Ther. 85°   Bar. 29.84   Long: 168°59′30 E.
Course NW by W.   141 m.   Wind. ENE & NE by N.

Today we have been quite busy. We had an exercise at our guns after which we shifted our fore topsail & foresail, replacing them in order to have those unbent repaired. We have had some very severe weather and our sails have suffered. The weather is terribly hot, and we have frequent and heavy rain squalls. Dull monotony reigns, and really it is painful. At night we put the ship under topsails. We have pretty steady NE trades, and are going along at the rate of 6 knots. Oh how much would I not give to hear from home.

At Sea, Wednesday March 29th 1865
Lat: 3°43′N.   Dist: 140.   Long: 166°55′E
Course NW by W 1/2 W.   Wind Variable, Sd & Ed & Ed
     Bar. 29.78 to 29.81.   Ther. 77° to 82°.

I never saw it rain harder and more continuously than today. Really in this region "it never rains, but it pours." By means of my standing tub I filled nearly all our tanks with nice rain water. The men employed their time in scrubbing their hammocks. At 4.45 P.M. just as it lightened up the joyous sound of "Sail ho" wound us all up. Sure enough there was a little schooner on our port or lee beam. We stood in chase. At 6 we came down to her and hove her to. She ran up the Hiawaiian [sic] flag, and upon boarding her she proved to be the Honolulu sch: *Pelin*,[10] 5 months out, trading. We stood on. This is the first sail we have seen for more than a month. She reported nothing at Strong Island, but four vessels at Ascension.

At Sea, Thursday March 30th 1865
Lat: 5°00′45″N.   Dist: 204   Long: 163°46′30″E
Course W.N.W.   Wind NE by N.   Bar 29.81 to 29.94
     Ther. 81° to 85°.

We now have the NE trades in earnest, and have slipped along 10, 10 1/2, 11 knots. At 1 O'c. P.M. concluding that we [were] very near Strong's Island, we got up steam. At 2.30 made low & high land ahead and on the Port bow. Furled all sails and steamed up and stood sufficiently close to see into Charbrol [sic] Harbour, and finding no vessels at anchor stood around the SE'tern

Extremity. Made all sail, worked off steam, hoisted the propeller, and went booming along. This is Strong's Island or "Onalan" of the Caroline group. The land is about 2000 feet above the level of the sea, and the scenery is fine. We were very close in and it looked like the portion of my dear old Virginia on the Virginia & Tennessee R. R. about Liberty. The cocoanut & banana trees are very thick. The island is some 15 miles long. The inhabitants are the same, or nearly so, as those on Drummond Island.

At Sea, Friday March 31 1865.
Lat: 6°06′N.   Dist: 150 m.   Long: 160°17′E
Course W by N 1/2 N.   Wind NE.   Bar. 29.87 to 29.77.
    Ther. 82°

Oh what splendid trades. We are fairly ripping along on our way to Ascension. While at quarters I thought I saw land on our starboard beam. It proved to be the island of McKascell [McAskill] bearing N by W distant 12 miles. This island's position is put down as doubtful. I went aloft and took a good look—there are two low islands and seem to be very close together. They are about half way from Strong to Ascension. At 9 P.M. being by reckoning about 12 miles from land, we wore ship to the Ed. and reduced sail to close reefed topsails, awaiting daylight to make land. Oh I trust we will make some prizes here.

Left to right, John Thomson Mason, Orris A. Browne, William C. Whittle, Jr., and Sidney Smith Lee, Jr. Before leaving England for Argentina, these officers of the CSS *Shenandoah* had their picture taken. They called themselves "The Old Dominion Company," after their native state. After receiving pardons, Mason and Browne returned to Virginia in 1867, Whittle and Lee in 1868. From Carte-de-visite. Copyprint courtesy of The Museum of the Confederacy, 1201 East Clay Street, Richmond, Virginia 23219.

Acting Master Irvine S. Bulloch, who served on the *Nashville,* the *Alabama,* and the *Shenandoah.* His navigational skills were excellent. When the *Shenandoah* neared the Irish Channel in November 1865, his landfall on the Irish coast occurred within two minutes of the predicted time. Copyprint courtesy of The Museum of the Confederacy, 1201 East Clay Street, Richmond, Virginia 23219.

Lieutenant Francis Thornton Chew, CSN, learned the practical aspects of being a watch officer on board the *Shenandoah*. He returned to Missouri from Mexico in 1867. Copyprint courtesy of The Museum of the Confederacy, 1201 East Clay Street, Richmond, Virginia 23219.

Lieutenant William Conway Whittle, Jr., CSN, executive officer of the CSS *Shenandoah,* and author of this journal, in a photograph taken during the Civil War or perhaps in England after the *Shenandoah* returned to Liverpool. Courtesy of Mary Beverley Dabney, granddaughter of William C. Whittle.

6

What an April fool to the poor Yanks . . .

April 1–May 19, 1865

At Sea, Saturday April 1st 1865.
Lat: In port.   Dist: Long: None. In port.   Wind NE.

Wore ship about 2 A.M. and made sail to topgallant sails, and stood for land. At 9.30 A.M. made the island of Ascension. At 10.30 furled all sails, got both anchors off the bows and steamed for the land. Discovered four vessels at anchor close in under the land. At 11.30 took a pilot for the middle harbor in which the vessels were, all but one with the detestable Yankee flag hoisted. Fearing some treachery on the Pilot's part we warned him that if he got us aground, death would be his instant portion. He was an Englishman named Thomas Harrocke. We had the English flag up and he supposed us to be the English surveying ship. The entrance is narrow but very deep. We steamed in and moored ship in 15 fathoms water. We were delighted. There we were safely moored close to four prizes and they thinking we were and [sic] English vessel. Some tried to come along side but we beckoned them off. As soon as possible we fitted out 4 armed boats—in charge of the following officers—1st, Lieut. Grimball & Passed Mid. Browne—2nd, Lieut. Lee & Pd. Mid. Mason—3rd, Lieut. Chew & Capt's. Clerk Blacker—4th, Lieut. Scales and M. Mate Minor—with orders to send the Captains, Mates & papers off. Oh what an April fool to the poor Yanks. There were no Captains onboard as they were at the lee harbor, on a "bust." The boats shoved off, we fired a gun & ran up our flag. What a time. There was one vessel which had up the Hiawaiian [sic] flag. Our prizes proved to be the Yankee whale ships *Ed. Carey* & *Hector* & Barks *Pearl* and *Harvest.* The latter was the only one about which there was any doubt, but as she had no bill of sale, a Yankee Captain & Mates, the same as before she was said to have been sold, with the same name, she with the rest was condemned as a prize. The mates were all put in irons. They said that the Capts. would soon be up. We had an armed boat at the gangway and their whale boat came through a short cut, they, not suspecting anything as our flag was down, pulled leisurely, looking at our ship. All were a little tight, they were singing, laughing & talking when our boat in charge of Lieut. Grimball pulled ahead of them. He hailed, "Boat ahoy!" "Halloo," "go alongside of that ship." "We don't belong there." "I don't care go alongside." Seeing him armed they obeyed, and over our gangway came Capt. Eldridge of the *Harvest,* Capt. Edwin P. Thomson of the *Hector,* Capt. Chase of the *Pearl* and Capt Baker of the *Ed. Carey.* What a perfectly April fooled party. When they learned what we were they were astounded. They were all put in irons except the Capt. of the *Harvest,* his deposition was taken, and the sale of the vessel was, as she had the same Capt. & Mates, all Yankees, the same name, and no bill of sale, considered bogus, and he was put in limbo with the rest. Having the Capts., 1st & 2nd Mates onboard and not knowing the feelings of the natives we withdrew our men, after having taken out all navigating instruments. And we all had a great rejoicing. This amply repays us for our monotony and is not a bad haul, as the cargo alone off one, i.e. 300 gallons of oil is worth $40,000. These raise our prize list to 11 & two bonded making 13. Of course we were soon surrounded with boats. All the natives in canoes, naked except a grass covering around the waists. The Pilot was delighted when he saw our flag and knew who we were, and said we would be heartily received by the natives. This is and [*sic*] island under none but local authority, and protection with no civilization and everything is under our guns. The Yanks were certainly caught napping this time. I only wish there were 50 instead of 4. If true, we have bad news from home. They say Hood has met with a terrible defeat at Nashville; Sherman has taken Savannah, and Porter Fort Fisher at Wilmington. All this, if true is very very bad. But "Thy will be done, O Lord." All will yet be well.

Island of Ascencion—Metaielirie or Middle Harbor
Sunday, April 2nd 1865

At 10 A.M. we sent the Pilot in the gig with an officer to bring off the King of the tribe of this portion of the island. He came off with some half dozen of his chiefs. The whole affair was very ludicrous. Each of the dignitaries was naked & covered with cocoanut oil. Each upon getting up the side sat in the gangway like monkeys and did not come onboard until some officer gave them the hand of friendship. Each had a covering about the waist made of grass or cocoanut bark, and each with a slit cut in the lower joint of the ear through which they stuck the stem of a common clay pipe, which after they took a turn was secure. The King's name is Nananierikie, is a short man of about 5 ft. 4 in. and quite stout. He had among other attendants his son, a young man of about 26 years old. They expressed astonishment at the size & general appearance of the ship. When he came up some fifty canoes escorted him. The Captain took him in the cabin and gave the party something to drink. And then told him at length the object of our visit. That we came to capture the Yankee ships. He was much delighted and begged that the prizes might be destroyed in the harbor so that they might get the copper. This was of course readily acceded to by us as it obviated the necessity of our taking them out to apply the torch. We took him all over the ship, and when he saw our guns he was astonished, and in the examination showed a good deal of sense. Before he left we promised to let him have a great many of the things from our prizes if he saw that no harm was done to our stern posts, or no thieving was permitted before we burnt our prizes. We made him a present of 22 old prize muskets, and an old sword. This last we made him buckle around his naked waist, the blade dangling about his legs, much to the injury of his shins. He left us the best friends, inviting all of us ashore, and declaring that we all had his hearty welcome. During the whole day we got quantities of cocoanuts, pineaples, pigs, chickens, bananas, plantins etc., giving tobacco in pay. We got some few articles from our prizes. We allowed some men to go onshore and all came off sober, because there was no liquor. We will be here some little time to get all our coal out of the forehold, etc., etc. We have much work to do, but we could not have a better time or place. The most of the day was spent in digesting the news. In the first place Sherman is said, after traversing the whole of the state of Georgia to have taken Savannah, our troops evacuating it. This if true leaves Charleston open to an attack in the rear, which will, I fear ensure its fall. Next, Hood has been terribly defeated by Thomas in Tennessee. This shows that we are weak and will I fear cause an evacuation of the ground gained. Next Porter is said to have taken Fort Fisher. This if true, closes our last port of Wilmington and closes all down to the world. Much allowance is to be made for this news coming via California, which it is well known is very unreliable. But I fear that there must be much truth in some of these reports. If they all be true, it is terrible. In God's hands I resign all, and in his Divine will, is my trust. I can never think that an Almighty and Merciful & all powerful God will allow such a people as ours to suffer subjugation. God grant us his blessing I pray. This harbor is called "Lodde" and the Island Punnapette. [Ponape]

Lodde Harbor, Ascension Island
Caroline Group, Monday April 3rd, 1865

Hard at work all day shifting coal. One boat Employed transferring stores from our prizes. In the Evening sent an officer with a boat, got the prize Bark *Pearl* underway, ran her on a reef, high up and destroyed her by fire. She is the eighth vessel burnt. Much small trade with the natives. The King bringing off many presents. Many officers went on shore, and all had something pricked in their arms [tattoos].[1] In destroying these prizes in port we were governed by the request of the King who said he would rather it should be done in port than that they should be taken outside. He pointed out the places for such destruction where the harbor would not be injured thereby.

Island of Ascension, Tuesday April 4th 1865
Having taken the prize ships *Hector* & *Ed. Carey* to the places pointed out by the King, we fired them. We have had rain nearly all day, which rendered it anything but pleasant. We brought the Barque *Harvest* nearer the ship in order to be more convenient for shifting stores of which we will want a good deal in order to feel up to our proper quantity.

Island of Ascension, Wednesday April 5th 1865
Cloudy weather with passing showers. Employed shifting coal from the Fore to the Main Hold and preparing the Forehold for the reception [of] pork, beef & other stores. The ship has been surrounded by Kanakas in their skiffs or canoes. Some of the officers went to "Windward" to see the ruins. "To Windward" means towards the North, from which the winds blow at nearly all seasons. "Lee harbor" is about 12 miles in the opposite direction.

Island of Ascension, Thursday April 6th 1865
Shipped Geo. Deas, Jno. Morris, Antoni Delombas (seamen) Joaquin Rodrigues (Lds) and Roberto Roselle (3rd c. Boy) from the *Hector*.[2] Hauled the Barque *Harvest* alongside & commenced getting stores out. It may be well here to state the reasons which actuated us in making prize of this vessel. She hoisted the Hiawaian [*sic*] Flag, but she had been sold as the Captain said since the war. She had nothing to show it, no bill of sale or bill of property, and has the same name, the same mates as before. She was said to have been sold, and these facts induced the conclusion that she was a lawful prize, the sale being sham.

Island of Ascension, Friday April 7th 1865
Employed shifting coal and stores. Weather pleasant. The officers making many purchases of curios paying for them with tobacco, cloth, etc., etc.

Island of Ascencion, Saturday April 8th 1865
Employed storing fore hold with provisions from our prize. The times of Simpson, Reid, Fox, Brosnan & Crawford expired. Brosnan reshipped for 12 months. Weather very pleasant. Surrounded by Kanakas.

Island of Ascension, Sunday April 9th 1865.
A day of rest. Let the port watch go on liberty in the forenoon & the starb'b watch in the afternoon, each armed with two plugs of tobacco. Pleasant.

Island of Ascencion, Monday April 10th 1865
Finished the shifting of stores from the *Harvest*, hauled her off and fired her. Her value together with 300 bbls of sperm oil, was $34,759. Pleasant weather.

Island of Ascencion Tuesday April 11th [1865]
Employed restowing the afterhold & painting ship. Pleasant weather.

Island of Ascencion Wednesday April 12th [1865]
Employed overhauling rigging and getting ready for sea—Pleasant weather.[3]

Island of Ascencion, Thursday April 13th [1865]
Paroled all prisoners, sent them in their boats with their personal effects on shore. Unmoored ship, got up steam and at 8 A.M. weighed [anchor] and stood to sea. At 8.30 discharged pilot, stowed anchors & chains. Hoisted propeller and made sail. At 2. P.M. Ascencion bore south distant 20 miles. Moderate NE trades which blow here at all seasons. I am rejoiced to be once more at sea.

Value of Prizes

			Total
Barque *Pearl*	vessel & cargo		$10,000
Ship *Edward Carey*			$15,000
Ship *Hector*	vessel	$35,000	
	cargo	$23,000	$58,000
Bark *Harvest*	vessel	$10,000	
	cargo	$24,759	$34,759
		Total	$107,759

[At this point in the journal Whittle kept a list of all prizes including the date taken, the name of the vessel, the name of the captain, the Rig, Tons, Fate & valuation. This list, with notes indicating discrepancies when compared with other lists kept in the official log and in private journals, has been reproduced in the appendix.—*Ed.*]

At Sea, Friday April 14th, 1865
Lat: 9°35′N.   Ther. 81°   Bar: 29.85   Long: 156° 03′ E.
Course NW   210 m.   Wind. NE.

Today we have been going steadily along under cruising canvass (i.e. topsails and foresail, Jib & F. Topmast Staysail). The ship is buoyant and in fine trim being about 18 1/2 feet aft and 16 1/2 forward. She is like a duck on the water; steers beautifully, and under short sail has averaged about 9 knots. This is splendid, and I consider that she is now in better trim & order than she has ever been. We have beautiful NE trades, which bring with them some sea. Jack Grimball is still very sick, having had a continuous fever all day. He is at times del[i]rious and talking all the time. Poor fellow he suffers very much, and is very impatient, thereby rendering his condition more painful. I have the greatest affection for him, and will nurse him, as I know he would nurse me.[4] A good many of our men are sick, but all are very slight ailings. I am delighted to be once more at sea, and hope to remain so until our work is done. I am a hater of port.

At Sea, Saturday April 15th 1865
Lat: 12°16′N.   Ther 80°   Bar: 29.90 to .83   Long: 154°16′E
Course NW by N   195 m.   Wind. NE.

Our steady NE trades continue and we slip along easily 8 knots under our cruising canvas of topsails & foresail. Today Jack Grimball is much better being now clear of fever, and I trust he will soon be well again. We are all gay.

At Sea, Sunday April 16th 1865
Lat: 14°45′N.   Ther: 80°   Long 152°23′E.
Course NW 3/4 N.   186 m   Wind NE   Bar. 29.82 to .90

Still we have our steady NE trades which in the morning send us on about 8 knots, growing lighter toward noon, we go 7, and freshening toward evening send us on at the rate of 9 1/2 knots per hour. This is all with a single reef in our topsails and our foresail. With all plain sail ie. Royals & Mainsail we would easily go 12 1/2. This is most wonderful sailing. Ah we have a fine ship and the blessing of God shows itself in many cases. Jack is out and nearly well, but very much pulled down. Today we have done nothing but muster the crew. We will soon be in a good cruising ground and day after tomorrow may bring us a prize. God grant it. Oh how I long to see my dear P[attie] and all at home.

At Sea, Monday April 17th 1865
Lat: 17°35′N.   Dist: 203 m.   Long: 150°27′E
Course NW by N.   Wind. NE   Bar. 29.90   Ther 80°

Here we are ripping along at the rate of 8 & 9 knots under double reefed topsails. Our noble ship is in splendid trim. Tomorrow we will be in a great track for prizes, ie. that from California to China. I trust we may see something and I hope that something will be a fine Yankee clipper. We are in no hurry. We have a noble NE trade and can run from almost any of their vessels of war.

We are busy blacking down, drilling and painting lower masts. Jack is nearly well, and all are happy.

> At Sea, Tuesday April 18th 1865
> Lat: 19°41′N   Ther. 81°   Bar: 29.96   Long. 150° 01′ E.
> Course N by W   129 m   Wind. ENE & East

At work rattling down. Five men's times expired today. Three out of the five re-shipped.[5] Drilled at great guns. We are now right in the Sanfrancisco [*sic*] & China track. In the evening wore ship to the Sd—to run across the track. All cheerful. Oh for good news from our dear Country, from my darling or a good prize. Either would be joyous. Today Jack Grimball was twenty five. We all drank his health in sherry.

> At Sea, Wednesday April 19th 1865
> Lat: 19°46′N.   Dist: 10 m.   Long: 150°10′E
> Course NE by E 1/2 E   Wind. East & E by N.   Ther. 79°
> Bar. 29.96

The day was variously employed, in rattling down the lower rigging, blacking down, drilling, sailmaking and carpentering. I hope soon to have the rigging in good order as we may soon have a gale of wind. We are cruising in a good track but we have seen no signs of a prize. The weather is getting much more pleasant and sleeping at night much more refreshing.

> At Sea, Thursday April 20th 1865
> Lat: 19°51′N.   Ther. 80°   Bar. 29.96 to .93   Long. 150° 30′ E.
> Course E by N   19 m   Wind. E by N.

The day has been employed in the same way as the past three or four. Our wind from the NE is growing much fresher and I fear that the change of the trades to the Sd & Ed will be attended with a gale. We are, in all respects, better prepared for it than at any previous time, but still I would rather not see it. I am not so romantic as to be able to see the grandeur of a gale. If I ever was, I have seen so many as to drive all such foolish admiration out of my head. Oh if I only knew that all was well in our dear Country. That God with his mercy will look upon us is my constant prayer.

> At Sea, Friday April 21st 1865
> Lat: 20°21′N.   Ther. 80°   Bar: 29.97   Long: 150°30′E.
> Course North   31 m.   Wind. Variable Eastward.

The same old routine. Standing across the track of the California & China Clippers. Not a sign of anything but constantly expecting to have better luck. Any vessel we might take would in all probability bring us news, later by nearly two [or] three months than any we have had. I shall receive it with fear and trembling. It may be bad; it may be good; just as God wills it. The latest news was from California of January 27th, and if true, which I very much doubt, it is very bad. Let it be ever so bad, our course & duty is clear, and every new disaster to our heroic armies at home should nerve us anew to do our duty like men. We will do it. God preserve and protect our dear country. We have seen much trouble, have lost many lives, have suffered from demoralization, devastation &c &c. God sees fit thus to punish us; but a merciful God never intends those who are, as are we, engaged in a holy & Just cause, to be subjugated or annihilated by our unrelenting enemies. Let us bide then, our time, and doing our duty to God, Country and Man, leave all in his hands. Trusting to his guidance & rule, we will & must succeed. God aid & comfort us I humbly pray.

At Sea, Saturday April 22d 1865
Lat: 20°11′N.   Ther. 79°   Bar. 29.95 to 30.00   Long: 150° 05′ E.
Course WSW   26 m   Wind. East & E by N.

We are still said to be cruising in the track as laid down by Maury, but thus far our cruise has availed but little. Not a sail have we see since we left Ascension and the last vessel seen was the wreck of the destroyed *Harvest*. Oh! I wish we could catch something. "Have patience," says a little whispering bird. We have finished our rigging and I consider that the ship never before was as clean, as sea worthy and in as good a condition, before [*sic*]. The Easterly wind continues, freshening to a strong breeze at night. Oh! if I could hear from my darling!! God guide, guard & protect her, I pray.

At Sea, Sunday April 23d 1865
Lat: 18°44′N.   Ther. 79 to 80   Bar. 29.95 to 30.00
 Long: 150°38′ E.
Course S by E 3/4 E   94 m.   Wind Eastward

Another day of rest. Except going to the ordinary morning & evening quarters, and inspecting the ship, nothing was done. The decks all looked cleaner, and everything in better order, than at any previous time. What an immense amount of good results from frequent use of sand and "holy stones." The trades continue fresh and are accompanied today by quite a lively sea. At night these trades always freshen in pretty brisk squalls. We have today, as we have for some time, just kept under short sail, and keeping close hauled, beating about, first heading North and then Sd & Ed to keep from running out of the reputed "track." I must say that I would prefer to see some more striking proof that it is the "track." Not a sail to be seen. This morning I read the "Morning Service" in my room, and in the evening, the "Evening Service," and . . . during the day finished Thackeray's "Adventures of Philip," gaining therefrom much useful information. How very long it will be before any one in the world knows where we are. Only think that since we left Melbourne for parts unknown more than two months ago, we have seen nothing which could report us for months. No doubt she (our ship) will be recorded as having been taken to Father Neptune's bosom. I trust that they may not get any such report at home, and if they do, I trust that they may only say that we are in God's hands.

At Sea, Monday April 24th 1865
Lat: 20°02′N.   Dist: 79   Long: 150°44′E.
Course N 1/2 E.   Wind. East.   Bar 30.00   Ther 76° to 49°

Today's routine has been the same as that of the past week with the same results. I do not know when I have felt worse than I have since I got up this morning. I, for some reason or other slept very little last night, but took a little medicine today and eat [sic] no dinner, and now feel very well. We have had squalls of wind & rain all day. I have felt awfully homesick, but tomorrow may bring us a prize.

At Sea, Tuesday, April 25th 1865
Lat: 22°09′N   Dist: 130   Long: 150°16′E.
Course N by W.   Wind. East.   Bar 30.00 to 29.95   Ther 78°

The wind prevails from the Ed, gradually backing in to the Sd as we go north. Finished blacking down. Not the sign of a sail. If this be "the track," I think we had better be making some tracks ourselves. I feel tonight as tho' we would catch something tomorrow. Nous verrons.

At Sea, Wednesday April 26th 1865
Lat: 23°56′N   Dist: 107   Long: 150°11′E   Ther. 79°
Course N 2° W.   Wind. East.   Bar. 30.00 to 30.05

Well here is another day gone and no sign of any prize. We are now, I fear, to the Northward of the track, but our time will come. This has been one of the lovliest days I ever beheld. The temperature is delightful. Some time in the forenoon we crossed the Tropic of Cancer (23° 28″) and are now in the Temperate Zone. At work all day painting yards, booms &c, exercising, and scrubbing the Berth Deck.

At Sea, Thursday April 27th 1865
Lat: 25°16′N   Dist: 80   Long: 150°18′E   Ther. 80°
Course N 1/2 E   Bar. 30.05 to 29.95   Wind. East, SE, SSE & S by E

This has been a very warm day, and nothing except the ordinary ship routine has relieved the monotony, except a fight between two marines the grog of both being stopped in consequence.

At Sea, Friday April 28th 1865
Lat: 26°45′N.   Dist: 86 m.   Long: 150°14′E
Course North   Wind SE, South & SSW   Bar. 29.89   Ther 79°

One of the most lovely days I ever saw in my life. Scarcely a cloud, pleasant and very smooth. One of our tanks being out we commenced to condense. Employed at scrubbing paintwork and drilling. I have felt in fine spirits all day. This morning made sail to royals on our course.

At Sea, Saturday 29th April 1865
Lat: 29°57′N.   Bar 29.70 to .80   Long: 150°19′30″E.
Course North   192 m   Wind Sd & Wd & Variable.   Ther. 75°

Employed holystoning the ship throughout. She is in pretty good order; far better than ever before. The terms of our two [F]renchmen who came to us from our first prize, the *Alina*, Louis Rowe and Peter Raymond, familiarly known as "Louis & Peter," expired today. They did not feel like re-enlisting but desire to leave the ship the first opportunity. This makes nine who await a similar opportunity, but no telling when it will come. I am very sorry that they do not re-enlist for when they get clear, we will probably be in a European port, and in the mean time they get no pay. Generally speaking they are excellent men, and have been as true as steel.

At Sea, Sunday April 30th 1865
Lat: 31°35′N.   Ther: 65° to 70°   Long: 150°26′E.
Course N 1/4 E.   98 m.   Wind. Variable.   Bar. 29.75 to 29.64

This day commenced with light baffling airs, but as the day advance[d] we began to get fresh squalls from the Wd and the barometer gradually falling, indicated bad weather. We prepared for it by furling the Miz. Topsail & close reefing the fore & Main. I trust we are not going to have a gale.

At Sea, Monday May 1st 1865
Lat: 33°01′N.   Bar. 29.67 to 30.00   Ther 64°   Long: 150°48′E.
Course N by E   88 miles.   Wind. West, W by N, WNW. Var.

Commenced clear with a strong breeze. This soon changed to a moderate gale and high sea. We lay to on the starb'd tack under a close reefed main topsail and fore storm staysail—got up preventer braces. Soon the gale moderated and we sent down preventer braces. Still a very high sea. This is the 1st of

May. I wonder how our dear country is getting along. God grant us success, I humbly pray.

At Sea, Tuesday May 2d 1865
Lat: 33°29'N.   Bar. 30.05   Ther. 64°   Long: 150°53'E.
Course N by E   29 m.   Wind. Nd & Ed East & East by South

This morning the weather was so much more moderate that we made sail to single reefed topsails & foresail, but it soon became evident that tho' moderated, the weather was by no means settled, and we reefed down to double reefed topsails & reefed foresail. We have seen a good deal [of] "whale food" and past [sic] some drift wood which looked like a portion of a wreck. Today I saw what I have heard was never seen north of the "Line" i.e. a large albatross. It is growing cool & bracing. I like clear, cool weather, but abhor cold rains, such as we have been blest with today.

At Sea, Wednesday May 3rd 1865
Lat: 35°47'N.   Ther. 60°   Bar 29.90 29.62   Long: 150°05'E.
Course N by W 1/2 W   143 m.   Wind. ENE, ESE, E by S.

This morning when I was called at 6.30, the Qr. master informed me that it was cloudy, rainy & squally weather. I went up to let Scales *fix his toilet* and found the ship under double reefed topsails & reefed foresail with a fresh breeze and high sea a little aloft the starboard beam and going 9 1/2 knots. The Captain said that this was too fast—reefed close down the fore & main topsails, took in the Fore topmast staysail, Foresail & mizzen topsail & brought by the wind & lay to on the starb'd tack. Tonight the gale has freshened, and as I write it is blowing a whole gale. This ship under our present sail with the helm half down will lay to & ride the waves like a duck, but the Captain orders that the helm must be kept amidships. This throws her in the "trough of the sea" which is very high, and she is laboring very much more than is safe, comfortable or necessary. In these things he is stubborn as a mule, and I fear that his stubborn[n]ess will some day do us harm. Oh how I do detest a gale of wind!!!

At Sea, Thursday May 4th 1865
Lat: 37°07'N.   Ther 64°   Bar: 29.40-29.38   Long: 149°17'E.
Course NW by N 3/4 N   89 m.
   Wind. E by S. Var. WNW. W by N & WSW

This has been, to all appearances, a fine day. The wind has been only moderate, and the only remaining evidence of the gale of yesterday was a sea. The wind hauled from the Nd & Ed to the Nd, then Nd & Wd & then to the Sd of West. The barometer remained all day very low at 29.45 and when the wind went to the Wd we wore ship. The low barometer is a bad sign and I fear we are going to have a heavy gale. Tonight the wind commenced to freshen, and now at 10.30 is blowing fresh from the Sd & Wd. I fear we are going to have a very heavy gale. God grant not. Our ship is, thank God, strong and in good order, but I detest a gale. I have seen too many not to appreciate them. Oh how much would I not give to hear from our dear ones. God protect them. I wonder if I will ever see my darling Pattie.

At Sea, Friday May 5th 1865
Lat: 39°06′N.   Ther.54° to 60°   Bar: 29.30 to 29.58
 Long: 149°40′ E.
Course N 3/4 E   122 m
 Wind. WSW, W, NW by W, W, & W by N.

Last night we had a strong wind the whole time, and every now and then a heavy squall of wind and rain, during which it blew fearfully and the water came down in torrents. The good old ship behaved most nobly. Today the barometer has remained below 29.45 and the wind has been fresh, with a high sea. The weather, [a]ffected as it is by the wind from the snow clad clifs of Japan is very chilly, but it is bracing and we are now by gradual transition being prepared for the intense cold before us. Going as we do, from extreme warm to extreme cold weather & back, must make us suffer, but what care we, in such a cause.

At Sea, Saturday May 6th 1865
Lat: 39°28′N.   Ther. 46°to 51°   Bar: 29.50 to 29.80
 Long: 149°47′E
Course N by E 1/4 E   23 m.   Wind W, W by N, W, W by S, WSW.

All day we have had a fresh breeze and a heavy sea, and we have been, I may say, lying to under close reefed fore & main topsails & F. storm staysail. The weather is quite cold. Our time passes monotonously, but there are so many of us, and all so cheerful that we manage to drive a good deal of care away. I expect that when we shape our course for our cruising ground, having given the ice time to drift clear, we will catch a good many Yanks. I trust it may be so—but Patience!!

At Sea, Sunday May 7th 1865
Lat: 39°28′N.   Ther. 58 to 61   Bar. 29.82 to .76   Long: 149°54′E.
Course East   6 m.   Bar 29.82   Ther 60°
 Wind WSW, SW, SW by W.

This being the first Sunday in the month we had inspection at quarters, muster and read "the Articles of War." The men all looked neatly and comfortably clad. The times of three more men were expired today and none desired to renew their engagement.[6] This makes twelve who are only awaiting an opportunity to get clear.[7] These are, thank goodness the last "six months men," and I am heartily glad of it. These taken from our 104 leave 92 souls all told belonging to the ship. From these after deducting 25 officers and 12 boys, stewards & cooks (37) leave us 55 all told, including firemen & marines—this seems small but when it be compared to the 46 all told, with which we started it will be seen that we are well off. Still under close reefed fore main topsails & in squally weather with a heavy sea.

> At Sea, Monday May 8th 1865
> Lat: 39°44′N.   Dist 24 m.   Bar. 29.70 to .64   Long: 149°32′E
> Course NW.   Ther 60°   Wind. SW.

The weather today was the same as on yesterday with the exception that we had today an occasional fall of drizzling rain. The wind the same; sea the same, and the ship under the same sail. Today Davey & West Capts of Tops, Jones (Jr. M.) and Griffiths (Cox) four of the best men I ever saw, whose times of service, among others had expired came forward and said that they would like to reship upon condition that they would be discharged at the first European port we got to. The Captain consented and they were shipped upon this condition. This raises the number of 92 souls attached to the ship as enumerated on yesterday to 96. Thank God for this.

> At Sea, Tuesday May 9th 1865
> Lat: 39°45′N.   Dist: 15 m.   Bar. 29.60, .70, .50   Long: 149°51′E
> Course East.   Ther 60° to 47°
> Wind Var. WbyN, NW & EbyN,E by S.

This morning the weather cleared off beautifully, the sea went down, and we wore ship to the Nd & Ed on our course; making sail to double reefed topsails & reefed foresail. No sails in sight. Oh! how I wish we could capture something. All will come in due time.

> At Sea, Wednesday May 10th 1865.
> Lat: 40°17′N.   Course NE 3/4 N   41 m.   Bar 29.40 .27 to 29.70
> Long: 150°23′E.   Wind East, calm, Nd & Wd, Var.
> Ther. 39° to 45°

Commenced very fresh winds which caused us to put the ship under close reefed fore & Main topsails, & fore storm staysail. The wind died out leaving a bad sea. Made sail to double reefed fore & Main & close reefed Miz. topsails, reefed foresail. The wind soon came out to N by W when we wore to the Nd.

A very heavy squall came up which nearly took us aback, and blew furiously. We ran off before it to the Sd. and reefed down. Very soon it was blowing a lively gale with a tremendous sea. We ran before it for 70 miles when we reduced sail, brought by with our head NE and lay to. The gale is heavy from NW and we lying to in the first tack, got up preventer braces.

At Sea, Thursday May 11th 1865.
Lat: 39°54′N.   Course E by S 1/2 S.   70 m.   Bar. 29.75 to 30.00
Long 151°55′E.   Wind NW, NW by W, WNW, W by S.
    Ther. 40° to 47°

The gale abated and sea gradually going down. Made sail cautiously. They say that we are likely to have continual gales until we get to the Northward of 45° or 50° N. How I do wish that we could get out of the "roaring forties," for I am sick and tired of gales. I have seen enough.

At Sea, Friday May 12th 1865.
Lat: 40°38′N.   Course NNE 1/2 E   50 m.   Bar. 29.98 to 29.80
Long: 152°25′E.   Wind Sd & Wd calm & Eastward.
    Ther. 43° to 46°

Light varying winds and passing drizzling rain, a heavy sea from the Eastward. It will be too bad if we have another gale.

At Sea, Saturday May 13th 1865.
Lat: 42°08′N.   Course NNE 3/4 E.   99 m.
    Bar. 29.70 to 29.10 to 29.40   Ther. 54°
Long: 153°21′E.   Wind E, SE, SSW, SW, W, WbyN, NE, NNE

As I feared we would be, we are, in the midst of a terrific gale.[8] At the commencement the wind was light with heavy rain. At 2 P.M. we had a sudden shift of wind to the Nd. reduced sail to close reefed fore & main topsails & the fore staysail. Set the Main staysail. Hauled up on the port tack. At 4 it was blowing furiously. The lee Main topsail sheet carried away and the sail blew all to pieces. Unbent the remnants letting all but the pattent [sic] blow overboard. Not being able to bend another topsail while by the wind we goosewinged the foresail, and got the ship before the wind and ran before a furious gale & terrific sea. Got up and bent another main topsail and set it close reefed. Gale blowing furiously.[9]

At Sea, Sunday May 14th 1865
Lat: 41°29′N.   Course South   40 m.   Bar. 29.47 gradually 29.50

Long: 153°21′E.   Wind N, NW by N, WNW & NW by W
Ther.42° to 38°

At 3 A.M. brought by the wind in the port back. Set the Main staysail. Gale moderating but a terrible sea. Toward night wind much more moderate but a high sea, made sail to close reefed topsails & foresail. It is bitter cold. Oh, I wish old father Neptune would let us alone.

At Sea, Monday May 15th 1865
Lat: 42°31′N.   Course NE 3/4 N.   78 m.   Bar. 29.70 to 29.90
Long: 154°25′E.   Wind Nd & Wd   Ther 40° to 35°

Today we had a fresh breeze. Made sail to Topgallant sails. Unrove studding sail gear and sent it below. Very cold.

At Sea, Tuesday May 16th 1865
Lat: 43°20′N.   Dist 83 m.   Bar 29.98 to 30.05   Long: 155°46′E.
Course NE   Ther 37° to 46°   Wind Nd by Wd Va'b'le Sd & Ed.

This has been a great relief after the bad weather for the last few days. The wind has been very light and from the Sd and the temperature quite mild and pleasant with a fine sun to dry our sails and decks. I trust we will be taken to the Nd of the 45th parallel without any more bad weather. Tonight a heavy swell from the Nd & Ed and a very high barometer, I fear are forerunners of fresh wind from that quarter. I witnessed today a peculiar sign of something. There was a very bright and distinct ring around the sun. I hope it indicates good weather. Oh how I would like to hear from all my dear ones. God protect them, I pray. I have had a strange presentiment that when we get back we will find the war over. I humbly pray to God that it may be true.

At Sea, Wednesday May 17th 1865
Lat 45°36′[N]   Dist: 127 m.   Bar. 30.02 to 29.60
 Long: 155°52′E.
Course N 2°E   Ther 32° to 40°   Wind SE, SSW & Sd & Ed

This morning I was called as usual at 6.30 and was told by the Qr. Master that it was blowing a strong breeze from the Sd & Ed & raining. I went on deck to relieve the officer of the watch as usual to bathe and found it blowing fresh, raining and [the] ship under close reefed fore & main topsail & reefed foresail, with the wind in the Starb'd quarter. This weather continues and the barometer continued to fall all day, and we expected a gale. A heavy sea getting up. The temperature of the water coming down to 30° and a heavy fog superceding the rain made us think that an iceberg was near, and the wind hauling to SW. We hove too [sic] on the St'b'b tack intending to lay so all night.

At Sea, Thursday May 18th 1865
Lat: 46°29′N.   Dist: 53 m.   Ther 30°   Long: 155°52′E.
Course North.   Bar 29.60, 29.35
   Wind. SSW, Calm, Nd & Ed, Nd & Wd

Rarely have I ever seen a worse day than this has been. Having lied to all night, I found that this morning we had no wind, or very little, and raining, the thermometer being down to 32° and some ice on deck. Throughout the day it continued calm, with a heavy mist & rain, being very raw & cold. The thermometer began to fall and at night it was very low.[10] The ship is under short sail & ready for any bad weather. I trust we may not have a gale, for the present temperature brought lower by a piercing NE gale would be trouble. Today we celebrated Bulloch's 23rd birthday.

At Sea, Friday May 19th 1865.
Lat: 47°32′N   Dist: 64   Ther 28°   Long 156°09′E.
Course N by E.   Bar. 29.63 to .42
   Wind W by N, W, S by W, WSW.

This has been a beautiful day and we have dried all our light sails. Toward the evening had a dense fog. Put the ship under short sail.

7

The news is bad, very bad

May 20–July 4, 1865

At Sea, Saturday May 20th 1865.
Lat: 49°04′N   Dist: 94   Ther. 28°   Long 155°40′[E.]
Course N by W.   Bar 29.44 to .60   Wind Wd.

Commenced with a thick fog but soon lightened up. Had a slight fall of snow. At 9 saw land "Onekotan" bearing (pe) NW by W. distant about 35 miles. Made all sail to try and make & enter the "Amphitrite" or "50th" passage but upon getting pretty well in the wind hauled in such a way as to induce us to think that it was blowing fresh through the passage and it coming on dark, we brought by the wind under close reefed Fore & Main topsails, with our head to the Sd & Wd or off shore.[1]

At Sea, Sunday May 21st 1865
Lat: 49°49′30″   Dist: 50 m.   Ther. 28° & 36°
 Long: 155°09′E
Course NNW 1/4 W.   Bar. 29.60 to 29.50.   Wind Sd & Wd

At an early hour wore ship and stood for the land. At 5 O'c we made land bearing NNW about 40 miles—this is Onnekotan [sic] Isd which is very long and has five high peaks on it. All the island was covered with snow and as we got the wind from it, it was as cold as anything. We commenced to steam and as we could not carry our square sails we furled them and set all fore & aft sail. We found it fresh through the Amphitrite passage and never would have gotten through but for our steam. At noon it was blowing very fresh and had a high sea, and the Island of Fronkonronskey which is just inside bore due west—and we found that we were snugly in the Okhotsk Sea. We now hoisted propeller and made sail. At night shortened sail to close reefed topsails, but stood on to get a good offing from the Kamschatska [sic] coast.

At Sea, (in the Okhotsk) Monday May 22d 1865
Lat: 51°37′N.   Dist: 138 m.   Ther: 30 to 43   Long: 152°54′E
Course NW 1/2 N.   Bar. 29.50 to 29.40   Wind SW & S by W.

This has been a delightful day, and most charming weather. It is a great relief after the bad weather which we have had.

At Sea, Tuesday May 23d 1865
Lat. 53°23′N   Ther: 31° to 41°.   Dist: 108 m.   Long: 153°15′E
Course N 3/4 E   Bar: 29.35 to 28.89   Wind S, SSE, E, SE by S.

In the morning watch loosed all the light sails to dry. It came up very foggy and commenced to blow. Reduced sail to close reefed topsails and got up preventer braces, and layed to under short sail. Barometer very low. It set in a cold & steady rain.

At Sea, Wednesday May 24th 1865
Lat: 54°08′.   Dist: 46 m.   Ther. 35° to 30°.   Long: 153°22′E
Course N 1/2 E.   Bar 28.80 to 28.75 to 29.38
Wind SSE, SSW, W & WNW

This morning weather more moderate. We filled away but very soon a most terrible snow storm set in. We brought by again and layed to. The snow storm continued, laying to with our head to the Sd & Wd.

At Sea, Thursday May 25th 1865
Lat: 54°55′N.   Ther. 31° to 39°   Dist 50 m.   Long: 153°01′E
Course N by W 1/4 W.   Bar. 29.50 to 29.80   Wind West to South.

Moderate breezes but overcast. Continued our plan of running in the day & hauling close to the wind with short sail. Cast the lead finding on bottom at 100 faths. Very foggy.

At Sea, Friday May 26th 1865
Lat: 56°30′   Dist: 96 m.   Ther 31° to 39°.   Long 152°29′E.
Course N by W   Bar. 29.50 to 29.60
Wind. SSE, S, S by W & SSW.

Very foggy, and disagreeable. At night brought by heading W1/2N.

At Sea, Saturday May 27th 1865
Lat: 57°07′N.   Dist: 41 m.   Ther. 28° to 37°.   Long: 153°01′E
Course NNE 1/4 E.   Bar. 29.50 to 29.54.   Wind. SW & Calm.

Filled away under close reefed topsails. As soon as the fog cleared up, we saw a large quantity of floating ice on the port beam. Very soon we saw a sail on the other side of the ice. Made sail standing around the ice for the sail. Made her out to be a bark standing for us, no doubt to "gam." Hove to and she came right for us—fired a gun. She hove too [*sic*] hoisting the Yankee flag. Sent a boat [to] bring onboard the Captain (Nye, Ebenezer) and all his mates. She proved to be the New Bedford Bark *Abigail*. We soon condemned the vessel. Put a prize crew onboard and commenced to transfer the personal effects of officers & crew, and remained by her all night. It is fine weather for our work as it is nearly calm. Lieut: Scales was placed in charge of her.

> At Sea, Sunday May 28th 1865
> Lat: 57°17′N.   Ther. 33° to 29°.   Dist 13 m.   Long 152°47′E
> Course. NW 1/2 N   Bar. 29.50 to 29.40   Wind Calm & N by E.

This has been a terrible day for me. We brought off a great deal of liquor[2] and many of our men and two officers got drunk.[3] Put all in irons, gagged & triced up, right & left. I never had such a time. Our men have heretofore been so clear of any such thing that it comes, as something new, still harder but I am determined that they shall not repeat it. Got onboard five hogs and many valuables from the prize and set her on fire. Paroled & cleared the crew (35) of the prize. This, our 14th prize was valued at $22,000. Saturday is our lucky day.

> At Sea, Monday May 29th 1865
> Lat: 57°27′N.   Ther. 29° & 27°   Dist: 13.   Long: 152° 30′ E.
> Course NW 1/2 N.   Bar. 29.29, 29.10, 29.25
> Wind. Nd & Ed & NNW

Just got through with our prize in time. This morning it was blowing a gale and snowing all the time. It has been a fearful day. Put Mr. Lynch (2d Carpenter) in irons for being again drunk. He being very insolent to me I gagged him. Lieut. Scales was suspended for bringing liquor from the prize for private use—such being irregular.[4] When the wind hauled to the Wd of North it cleared up.

> At Sea, Tuesday May 30th 1865
> Lat: 57°48′N.   Ther. 32° & 37°.   Dist. 22 m.   Long 152°24′E
> Course N 3/4 W.   Bar. 29.34 to 29.46.   Wind Calm & W by N

A lovely day. Loosed sail to dry. Saw land to the Nd from N by E to NW. We being in the mouth of NE bay, with Kamshatska [*sic*] on starb'd bow & Siberia on port bow, all covered with snow and distant about 80 miles. This is a droll part of the world. It is never dark as you can read on deck all night. The sun rises at 3 A.M. & sets at 9 P.M. We learn from one of the prisoners whose sympathies are with us that all the whalers are at St. Jona's Island in the ice and we will remain here until they come up to enter the NE bay, and pick them up then.[5]

At Sea, Wednesday May 31st 1865
Lat: 57°08′N.   Ther. 32° to 40°   Dist: 45 m.   Long 152° 59′ E
Course SE By S 3/4 S.   Bar. 29.40 to 29.57   Wind W by N.

I never saw a more beautiful day than this last day of May, and I trust it will continue. The weather here in June & July is generally good. Today we got our heavy boats off the gallows and got one which was on the port side down on chocks and the other to the Stb'd Davits destroying the gig which was there. This releaves [sic] us of a great deal of top hamper. Lieut: Scales was restored to duty & Lieut: Chew put on watch. This places all four Lieuts on watch, from which the Master is excused.

At Sea, Thursday June 1st 1865
Lat: 58°00′N.   Dist: 54 m.   Ther. 48° to 36°.   Long: 153° 25′ E.
Course N by E 1/4 E.   Bar. 29.53 to 29.82.   Wind Nd & Wd & Calm

At sun rise (3 A.M.) made high land ahead. This we took to be the land near Tausk Bay, and supposing that there might be some whalers there we got up steam & steamed near the land but found the Bay entirely closed by thick ice. We then brought by the wind at about 30 miles from land, hoisted the Propeller, lowered a boat & scrubbed [the] ship. It is perfectly calm.

At Sea, Friday June 2nd 1865
Lat: 58°28′N.   Dist: 70 m.   Ther. 42° 37° 35° 34°
 Long: 151°25′E
Course WNW.   Bar. 29.68 .60 .58 .46 .44 .45
 Wind.NNE, ENE, E by N

Stood along the shore and down to Tausk Bay but it came on to blow & seeing ice all to leeward of us, layed too [sic] under close reefed main topsail & Fore storm staysail, head to sea. This afternoon saw a vessel to windward but made it out to be a brig, and as there are no American brigs used as whalers we did not make chase supposing him to be a Dutchman. We will remain here all night laying to.

At Sea, Saturday June 3rd, 1865.
Lat: 58°00′N.   Dist: 35 m.   Ther: 34° to 32°   Long: 150°46 E°
Course SW 3/4 S.   Bar 29.48 .45/.40/.38/.30/.28
 Wind E by N, SE by S & East.

This morning we filled away and stood about WNW, towards St. Jona's Island. It commenced to rain & hail and the rain froze as fast as it fell. We soon saw ice ahead and we brought by under close reefed fore & main topsails and fore staysail on the stbd tack. I have never seen such weather at sea in my life—the rain as fast as it fell on the sails, ropes, masts, deck, yards & rigging froze into

solid ice, and the ship had the appearance of being made of glass. None of
the braces or gear would work, and the ship's side was solid ice. The sight was
certainly beautiful & grand but was most severe. We are very much blessed.
Our quarters for men & officers are most roomy, comfortable & warm. With
our galley on our nice large berth deck and our little stove in our ward room
we are very snug. The watch officers and Qr. Master are really the only parties
much exposed. Oh! how I thank God for his numerous blessings. Oh! if I but
knew that all was well with our dear country. I leave all in God's hands trusting in him as the supporter of what I consider the Just Cause. I trust we may
have a good day tomorrow, for I am sure that there are sails near us. Our ship
being under close reefed Fore & Main topsails we ranged ahead and soon
made ice ahead & on both bows, and on the starb'd bow. Tried to work the
braces, but could not but by the helm kept away, ran to leeward and are now
laying to under the lee of the ice, on the St'b'd. tack, as smooth as a mill pond.
Ice about 1 1/2 miles to windward. God bless, protect & guard my dear ones.

> At Sea, Sunday June 4th 1865.
> Lat: 57°21'N.   Dist. 17 m.   Ther. 32°   Long: 150°18'E.
> Course SW by W1/4W.   Bar. 29.27/.25/.30/.23/.15/.10/
>   Wind. E by S, ENE & NE.

Last night I went to sleep feeling content that the ship lying to under the lee
of an immense floe of drift ice was perfectly safe. She was unfortunately under close reefed fore & main topsails and under this sail ranged ahead too
much. We could not take in the fore topsail as we could not use our clew lines
or buntlines or overhaul our sheets and the sail itself was like a board, being
frozen stiff. Not a brace could be started and the whole ship was literally frozen up. At three A.M. I was aroused by heavy thumping. I jumped on deck and
found that being entirely unmanagable she had ranged ahead into an immense floe of ice which without our knowledge was on the lee bow. Lee was
officer of the deck and had all the watch, with belaying pins using every possible means of beating the ice clear of the braces and it took his relief (Chew)
until 6 O'clock (3 hours) to get them so that they might be used imperfectly.
We then braced aback to force her out stern first but this brought such a strain
on the rudder that we we[re] afraid of splitting it. We filled away and forged
ahead. Her head was SW and we knew that we were getting further & further
in. The ice tho rotten was very large and but for some punch mats on the fore
foot & bows we might have ripped off our stem copper or stove our bows.
The ship was so locked up in the ice that we scarcely thought it possible to
wear to the Nd. but thank God just ahead was seen a small clear or comparatively clear spot of about 40 feet square. This was our only chance. We hoisted
with great difficulty the fore topmast staysail & fore topsail and wore with

much difficulty and very slowly to the NW & Nd and then just using sail enough to work very slowly ahead we finally pushed our way back the way we came. At 8.45 we were out of the heavy ice, and made sail to get well clear. I was very uneasy and feared the stoving in of our bow. Some pieces were thirty feet deep and fifteen yards square. The mats alone saved our cut water and copper, and I would warn any one coming here to have a good supply. God again favored us. A warm day aided in its work by belaying pins, capstan bars etc. cleared our rigging and sails of ice and we are now all right sailing to the Nd, keeping a bright look out with neither the desire or intention of trying over so hazardous an experiment. The ship from the water line up was ice 1/2 an inch thick. It is now snowing heavily, and I fear a rain. The ice has by falling made every man look out for his head. I never did see any thing like it nor never wish to. All Arctic men I warn to have a plenty of mats—without them our ship would have been ruined if not sunk and with them she has sustained no injury. Meeting ice here, at some two hundred miles from St. Jonas Island proves to us that we can't go near there for whalers, and must content ourselves in picking them up as they go North into the Bays after the ice is broken away. The sides of our ship are thin and are in no way suited, like the bluff bowed & sheathed whalers, to go into ice. I give my vote to keeping out of all ice, as necessary to the safety of the ship. I trust we will catch a great many before they get into the Bays.

> At Sea, Monday June 5th 1865
> Lat: 58°05′N.   Dist: 15 m.   Ther. 32° to 34°   Long: 150°27′E
> Course N by E 1/2 E.   Bar. 29.00/29.10/.15/.20/.30/.40/
>   Water 30° to 32°   Wind. Nd & Wd, Calm & Nd & Wd

At midnight I was again aroused by thumping and hurried on deck. I found the ship in heavy ice. Grimball had relieved Scales and got her clear without damage. It has been calm or nearly so the whole day with a heavy swell. The barometer has been very low but is gradually rising. The question arose today whether it was proper & safe to take the ship into the ice toward Jona's Island in pursuit of the whalers. I am utterly and entirely opposed to it, as I am sure that, without any sheathing or fixings we are entirely unfit for it, and if we did not materially endanger the safety of the ship (and all hands) we would lose our copper, thereby ruining our sailing qualities and our more important work hereafter. My idea is to catch one vessel, put a crew on her and let her go in the ice, fitted as she will be for the purpose, keeping our vessel out which can catch them as they come up to go into the Bays. If this vessel be fitted out as I most earnestly do and will recommend, I will try and command her. The Captain agrees with me in that this vessel should not go in, but to additionally arm & secure himself against any future censure, he determined to call a consultation of Lieutenants & Masters. Lieuts: Lee, Chew, Scales & I were of the same opinion, i.e. that we ought to keep out. Lieut. Grimball & Master Bulloch thought we ought to go in. He (the Capt:) will act by his own opinion & that of the majority. I am glad for when I consider that one ordinary merchant vessel is worth three or four ordinary whalers, I am convinced that we should risk nothing for the uncertain destruction of the latter to unfit our vessel's cruize against the former.

    At Sea, Tuesday June 6th 1865
    Lat: 58°28′N.   Dist: 26 m.   Ther. 36° to 41°   Long 150°49′E.
    Course NNE 1/2 E   Bar. 29.40/45/50/55/60/65
      Wind. WSW, W, WNW   Water 32° to 36°

This has been a beautiful and delightful day. We have had a fine day for drying all damp clothes, wet sails, scrubbing our berth deck and airing bedding and we have fully availed ourselves of the good opportunity. This morning early we made the snow clad cliffs of Siberia and with light airs we stood for them nearly all day. This land is the same that we left the other day i.e. the land at the mouth of Tausk Bay. Olski Island which is in the centre of the Entrance was on the port bow and Cape Alivian [Alevina] the right hand point of the Eastern Entrance on our starboard bow. After standing sufficiently close to the land we stood to the Nd & Ed along the coast. At 7 P.M. we made ice ahead and all on the starb'd bow. We are in fact surrounded by land & ice. I shall use all my p[e]rsuasion to keep the ship out of the ice. Tonight we are under "night sail" i.e. three close reefed topsails & storm staysail. The distances at which you can see land in this atmosphere are most d[e]ceptive. You can in the clear atmosphere see the snow clad clif[f]s at a distance of 80 miles.

    At Sea, Wednesday June 7th 1865
    Lat: 58°15′N.   Dist: 50 m.   Ther. 35° to 38°   Long 152°19′E.
    Course E by S 1/2 S.   Bar. 29.66/67/69/.70
      Wind. WNW, ENE, E by S

This has been another beautiful day. The high state of the barometer indicates Easterly weather and as the day advanced the gentle breeze hauled to the Eastward of North. This morning we ran along the land between the Tausk & Babushkin Bays, just before getting up to the Cape to the westward of the Entrance to the latter Bay we made ice which extended to the Eastward or Sd & Ed as far as we could see. This we made out to be very high & very thick and extending up to the Nd & Ed as far as we could see. To enter it would be folly and we determined to skirt along it. This we have been doing all day and have not yet come to its end. This is undoubtedly the ice coming from the NE bay, and occupying the whole entrance from the Siberian to the Kamschatski [Kamchatka] coast. No whaler would attempt to go through it and we are safe in concluding that there are no whalers in that arm of the sea. Meeting as we have done ice everywhere, and not considering it safe to enter the ice in the ship, our chances of [a] capture are very remote. Our only hope lies in the possibility of our picking up some vessel off this entrance and sending her in the ice after the rest. If we can only get the vessel this will be good, but if we are not so fortunate I am entirely opposed to endangering the safety of this ship and all onboard to attempt to catch six or eight whalers. The Capt: and a majority of our officers are of my opinion, and this will be our plan.

At Sea, Thursday June 8th 1865
Lat: 56°55′N.   Dist: 90 m.   Ther. 37° to 49°   Long: 153°36′E.
Course SSE 1/2 E   Bar. 29.75/.80/.84   Wind. Sd, Nd & Ed.

This has been another beautiful day. All the time we have had all plain sail set, and sailing comfortably along with a light breeze. The Captain came to a somewhat sudden conclusion in deciding to quit this sea and accordingly changed the course at noon for the Amphritrite or 50th passage. When the main object of our cruize was to do work in this sea, I can but deeply regret coming so far and destroying but one vessel. I was entirely opposed to taking this vessel into the ice, deeming such a course most imprudent and dangerous, not alone to the sailing qualities of the vessel by the loss of her copper, but to her safety. I was however in favor of remaining a short time and trying to pick up a vessel off the NE gulf, and sending her, fitted as she would be into the ice after the rest. The Captain however thinks that this even if successful would cause too great a loss of time. He says that he has found out upon good authority that while there are but about twelve whalers here there are some sixty or eighty in the Arctic & Berhing [sic] Seas, and by remaining here he would lose so much time as to prevent his going there. If all these facts are correct he is right in going on. Whatever he decides upon I will do all I can to assist in carrying out. So here we go for Berhing [sic] Sea, I trust with good luck ahead. As to a commanding officer pleasing all hands, it is impossible. If he steers to the Nd, the question at once arises "Why don't we go to the Sd, what the devil are we going North for?" and if he goes to the Sd, the same question is asked. It is disgustingly true that men are bound to differ at all times. We saw today the snow clad mounts of Kamshatka [sic] distant 76 miles!!!

At Sea, Friday June 9th 1865.
Lat: 55°09′N.   Long: 153°58′E.   Wind. North & NW (light)
Course S 1/2 E.   Ther. 39° to 51°   Bar. 29.80-.90   Dist: 107 m.

During the whole day we have been [in] a dense fog, so dense that we could see but a short distance. Towards night a gentle westerly breeze cleared away the fog, and then fell calm. I have felt very, very sad all day. It is only now when I have little to do that my troubles come more heavily upon me. The sad fate of my dear uncle Capt. Arthur Sinclair, reported drowned in the *Lelia* near Liverpool, renders me sadder than I can express. The loss of so noble & affectionate an uncle is, of itself bad enough; but when I consider the state of poverty & grief of his dear wife and children, I am thrown into a sad state of gloom.[6] My constant prayer is that God will be merciful to my country and dear ones. In his hands, and to him, as a just God, I am happy to trust all. The latest news, representing the taking of Savannah & Wilmington is calculated to distress us, but at the same time it is an incentive to me to make a greater exertion to do my full, whole & highest duty. Our cruize thus far has been commenced & vigorously prosecuted amid unprecedented difficulties and we are certain, with a proper degree of energy to come out with flying colors. God aid us, I pray.

> At Sea, Saturday June 10th 1865
> Lat: 54°18′N.   Course S 1/2 W Wind Sd & Ed   Ther 32° to 47°
> Long: 153°47′E.   Dist: 52 m.   Bar. 29.95 to 30.00

During the whole day we have been in a dense fog and the greater portion of the time in a perfect calm. Several whales (finbacks) played close around the ship. Today it was reported to me that Capt: Nye late of the prize *Abigail,* had been using every argument in his power to prevent some of the "*dagoes*" of his crew from shipping telling them that a Yankee man of war would catch us and hang them. We want men and as these are not Yanks, and can haul in ropes we would like to get some of them—besides such talk would discourage any of our men who were at all weak nerved. I sent for him and told him that if he continued to talk in this way I would put him in double irons. Today Thos: S. Manning, late second mate in the *Abigail,* from Baltimore, came forward and said all his feelings were Southern and he had long wanted to join her cause, and shipped as Seaman. The Captain rated him Ship's Corporal. I am glad to have him, as the more Southerners we have the better. Besides, he is an old arctic whaler and may prove a valuable man to us.[7] I trust he may soon recover from his present painful complaint. He is a fine looking fellow.

> At Sea, Sunday (Trinity) June 11th 1865.
> Lat: 53°27′N.   Course S 3/4 E   Dist 52 m.   Ther 36° to 44°
> Long: 154°10′E.   Wind WSW, W, WNW.   Bar. 30.00, 29.98

This has been one of the loveliest days I have ever beheld, a soft, gentle breeze, smooth sea, and a perfectly clear horizon. This being Trinity Sunday I read the whole service for the day, in the little book which my darling Pattie gave me. It seems to me that I love her more and more every day. God protect her I pray. My great effort is to make myself worthy of her love. I have been happily engaged in rereading her dear letters and those of my dear ones at home. What would I not give to know that they were all well. Oh for but a line. We had today general muster & read the "Articles of War." All day we have a great number of whales spouting all around us. I had no idea we could see them so far. These I saw at a great distance and I at first thought they were sails. The "spouts" looked like volumes of smoke or steam. I trust we will see a sail, but I scarcely think we will catch any until we get to the Berhing [*sic*] Sea which is 1600 miles from the Amphitrite Strait. I trust we will succeed. I am sure we will do our best.

> At Sea, Monday June 12th 1865
> Lat: 51°08′N.   Course South.   Wind NW, North, WNW.
> Long: 154°14′E.   Dist: 139 m.   Bar. 29.92/.89/.85.
> Ther. 36°to 54°

During the whole day we have had a light breeze. At an early hour in the fore noon we saw high land a little on the port bow. We soon made out that this was the Peak of Aliad. We altered our course a little and tonight it is on the port beam. You can easily imagine how clear the atmosphere is when we saw this land at a distance of 65 miles. I turned around to an old sailor and asked him how far it was[;] he looked at it and sagely replied "about 15 miles"[;] it was then 63. We soon saw Schrinsky island and are now standing for it, Borunsky Island being on the Stbd: bow. At 8 we were about 38 miles from the Entrance. Today we shipped twelve men nearly all Sandwich Islanders or "Kanakas." Such names I never read, among them were Jim California, John Boy &c. one[']s name was from his being so tall was "Long Joe," but some one suggested that he had better reverse it, so he put himself down as Joe Long. They are a poor looking set but they can haul on the ropes.

> At Sea, Tuesday June 13th 1865
> Lat: 49°51′N.   Course SE 1/2 S.   Wind Nd & Wd, Wd & South
> Long: 155°54′E   Dist: 101 m.   Bar 29.82/.79/.75/.60
> Ther 37°to 51°

This morning I got up as usual at 6.30 and went on deck. I found the ship going 6 knots through a dense fog, but when I relieved the officer of the deck to *arrange his toilet* or as we say, "get a wash," I was informed that we were going through the Amphiatrite [*sic*] Strait. Still we could not see land on either side although the passage is only 20 miles wide. At 7.30 I hauled up to East, and very soon we could see the peaks on each side away above the fog.

We were fairly through, and during the day have with a very light breeze been going about N.E. very slowly. The mainland of Kamschatka in sight on our port bow, and Shrinsky & Borunsky isles in plain sight. Today I organized another gun's crew, which will give us four guns on a side with full crews. Late last night I shipped another man a Prussian (Burnett) as a marine, also our two [F]renchmen Peter Raymond & Louis Rowe, whose terms expired on the 29th of April [and who] resigned. This gives us upwards of 110 men exclusive of officers.

> At Sea, Wednesday June 14th 1865.
> Lat: 50°47′N.   Course NE by E 1/2 E   Wind. South
> Long: 158°28′E.   Dist: 112 m.   Bar: 29.78/.75/.80
>   Ther 36°to 41°

All day we have had a nice breeze from the Sd & Ed which sends us along about 7 1/2 knots. The fog during the whole day has been a kind of "Scotch mist" or small sized rain. Of this kind of weather we may expect a great deal in this region and in the Berhing [*sic*] Sea and Arctic. I trust that we may not run into any ice in this kind of weather. Today I cleared out the after "'tween decks" which I shall use for prisoners. It is where we had coal, but when clean, will be more comfortable than our Berth deck of which it formed a part.

> At Sea, Thursday June 15th 1865.
> Lat: 51°59′N.   Course ENE.   Ther 37° to 40°   Wind Sd & Ed.
> Long: 163°06′E.   Dist: 188 miles.   Bar. 29.80/.79/.77/.80/.70/.69

During the whole day we have had a pretty fresh breeze from the Sd of West attended by a high barometer and a heavy fog. Towards ten P.M. the Barometer commenced falling which indicated either a gale or Westerly weather. We are truly fortunate in getting this breeze as it enables us to go along at about 8 1/2 knots on our course. At one time this morning we went for two hours 11 knots per hour, under topgallant sails. This is good sailing. I shall be glad when we have finished our cruising in this region and get to where we have more sunshine. Here although the sun is above the horizon about 18 hours in the 24 we rarely see it, and at times cannot see 100 yards ahead. We are now (10.30) not more than 142 miles from Copper Island which is one of the Behring group.

> At Sea, Friday June 16th 1865.
> Lat: 54°30′N.   Course NE 1/2 E.   Ther: 40° to 47°
>   Wind Sd & Ed.
> Long: 168°00′E.   Dist: 232 m.   Bar. 29.65/.60/.56/.44/.41/.37

During the whole day we have been in a dense fog or fine rain. At noon we were standing on with a nice breeze under topgallant sails, when the fog slightly lightened and to our astonishment we saw land right ahead an[d] on both bows not more than 6 miles off. We backed at once and stood to the Sd & Wd. Not having had an observation for three days we had run by dead reckoning and estimated that we were about 34 miles to the Sd & Ed of Copper Island and about 60 from Behring Island. We did not know where we were and which of the two we saw, but let be either one or the other, and it proved that we had a current setting us to the Nd & Wd. We ran SW about 16 miles when it fell calm. If it was Copper Island which we saw, the current would set us right on Behring Island, so we very sensibly got up steam and steamed to the Sd & Ed so that we will be clear in either case. The fog is very dense, and had it not lifted when it did this forenoon, our ship's ribs would most certainly have been in an uninhabited island. Surely God is with us. The Barometer is very low, and either indicates a gale or westerly weather. I trust the latter as then we will find our position. Today another Sandwich Islander shipped, his name is "Joe Kanaka." The 4th mate of the late *Abigail* also shipped. We now muster strong.

At Sea, Saturday June 17th 1865
Lat: 54°23′N.   Course E3/4S.   Ther 40° to 46°
  Wind Sd & Wd & Sd & Ed.
Long: 170°08′E.   Dist. 129 miles   Bar 29.32/.40/.41/.44/.45

This morning I got up at 6.30 as usual. What with the noise of the propeller and the anxiety felt as to the true position of the ship, I slept very little and awoke feeling fatigued rather than refreshed by my last night's restlessness. Last night having run under steam some 40 miles SE, a westerly breeze set in and we stopped steam, hoisted the propeller, made sail and stood on a ENE course, which we consider perfectly safe even if the land seen yesterday chanced to be Copper Island. The day cleared up very nicely and enabled us to get our position accurately. It was found that we were about 50 miles to the Eastward of Copper Island which was nearly due west from us. By working back it was found that the land made on yesterday was Copper Island which was then but ten miles from us. We are now fairly in [the] Behring Sea, standing with a gentle Southerly breeze for the fishing ground with nothing to look out for, for about 400 miles, but ice.

At Sea, Sunday June 18th 1865.
Lat: 55°47′N.   Course NNE1/2E.   Ther 40° to 38°

Wind. Variable.

Long: 171°28′E.   Dist: 96 m.   Bar. 29.35/.22/.28/.25/.27/.30

A day of rest. All day the weather has been very disagreeable; overcast with fog & rain, cold & dreary. Towards night the wind freshened and we may have it fresher. I only feel apprehensions about ice, but "on dit" that we will not see any so far south. I trust not. I am growing impatient to have our work up here finished. I want to go where we can see more of the Sun, and of the Enemy's property; the latter I am certain we will find further north. The day I have spent in reading my prayer book given me by my dear Pattie and her sister. Oh! how much I do wish I was a Christian.[8] I will pray & try. How much would I not give to know that all was going well in our dear country. God uphold our cause, I humbly pray.

At Sea, Monday June 19th 1865.
Lat: 57°19′N.   Course NE3/4E.   Ther. 38° to 40°
   Wind Nd & Wd, Wd, Sd & Wd
Long: 175°06′E.   Dist: 152 m.   Bar. 29.28/.25/.20/.17

This has been a lovely day with a bright sun and leading Westerly breeze gradually increasing towards evening. Towards night or rather when night might [start] to commence (for the sun does not set until 9, and it never gets dark) the sky became overcast and the wind came out fresher from about WSW. We ran from 9 knots, gradually increasing up to 11 1/2 under topgallant sails. We were going too fast for this icy region and we shortened sail to single reefed topsails. We are now in a region which will not allow us to run too fast as we might be roused up at midnight by striking floe ice. This ship should never go into ice—she is to[o] frail. With these whalers, who come prepared with sheathing, iron cutwater and outside planking it is very different.

At Sea, Tuesday June 20th 1865.
Lat: 60°04′N.   Course NNE3/4E.   Ther 38° to 43°
   Wind Sd & Wd.
Long: 178°16′E.   Bar 29.17/.15/.11/29.00   Dist 192 m.

During the whole day we have had overcast and gloomy weather with fine rain. Our breeze has nobly stuck to us and with it we have been enabled, assisted by the current to get very high up. Tonight it is almost calm and if, as is highly probable, we make some of the whalers, a calm is the very thing we would desire. There are some sixty vessels up here and we would scarcely see a vessel alone, indeed we might see ten at one time and if there was a calm we could with our steam catch the party, but if there was a breeze I am sure, apprized of our character two thirds might escape. A great deal of good,

sound judgement must be brought to bear. We have been very much blessed
so far, and I pray God to continue his blessings. All of us are now further
north than ever before.

At Sea, Wednesday June 21st 1865
Lat: 62°11′N.   Course NNE.   Bar. 29.08/10/12/13/19/25
Long: 179°57′E.   Dist: 136 m.   Wind Varble Nd & Ed
    Ther 38° to 36°

This morning I awoke after a restless night. We got up steam in the first watch
so that I was up during that watch, and afterwards got very little sleep. We
stood towards Cape St Thadeous which is the southern cape of Anadie Bay
[Anadyr]. When we got within 15 miles of it the fog became so dense that we
did not deem it prudent to go any closer. When it cleared a little we saw Cape
Navarin which is about 28 miles from Cape St. Thaddeous and separated
from it by the Bay of the Archangel Gabriel. Off Cape Navarin we saw what
we supposed to be a sail, but standing for it we made it out to be a "sail rock"
right near the cape and hauled up again for St Thaddeous which we soon
made but finding no sails near it and being unable to weather it we tacked.
Cape St Thaddeous is a high flat table land which can be seen in clear weather
some 35 miles. During the day we have had alternately fog (dense), rain, snow
& hail. This is a day which a man may go to sea a long time and not experience. If you sail from England to the Eastwards and go around the world,
returning to England say on the 21st of June you will find that if you have
not kept up the necessary corrections for change of longitude your 21st is
their 20th or that you have gained a day. We today crossed the 180th meridian
from Greenwich and are therefore 12h ahead of them or tomorrow being
by our account is regularly Thursday June 22nd it is with them Wednesday
June 21st. So that in order to keep our time with them we will have to call
tomorrow Wednesday June 21st or in other words we will have a week with
two Wednesdays, a month with two 21st's, and June with 32 days. We will
also for tomorrow have to take out the the same declination, Equation of nine
etc as we did today. This will puzzle some of our old sailors when Sunday
comes to find that the day on which they expected Sunday, Saturday's work
will be done. We expected to see some prizes today but are disappointed and
expect them further to the Ed near St Lawrence Island. We passed a great deal
of whale "blubber" showing that the whalers are not far off. I trust that tomorrow will bring them.

At Sea, Thursday June 22nd 1865
Lat: 62°23′N   Wind Nd & Ed   Bar 29.40   Dist: 13 m.
Long: 179°46′E   Ther 35°   Course. NNW.

Yesterday I was too soon in saying that we would have two 21st's & two Wednesdays as we did not cross the 180th meridian as today we we [*sic*] were but fourteen miles from it, we will have two Thursdays instead. At 9 O'c A.M. we made two sails on our port quarter. Furled sails & stood for them under sail. At 11 O'c hove to and boarded the six topsail yard whale ship *William Thompson* of New Bedford Mass—Capt. Smith. Put a prize crew onboard & brought the Captain & Mates onboard our vessel and stood in chase of the other vessel. At 12'05 boarded the whale ship *Euphrates* of New Bedford Mass —brought the crew with their personal effects onboard and fired the prize. The fog is very thick. The prize *Wm. Thompson* came near us & hove too [*sic*]. We now commenced to get from the prize beef, pork & provisions when we saw a sail to the Nd & Wd.[9] We gave chase[.] She proved to be the English whaling Barque *Robt: Townds* of Sidney, Australia.[10] We stood back to our prize—which we had some trouble in finding as the fog became very dense. When we found her we continued getting stores onboard. I will now say something of the news which has this day come to us. Capt. Smith gave us all he seemed to know. We heard first of the assassination of Mr. President Lincoln and a similar attempt upon the life of Mr. Seward. I only fear that these attempts will be put to the credit of some Confederates, but I am certain that it was not done by anyone from our side. I am very much cast down by the news, which if true is very bad. Charleston; Savannah & Richmond taken. How awful this is. The two first I looked for, and I was certain that upon the fall of Wilmington, Richmond must be evacuated, but Genl. Lee is reported to have surrendered after his evacuation of Richmond at Appomattox, with his whole army, and rumors of Genl. Lee's negotiating for peace etc., etc. All this last I put down as false. Genl: Lee may have left a portion of his force to protect the retreat of his army, and even he might have been taken with this portion, but as to his surrender of his whole army, and of his treating with Gen Grant for peace I do not believe one single word. There is no doubting the fact that the Confederacy has received in prestige a heavy blow, but further I do not believe. With Richmond we must lose for a time, if not permanently, Virginia my own dear state, which to me as a Virginian, and to every true Confederate is a great blow. One would think who read some of the papers, that the Confederate States were subjugated but I know too well the falsehood letting propensities of our enemies to place much confidence in their statements. The news is bad, very bad, and it is well calculated to make a "person feel blue." My heart is heavy! heavy!! heavy!!! but my prayers to an Almighty God, give me great relief. God alone knows what will become of my darling little Sisters, if our dear old state should be given up to our cruel and relentless foes. There they are with no means of support and in a country already devastated by invasion. God grant them protection I pray most fervently. With the fall of Richmond, Virginia must be evacuated and I fear it will never be ours again. God protect us I pray. During the day my thoughts have been running on my home and dear ones and really I have almost gone mad over the helpless and destitute condition in which the[y] must be placed. In my anguish I sought consolation in reading my little prayer book which my dear Pattie gave me, when my eyes fell on these words. "I have been young, and now am old; and yet saw I never the righteous forsaken, nor his seed begging their bread."[11] God help us I pray. Oh! God protect us.

At Sea, Thursday June 22nd 1865
Lat: 62°40′N   Course NE by E 3/4 E   Wind Nd & Ed & Nd.
Long: 178°50′W   Dist: 42 m.   Bar 29.64.   Ther 38°
[The *Shenandoah* crossed the International Date Line.]

Having gotten water & provisions from our prize the *Wm. Thompson* and brought off the prisoners and their effects we fired her and steamed away. We very soon made a floe of ice which we skirted stopping when it became foggy. At 1 we made nine sails. Stood for one which proved to be the whale ship *Milo* of New Bedford—bonded her for $46000, sent all prisoners on board and keeping her papers ordered her to follow us.[12] Chased the next vessel a ship which put on all sail, running into the ice, we gave her two shot which hove her too [*sic*]. We boarded her, she proving to be the ship *Sophia Thornton* a New Bedford whaler. Threw a prize crew onboard keeping as prisoners the Capt & mates, and ordered her to follow. There were four sails the other side of the ice to windward and besides the two captured three on this side, one was a Frenchman [*Gustave*, of Havre, Captain Vaulpré], one a Hiwaian [*sic*] [either the *Kohola*, Captain Barney Cogan, or the *Hae Hawaii*, Captain John Heppingstone][13] and the third a fast Bark which had taken the alarm & clapped on all sail to escape. We gave chase and after an hours[14] run, hove too & boarded the clipper whale Bark *Jireh Swift* of New Bedford. Taking off the officers & crew with their effects we fired her, and stood for our prizes.

At Sea, Friday June 23rd 1865
Lat: 62°48′N.   Course NW.   Bar 29.85   Ther 38°
Long: 179°04′W.   Dist: 9 m.   Wind Nd & Wd & Sd & Ed

Received a few stores from the prize *Sophia Thornton,* cut her masts away, and left her in charge of the bonded prize ship *Milo* Capt: Hawes to get provisions for his passengers. After which he had orders to fire her. He now had on board, paroled prisoners from his vessel, the Bark *Abigail* burnt in the Ok[h]otsk, ship *Wm Thompson, Euphrates, Sophia Thornton* & Bark *Jireh Swift,* in all, about two hundred men.[15] Made a sail to the Sd & Wd, stood for her. She proved to be the American Brigantine *Susan Abigail* a fur trader from San

Francisco. Taking off the crew & officers with their effects we fired her. Standing to the Nd & Ed passed the *Sophia Thornton* burning. We shipped several men from our various prizes. Towards night stopped steaming for fear of getting into ice as it is very foggy. The vessel which we captured today is one of the latest arrivals from San Francisco and brings the confirmation of the assassination of Lincoln, fall of Charleston, Savannah, Wilmington, Richmond and the surrender of Genl: Lee with 16000 men. The news is, if true very bad, but "there's life in the old land yet." "Let us live with a hope." "The God of Jacob is our refuge." Oh let us trust in him.

> At Sea, Saturday June 24th 1865
> Lat: 63°26′N.   Course NE by E 1/2 E   Bar 29.90   Dist: 80
> Long 175°16W   Wind East   Ther 34° to 40°

This has been a bad day. The high barometer indicated East winds which bring heavy fogs. It was certainly so today, for the fog was like rain. As it brightened up so that we could see any distance we steamed but frequently stopped for fear of running into ice. Shipped two more men who came from the *Abigail* (*Susan*) The fact of their joining shows how much faith they put in the news. They all agree in saying that there is very little confidence to be put in it, and that very little of it was believed. On the other hand they say that there are riots all through the North, and that the public mind there is most feverish. God grant us his aid I pray. Saw St Lawrence island on the port Bow.

> At Sea, Sunday June 25th 1865
> Lat: 63°50′N   Course E by N 1/2 N.   Bar 29.79 to 29.65
> Long 172°59′W   Wind Nd, Nd & Ed & West   Ther 37° to 40°
> Dist 93 m.

At 2 A.M. commenced steaming, St Lawrence island bearing NE.

Main land insight [*sic*]. Made large fields of ice ahead, slowed down and hauled to the Nd. Made two sails on our port Bow, stood in chase but one was a Frenchmen and the other a Hiawaiian [*sic*].[16] Soon after saw a sail on the Starb'd bow. Stood in chase—found her close under St Lawrence island trying out. She proved to be the Whale Ship *Gen'l: Williams* Captain Benjamin of New London, Connecticut. We got the prisoners with their effects off and burnt the prize. Several Esquimaux from St Lawrence island visited the ship in their canoes made of the skins of walrus stretched over a wood frame work. [They are] a miserable looking race of people of a light copper color, with straight black hair, but well formed and muscular. They were dressed from head to foot in skins of the thickest kind. They live on fish & whale blubber, and are known to be no more choice in their diet than are buzzards. Placed master's mate C. E. Hunt and Capt's Clerk J. C. Blacker under arrest for fighting. Upon investigation the former was restored to duty. Made Mr. Thos: S. Manning (Ship's Corpl.) Master's Mate for his most valuable services as a pilot.[17] Paroled all our prisoners but kept them under guard. At midnight saw three sails ahead. Steamed for them passing threw several fields of ice.

At Sea, Monday June 26th 1865
Lat: 64°21′N.   Course NNE 1/2 E.   Bar. 29.75   Dist 36 m.
Long: 172°20′W.   Wind Variable   Ther 40°

Commenced clear, pleasant with very light airs. Came up with the three vessels which proved to [be the] Whale Barks *Wm C. Nye, Catherine* & *Nimrod,* all of New Bedford, Massachusetts. Took off all the prisoners, with their effects, paroled them and took them in tow with their baggage in their own boats—and set fire to all three of them. Five sails insight [*sic*] to the Nd. Stood in chase of the four closest together. At 8 A.M. came up with them in succession and took possession of the Barks *Genl. Pike, Gipsey* and *Isabella*—the fourth the *Robt: Cummings* [*Benjamin Cummings*],[18] had the small pox and we only satisfied ourselves of the fact and for fear of its getting among our crew & prisoners we let her go. The *Genl Pike,* being the slowest we decided to bond her and send all prisoners onboard—accordingly she was bonded and we paroled our prisoners from the *Susan Abigail, Genl. Williams, Nimrod, Catharine, WC Nye, Isabella, Gypsey* & *Genl Pike* in all about 300 men & sent them onboard. We set fire to the *Gypsey* and cutting the masts out of the *Isabella* got her alongside, got out all her provisions, water and everything useful, working all night & day.[19] The weather favored us as it was foggy & calm. This gives us a fine supply of water & provisions. We having finished at midnight and set her on fire, and stood in chase of two sails to the Sd & Ed.

At Sea, Tuesday June 27th 1865
Lat: 65°19′N.   Course NE 3/4 N.   72 m.   Bar 29.54 to 29.65
Long: 170°39′W.   Wind Calm & N by E   Ther 40° & 36°

Passing threw a great deal of ice. Saw five sails all to windward beating up, the wind being fairly fresh we knew that if it came up fog we would certainly loose [*sic*] our prized [*sic*] or at least some, so that we stopped steaming, hoisted the propeller[,] made sail and commenced to beat up the straits in company, but a good way off from what we knew to be a fleet of Yanks. We passed & repassed several times, but they saw that we were a steamer but were as unsuspecting as babes—so that we will wait till it falls calm and then pounce upon them. It does make me feel sorry for them, but when I reflect that they have burnt the houses over the heads of our women, stolen their clothes and all kinds of property and inflicted hardships and perpetrated outrages which it makes me blush with shame for them, and maddens me to a degree which I never thought myself capable of reaching, when I think of this I say, everything like compassion gives place to intense hatred, and a determination in this cruel and relentless war to fight the devil with fire. The laws of Nations on war respect private property on shore but not on the sea. And all I can say is, I will burn as many as it is my good fortune to catch. All day we have been beating up insight of several sails, waiting for a calm, when we can bag the whole party.

At Sea, Wednesday June 28th 1865
Lat: 65°39′N.   Course NE by N   24 m.   Ther 37° to 38°
Long: 170°08′W.   Wind light Nd & Ed.   Bar. 29.65 to 29.72

What a day's work we have had today. At 6.30 A.M. Diomede island bore (pc) NNE about 12 miles. Ten sails insight [sic] to windward. Saw a great deal of floating ice. The sails to windward cannot get away as the wind is too light. At 8.15 saw a sail to the Southward, stood in chase under steam. At 10 came up with chase and captured the Whale Bark *Waverley* of New Bedford. Took off the prisoners with their effects, and burnt the prize. At 11 stood to the Wd to avoid ice and then stood to the Nd for ten sails insight [sic] all very near each other. At 1.30 P.M. came up with the fleet of ten sails all at anchor and all hoisting the Yankee flag. One vessel, the Bark *Brunswick,* was last night stove in running through some ice and the others were assisting her. We called away and manned all boats and boarded in succession the following vessels, all Yankee Whalers. Ships *Hillman, James Maury, Nassau, Brunswick, Isaac Howland* and Barks *Martha* (Second) and *Congress* of New Bedford, Mass. Barks *Nile* of New London, Connecticut, *Favorite* of Fair Haven, Mass and *Covington* of Warren, Rhode Island, capturing all ten which were made prizes. The *James Maury* having a lady on board, the widow of the Captain (Gray) who died at sea, we bonded for $37,000 and sent half the prisoners paroled onboard to be taken to San Francisco. We picked out the next slowest vessel, the Bark *Nile* of New London and bonded her for $41,600 and sent the rest of the prisoners paroled on her for a similar passage. We then towed the rest clear of those bonded, anchored them and burnt the whole party. We could still see the *Waverley* burning so that there were nine in sight in flames at one time. It is a gloomy sight to see these magnificent and valuable works of man so summarily destroyed, but do our enemies in their hellish acts of barbarity of burning the houses over the heads of helpless, defenseless and unoffending women & children consider this. No; it is an awful sight, but suffering as we have suffered from the ruthlessness of an inhuman foe, we can but consider that we are doing our duty in punishing them, as the only hope of bringing them to their proper senses—for if you touch a Yankee pocket you wound him in a sensitive and vital part. This day we have destroyed property to the amount of $400,563 and bonded property to the amount of $78,600. This will create an excitement. I trust it will do our hearts good by encouraging our noble people. Tonight it came on so foggy that we were afraid to run for fear of ice. We let go a kedge[20] under the lee of East Cape in twenty three fathoms water, but as the fog lifted sufficiently to see about a ship's length ahead we hove up the kedge and steamed slowly through Berhing [*sic*] Straits, Cape East being on our port bow and the Diomedes on the Starboard bow.

> At Sea, Thursday June 29th 1865
> Lat: 66°14′N.   Course NNE 3/4 E   42 m.   Ther 37° to 41°
> Long: 169°06′W. Wind Sd & Ed Sd & Wd & Calm.
>   Bar 29.80 to 29.90

This morning there was a dense fog, but what with steaming and a current of about 2 1/2 or 3 knots per hour to the Nd & Ed we felt sure that we were through Berhing [*sic*] Straits and fairly in the Arctic Ocean. About 6.30 the fog lifted and as we expected Cape East bore S 1/2 W & Diomede Island ESE. At 10 we saw ahead and all around very heavy ice, floe & packed and not considering it safe to attempt to pass threw it we stood to the Sd for the Straits. We went inside of the Arctic Circle as was shown by our bearings. I suppose Yankeedom will be astonished at our coming away [up] here after them. Soon after getting through the Straits we encountered ice, and as we could not get around it, we had to down mats and work through. Again our mats were our salvation or rather the salvation of our copper. In the ice we hove to a French ship and the Hawaiian Brig *Kohola* who told us that the Northern President had been killed & Gen: Lee had surrendered. News anticipated.

> At Sea, Friday June 30th 1865
> Lat: 64°24′N.   Course SW by S   108 m.   Ther 34° to 39°
> Long: 170°04′W.   Wind WSW.   Bar. 29.90 to 30.05

Early in the day set all staysails. At 8 A.M. worked around ice to the Ed. At 10 standing on our course through open ice. At 12 a very thick fog, but it being a little rough we took it for granted that we were not near any heavy ice. At 7.45 the fog continued but as the sea was not smooth we took it for granted that [we] were not near any ice. Made sail to topgallant sails, hoisted the propeller & lowered smoke stack. I went to bed feeling very uneasy for fear of ice.

> At Sea, Saturday July 1st 1865
> Lat: 63°09′N.   Course SW 1/4 S   88 m.   Ther 35° to 42°
> Long: 173°56′W.   Wind WSW & SW.   Bar 29.90 to 30.15

At 1 o'clock in the mid watch I got up having dreampt [*sic*] that we were in ice. I went on deck and found the ship going very nicely 6 knots. It was very smooth and a dense fog. I asked Lee how long it had been so smooth and he said for all his watch and two hours of Grimball's. I told him my dream and said that we were very near ice. He did not think so. I went to my room for my overcoat, and had not gotten to the door before the startling report of land dead ahead was given—it was soon reported to be high ice. We were within a ship's length of it before it was seen as there was a very heavy fog. Everything was thrown aback, but before she stopped her headway she struck very heavy ice hard enough to wake everyone up. The shock was very heavy and those below thought that she had knocked a hole in her bow, but as it turned out she sustained no injury. I went forward, lowered the mats while Lee took in all sail. Before he did this she was well in the ice and going rapidly astern. I feared the loss of the rudder, went aft and found it aport. Just had time to put it amidships and put three men to hold it when it struck with great violence against a heavy piece of ice—holding it amidships alone saved it. When it received the shock the rudder chain was broken, and the relieving tackles were hooked in time to save it. The ship was in great peril. The ice was high, hard and heavy and the fog very dense so that we did not know which way to go. We lowered a boat and ran out a grapnel to the Wd of North, hooked it to a heavy cake and winded [*sic*] her head in that direction—ran it to another and hauled her ahead. Got up steam[,] lowered the propeller and by means of oars and poles kept the ice clear of the propeller while we steamed very slowly—hoisted our boat. At 4.30 got out of the heavy ice but during the early part of the day up to 9.30 A.M. we were passing through heavy floes. At 9.30 got clear, and I trust we may never see any more.

At Sea, Sunday July 2nd 1865
Lat: 60°13′N.   Course S 2° W.   176 m.   Bar 30.10 to 30.22
Long 174°08′W   Wind SW, Var, ESE & E by S   Ther 38° to 41°
Ship under steam & staysails. Mustered the crew & read the "Articles of War." Fresh breezes. At 7 saw a sail ahead but it came in a dense fog and we lost her. I occupied the day in reading in my room, the services for the day. Most fervently did I pray for our dear country and loved ones. God protect & feed them I pray.

At Sea, Monday July 3d 1865
Lat: 56°56′N.   Course S 7°E   198 m.   Bar. 29.90 to 29.45
Long: 173°19′W.   Wind. ENE & SE by E.   Ther 40° to 43°.
The Sea being rough and the wind fair for the 172d passage we hoisted propeller, banked fires and made sail to Topgallant sails. During the whole day it

has been foggy with drizzling rain. At night shortened sail to topsails. We are beginning now to have night, as in days of yore. I shall be very much rejoiced when we get out on the broad Pacific once more. I shall hail it with joy.

At Sea, Tuesday July 4, 1865.
Lat: 53°52′N.   Course S 1/4 E   185 m.   Ther. 43° to 44°.
Long: 173°00′W.   Wind Sd & Ed.   Bar. 29.45 to 29.52

The sea being smooth and the wind light and ahead we furled sail and started under steam. This is the 4th of July—who can celebrate it? Can the Northern people, who now are, and for four years have been waging an unjust, cruel, relentless & inhuman war upon us, to take from us the very independence, the declaration of which 90 years ago, made this a day to be gloried in, can they glory in the day. Have they the bare faced audacity, when five of the original 13 are now battling against more greivous [sic] wrongs from the others than they could ever urge as a support to their cause. Should they not rather blush with shame at their present course, and relent. Yes, they have the audacity. Their honor, honesty, christianity, civilization is all gone. They blush at nothing except that which may be honest & honorable, and in their own acts they rarely blush for even these causes. Oh God mete out confusion & discord to their counsels. If any people can celebrate the day the Southerners are the ones, for they now are battling [for] the same rights, aggr[a]vated by causes ten times as strong, as those for which in 1775 they fought, but if such a thing be possible and these wicked men be successful, I for one would regret from the depth of my heart that we ever knew a 4th of July for tomorrow I would rather be ruled over by the President of Liberia than by the Yankees. Yes I would rather see the most worthless negro in the whole world rule over us than the Yankees. Who I consider a race of cruel, fanatical Scoundrels, lost alike to honor, decency, honesty & christianity. Any but those cruel, inhuman traites [sic], baser than the basest. They will celebrate the day with even more enthusiasm than before. To the world they say that they are fighting to free the slave, because they have in such a war the sympathy of the world, to their soldiers they cry union and the old flag, as the cry best calculated to make them rally; whereas in their now cruel, cowardly, dishonest and inhuman hearts, their sole object is gain, and not a single one exists but that has his eye on the rich spoils in land property to be had in the South. Let us free & arm our slaves; let every old man, every young woman in the South be armed, let their principle, practice & cry be to shoot dead the invader, whenever & wherever he be found, putting their trust in the justice of an Almighty all powerful & all just God. "The God of Jacob is our refuge."

8
The darkest day of my life . . .

July 5–September 28, 1865

At Sea, July 5th Wednesday 1865
Lat: 52°02′N   Course SE by S 1/4 S   128 m.   Bar 29.52 to 29.70
Long: 171°12′W   Wind Calm, Sd & Ed & Sd & Wd
  Ther 42° to 52°

The day commenced with a thick fog—ship under steam. At 5. the fog lightened up & saw on the port bow Tchagula [Chagulak] and Amaukhta [Amukta] Islands the most easterly being a burning volcano. The sight was beautiful— Smoke rushing from the crater. At 12 O'c being, thank goodness[,] well out into the Pacific, made sail, hoisted propeller, hauled fires & ran out the boiler. It is almost calm.

At Sea, Thursday July 6th 1865
Lat 51°37′N.   Course SSE   27 m.   Bar 29.69
Long: 170°56′W.   Wind SW, Calm & SE   Ther. 44° to 50°

Commenced with light airs & mist, died away calm and light winds sprung up from the Sd & Ed, which went on gradually increasing until at 12 Mid. she was going 9 1/2 knots. We are once more on the broad Pacific with no land or ice to make us uneasy. All hail it with delight.

At Sea, Friday July 7th 1865
Lat: 49°33′N.   Course S by W3/4W.   132 m.   Bar. 29.65 to 29.40
Long: 172°06′W.   Wind EbS, ESE, EbS, ENE, NE by N, NW & West.
  Ther 46°

Today we have been going along nicely. The weather has been very unpleasant there being a heavy Mist.

At Sea, Saturday July 8th 1865
Lat: 47°49′N.   Course SE1/2S.   134 m.   Bar. 29.55 to 29.80
Long: 170°00′W.   Winds from S to WSW.   Ther. 46° to 43°.

Another misty day but we have be[en] jogging nicely along, close hauled all day. The last two hours have been calm.

At Sea, Sunday July 9th 1865
Lat: 46°43′N.   Course SE 1/2 E   104 m.   Bar: 29.70 to 29.65.
Long: 168°03′W.   Wind NE.   Ther. 45° to 48°.

A day of rest. Occupied reading in my room. First three hours calm, when a gentle breeze from the Nd & E pushed up along nicely. Cloudy rainy & cool.

At Sea, Monday July 10th 1865
Lat: 45°37′N   Course SE   92 m.   Bar. 29.60 to 29.72
Long: 166°32′W.   Wind NW.   Ther 49° to 51°

The first hour the wind was from the NE, but it hauled into NW & continued light all day. Sent aloft all studding sail booms, rove off the gear and set the sails.

At Sea, Tuesday July 11th 1865
Lat: 44°57′N   Course SE   58 m.   Bar: 29.66 to 29.56
Long: 165°33′W.   Wind Variable   Ther: 41° to 56°

During the greater portion of the day it has been almost perfectly calm—with a smooth sea. We got our stages out and painted the ship thoroughly outside. Towards the evening a gentle breeze from the Sd & Ed sprang up.

At Sea, Wednesday July 12th 1865
Lat: 44°10′N.   Course ESE   132 m.   Bar 29.50 to 29.72
Long: 162°40′W.   Winds SW & S by W.   Ther. 50° to 55°

Today we have been ripping nicely along with a full breeze and all sail set in a wind. The ship sails well, very well. She has had only a moderate Royal breeze commencing with light airs. She went 5 at 1 A.M. increasing to 7 at 10 A.M. At 11 she went 9 and during the rest of the day she went 10. The sea is smooth.

At Sea, Thursday July 13th 1865
Lat 42°17′N.   Course SE by E   209 m.   Bar 29.75 to 29.40
Long 158°38′W.   Wind. Variable Sthly   Ther 54° to 57°

This is Captain Waddell's 41st birthday, and by invitation he took a nice dinner with us in the wardroom—as it was blowing a gale I only was present to drink his health, and then went on deck. The movements of the wind today have been peculiar, at first it was South, then variable then SE, went to South, went then to S by E and then hauled to S by W, SSW up to SW by S. At 1 from Royals we commenced to reduce sail as the winds increased. At 4 we were under close reefed Fore & Main Topsails & Fore staysail. At 4.30 blowing a fresh gale we furled the Fore Topsail & laid to under Main Spencer, close reefed Main Topsail & Fore Staysail. As the wind hauled to the westward we decided to run out of it by going about East but made sail to close reefed Fore & Main Topsails and reefed foresail and ran with the wind on our starboard quarter. There was a heavy sea, and she rolled fearfully. Everything was playing "Isaac and Josh." No one could account for the gale until it was reported that the cat was overboard. As soon as this was known there was no doubt of the cause. I thought the cat was overboard as I had intimated to the Master at Arms that such an expenditure would be agreeable to me, but I was by no means one of the superstitious ones. All were scolding me as the Jona [sic] when up walked the cat. No one was more surprised than I, for I thought poor pussy gone. I gave orders to let the cat live. Ship is rolling fearfully but easily, being in fine trim.

> At Sea, Friday July 14th 1865
> Lat: 41°21′N.   Course ESE   150 m.   Bar 29.57 to 30.18
> Long: 155°30′W.   Wind Nd & Wd.   Ther. 54° to 59°

This morning the gale was broken but the sea was high but went on gradually decreasing. During the morning watch we made sail from close reefed topsails gradually to Royals & Studding sails. I was up all last night being uneasy for fear something might break adrift, and she rolled so that I could not sleep. Jack Grimball is today quite sick with a high fever. A sad accident occurred today. One of our Kanakas John Boy got his right hand entirely crushed in the upper gin block of the Main Topsail hallyard [sic]. I fear he will lose the hand.

> At Sea, Saturday July 15th 1865
> Lat 39°39′N   Course SE 1/2 S.   Bar. 30.17 to 30.15
> Long 153°38′W.   Winds WNW.   Ther. 57° to 61°

This has been a beautiful day. The wind nearly aft, with a smooth sea & bright sun. It was reported to me this morning that Michl: Reid Master at Arms had gone to the room of our Sergeant of Marines to enquire after his health when the latter gave him, very improperly, a drink, he still lingered around the room and finally took a drink without being asked; he was then told by Mr. Canning to leave the room, which he did but afterward was found there trying to find still more. I sent for him and he denied it, but afterwards acknowledged that it was true. His position onboard ship rendered it absolutely necessary to the proper maintenance of discipline to have him punished. I told him that to find him, whom I had so implicitly trusted guilty of such conduct was very painful, but that his offense had no palliation and I intended to have him disrated. I did so and Chas. McLaren C. F. Castle was rated in his stead. Wm Warren whose term of enlistment expired on the 8th of April came forward to reship. I reshipped him and upon my recommendation he was rated C. Forecastle in McLaren's place. Warren is a man for whom I feel a great sympathy. He is a pensioner on the British Government for £15 per annum for wounds received at Savastopol. By the English rule these pensioners have to receive in person their pension. We have had no opportunity of getting him out of the ship for him to be at home in October the time when he should be there. And he will lose his life pension. I am very sorry for him. Employed holystoning the lower & upper decks, both of which have become very dirty from the dust from the coal which we have been trimming. We had a fine drying day, and made good our chance.

At Sea, Sunday July 16th 1865
Lat: 38°33′N.   Course SE by E1/4E   129 m.   Ther. 58° to 64°
Long: 151°14′W.   Winds, from SW to WNW.   Bar 30.15 to 29.96

A day of rest. How very rapidly the weeks pass by—Sunday seems but to have been on[ly] yesterday. How changed I feel myself. I remember when this day of rest was considered very uninteresting and tiresome. Now, I hail it with joy. It is a day of rest for all, and when there is no work going on I feel at liberty to retire to my room and have my time to myself. This I always do on Sunday, when I commune with my God, and read my letters. Oh! how I wish that I was a christian! And why am I not? Why can I not be? Most humbly do I pray God to assist me in my desire and attempt to become one. I read today the morning & evening services and many consoling passages cheered my poor heart. Were it not for my belief in his almighty Justice, my reflections about the condition of my dear sisters and country would run me mad. I pace the deck and my thought[s] all revert to them, and are gloomy, sad and distracting almost to insanity: but then I think of the blessed assurances from God, and Oh: how consoling: Oh! God teach me to trust in thee!! Today we have had strong breezes and occasional rain, and our noble Shenandoah has skipped merrily along. How very much we have been favored with fair winds. Truly God is with us. In reading over my letters from my darling Pattie which always give me so much courage, hope and encouragement, truly sad thoughts came into my head. If anything should happen to cause our dear country to lose the freedom for which we are contending and that we should be subjugated could I a poor creature, without money, country or profession ever look for a consummation of my fondest hope to call her mine. In her words "hope on, hope ever." Trust in the Lord. Oh: God! protect our dear country.

At Sea, Monday July 17th 1865
Lat: 37°16′N.   Course SE by E3/4E.   190 m.   Bar. 30.15 to 29.96
Long: 147°38′W   Winds from WNW to W.   Ther. 58° to 62°

Employed repairing sails. This has been a very nice day but occasionally a fog would pass over. Tonight we see a great many stars, which increase in number. In the Arctic region we never saw one. Again we too have night and day, but in the Arctic it was never dark. It is as mild as is comfortable. Well here we are to the Sd of San [F]rancisco and running bravely on. They will first hear of our exploits in the Arctic & Berhing [*sic*] & Okotsh [*sic*] Seas from the *Milo* the ship first bonded, and she will spread a panic, but she will not tell all for there are three behind who will by their arrival only add to the distress. I have no doubt, (as they probably have not heard of us since we left Melbourne, nearly six months ago), that we have [been] reported and rejoiced over as wrecked. But in August they will hear of our work at Ascension, and in this month they will hear of us three months afterwards in the Arctic regions. The *Milo* must be behind us as we are a far better sailer and altho she started a week before us still while she was no doubt . . . becalmed in Berhing [*sic*] Sea, we steamed out. I think that about a week from now she will arrive in San [F]rancisco, and report us in the Arctic when we will be booming along some 800 miles from San [F]rancisco, and some thousands of miles [from] where their whole fleet will be looking for us.[1]

At Sea, Tuesday July 18th 1865
Lat: 36°03′N   Course SE by E3/4E   167 m.   Bar. 30.01 to 30.10
Long: 144°31′W.   Winds. Sd & Wd   Ther. 65° to 74°

Our breeze from the Westward still continues and we are going along finely under all sail. I trust it may last until we get the regular NW breezes which are to run us down to where we catch the regular trades. Surely we have been blest with fair winds, for really, by reference to the log, we find that we have had very little head winds. I trust we may be so fortunate as to pick up a vessel from San Francisco to China which will give us late news. God grant that it may be good, and that the views of some of our officers may not be consummated.

At Sea, Wednesday July 19th 1865
Lat: 35°18′N.   Course E by S3/4S   128 m.   Bar. 30.10 to 30.14
Long 142°05′W.   Wind S by W & SSE   Ther. 65° to 71°

This has been a most lovely day, a bright sun, a smooth sea, and a gentle breeze. What more can we ask of old Neptune. The old gentleman in some of his levees has pitched into us pretty harshly, but altogether he has been kind and merciful to us. This morning we went to Genl: Quarters and fired two blank cartridges from each of our Starboard guns firing by broadside.

Considering that it was our first time we did remarkably well, but we need practice and without it we cannot expect to be perfect. I was much gratified by the working of the guns. Our 8 in. shell guns which I thought would by their recoil strain our bulwark, brought no strain upon it, as they only recoiled about three or four feet.

At Sea, Thursday July 20th 1865
Lat: 34°39′N.   Course E by S 1/2 S   131 m.   Ther. 67° to 71°
Long: 139°32′W.   Wind S by E to West.   Bar. 30.12 to 30.15
Today we have been making the best of our way with a light breeze, using all drawing sail. The sea is almost perfectly smooth. We went to General Quarters again and the men did much better than on yesterday showing that they only need practice to become proficient.

At Sea, Friday July 21st 1865
Lat: 34°12′N.   Course SE by E 3/4 E   62 m.   Bar 30.05 to 30.18
Long: 138°24′W.   Wind Var. Calm & NW to NE.   Ther 68° to 79°
Today we broke out and restowed the after hold. This is about the 7th time we have had to do this tedious work. Receiving as we have been doing fresh installments of provisions from every prize it is impossible to keep the holds in order. The NE breeze today came to us & commenced very light and went on increasing.

At Sea, Saturday July 22d 1865
Lat: 32°55′N.   Course SE by E 1/2 E   156 m.   Ther 68° to 79°
Long: 135°41′W   Wind Nd & Sd   Bar. 30.05 to 30.18
The NE breeze continued and gradually freshened, coming on in squalls, these squalls coming up in fog. Up to a late hour we carried on all sail, staysails & port studding sails. Tonight we took in studding sails and hove the long [log], she ran out all the line 12 knots. The breeze freshened, took in Royals and Staysails and found her going 13 knots. This was done under Topgallant sails and nearly close hauled. This is splendid work.

At Sea, Sunday July 23d 1865
Lat: 30°14′N.   Course SE 1/2 S 208 m.   Ther. 67° to 69°
Long: 133°07′W Wind NE   Bar. 30.07 to 30.00
All hail another day of rest. I feel that I enjoy this holy day more and more as they come. I feel now that I would like to be a good man, a christian. I feel more in earnest when I commune with my God and I feel more faith in my prayers being heard, listened to and answered than formerly. God grant that I may lead such a life, as justly to lead one to expect to be saved; but oh! what a vast change is yet to be undergone. Like everything else the more you see,

the more you appreciate what remains to be seen. Today we have done better sailing than ever before. We were under all staysails & Royals close to the wind with our light sails lifting most of the time and for four consecutive hours we went 13 knots. With the same wind two points aloft the beam, same sail, yards a little braced in I am sure we would have gone 15 or 16 knots. This is fine work.

> At Sea, Monday July 24th 1865
> Lat: 27°12′N.   Course SE 1/4 S   249 m.   Ther 66° to 69°
> Long: 129°56′W.   Wind NE to ENE.   Bar. 29.97 to 28.97

Today we have been slipping along very much under all sail by the wind steering so as to clear Henderson's, a small island distant about 240 miles.[2] This will be the last island which will probably give us any uneasiness. The greatest pest of the ship, Henry Canning (Lds) was reported to me for fighting. I triced him up for three hours. He is more trouble than he is worth. I wish he was out of the ship. We have a fine trade sky, smooth sea & moderate breeze.

> At Sea, Tuesday July 25th 1865
> Lat: 25°25′25″N.   Course SE 1/4 S   147 m.   Bar. 29.85 to 29.90
> Long: 128°04′W.   Wind NE by E to NNE   Ther. 68° to 73°

This morning I got up early and found it nearly calm, we having lost what were supposed to be the NE trades. We must have been too hasty in coming to the conclusion. Today we have had light, baffling airs from the Nd & Ed, which may be the dolldrums [sic] and which I trust will turn into the regular trades. We have been under all sail, wind on the port beam until tonight when we took in our studding sails. We exercised at Genl. Quarters and the men did pretty well. All day I have been thinking of my dear ones at home, and taking the report about the occupation of Virginia as true my thoughts are sad! sad!! sad!!! Sometimes (for I am always thinking of them), when I reflect upon the helpless and perfectly destitute condition of my dear sisters, I am driven almost to madness. Then comes the warning "trust in the Lord." Oh! God grant me this power of trusting, I pray.

> At Sea, Wednesday July 26th 1865
> Lat: 24°40′N.   Course SE   63 m.   Bar. 29.90 to 29.93
> Long: 127°16′W.   Wind Varble Nd & E   Ther. 70° to 72°

Today we have had light variable airs and conclude that we were too hasty in concluding that we had taken the trade winds so high, and that we have not yet caught them. I trust we may soon have them. This afternoon Smith Lee was taken sick and I took his watch.

At Sea, Thursday July 27th 1865
Lat 23°22′30″N.   Course SE 1/4 S   107 m.   Bar. [29.91-29.94]
Long 125°50′W.   Wind [Nd & Ed Var]   Ther. [68°-74°]

The early part of the day we had light airs and the latter part we have the breeze from the Nd & Ed which we hope is the regular trade wind. Jack Grimball came off the [sick] list, and Smith Lee went on. I shall take his watch so as to prevent them going into three watches, as I do not think Grimball able to keep them.

At Sea, Friday July 28th 1865
Lat: 21°19′N.   Course. SE 1/2 E   190 m.   Ther. 70° to 76°
Long: 123°01′30″W.   Wind. Nd & Ed   Bar. 29.86 to 29.75

All day we have been ripping along nicely under all plain sail and staysails. Towards night we reduced sail to double reefed topsails. Weather pleasant. During my watch we made in four hours 44.2 miles which is about 11 knots an hour. This is doing very well.

At Sea, Saturday July 29th 1865
Lat: 19°17′N.   Course. SSE 1/4 E.   135 m.   Ther. 76° to 81°
Long: 122°00′W.   Wind Nd & Ed, Ed & Ed & Sd
Bar. 29.68 to 29.78

Strong breeze and high sea; both moderated towards night. Made sail to whole topsails.

At Sea, Sunday July 30th 1865
Lat: 17°49′N.   Course South   88 m.   Bar. 29.75 to 29.85
Long: 122°00′W.   Wind ESE & Var.   Ther. 77° to 87°

Made all sail to Royals. Towards night the wind grew very light. Another day of rest. I have spent it nearly all the time in my room, except when I was on watch. I read the church service, and reread my letters. Oh what a consolation it would be if I only knew that all was going on well in our dear country. When I think how long it has been since we heard from there and how many changes may have taken place it makes me very sad, and when I get back I will be afraid to ask for anyone, for fear, by the chances of war, some accident may have happened. God grant thy protection I humbly pray.

At Sea, Monday July 31st 1865
Lat: 17°52′W [N]   Course W 1/2 N   32 m.   Bar. 29.84 to 29.90
Long: 122°33′30″W.   Wind Calm, West & NW   Ther. 79° to 84°

Until now it was a dead calm. We have lost our NE trades entirely I fear. This is the last day of July. We have traversed three tracks of vessels i.e. to China,

Japan and [the] Sandwich Islands and have not seen a single sail. I wish we could see a vessel if but to get some news. We have none since we heard of the death of President Lincoln. I trust that none of our people had anything to do with it. If he had been killed in battle 'twould have been the fate of war; but not to be assassinated.

At Sea, Tuesday August 1st 1865
Lat: 17°10'N.   Course SE 1/2 S   54 m.   Bar. 29.90 to .85.
Long: 121°58'W.   Wind Nd & Ed, Nd   Ther. 81° to 78°
We have had light breezes all day. Had all sail set.

At Sea. Wednesday August 2d 1865
Lat: 16°20'N.   Course SE 1/4 S.   68 m.   Bar. 29.78 to .86
Long: 121°11'W.   Wind NW, N by E, Calm & SE.   Ther. 78° to 87°
The darkest day of my life. The past is gone for naught—the future as dark as the blackest night. Oh! God protect and comfort us I pray. In a few words I will say why we are plunged into the deepest distress that ever men were thrown. At 12.30 made a sail bearing NW. Got up steam and made chase. Overhauled the chase which hoisted English colors, an iron Bark. Boarded her: she proved to be the Bark *Baracouta* from San Francisco 13 days ago, bound to Liverpool. She brought us our death knell, a knell worse than death. Our dear country has been overrun; our President captured; our armies & navy surrendered; our people subjugated. Oh! God aid us to stand up under this, thy visitation. There is no doubting the truth of this news. We now have no country, no flag, no home. We have lost all but our honor & self respect, and I hope our trust in God Almighty. Were men ever so situated. The Captain gave me an order to dismount & strike our battery, turn in all arms except the private arms, and disarm the vessel, as no more depredations, of course, upon the United States shipping will be done. We went sorrowfully to work making preparations but night coming on, we will await tomorrow to finish our work. Hoisted propeller and made all plain sail. I feel, that were it not for my dear ones at home, I would rather die than live. Nearly all our work in the Arctic must have been done after this terrible visitation, but God knows we were ignorant. When I think of my darlings at home, and all our dear ones, my heart bleeds in anguish. From my father's position I can form no idea what they will do with him. He is excluded from their amnesty proclamation, and God's intervention alone can induce them to act so leniently as to spare his life. Beverley was in the army, but I pray God that he may be spared. What is then to become of my five sisters and two little Brothers. They have no means, no property, and God alone knows what is to prevent them from starving. Trust in the Lord. "I have been young, and now am old, but never have I seen the righteous man forsaken, or his children begging bread." Let this be my

motto until I can get safely to some port. Oh! God protect them for Christ's sake. I am almost mad, and will lay down my pen.

At Sea, Thursday August 3d 1865
Lat: 15°52′N.   Course SW 1/4 W   42 m.   Bar. 29.77 to 29.83
Long: 121°44′W   Wind. SE, E by S, Var.   Ther. 79° to 84°

Today we have been going slowly & sorrowfully along with a very light breeze. In obedience to the order which I received from the Captain upon the receipt of the melancholly news which reached us on yesterday, I struck all our battery below, dismounting the guns and striking down also the carraiges [sic]— also fired off all the pistols and muskets and boxed them up, disarming the ship. This will prove to any but the most prejudiced enemy that we are no longer a vessel having any intention of making any captures. I never undertook a more painful piece of work, rendered so by the attending causes. When I think that all our privations, trials, loss of life & blood since the war have such an end, I scarce know what to think or do. We are certainly a pitiable people. To think of our fair country being overrun, and our people subjugated, conquered and reduced to a state of slavery which is worse than death. This, of itself, is enough to distract me, but what of my dear ones. Who will protect them? Who will feed them? Who will comfort them? There is but one who can. He who afflicts can comfort—God!!! All powerful!! All mighty!! Oh! God give me the christian eye to see threw all this darkness thy power to save! Teach me to resign my all to thee!!

At Sea, Friday August 4th 1865.
Lat: 14°11′N.   S 3/4 E 102 miles.(course)   Bar. 29.80 to 29.83
Long: 121°29′W.   Wind ENE & NE.   Ther. 80° to 88°.

All day we have had light airs and calms. It is deemed proper that we should cross the Equator to the Eastward of 115 W. in order to clear with the SE trades the Tahita [sic] group of islands.[3] We are making a poor out at our attempt. I trust that we may soon have a change for the better. All day my mind has been distracted by the most painful thoughts. Oh! that I were a good Christian that I might with true faith resign myself to my fate.

At Sea, Saturday August 5th 1865
Lat: 12°44′N.   Course S by E 1/2 E.   92 m.   Bar. 29.75 to .82
Long: 121°03′W.   Wind Nd & Ed, Var'ble & calm.
    Ther. 80° to 86°

Today we dismounted our two signal 12 pdrs, and struck the carraiges [sic] below but having no room for the guns, we secured them on deck. The wind is so light and adverse that we got up steam & commenced to use our engines.

At Sea, Sunday Aug: 6th 1865
Lat: 10°07'N.   Course SE 3/4 S.   193 m.   Bar. 29.75 to 29.86
Long: 119°13'W.   Wind Sd & Ed, Sd & Sd & Wd.
  Ther 74° to 84°

Getting a breeze from the Sd & Wd we hoisted propeller and made all sail, taking it in as necessary. A day of rest. I read the morning service, and read my letters. Those of my darling Pattie! Oh the fondest wish of my heart was to call her mine. All, all is blasted! All, all is gone save honor, self-respect and love. They are fresh as ever.

At Sea, Monday August 7th 1865.
Lat: 9°14'N.   Course E by S 1/2 S.   171 m.   Ther 71° to 82°
Long: 116°29'W.   Wind S by W, SSW & Var.   Bar. 29.80 .85

Commenced overcast & squally with strong breezes. Double reefed the fore & main topsails; afterwards made sail. At 5 P.M. as the wind headed us off to ENE, we wore ship to the SE. I rove off a new, full set of braces. I feel so melancholy that I can scarcely keep a cheerful face. How difficult it is to act what you can't feel.

At Sea, Tuesday August 8th 1865
Lat: 8°41'N.   Course E by S   188 m.   Bar 29.80-.85
Long: 113°22'W.   Wind Sd & Ed & Sd.   Ther. 78° to 81°

Employed making all necessary preparations for bad weather, i.e. the "brave westerlys." Got our boats inboard. Oh! God how cast down I feel, when my thoughts revert to my country & dear ones, and they rarely stray therefrom. I feel that God alone can give me strength to bear such adversity.

At Sea, Wednesday August 9th 1865
Lat: 8°07'N.   Course E by S 1/2 S   128 m.   Bar. 29.80/.87
Long: 111°17'W.   Winds Variable   Ther. 78° to 80°

Ship under all plain sail; reducing to occasional rain & wind & squalls. Rove off our running gear fore & aft. To know how I feel would give anyone the blues. How my position is altered; no country; no home; no profession, and alas, to think the fondest wish of my heart, i.e. to marry, must be abandoned. Oh! my darling Pattie; how can I give thee up?!! God grant me support!!!

At Sea, Thursday August 10th 1865.
Lat: 7°28'N.   Course E by S 3/4 S   108 m.   Bar. 29.80/.88
Long: 109°25'W.   Winds Variable   Ther. 78°/81°

Occasional rain squalls. At 1 P.M. headed off to E by N tacked to the Wd. Ship under all plain sail, which was reduced as necessary. I am continually thinking of my dear ones. What is to keep them from starving I cannot imagine.

And my poor dear old father what will be his fate. I dread to dwell upon it, but I am prepared to hear the worst. I fear that they will deal out harshness.

At Sea, Friday August 11th 1865.
Lat: 6°19′N.   Course SE by E   121 m.   Bar. 29.77/29.86
Long: 107°45′W.   Winds. Sd, Variable   Ther. 80°/77°

At 3.30 tacked to the Sd & Ed at 3. P.M. tacked to Sd & Wd. at 6.30 wore to the Sd & Ed. We are literally beating to the Sd. when we should have the NE trades—these have entirely failed us. I suppose that the Sun's declination being about our latitude causes this. Our winds are from the Sd & very light but with heavy squalls. We are all wonderfully blue. All will be adrift as soon as we get ashore.

At Sea, Saturday August 12th 1865
Lat: 5°57′N.   Course SW1/2S   43 m.   Bar. 29.75/.85
Long 108°13′W   Winds Var'ble, Sd.   Ther. 75°/79°

All day we have had moderate & variable winds from the Sd, and kept the ship, as the winds veered & hauled on that tack upon which we could make the most Southing. My spirits are no better. I feel ten years older than I did before this news reached me. Oh! God give me the power to look up to Thee and with Christian resignation to say "Thy will be done."

At Sea, Sunday August 13th 1865.
Lat: N. 5°29′   Course W by S 1/4 S   116 m   Bar. 29.80/.88
Long: 110°05′W.   Wind Variable.   Ther 76°/80°

Still have adverse winds—beating to the Sd, going about when by so doing we could make more by it. Oh! how carefully I read my morning service today. How earnestly did I pray Almighty God to give our afflicted people his kind protection. I read my darling Pattie's letters. Oh how sad was this perusal compared with the former ones.

At Sea, Monday August 14th 1865
Lat: 5°20′N.   Course W 1/4 S   134 m.   Bar. 29.89/.95
Long: 112°19′W.   Wind Sd & Variable.   Ther. 74°/75°

Still making a dead beat of it. Started to get up steam but broke one of the screws of a guide rod, and had to delay until 8.20 P.M. for repairs, when we started Engine on our course under steam & fore & aft sail. Stowed afterwards all fore & aft sail.

At Sea, Tuesday August 15th 1865
Lat: 3°09′N.   Course SSW 1/2 W   146 m.   Bar. 29.88/.98
Long: 113°27′W.   Wind Sd & Sd & Ed.   Ther. 72°/75°

Set fore & aft sails. At 7 P.M., the wind being fair made sail, and stopped steaming, hoisting the Propeller. We are all gloomy and will be so until we get to port and hear what is the fate of our dear ones—for the present we can only pray to get safely to some neutral port without capture.

At Sea, Wednesday August 16th 1865
Lat: 1°10′N.   Course SW   170 m.   Bar. 29.77/.85
Long: 115°29′W.   Wind Sd & Ed.   Ther. 71°/76°

With good weather we feel better—I, simply because I know that each friendly breeze takes me closer to a port where I can hear of my dear ones. I care not for myself, for had I no dear sisters & brothers & father dependent on me, and no dear Pattie to love more than aught else, I would just as willingly die as live. Under all sail, going nicely along.

At Sea, Thursday Aug 17th 1865.
Lat: 00°48′S   Course SW 3/4 S   146 m.   Bar. 29.80/.85
Long: 116°56′W.   Wind. SE & SE by S.   Ther. 71°/75°

Some time in the morning watch we crossed the "Line." Again we are in the Southern Hemisphere, and its numerous stars are brightly lighting our weary way. The Southern Cross, Antares, and the Sickle are looking brightly on us. Oh how I wish we were just going into the Northern Hemisphere on the Atlantic side. All will be well, if God so wills it. Trust in Him.

At Sea, Friday Aug 18th 1865
Lat: 3°05′S.   Course SW 1/2 S   176 miles   Bar.29.79/.87
Long: 118°46′W.   Wind. SE & SE by E.   Ther. 75°/77°

During the whole day we have had a fine breeze which sent us nobly on at from 9 to 11 knots per hour. We were under all sail by the wind only reducing to squalls. I trust that these winds may keep by us, and send us quickly to where our dear ones may learn that we are still alive. I have no doubt but that we have been repeatedly reported lost. I trust that those at home may not credit any idle reports.

At Sea, Saturday August 19th 1865
Lat: 6°11′S.   Course SW by S   225 m.   Bar. 29.80/.95
Long: 120°52′W.   Wind SE, SE by E, ESE   Ther. 75°/79°

Our fine winds continue sending us along nicely. They fresh[en]ed so that we had to reef down to them but we soon ran up our topsails again. Our ship is getting light and we have to watch her carefully. Having been out so long it stands to reason that her weight is greatly decreased. The guns being below make a most perceptible difference in her stability.

At Sea, Sunday August 20th 1865
Lat: 9°08'S.   Course S by W 3/4 W   188 m.   Bar 29.85/.90
Long: 121°04'W.   Wind ESE, SE by E, SE   Ther. 76°/80°

Still our wind holds. Most of the time we had Royals set but sometimes reduced sail to squalls. During the afternoon she has gone from 9 1/2 to 12 knots per hour. I find it impossible to keep a cheerful face. I cannot act such deception. Our Paymaster W Breedlove Smith was 24 years old today. We celebrated it without any extra show, as salt beef is the go.

At Sea, Monday Aug. 21st 1865
Lat: 12°20'S   Course S by W 3/4 W   205 m.   Bar. 29.90/29.84
Long: 123°07'W.   Wind. SE & SE by S.   Ther. 75°/78°

Our wind still holds and we are getting rapidly on. We made & reduced sail as necessary. Our ship is sailing very well. I will not attempt to put my painful thoughts on paper. Were the paper white, they would render it blue. Our diet is regularly slim, regularly salt, and I would be ashamed to look a salted pig or cow in the face. What we have however is very good in its way but it is a salt road.

At Sea, Tuesday August 22d 1865.
Lat: 15°30'S.   Course SSW 1/2 W   214 m.   Bar. 29.88/.96
Long: 124°47'W.   Wind. Sd & Ed.   Ther. 75°/77°

The same winds continue. Sometimes we are under topgallantsails, and fifteen minutes afterwards we are under double reefed topsails. These are noble trades. Oh! how I wish I knew the fate of my dear ones. My dear father. Will he be pardoned or will he be hung as they would hang a dog. Oh! my God: how sorely thou hast afflicted us !! Give, oh! Give us power to stand up under it.

At Sea, Wednesday August 23rd 1865
Lat: 19°02'S.   Course S by W 3/4 W   227 m   Bar. 29.91/30.05
Long: 126°12'W.   Wind ESE to SE   Ther. 75°

And still these good trades hold. We have gone from 7 knots to 12 1/2. The ship is sailing beautifully. Made & reduced sail as necessary. A great many of my messmates outwardly appear cheerful. I cannot rally. When I smile I feel astonished at myself. Oh! God give us the power with Christian resignation to support the terrible, prostrating blow with which we are visited.

At Sea, Thursday August 24th 1865
Lat: 22°26'S   Course S by W 1/2 W   214 m   Bar. 30.07/30.00
Long: 127°15'W.   Wind ESE, E, & Baffling   Ther. 73° to 75°

Our trades I fear are failing us, at the latter part of the day we have had baffling airs from the Wd of South—however we are going nicely on. Today was Chew's 24th birthday. We are I expect the youngest set of officers who ever went to sea. The oldest member of our mess (Dr. Lining) is but 31 and the others range from 28 to 24. There are but four older than I am, and I am not 26.[4]

At Sea, Friday August 25th 1865.
Lat: 25°06′S.   Course South   160 m   Bar. 30.05/29.97
Long: 127°19′W.   Wind ENE, NE, NW, North   Ther. 72° to 80°

The winds today have been baffling, and very changeable. I care not how soon we get the "brave westerlies" which are to run us around. The book of Job would be thrown in the distance if I were to record my feeling. "Let us live with a hope," or as my darling Pattie says "Hope on; hope ever."

At Sea, Saturday August 26th 1865
Lat: 27°28′S.   Course. South   142 m   Bar. 29.95/.69
Long: 127°20′W.   Wind North & NW by N & W by S
Ther. 72° to 75°

Wind changeable. At 5.15 we were under all studding sails when the wind suddenly shifted in a rain squall seven points; reduced sail to close reefed topsails, afterwards making sail again. Tonight we have what we hope may prove a good westerly breeze. I trust our conjectures may prove correct.

At Sea, Sunday August 27th 1865
Lat: 30°06′S.   Course SE 1/4 S   206 m   Bar. 29.61/30.00
Long: 124°50′W   Wind. Sd & Wd.   Ther. 50° to 60°

This morning we had moderate gales from the westward. We made sail as it abated which was not long. Towards night the wind became quite light. Spent my sabbath nearly entirely in my room reading the service, and my darling's letters. Oh! what a trial it is to think that I may never be in a position pecuniarily to ask her to be mine. It seems to me that I love her more than I ever did.

At Sea, Monday August 28th 1865.
Lat: 31°05′S.   Course SE1/2S   79 m.   Bar. 30.00/30.13
Long: 123°52′W.   Winds Sd & Wd, Nd & Wd & Var.
Ther. 60°/62°

Winds very light and variable—made the most of them by making all sail. The weather now is delightful, neither too warm nor too cold and if we only had a good wind to send us in we would be a blessed people. As it is, never did a set of men have it more clearly proven that God was with them. Oh! if our dear country were free, how happy I should be.

At Sea, Tuesday August 29th 1965.
Lat: 33°05′S   Course S1/2E   120 m.   Bar. 30.10/29.58
Long: 123°36′W.   Winds North.   Ther. 61° to 66°

Winds gradually freshening all day. Made sail to all studding sails on both sides, afterwards reduced down to Royals and later, as the wind freshened, took in Royals. At 10 the ship was going 13 1/2 knots under topsails and courses nearly before the wind. This is remarkably good sailing. Oh! how I long to know the fate of my dear ones.

At Sea, Wednesday August 30th 1865.
Lat: 36°44′S   Course S3/4E   221 m.   Bar 29.55/29.30
Long: 123°01′W   Wind N, W, WSW & NW   Ther. 60° to 61°

Commenced fresh—double reefed the fore & main topsails—afterwards made sail to Royals. Towards night it came in fresh and squally from the NW and we reduced down to topsails. My thoughts are continually of my dear ones, and are most painful. If I only knew that they were all alive and not starving, Oh! how happy I would be.

At Sea. Thursday August 31st 1865.
Lat: 39°18′S.   Course SE1/4S   209 M.   Bar. 29.39/29.56
Long: 120°02W   Winds. W.N.W.   Ther. 52°/57°

The ship has been sailing well, very well, all day, going for hours in succession 13 knots with the wind nearly aft. Made and reduced sail as necessary. At night under all plain sail. Well, this is the last of August. Looking at what I have gone threw with during this month, I will always recall it as the most trying time of my life.

At Sea, Friday September 1st 1865.
Lat: 42°02′S.   Course SE 1/2 S   211 m   Bar. 29.43/29.40
Long: 117°08′W   Winds W NW, NW & Calm   Ther. 50°/57°

Carrying all studding sails in day time and reducing down to plain sail at night. Towards midnight it died out to a calm. At midnight wore ship to the Sd & Wd. Sent Vanavery to the mast head for insolence and kept him there for nine hours. When he came down he was like a lamb. A good thrashing would do him great good.

At Sea, Saturday September 2d 1865
Lat: 45°07'S [43°07'S]   Course SE 3/4 E   68 m   Bar. 29.40/29.70
Long: 116°39'W.   Wind Sd & Ed   Ther. 45°/50°

Commenced with strong wind from Sd & Ed. barometer low, and threatening appearances. Close reefed the topsails. Afterwards made sail to Topgallant sails. Wore ship several times during the day. Last two hours it was calm. Wore to SSW. Sent Peter Raymond & Thos: Evans to the mast head for fighting. It is getting quite cold.

At Sea, Sunday September 3rd 1865
Lat: 43°08'S.   Course. W by S   5 m.   Bar 29.70/.85
Long: 116°46'W.   Wind. Calm & Variable   Ther. 44° to 50°

Winds very light and variable. We made only about 5 miles in the 24 hours. This is in consequence of weaving about so often. Oh how I wish for our "brave westerlys." Here we ought to have a strong wind from the NW. but we have nothing of the sought [sic]. Spent the day in my room, read service and my letters.

At Sea, Monday September 4th 1865
Lat: 43°15'S.   Course SE by S   8 m.   Bar. 29.80/.90
Long: 116°40'W.   Wind Calm & South   Ther. 44° to 47°

Wind from various Southerly points and calm. Our runs are so small that I feel that we are doing nothing to forward the most earnest wishes of all onboard to get where we can hear from our homes. Oh! for the "brave westerlys," of which we are told so much. It is quite cold.

At Sea, Tuesday September 5th 1865
Lat: 43°42'S   Course E by S 1/2 S   93 m.   Bar. 29.90/30.00
Long: 114°38'W.   Wind. Varble, Sd & Ed & Sd   Ther. 44° to 47°

Wind very changeable—and light. I trust that we may not have many more such idle days as the last three. Wore ship several times during the day trying to make southings.

At Sea, Wednesday September 6th 1865.
Lat: 45°43'S.   Course SE 1/2 E   190 m   Bar. 29.93/.90
Long: 111°14'W   Wind S SSW   Ther. 44° to 46°

We have had a moderate SW sea all day accompanied by a light breeze. We have carried all plain sail. Unbent all our studding sails. I trust this breeze will haul to the NW and shove us along on our course. I am weary, weary, weary. No language can express my broken hearted feelings.

At Sea, Thursday September 7th 1865.
    Lat: 47°16′S.   Course SE 1/4 S   139 m   Bar. 29.90/.67
    Long: 108°46′W   Wind NNW to NW   Ther. 44° to 48°

As I hoped the SW wind hauled to the NW, and we right before it in our course. Ship under all plain sail.

At Sea, Friday September 8th 1865.
    Lat: 49°42′S.   Course SE 1/2 S   192 [m.]   Bar. 29.60/.28
    Long: 105°41′W   Wind NW to WNW   Ther 42°/45°

Fresher breeze all day and we going nicely on our course right before it. Sent down Royal yards. The ship was at 11 A.M. going 14 miles per hour—from 1 to 10 P.M. she went 14, 14 1/2 & 15 for each hour—this was under topgallant sails & foresail. At 8 the wind hauled a little on the Port quarter—gave her the mainsail and she went 16 1/2 knots. This is fine work.

At Sea, Saturday September 9th 1865
    Lat: 51°50′S   Course SE by E 1/4 E   262 m   Bar. 29.28/.50
    Long 99°40′W.   Wind. SW to W by S   Ther. 40°/45°

During these twenty four hours, that is from noon yesterday to noon today, she has made *262* miles good—this is the best she has ever made with us—being an average of 11 knots per hour. By log she ran 278 miles but she had a current of 16 miles against her. The wind hauled to SW and then to West.

At Sea, Sunday September 10th 1865.
    Lat: 52°49′S   Course E by S 1/2 S   204 m.   Bar. 29.55/30.00
    Long: 94°20′W.   Wind. W by S   Ther. 43°/44°

Going along nicely under topsails, foresail, Fore & main topmast staysail. Heavy sea from the westward. Read the services for the day and my letters from my dear Pattie, commencing with my God and my darling P——.... [Sentence scratched out, but some words can be read.—*Ed.*] [... I have lost her. I can never love another.] My love for her was under the circumstances most peculiar.

At Sea, Monday September 11th 1865.
    Lat: 53°40′S   Course E by S 1/2 S   188 m.   Bar. 29.60
    Long: 89°24′W   Wind WNW to W by N.   Ther. 40° to 42°

Ship under all sail. Crossed the Royal yard. Here where we have been led to believe that we might expect the most terrible weather, we are having as fine weather as I ever want to see. It is a little cold but that is nothing. I suppose that the weather off the pitch of Cape Horn will make up for all this. Nous verrons.

At Sea, Tuesday September 12th 1865.
Lat: 54°36'S   Course E by S 1/2 S   168 m   Bar. 29.55/.60
Long: 84°54'W   Wind. N, to NNW.   Ther. 42°/39°

Ship generally under all plain sail, made and reduced as necessary. Saw a large ship on the beam about 10 miles off heading a little higher up to the Ed than ourselves. Kept in company. This is the first sail of any kind which we have seen since the *Baracuta*. We are now getting into the thoroughfare.

At Sea, Wednesday September 13th 1865.
Lat: 55°46'S.   Course E by S 1/2 S   230 m   Bar. 29.67/.65
Long: 73°31'W.   Wind NNW to N by W.   Ther. 37° to 42°

Fresh breeze; saw the ship on the lee beam, she hoisted English colors & signalized but we did not reply.[5] She walked right away from us most shamefully —got up the Port Fore Topmast studding sail but she still beat us.[6] Past [*sic*] the Eng: ship *West Australian* Cardiff to Valparaiso but did not reply to signals. Passed three other vessels bound to the Westward.

At Sea, Thursday September 14th 1865.
Lat: 56°50'S   Course E by S 1/4 S   240 m.   Bar. 29.65
Long: 71°39'W   Wind NNW to N by E   Ther. 42° to 45°

Ship under Topgallant studding sails. Tonight at 12 O'c: we passed about 50 miles to the Sd of Diego Ramerez rock which is to the Sd of Cape Horn and about 90 miles to the Westward. The weather remains fine but the wind's hauling to the Eastward of North is very unfavorable. I never saw better weather. Passed two sails going to the Westward.

At Sea, Friday September 15th 1865
Lat: 57°24'S.   Course. E by S   204 m.   Bar. 29.65/.55
Long: 65°31'W.   Wind. NW by W/NNW   Ther. 42°/39°

Today we passed Cape Horn, and we got a tartar. Commenced with a fresh gale from NNW. We reduced down to three close reefed topsails and reefed foresail & fore staysail. Beautifully clear weather, but blowing like scissors, with a heavy sea. Getting on about 5 knots per hour. Quite cold. I suppose we will have it heavy.

At Sea, Saturday September 16th 1865
Lat: 57°22'S   Course East   109 m.   Bar. 29.55/29.40
Long: 62°09'W.   Wind Nd & Wd.   Ther. 38°/36°

Moderate gales and strong winds, with heavy sea, and heavy rain squall. Under close reefed topsails & staysails & foresails reefed. About 1 P.M. set the mainsail reefed, also the main storm staysail. I trust that we will soon be out of the squally influences of Cape Horn. The next thing which we have to look out for will be ice bergs.

At Sea, Sunday September 17th 1865.
Lat: 56°27'S   Course E by N 1/4 N   228 [m]   Bar. 29.55/.90
Long: 55°22'W.   Wind West to North   Ther. 36°/40°

Today we have had fresh winds. Mastheaded the topsails and gave her the outer & inner jibs. These Northerly winds are crowding us too far to the Eastward but to look out for the Georgian islands and Shag rock, together with ice bergs.[7] O! how I wish that our dear ones could know that we are still in the "water of the living." I have no doubt that a great many think us lost.

At Sea, Monday September 18th 1865
Lat: 54°17'S.   Course NE by E   236 [m]   Bar. 30.35/30.07
Long: 49°39'W.   Wind WNW/NW by W   Ther. 39°/37°

Strong winds, moderate gales and heavy sea. Ship under whole topsails and courses. From noon yesterday to noon today we made a good run, but our winds are cold and disagreeable, but thus far "rounding the Horn" is a very small affair, and we are going cheerfully (?) on.

At Sea, Tuesday September 19th 1865.
Lat: 52°46'S   Course NE 3/4 E   153 m.   Bar. 29.55/29.25
Long: 46°13'W   Wind NW by W to NW.   Ther. 35°/38°

Moderate gales, strong winds and heavy sea continue. Closed [sic] reefed the Mizen, double reefed fore & main topsails & reefed courses. Passing rain showers at intervals. Thank goodness we are now well clear of Shag Rock.

At Sea, Wednesday September 20th 1865
Lat: 51°16'S   Course NE by E 1/2 E   191 m.   Bar. 30.02/ 29.61
Long: 41°39'W.   Wind. NW/N by W   Ther. 34°/39°

Weather much more moderate. Made sail to whole topsails, courses & Top Gallant sails. Set the Royals but soon took them in. Sea rapidly going down. Today our enemy, ice, made its appearance. At first we saw a small piece and then several large ice bergs, some of which were very close, heavy fog occasionally. Doubled the watch to look out for ice.

At Sea, Thursday September 21st 1865.
Long: 38°36'W.   Course E by N 1/4 N   191 [m]   Bar. 29.20/.10
Lat: 51°49'S   Wind. N to WNW   Ther. 36°/39°

This wind is "bousing" us too far to the Ed. We wore ship this morning to the Wd and afterward to the Ed. Passing icebergs all day. Some of them are tremendous. The weather is pleasant but foggy in the vicinity of ice. The air from the ice is very cold but the water does not seem much [a]ffected. Some of the bergs seen today were upward of 300 feet high.

At Sea Friday September 22 1865.
Long: 36°00′W   Course NE   140 m.   Bar. 29.40/.44
Lat: 49°11′S   Wind Var. Nd & Ed & Nd & Wd
  Ther. 36°/42° & 44°

Smooth sea, pleasant weather, but the wind forcing us to the Ed. I trust we are out of all ice as the thermometer remains steadily up at from 40° to 44, though this morning it was 36°. Sent up all studding sail booms and made all plain sail by the wind.

At Sea, Saturday September 23d 1865
Lat: 47°58′S   Course NE by E 3/4 E   [166 m.]   Bar. 29.40/.45
Long: 32°17′W   Wind Nd & Wd   Ther. 44°

Our Northerly & NWterly winds continue. This is beyond doubt the Equinoctial weather, as the Sun crossed on yesterday. No more ice and I trust I may never see any more at sea. Ship under sail from Royals to Topsails as necessary.

At Sea, Sunday September 24th 1865.
Lat: 46°54′S   Course NE by E   115 [m]   Bar. 29.55/29.00
Long: 29°55′W   Wind Nd & Ed, Nd Vable & West & WSW
Ther. 42°/45°

Heavy sea from the Nd commenced with strong gales from the Nd & Wd & Nd & Ed. Ship under close reefed topsails. At 5 P.M. it died out nearly calm heading NW. We expected the wind from the Wd wore ship and had barely gotten round when it came out very fresh. Ship under close reefed fore & main topsails going through a heavy head sea, nearly before the wind.

At Sea, Monday September 25th 1865
Lat: 44°49′S   Course NNE 1/2 E   141 [m]   Bar. 29.30/.68
Long: 28°23′W   Wind W to NNW   Ther. 45°/48°

Moderately fresh breezes all day. Most of the time the ship was under all plain sail. Last night as soon as the head sea went down we made sail to Topgallant sails. All today it has been gradually hauling to the Nd.

At Sea, Tuesday September 26th 1865.
Lat: 43°41′S   Course NE by E 1/4 E   152 [m]   Bar. 29.50/00
Long: 25°20′W.   Wind. Nd, Nd & Ed & Sd & Wd   Ther. 48°

Wind hauled from NW to Nd & Ed and blew fresh we kept on the tack which gave us most northing. Passing showers. There was a short lull at 10 P.M. and we expected a similar shift to day before yesterday's. We wore to the Nd & Ed and barely got around before the wind, as we expected came out very fresh from W.S.W., blowing a gale.

At Sea, Wednesday September 27th 1865
Lat: 41°14′S   Course N by E   151 miles   Bar. 29.02/.50
Long: 24°40′W   Wind SW, WSW/W by S.   Ther. 44°/51°

Wind moderated but remained from the same quarter. We made sail to all studding sails, reducing as necessary. Got up our main Royal studdingsail booms and set the port sail. The ship now has bent and ready 3 Jibs, 3 topsails, 3 Courses, 3 Top Gallant sails, 3 Royals, 8 Staysails, 1 Spencer, 1 Spanker, 1 Gaff topsail and 12 Studding sails, making in all 38 sails. This is tremendous, is it not? She sails remarkably well under all circumstances, but being light, would not beat well.

At Sea, Thursday September 28th 1865.
Lat: 38°25′S   Course North   169 mi.   Bar. 29.45/.07
Long: 24°38′W   Wind Sd & Wd.   Ther. 45°/57°

Our wind still hangs on and we are going swiftly on our course. The wind is fresh, and is the same as that which is known at the Falkland Islands as the Pamparo [Pampero]. I hope it may continue as we are driving on under every stitch of drawing sail. Of course when we have a fair wind we feel more cheerful than with any other. God grant us a safe and speedy relief from our unfortunate position. God bless our dear ones.

9

In the name of honor . . . let us support the Captain . . .

September 29–November 3, 1865

At Sea, Friday September 29th 1865.
Lat: 34°25′S.   Course N 1°E   240 [m]   Bar 29.56/.90
Long: 24°36′W   Wind SSW, S by E   Ther. 54°/66°

The minds of a good many who were in favor of going to Cape Town seem very little quieted. There is a feeling approaching a panic among them which I consider very disgraceful and injurious. Some look as though they had already been hung. In the name of honor, birth & propriety let us support the Captain. Even if we are caught & hung, why, are we not men? Cannot we stand our fate like men, a fate which, unjust tho' it would be & has been, has been stood & met by men of all countries. No! let us throw aside this childishness, and trusting in God, stand like men to brave all consequences of our participation in the struggle now ended by Divine will, for all that is dear to man. God has afflicted us for some just & holy cause; by his will alone can even a sparrow fall. If we are captured, which is most improbable, it will [be] by his will; trust in him & him alone!!! Tonight we crossed our track of Nov: 29th 186[4]—ten months ago. In that time we have travelled over 45000 statute miles of water; we have been around the world, the first to carry our down-trodden flag around. We have done our work nobly, and honorably except in the eyes of our prejudiced enemies, who no doubt place us in the same category with Captain Kidd. Some 77 men signed the paper last night sent in, in favor of going to England and expressing their unbounded confidence in the Captain, and their determination to stand by him in anything he attempts.[1] Tho' I differed with him for reasons known to all, and thoroughly canvassed in my own mind, he has my unbounded support. I am willing to run any risk that he may incur. I humbly pray God to protect us. Grimball, Lee, Scales &

McNulty sent in a paper in which they heartily agree in his decision to go to England. Papers, petitions &c, &c. are not my fort[e] and as Executive Officer I will have nothing [to] do with them, for he has my support in anything except one, & that would be any attempt to go to a Yankee port. A large majority of the officers [who] are vehemently opposed to running the unnecessary risks of going to England, are in favor of going to Cape Town. I am very sorry to see so much temper shown on both sides. I myself am of the opinion that in a matter of such individual vital importance more weight should be given to the opinions of those officers who were not called into consultation. As I do not think that because a person has a Lieutenant's commission he is any better able than anyone else to decide a matter of common sense.[2]

At Sea, September 30th (Saturday) 1865.
Lat: 32°23′S.   Course North   122 m.   Bar. 29.92/30.00
Long: 24°28′W   Wind South.   Ther. 62°/66°

I never saw a more lovely day at sea than this has been, with a bright sun and smooth sea, and just breeze enough to prevent its being too warm. I wish we could strike the glorious SE. trades. These are sometimes even taken as far as 43° South, but as we will take them well up it is fair to suppose that we will be late in losing them. The breeze now is very light, but with all studding sails on both sides we are fanning ourselves along at the rate of 4, 5 & 6 knots. The fact is that she is so light that she go[es] well before the wind.

At Sea, Sunday October 1st 1865.
Lat: 30°37′S   Course N 2° W   106 [m]   Bar 29.97/30.00
Long: 24°32′W.   Wind Southerly   Ther. 58°/75°

Rarely have I ever seen a finer day. We have been fanning quietly along, until toward night we got the breeze light from SE. I trust that it is the commencement of the long wished for SE trades. I spent most of the day in my room, reading the Services for the day and reading the letters of my darling Pattie. Oh! how awful it is that there seems to be no prospect of my ever being able to ask her to be mine. When I asked before I had a profession to support us, but how changed!! I have lost all and have to commence again, with a dark future. Oh! how I love that dear girl!! Oh! how sad & heartbreaking to give up all hope of her being mine. This is the 1st day of October.

At Sea, Monday October 2d 1865.
Lat: 28°46′S.   Course North   110 m.   Bar. 29.90 29.85
Long 24°30′W.   Wind ESE & SE.   Ther. 60° to 66°

A beautiful day. The SE trades I verily believe are regularly set in. Gradually they freshened towards night. At 10 P.M. we were going 10 knots with the wind on the Starb'd beam or abaft with all (29) sails set. Got up a main top-mast Studding Sail, the first I ever saw set. I think it is one of the loveliest nights I ever beheld, clear, pleasant, good breeze & perfectly smoothe.

At Sea, Tuesday October 3rd 1865
Lat: 26°01'S.   Course N 1/4 W   165 m.   Bar 29.75/.88
Long: 24°43'W.   Wind Sd & Sd & Ed & SW (light)
    Ther 64°to 71°

Today our SE wind has failed us and has come out to the Westward of South. This rather shows that we were mistaken in supposing that we had the regular trades. We are however going ahead at about 5 miles per hour. Oh how I wish I could hear from my dear ones at home. I leave them in God's hands, as the sole remaining friend. How very anxious they must be about us.

At Sea, Wednesday October 4th 1865.
Lat: 23°51'S.   Course N 1/2 E   132 miles.   Bar. 29.82/.90
Long: 24°27'W.   Wind Varble, WNW, W, SW, S.   Ther. 67° to 74°

No trade wind yet. During the whole day we have had light, baffling airs from the Sd & Wd, Wd & Nd & Wd. I hope we may get them tomorrow. At 8 P.M. we were in 23°27'S latitude which places us just one mile to the northward of the Tropic of Capricorn. At 8 we had a partial eclipse of the moon which was very pretty. In looking at it I could but think that so many eyes so dear to us all are looking at it. This is in common and they no doubt have the same thoughts.

At Sea, Thursday October 5th 1865.
Lat: 22°22'S   Course N 1/4 E   90 m.   Bar. 29.80/.90
Long: 24°20'W.   Wind SSE to ESE   Ther. 68° to 70°

All day we have had a nice SE breeze which has been gradually freshening. This is, no doubt the SE trade wind which we so much desire. All hail it with joy, and all hearts leap with joy at the prospect of soon reaching a port at which we can obtain news from our afflicted country and of the fate of our dear ones. Our ship is now (10 P.M.) dashing nobly on at the rate of 9 1/2 miles per hour, with all sail set for a good breeze on the Starboard beam or quarter (for it is between the two). Oh how my poor heart yearns to know the fate of my dear ones. My dear father; have they bathed his silvery locks with blood; my dear brother; have they slain my dear sisters and brothers are they suffering *from want of food?* These thoughts harrow my brain. The answer is, God alone can tell. He alone can afflict, and He alone can comfort when afflicted!

At Sea, Friday October 6th 1865.
    Lat: 19°01′S.   Course N 2° W   201 miles.   Bar: 29.80/.95
    Long: 24°28′W.   Wind E by S, E by N, E by S, E   Ther: 70° to 74°

Our trade wind still continues and we are getting along comfortably and nicely. Employed in getting casks filled with salt water for ballast. I have been thinking all day long about my home and dear ones. The more I attempt to penetrate into the future, the darker it appears, and the more impenetrable seems its darkness. I cannot see what in the world I can do after I get onshore to support my darlings. Oh! God help me.

At Sea, Saturday October 7th 1865.
    Lat: 15°26′S.   Course N 2° W.   215 m.   Bar. 29.85/.90
    Long: 24°35′W.   Wind from E to ESE   Ther. 73° to 75°

Our trades continue more or less fresh during the day, and freshening during the evening and night. Ship under all starboard studding sails & staysails. Towards night took in Main Royal studding sail & Staysail. This morning at 3 A.M. passed close to a bark standing to the Wd. From the cut of her sails I should say she was English. Employed stowing casks of salt water in the hold so as to have our coal clear. At 8 the ship going about 12 knots. If the breeze continues will make a good run.

At Sea, Sunday October 8th 1865.
    Lat: 11°14′S.   Course N 1/4 W   252 miles   Bar: 29.80/.73
    Long: 24°48′W.   Wind from ESE to ENE.   Ther. 76° to 78°

Our trades still hold and we are ripping along at the rate of from 10 1/2 to 11 1/2 knots per hour. The ship is sailing beautifully. We are carrying all sail except the Main Royal Staysail and studding s'l. A day of rest. I read the service for the day and read over my letters. These last, which before always cheered me up, now make me feel very, very sad. I can't help from contrasting the present and past conditions of the writers of them. It is a great consolation to know that at our present rate, they will soon be relieved of any anxiety about my safety. One year ago today I sailed in this ship from London. It has been a year of constant anxiety and labor from then till now. And all to have such a sad, inglorious, pitiable & miserable end, is truly heartbreaking, but God ruleth.

At Sea, Monday October 9th 1865
    Lat: 7°00′S.   Course North   254 miles   Bar. 29.80/.75
    Long: 25°00′W.   Wind East to ESE.   Ther. 77° to 78°

Again we have made an excellent run, from noon yesterday to noon today being 254 miles. This is fine work for although we have a good trade wind, it is well abeam, some times forward and not very fresh. I sincerely trust that we may be run well to the north of the "line" by it. At 8 P.M. we were in about 5° S. latitude which again puts us to the northward of the Sun whose declination is six south. The weather will now as we leave the Sun be gradually getting cooler. How rapid and frequent have been our change[s] of temperature in the last year! Today three cases of scurvy made their appearance; I trust this disgusting and terrible complaint will not extend much further for it is painful, disagreeable and very often most terribly fatal. All day I have thought of my dear ones.

At Sea, Tuesday October 10th 1865.
Lat: 3°7'S   Course N 2° W   213 miles.   Bar 29.70 to 29.78
Long: 25°08'W.   Wind. ENE to ESE.   Ther. 78° to 80°

During the day our trades have continued but are not as fresh as before. Last night Mr. Alcott our sailmaker went to his room and found that someone had forced his chest open and taken out of it a pair of opera glasses. I determined to have a search as this is one of very many instances of theft. I had the berth deck cleaned and overhauled each bag but did not find the thief. Dr. McNulty got on one of his periodical drunks and was so abusive to some that he was reported to me. I by order of the Captain ordered him to confine himself to his quarters. He is a poor unfortunate whom I greatly pity on account of his weakness.

At Sea, Wednesday Oct: 11th 1865.
Lat: 0°5'30"S.   Course North   202 miles   Bar. 29.75 to 29.65
Long: 25°06'W.   Wind ESE to SE by S.   Ther. 78° to 82°

Our trades still hang to us. We crossed the "Line" today at 12:45 or thereabouts going 8 knots per hour. We are once more in the North Atlantic, and I for one, never expect to go out of it again, however we can never tell what may become of us. This morning the Captain told me to relieve Dr. McNulty from suspension if he was sober. I did so. The Captain had a conversation with him and afterwards told me the sum and substance of it. He said that he was not drunk, that his language to Mr. Blacker was caused by the latter using abusive language about the Captain, and that the pistol which I took out of his hand was only taken out by him to show to me. I at once sent for two officers who sustained me in saying that he was drunk. I learned from two sources that the quarrel between himself & Mr. Blacker originated in his own abusive language and that Mr. B—— said nothing of the Captain, and taking everything in connection I conclude that he tried to make it appear to the Captain, 1st that he was a partisan of his, and 2d, that my report about his being drunk & drawing the pistol, was an act of cruelty on my part. I made up my mind that my report should not be so treated or considered—for his every ground was false. I went to Scales and said that I wanted some one present when I had a conversation with him and Scales agreed to be present. I asked him if he intended to deny my report—he said "All I say, Sir, is that I was not drunk." I asked him if he was not intoxicated—he said he was. I asked him why he did not tell the Capt: so instead of leading him to believe that my report was false—he simply said, "Well, didn't I," I replied, ["]no.["] I then asked him if he took the pistol out to show to me—he said, "Yes." I said that he did not—he asked "How do you know." I replied that I was certain of it, and that I believed furthermore that he knew that he did not. He said, "Well, Sir, when we get onshore there is a way to settle this thing." I would be ready to do so. He said "Well then, 'You waive.'" ["]Yes, Sir,["] I replied, ["]I waive everything.["] I am sorry the whole thing took place, but after making the report and having pretty good evidence that he lied I was determined to tell him what I thought of what he said of my report. I suppose as I have told him he will challenge me. I certainly cannot tell him that he did not lie when I think that he did, and when every single thing goes to show it. Scales came to me afterward and said that McN—— wanted him to be his friend and bring me a challenge to settle it at once. S—— declined as he was already too much mixed up in it. He then went to Lee who consented. I suppose tomorrow will bring his mandate.

> At Sea, Thursday Oct: 12th 1865.
> Lat: 2°42′N.   Course N 1/2 W   168 m.   Bar. 29.60 to 29.75
> Long: 25°24′W.   Wind SSE & Variable.   Ther. 80° to 86°

We are beginning to lose our nice trade winds. This is the first day for the last seven that we have not made more than 200 miles. Ship under all sail. Saw a great many vessels passing to the Sd & Wd & Sd & Ed. This morning I was called on by Lieut: Lee, who is the only man in my mess with whom I am not on good terms and was given this note.

> (Copy). Str: *Shenandoah* At Sea Oct 12th 1865
> Lt: W. C. Whittle
>   Sir, I demand an explanation and withdrawal of the language you applied to me in the presence of Lt: Scales last evening. Should the demand appear extravagant, such other satisfaction as is looked for between gentlemen is expected at your earliest convenience. Lt: Lee will bring me your reply, Yours &c.
>   (Signed) Fredk. J. McNulty

I asked Scales if it were possible to settle this thing onshipboard [sic]—he replied no. I called Dr. Lining and asked him to act [as] my friend—he said he would—he agreed with me that he did not think that the thing could be settled until I got on shore. I told him that I agreed with him but that as I had given him an insult onboard I regretted that I could not give him satisfaction also. I told him to take this note to Lt: Lee, in reply.

C.S.Str: *Shenandoah*

At Sea, Oct: 12th 1865
Dr. F. J. McNulty

Sir, I have to acknowledge the receipt of your note of this morning through Lieut: Lee. My language to you on last evening in the presence of Lt: Scales explained itself. Under the circumstances I have but to accede to your demand for such satisfaction as you desire. As the ship is not a place where such things can be settled, as soon as we get onshore, full satisfaction will be given you.

Yours &c,
W. C. Whittle, Jr.

I told Lining to confer with Lee and if they could in any way arrange a plan for an earlier settlement to do so, if not, send the note. He told me that Lee agreed that under the circumstances it could not be settled at present—the note went, and I received as an answer that its terms were agreed to. Thus ends for the present this disagreeable affair. It must come off when we get onshore. I have always been opposed to duelling, but I have given an insult and really think that he (MN) did tell a lie. I must give him satisfaction and will meet him. I may have been wrong in not keeping my opinion that he had lied to myself but I could not do it, and will give him any satisfaction he may require in the fighting line. I think that Dr. MN's conduct is very discreditable. His statements about the origin of the quarrel between Mr. Blacker & himself was a fabrication and was used to induce the Captain to think that his trouble was caused by taking his part.[3]

At Sea, Friday Oct: 13th 1865.
Lat: 4°38′N.   Course N by E 1/2 E   123 m.   Bar. 29.60/.70
Long: 24°45′W.   Wind. Variable-Wd.   Ther. 80° to 84°

We have lost our trades and have light variable airs, and light rain. The weather is very hot.

At Sea, Saturday Oct: 14th 1865
Lat: 6°07′N.   Course N 1/2 E   90 miles.   Bar. 29.55/.66
Long: 24°36′W.   Wind SW to WNW.   Ther 79° to 80°

Light variable airs. Ship under all sail fanning along. At 3.30 it fell calm and started to get up steam but a light breeze springing up from the SW hauled the fires. Passing squalls of heavy rain. Employed catching drinking water. A great many sails insight [*sic*]. If we were as we used to be, we would have been running every which way to catch a prize. At 12 (mid) I was aroused by Chew's giving the order to haul down the Topmast studding sails—and then let fly studding sail tacks &c & let go Royal & Topgallant halliards. I jumped on deck and found that it was raining in torrents and we flat aback with a fresh NE squall. I took the deck, shortened sail, keeping the ship off before the wind, and then brought by. The squall was very fresh & blew our miz: royal away, & carried away the m'n royal studding sail boom. I was as wet as a drowned rat, and caught cold. I never saw it rain so in all my life.[4]

At Sea, Sunday October 15th 1865.
Lat: 7°59′N.   Course N 1/2 E   113 m.   Bar. 29.65/.70
Long: 24°21′W.   Wind Variable.   Ther. 82° to 86°
It has been hot all day—112° to 120° in the Sun. Passed a great many sails. Wind changing about all the time. Kept on that tack in which we could make most northing. Spent the day in my room, read the service & some of my letters.

At Sea, Monday October 16th 1865
Lat: 9°23′N.   Course N 1/2 W   85 m.   Bar: 29.75/.65
Long: 24°32′W.   Wind ENE to ESE
    Ther: 80° to 95° (in the shade) 110° (in Sun)
Slight airs and calms, and very warm weather. Towards midnight the clouds looked as though we might have the NE trades before daylight. I hope it may be so for I am getting tired of the slow work. During the day we saw three vessels standing to the Sd & Wd. One of these telegraphed her name as the *Annie Cheshia*. We made a calculation today of the distance we have run—by which we found that on the 12th of this month our runs by observation gave us 39,282 knots or upwards of 44,000 miles since we have been in commission.

At Sea, Tuesday October 17th 1865
Lat: 10°22′N.   Course N 3/4 W   60 m.   Bar. 29.65 to 29.70
Long: 24°42′W.   Wind. Var'ble NNE to SSW   Ther. 80° to 86°
Well here we are in an almost perfect calm. We are living now on the hope that we will have the NE trades tomorrow. I hope that we will not miss them as we did in the Pacific. Painted ship outside. Passed two vessels bound to the Sd & Wd. The weather is very hot.

At Sea, Wednesday October 18th 1865
Lat: 11°21′N.   Course NW 3/4 N   73 m.   Bar. 29.60/.75
Long: 25°25′W.   Wind. NE to NE by E   Ther. 78° to 83°

During the whole day we have had a moderate breeze from the NE which we hope is the regular NE trade. We have made the most of it being under all plain sail. This evening we passed a Bark standing about SSW. She was, judging from her sails, American. This with all of us, and particularly myself [was] an important anniversary. It is the day on which the little steamer *Laurel* and this ship met at Madeira one year ago. The day upon which we took onboard our battery, stores & officers, and in fact the birthday of the *Shenandoah*. Since this day 12 months ago, how many changes have we gone through. Then we were all rejoiced at and proud of having an opportunity of serving our country; alas, how changed; now, we are plunged into the most heartbreaking despair at having no country to serve. Oh God! give us the strength and faith to resign ourselves to thy will. To me the day is more dear in as much as it is the birthday of the dearest being on earth to me. This day twenty two years ago my darling Pattie was born. Most solemnly do I invoke God's blessing upon her. Oh! God! guard, rule and lead her I humbly pray, and grant that I may yet be able to call her mine own. It is the fondest wish of my heart, next to seeing my country free. Are not both hoping without hope? It would appear so, but the same hand which afflicts, can bless and aid. At dinner today, I filled my glass with port wine and silently drank her health. Oh! may she have many happy returns of the day. Many anxious thoughts has she had for me, for she loves me most dearly. And only to think that if the Yankees refuse us permission to enter the country, which I think more than likely, I may never see her again. The thought almost maddens me, but her motto "Hope on, hope ever," shall be mine.

At Sea, Thursday October 19th 1865
Lat: 13°37′N.   Course NW 1/4 N   182 m.   Bar. 29.60/.70
Long: 27°29′W.   Wind NE.   Ther. 80°/90° (shade) 100° (Sun)

All day we have had moderate trades, but they are rather too far to the Nd, to enable us to head our true course N by E. At 12 today we were almost exactly where we were one year ago on the 30th of October, which was the day after we took the *Alina* our first prize. We crossed our old track probably for the last time. We are now not more than 150 miles from Brava one of the Cape de Verdes. Today I witnessed one of the most beautiful sights I ever saw. It was the ann[u]lar eclipse of the sun. It commenced about 2.30 p.m. and lasted 'till about four. In the middle of it the moon's disc was right in the center of the sun, with a bright circle of the latter all around it. It was really beautiful. All these things take my thoughts back to my dear ones, feeling assured that they are looking at & admiring the same scene. All these things are sights admired by all however separated in distance.

At Sea, Friday October 20th 1865
Lat: 16°30′N.   Course NW by N   209 m.   Bar. 29.70/.80
Long: 29°30′W.   Wind. NE by E.   Ther. 78°/80°

All day we have had a fine NE trade wind which gradually freshened toward night, raising our hourly speed from 8 to 10 knots per hour. We saw a large ship at 10 A.M. ahead standing as we are, and at sundown she was hull down on our lee (port) quarter. Passed a ship heading about SW. We are once more to the Nd of the Cape de Verde Islands.

At Sea, Saturday October 21st 1865
Lat: 19°23′N.   Course NNW 3/4 W   204 m.   Bar. 29.78/.90
Long: 31°21′W.   Wind NE by E   Ther. 76° to 78°

During the whole day we have had moderate trades, which are very steady. I never saw more beautiful sailing. Since we left 50° S. upwards of 4200 miles in latitude alone we have had the sea so smoothe that we could with safety keep our airports all open on the berth deck and carry royal studding sail. This morning at 6 we saw a large ship under all sail hull down ahead standing as we were, at sunset she was hull down astern. She was the Eng: ship *Belvedere* 81 days from Madras to London.

At Sea, Sunday October 22nd 1865.
Latitude 22°10′N.   Course NNW 1/2 W   189 m   Bar. 29.78/.90
Longitude 32°56′W.   Wind ENE   Ther. 76°/78°

All hail another day of rest. I spent it as I generally spend my sabbaths, in my room. I read the service and read over my letters from my dear Pattie and from my dear ones at home. I can now begin to count the days which will probably pass before I will be where I can communicate with them. I give our noble old vessel about fifteen more days to land us safely in some English port, after having borne us over upwards of 50,000 miles of water on the most wonderful and eventfull cruises ever made. What will become of us after we get there, God alone can tell. For myself I have little or no faith in the existence of honor among nations when that honorable course may clash with interest. Oh, God, never were any men in such a terrible situation of suspense and misery. Here we are heart broken, with no country, no home, no profession, no means, and for aught we know, no relatives or friends. Of the latter, if there be any, our thoughts are maddening. What will become of my little brothers, sisters and dear old father? God alone knows. Merciful God give me faith to say with christian resignation "Thy will be done." We passed several vessels bound south. Tonight we will be once more out of the Torrid Zone & in the North Temperate.

At Sea, Monday Oct: 23rd 1865
Lat: 25°30′N.   Course N by W 3/4 W   214 m   Bar. 29.90/.95
Long: 34°16′W.   Wind ENE & E by N   Ther. 76°

All day our gallant trade has continued being a good deal fresher and further aft. Two of our men are very ill. One William Bill (Sea) a Kanaka from the Sandwich Islands is insensible and dying, and will probably breathe his last before morning. The other, Sergeant Geo: P. Canning of the Marines is as low as he can be. The other is a well educated young Englishman who was in our army on Gen: A. Sidney Johnston's Staff who dies from the effects of a wound received at the battle of Shiloh. Oh! how I pity the poor fellows, because neither is prepared to die. God have mercy on their souls I pray. Passed two vessels (probably Yankees) bound to the westward.

At Sea, Tuesday October 24th 1865
Lat: 29°16′N   Course N by W   231 m.   Bar. 29.90/.95
Long: 35°06′W.   Wind E and E by N.   Ther. 76°

All day our NE trades have continued but toward midnight there were signs of their dying out. They have run us well up. Contrary to all belief Wm Bill is still alive, but his complaint is such that he can't get well. Mr. Canning is still very low. Our ship is sailing well. We are now nearer our dear ones than we have been for a long time, being not much more than 2300 miles from Charleston which is very little to the Nd of West from us. I wonder if we will ever be any nearer. God grant it. I trust that we may get to England safely. Some fourteen days will determine it. It has now been 112 days since we saw land, and 195 days since we were on shore at the savage island of Ascencion. Since we have been ashore in a civilized place it has been 248 days—and in 12 months (365 days) we have been at sea 330 days. That is right "hefty."

At Sea, Wednesday October 25th 1865
Lat: 31°40′N.   Course N 1/2 W   147 m.   Bar. 29.95/.90
Long: 35°24′W.   Wind East & Variable   Ther. 75°/78°

Today we have been going very slowly along with light airs. Towards 4 P.M. a sail was reported two points on the port (lee) bow standing to the westward. She was made out to be a brig with great drift between her masts, no mainsail, staysail or studdingsails or Royals set. This of itself made her clearly no merchant vessel; very soon she was seen to get on the same tack as ourselves, and standing higher than we was crossing our bow. All this looked so suspicious that as soon as it was dark, we wore short around, got up steam and when ready took in all sail, steamed dead to windward for 16 miles and then went on our course, putting out all lights. If she be a Yankee[5] she will be somewhat astonished tomorrow morning to find no vessel insight [sic], but no doubt will conclude that it was really the "Shenanagin" but she will have a sweet time finding us as we will remain under steam until we get a good breeze. Employed painting.

At Sea, Thursday Oct 26th 1865
Lat: 33°54′N.   Course N3/4E   132 m.   Bar 29.90/.97
Long: 35°00′W   Wind. ENE, Calm & NW.   Ther. 73°/76°

Under steam all day—no signs of our last night's friend. I am sure that he was a Yankee gunboat. Passed a brig going to the Sd. Poor W*m* Bill died at 5 p.m. He was such a sufferer that we cannot regret that he is relieved. God have mercy on his benighted soul, I pray.[6] It has been nearly calm all day.

[Nearing the end of their voyage, Lt. Whittle became erratic in his entries. Bracketed material is from the log copied by Midshipman John T. Mason.—*Ed.*]

At Sea, Friday October 27th 1865
Lat: [36°49′N.]   Course [N1/4E]   [175 miles]   Bar. [29.75–29.90]
Long: [34°40′W.]   Wind [WSW]   Ther. [72°–76°]

This morning early a light westerly breeze sprung up which changed into SW and supposing it to be the counter trade which we expect, stopped steam, hoisted the propeller keeping banked fires, and made all sail with the wind on the port quarter. During the day the breeze has freshened and by the falling of the barometer we infer that we can expect westerly weather. If it is not a gale it will suit us exactly. At 9.15 a.m. we performed funeral service over the remains of poor Wm Bill and committed them to the deep.[7] We half masted our poor down trodden flag. At all times a burial is sad, but particularly at sea. And when I saw our poor flag weeping I could but be plunged into the depths of thought connected with it which made me still more melancholy. Our poor downtrodden country, our weeping flag. We are as it were the rear guard of the armies of the South. Oh! God how thou has afflicted us. Teach! Oh! Teach! us to say "Thy will be done." This is our first & I trust our last death onboard; although poor Mr. Canning is nearly gone. We overhauled & rapidly passed a Brig under all sail standing as we are. We are getting on nobly. As I am writing I am about a little north of the latitude of my dear old home and about 2000 miles to the Eastward of N[orfolk]. How much would I not give to be there now! When may I expect to be near it? God only knows. God be merciful to my darlings and our afflicted people. Protect & lead them I humbly pray.

At Sea, Saturday October 28th 1865
Lat: 40°20′   Course [NNE]   [226 miles]   Bar. [29.30-29.70]
Long: 33°07′   Wind [Var (SW, NwbyN)]   Ther. [62°–72°]

Up to twelve today we made an excellent run getting to the Nd of the most northward of the Western or Azore Islands and shaped our course for Cape Clear, the southern cape of Ireland. Our counter, SW trade continued and freshened to a fresh gale accompanied by a tremendous sea, the height of which I never saw equaled except off these very islands when I was on the Str: *Nashville* in February 1863 [1862]. It was favorable for us and we ran before it at the rate of 12 knots. At 12 the SW gale abated and sea went down rapidly, the wind hauled to about NW and blew in fresh squalls. I trust it will haul to the westward and enable us to put more sail on as we are now by the wind, and from the ship's being light can't "carry on." I trust we may yet get in in [*sic*] the course of 7 or 8 days. I am afraid that the English Government will give us up. Nous verrons. J'espère que non, mais Je le crois.

At Sea, Sunday October 29th 1865
Lat: 42°36′N.   Course [NE1/4N]   [185 miles]   Bar. [29.70–30.00]
Long: 30°21′W.   Wind [NW]   Ther. [58°–62°]

Last night and all today we have had fresh breezes, and very heavy squalls from the NW, together with a heavy sea. I trust that we may soon run out of this disagreeable weather. We made a much better run than any one supposed we would have done from noon to noon. As usual I read the service for the day and when not on deck, read some of my dear Pattie's letters. God grant that she may be safe, and that her heart may be soon gladdened by the intelligence of our safety. I have no doubt but that we have been given up as lost, by a great many, having last heard of us 123 days ago in the ice in the Arctic Ocean, since which time we have sailed on straight lines joining the positions on the consecutive days 18,434 miles, so that this is about the last place in the world that they would expect to hear of us.

At Sea, Monday October 30th 1865
Lat: [43°47′N]   Course [ENE]   [174 miles]   Bar. [29.07–30.10]
Long: [26°46′W]   Wind [NNW Var]   Ther. [56°–59°]

During the day the weather has been very unsettled, with a NW wind and very heavy sea. The wind moderated towards evening and we gradually made sail from close reefed Fore & Main topsails, reefed Foresail, Fore & Main topmast staysails to Fore & Main topgallantsails, whole courses & all staysails. We had our Main topmast staysail, Foresail, Inner jib, Mainsail, all split at different times, and all repaired. I can't tell how the wind will come out, but I trust it will be favorable. Oh! how anxious I am to get on. This evening at about 5.30 poor Sergeant Canning died.[8] He will be buried tomorrow. His death was very sad. The poor old negro (Weeks) who waited on him, was by him terribly abused, and he cursed him most terribly up to the very last. Oh! it is a terrible sight at any time to see a soul take flight, but when you see a man die who up to the last breath is a sinner the sight is awful. Oh! God let us prepare to die.

At Sea, Tuesday October 31st 1865
Lat: [44°36′N]   Course [NE by E 3/4E]   [113 miles]
  Bar. [30.00-30.10]
Long: [24°25′W]   Wind [NNE, SW]   Ther. [55°-59°]

This morning at 9.45 the solemn call of "All hands to bury the dead," was passed, and after the Catholic burial service was read by Dr. McNulty the remains of poor Sergeant Canning were committed to the deep. It was an affecting sight. During the whole day we have had an almost perfect calm with a very heavy NW swell. Toward night a light SW breeze sprung up which I hope may increase, remain steady and drive us to land. I am becoming awefully [sic] impatient to get where I can hear from my dear ones, and relieve their uneasiness about us. God grant us a safe arrival I pray.

At Sea, Wednesday November 1st 1865.
Lat: [46°16′N]   Course [NE]   [141 miles]   Bar. [29.80-29.92]
Long: [22°04′W]   Wind [SSW–NbyE]   Ther. [55°-60°]

Up to about 10 A.M. we had a fresh SW wind which was driving us nobly on, but at that hour it commenced to moderate and at 12.10 there was a sudden shift of about NNE (pc.) and freshening. We close reefed our topsails in consequence of the squally appearance and hauled up as near our course as we could lay with the wind. At 12 we were almost 600 miles from Cape Clear and about 900 from Liverpool. Oh how near this seems after the tremendous distances that we have been in the habit of dealing with. In the afternoon we saw a small Hermaphrodite Brig standing about SE, supposed to be bound to the Mediterrenean [sic]. Towards night we made sail. We are getting slowly but surely on. Some how or other I look forward to our safe arrival in an English port with very little hope. I feel some way or other as tho' some great calamity was hanging over me. Why, I can't divine—or what I can imagine, as it really seems to me that our cup of grief is already full. I trust that I am only gloomy without cause. God grant it. Oh God grant us a safe asylum that we may be assistants to those dependent on us. When I consider how much sad news awaits us, I am plunged in gloom. God support us.

At Sea, Thursday November 2nd 1865
Lat: [46°43′N]   Course [E3/4N]   [170 miles]   Bar. [29.90-30.00]
Long: [18°15′W]   Wind [NE Var]   Ther. [53°-55°]

During the whole day we have had the wind from the Eastward of North, and very flawy and baffling. At daylight we saw a six topsail yard ship and a bark ahead standing as we were, they were soon come up with and at 4 P.M. were hull down & out of sight astern. They had as much sail as we so that the beat was a thorough one. At noon we were about 400 miles from Cape Clear, and the wind remaining adverse, we got up steam and started ourselves ahead at the moderate speed of 7 knots per hour on our course. At our present rate we ought to get to Liverpool in four days. I feel that we are men with something awful hanging over us. Some way or other I do not look forward to our arrival at an English port with as much hope and good cheer as the rest. Why is this? I can't say. I feel that we have only done our duty, and would be willing under similar circumstances to go through with twice as much again—but the truth is that I have very little faith, in dealing with Governments, in honor versus interest. In other words I fear that upon our arrival in an English port, if the Yankees were to declare a refusal to give up our persons a just cause for war, and England's interests were opposed to a war, the English Government would make a sacrifice of honor to interest. I trust that my view may be erroneous. But still, this is a matter which sooner or later must be put to the test, and therefore the sooner our minds are relieved the better. Of the future I will only think, without putting any thoughts on paper. More and more each day do I see that our destinies are in the Almighty's hands, and my future cannot be fathomed. God give me faith and trust, hope, industry, fidelity and health, that I may assist the darlings at home, who are at this moment so anxious about me. Oh how clearly I can picture to myself, the dear hearts replete with joy, when the joyous news of our safe arrival in an English port is made known to our dear ones at home. The problem will soon be elucidated, and my fate will soon be known. Once inside of Cape Clear, unless a gross violation of neutral waters be submitted to, we will be safe from capture even if we were to fall in with an American man-of-war, for in the St. George's Channel, England owning the country on both sides, it is most emphatically English water, which is English soil—but I would rather not have the experiment tried. Nous verrons. Restons tranquile [sic].

At Sea, Friday November 3rd 1865
Lat: [48°01′N.]   Course. [NE by E 1/2E]   164 m.]   Bar. [29.92-30.00]
Long: [14°43′W]   Wind [NNE; Var.]   Ther. [52°-57°]

All day we have been under steam and all fore and aft sail, going bravely along in our course. We have seen and past [sic] a great many sails. One was a six topsail yard ship, with very white canvas, and every indication of her being a Yankee. Today at noon we were just 280 miles from Fastnet or Cape Clear light and at 8 P.M. we were 210. We are gradually approaching the end of our journey. Oh how much I would give to have it finished favorably, of which there is now, as far as we are concerned every probability. God grant it, I pray. I gave the spar deck today a thorough holystoning and it really looks very well. To-day they commenced to pay the officers and men the money due them as far as possible. Upon calculation it is found that it would take some $30,000 to pay which we have about $4,000, this deducting the probable cost for pilotage &c—will give every man on the ship one dollar in each $7.10 he has due him. Upon this I got $45.90 having some $326 due me.[9] This is probably the last money I will have for a long time, and it only grieves me to know why.[10] I do not love money, and have no desire to be rich. All I want is enough to live on and support my darlings at home. "Where there is a will there is a way," and this shall be my motto. I am sure not to starve on it.

Epilogue

[Lt. Whittle's entries in the journal ceased on 3 November 1865. Three days later the *Shenandoah* tied up in Liverpool next to the HMS *Donegal*, surrendering to Captain J. C. Paynter of the *Donegal*. Whittle's account of the surrender and the ultimate fate of the *Shenandoah*, written several years later, follows.][1]

On November 5, 1865, we entered St. George's Channel, making Tuskar Lighthouse, which was the first land we had seen for one hundred and twenty-two days, after sailing twenty-three thousand miles, and made it within a few moments of when it was expected. Could a higher proof of the skill of our young navigator, Irvine S. Bulloch, be desired? That night, we took a Liverpool pilot,[2] who confirmed all the news we had heard. He was directed to take the ship to Liverpool. On the morning of November 6, the brave ship steamed up the River Mersey, with the Confederate flag at her peak, and was anchored, by the pilot, by Captain Waddell's order, near H.B.M. Guard ship *Donegal*, Captain [J. C.] Paynter, R.N., Commanding. Soon after, a lieutenant from the *Donegal* came on board to learn the name of our vessel, and advised us officially of the termination of the war. At 10 A.M., November 6, 1865, the last Confederate flag was hauled down, and the last piece of Confederate property, the C.S.S. *Shenandoah* was surrendered to the British nation, by letter to Earl Russell, from Captain Waddell, through Captain Paynter, R.N., commanding H.M.S. *Donegal*.

The gallant little ship had left London thirteen months before, as the *Sea-King*, and had, as a Confederate cruiser, defied pursuit for twelve months and seventeen days; had captured thirty-eight vessels, valued at $1,172,223.00, bonding six and destroying thirty-two—second only to the C.S.S. *Alabama*, in number; had circumnavigated the globe, carrying the brave flag around the world and into every ocean on the globe except the Antarctic, traveling over a distance of about sixty thousand miles, without the loss of a single spar.

Captain Waddell's letter to Earl Russell set forth the unvarnished facts and work of our cruise, and surrendered the vessel to the British nation. The *Shenandoah* was placed under custody of British authorities, the Gun-boat *Goshawk* being lashed alongside.

U.S. Minister Adams, on November 7 addressed a letter to the Earl of Clarendon, Secretary of State for Foreign Affairs, requesting that necessary steps be taken to secure the property on board, and to take possession of the Vessel with view to her delivery to the United States. Minister Adams's letter, with that of Captain Waddell, with other documents relating to the *Shenandoah*, were referred to the law officers of the Crown on November 7, 1865, who advised in substance as follows:

> We think it will be proper for Her Majesty's Government, in compliance with Mr. Adams' request, to deliver up to him, in behalf of the Government of the U.S., the ship in question, with her tackle, apparel, &c., and all captured chronometers of other property capable of being identified as prize-of-war, which may be found on board of her. . . . With respect to the officers and crew . . . if the facts stated by Captain Waddell are true, there is clearly no case for any prosecution on the ground of piracy in the courts of this country, and we presume that Her Majesty's Government are not in possession of any evidence which could be produced before any Court or Magistrate for the purpose of contravening the statement or showing that the crime of piracy had in fact, been committed. . . . With respect to any of the persons on the *Shenandoah* who cannot be immediately proceeded against and detained under legal warrant upon any criminal charge, we are not aware of any ground upon which they can properly be prevented from going on shore and disposing of themselves as they think fit, and we cannot advise Her Majesty's Government to assume or exercise the power of keeping them under any kind of restraint.

The law officers who gave this advice and these opinions, and whose names were attached thereto, were Sir Roundell Palmer, Sir R. P. Collier, and Sir Robert Phillimore.

In consequence of these opinions of the law officers of the Crown, instructions were sent to Captain Paynter, of Her Majesty's ship *Donegal*, to release all officers and men who were not ascertained to be British subjects. Captain

Paynter reported, on November 8, that, on receiving these instructions he went on the *Shenandoah*, and being satisfied that there were no British subjects among the crew, or, at least, none of whom it could be proved were British subjects, he permitted all hands to land with their private effects.

Thus ended our memorable cruise: grand in its conception, grand in its execution, and unprecedentedly,[3] awfully, grand its sad finale! To the four winds the gallant crew scattered, most of them never to meet again until called to the Bar of that Highest of all Tribunals.

The ship was handed over to the U.S. agents. A Captain Freeman was appointed to take her to New York, but going out and encountering high west winds, lost light spars, and returned to Liverpool. It was not tried again. The noble vessel was put up, and sold to the Sultan of Zanzibar. She finally was lost on a coral reef in the Indian Ocean in 1879, fourteen years after the last Confederate flag was hauled down.

Appendix. List of Prizes Taken by the CSS *Shenandoah*. Kept by Lt. William C. Whittle, Jr.

Dates	Name of Vessel	Name of Capt.	Rig	Tons	Fate	Valuation
1864						
Oct. 29	*Alina*	E. Staples	Bark		Sunk	$95,000
Nov. 5	*Charter Oak*	Gilman	Schooner		Burnt	$15,000
" 7	*D. Godfrey*	Hallett	Bark		Burnt	$36,000
" 10	*Susan*	Fred Wm Hansen	Brigantine		Sunk	$5,436
" 12[a]	*Kate Prince*	Henry Libby	Ship		Bonded for	$40,000
" 13	*Lizzie M. Stacey*	Wm. F. Archer	Schooner		Burnt	$15,000
Dec. 4	*Edward*	Chas. P. Wirth	W. Bark	274	Burnt	$20,000
" 29	*Delphine*	Wm. G. Nichols	Bark	705	Burnt	$25,000
1865						
April 1	*Edward Carey*	Geo: O. Baker	W. Ship	353	Burnt	$15,000
"	*Pearl*	Wm. O. Bush	W. Bark	194	Burnt	$10,000
"	*Hector*	Amos A. Chase	W. Ship	380	Burnt	$58,000
"	*Harvest*	H. Hackfeld	W. Bark	352	Burnt	[b]$52,016
May 27	*Abigail*	Ebenezer T. Nye	W. Bark	310	Burnt	$16,705
June 22	*Wm. Thompson*	T. C. Smith	W. Ship	495	Burnt	$40,925
" "	*Euphrates*	T. B. Hathaway	W. Ship	364	Burnt	$42,320
" "	*Milo*	Hawes	W. Ship	401	Bonded for	$46,000
" "	*Sophia Thornton*	Moses G. Tucker	W. Ship	424	Burnt	$70,000
" "	*Jireh Swift*	Thos W. Williams	W. Bark	453	Burnt	$61,960
" 23	*Susan Abigail*	T. S. Redfield	H. Brig	124	Burnt	$6,500
" 25	*Genl Williams*	Wm. Benjamin	W. Ship	419	Burnt	$44,740
" 26	*W. C. Nye*	P. H. Cooley	W. Bark	389	Burnt	$31,512
" "	*Nimrod*	James M. Clark	W. Bark	341	Burnt	$29,260

"	"	*Catherine*	Wm. H. Phillips	W. Bark	385	Burnt	$26,175
"	"	*Gen. Pike*	Crowell	W. Bark	313	Bonded	$45,000
"	"	*Isabella*	H. Winslow	W. Bark	315	Burnt	$38,000
"	"	*Gipsey*	O. G. Robinson	W. Bark	360	Burnt	$34,369
"	28	*Waverley*	Richd Holley	W. Bark	327	Burnt	$62,376
"	"	*Martha 2nd*	Josh L. Macumber	W. Bark	360	Burnt	$30,607
"	"	*Hillman*	Jno. A. Macumber	W. Bark		Burnt	$33,000
"	"	*Jas: Maury*	Cunningham	W. Ship		Bonded for	$37,000
"	"	*Nassau*	Saml Creen	W. Ship	408	Burnt	$40,000
"	"	*Brunswick*	A. J. Porter	W. Ship	295	Burnt	$16,272
"	"	*Issac Howland*	Jerry Ludlow	W. Ship	399	Burnt	$75,112
"	"	*Congress*	D. D. Wood	W. Bark	376	Burnt	$55,300
"	"	*Nile*	Fish	W. Bark	322	Bonded for	$41,600
"	"	*Favorite*	Young	W. Bark	298	Burnt	$57,896
"	"	*Covington*	J. S. Jenks	W. Bark	350	Burnt	$30,000
					^cTotal		$1,399,080

a. On November 12, 1864, the *Shenandoah* captured the *Adelaide*. It is listed in the log in the *ORN*, ser. 1, 3:792, as bonded for $24,000. Whittle explained in his entry of November 12 that they discovered the cargo belonged to a Confederate sympathizer named Pendergrast and bonded the ship to prevent the Union authorities from confiscating the cargo. Whittle failed to list this ship because he obviously did not consider it a true prize of war. Midshipman John T. Mason's journal confirms Whittle's explanation but listed the bond as $25,000.

b. Whittle's entry of April 13 indicates the value of *Harvest* as $34,759. There is no indication in the journal as to why this error occurs. Lining's journal contains the same error.

c. Whittle's total value of ships and cargoes destroyed is obviously in error. Subtracting the erroneous figure for *Harvest* and adding the correct one, and adding the $24,000 bond for the *Adelaide*, gives a figure of $1,405,823.

Notes

Introduction

1. Philip Van Doren Stern, *The Confederate Navy: A Pictorial History* (New York: Doubleday & Company, 1962), 9, hereafter cited as Stern, *Navy*.

2. Ibid., 7, 34; James Dunwody Bulloch, *The Secret Service of the Confederate States in Europe, or How the Confederate Cruisers Were Equipped* 2 vols. (New York: Putnam, 1884; reprint, New York and London: Thomas Yoseloff and Sons, 1959, with an introduction by Philip Van Doren Stern), 1:ix–x, hereafter cited as Bulloch, *Secret Service*.

3. James Dunwody Bulloch to James Iredell Waddell, 5 October 1864, in U.S. Department of the Navy, *Official Records of the Union and Confederate Navies in the War of the Rebellion* (Washington, D.C.: Government Printing Office, 1894–1927), ser. 1, 3:749, hereafter cited as *ORN*.

4. Journal of William Conway Whittle, Jr., private collection of the Whittle Family, Norfolk, Virginia, now deposited in the Eleanor S. Brockenbrough Library, Museum of the Confederacy, Richmond, Virginia, 5 November, 5 December 1864, hereafter cited as Whittle, Journal.

5. Peter Karsten, *The Naval Aristocracy: The Golden Age of Annapolis and the Emergence of Modern American Navalism* (New York: The Free Press, 1972), hereafter cited as Karsten, *Aristocracy*. See p. 385 for Karsten's definition of the American naval aristocracy.

6. Wyndham Robertson and R. A. Brock, *Pocahontas, Alias Matoaka, and Her Descendants through Her Marriage at Jamestown, Virginia, in April, 1614, with John Rolfe, Gentleman* (Baltimore, Md.: Genealogical Publishing Co., 1974), 54–55, 74–75; Whittle Family Genealogy in Stafford Whittle Family Papers, 1753–1960, Accession

#7973, Box 6, Folders 1 and 2, Albert and Shirley Small Special Collections Library, University of Virginia, Charlottesville, hereafter cited as Stafford Whittle Family Papers, 1753–1960; Obituary of Fortescue Whittle, undated clippings in Lewis Neale Whittle Papers, Southern Historical Collection, Library, University of North Carolina at Chapel Hill, hereafter cited as Lewis Neale Whittle Papers; Senate, Senate Executive Document No. 1, 31st Cong., 2d sess., 220; Karsten, *Aristocracy,* 122.

7. William Conway Whittle, Sr., to Lewis Neale Whittle, 13 December 1850, 22 July 1852, Lewis Neale Whittle Papers.

8. Service of Commander William C. Whittle, USN, in Stafford Whittle Family Papers, 1753–1960, Box 6, Folders 2 and 6; John Thomas Scharf, *History of the Confederate States Navy,* 2 vols. (New York: Rogers & Sherwood, 1887), 1:300, hereafter cited as Scharf, *Confederate Navy; Annual Report of the Secretary of the Navy,* Senate Executive Document No. 1, 33d Cong., 2d sess., 386; House, *Letter from the Secretary of the Navy Reporting Appointments . . . to the Naval School,* 6 December 1854, House Executive Document No. 5, 33d Cong., 2d sess.

9. Karsten, *Aristocracy,* 23–30, 37–45; Charles Todorich, *The Spirited Years: A History of the Antebellum Naval Academy* (Annapolis, Md.: Naval Institute Press, 1984), 78–79, hereafter cited as Todorich, *Academy.*

10. Karsten, *Aristocracy,* 24, 70, 78–80, 91–93; George Dewey, *Autobiography of George Dewey, Admiral of the Navy* (New York: Charles Scribner's Sons, 1913), 20, hereafter cited as Dewey, *Autobiography;* Whittle Family Genealogy in Stafford Whittle Family Papers, 1753–1960, Box 6, Folder 1.

11. Dewey, *Autobiography,* 14; Diary of William Conway Whittle, Sr., 13 June 1858, in William Whittle Papers, 1753–1871, Accession #7973, Albert and Shirley Small Special Collections Library, University of Virginia, Charlottesville, hereafter cited as William Whittle Papers, 1753–1871.

12. Edward Chauncey Marshall, *History of the United States Naval Academy* (New York: D. Van Nostrand, 1862), 133, hereafter cited as Marshall, *Naval Academy;* Reminiscences of Francis Thornton Chew, 3, Francis Thornton Chew Papers, Southern Historical Collection, Library, University of North Carolina at Chapel Hill, hereafter cited as Chew, Reminiscences; *Report of the Board of Examiners to the Secretary of the Navy,* 16 June 1855, Senate Executive Document No. 1, 34th Cong., 1st sess., 70; 23 June 1856, Senate Executive Document No. 5, 34th Cong., 3d sess., 473; 17 June 1857, Senate Executive Document No. 11, 35th Cong., 1st sess., 594; 17 June 1858, Senate Executive Document No. 1, 35th Cong., 2d sess., 431.

13. Dewey, *Autobiography,* 14, 17; Alfred Thayer Mahan, *From Sail to Steam: Recollections of Naval Life* (New York: Harper & Brothers, 1907), 74–75; Richard S. West, "The Superintendents of the Naval Academy," *Proceedings of the United States Naval Institute* 72 (April 1946):60–61.

14. Diary of William Conway Whittle, 13 June 1858, in William Whittle Papers, 1753–1871, Box 2; L. M. Goldsborough to Mrs. E. B. Whittle, 20 June 1855, in William Conway Whittle, Jr. Papers, Sargeant Room, Kirn Memorial Library, Norfolk, Virginia, hereafter cited as William Conway Whittle, Jr. Papers, Kirn, Norfolk.

15. Marshall, *Naval Academy,* 137–38; Isaac Toucey to William C. Whittle, Jr., 19 April 1860, private collection of Mary Beverley Dabney, Norfolk, Virginia; Murat Halstead, *Life and Achievements of Admiral Dewey from Montpelier to Manila* (Chicago: Our Possessions Publishing Company, 1899), 106–7, hereafter cited as Halstead, *Dewey;* Karsten, *Aristocracy,* 63; Todorich, *Academy,* 32, 83–84.

16. Senate Executive Document No. 17, 35th Cong., 2d sess., 21; William Conway Whittle, Sr., to Lewis Neale Whittle, 9 April 1859, in Lewis Neale Whittle Papers; U.S. Department of the Navy, *Dictionary of American Naval Fighting Ships,* 9 vols. (Washington, D.C.: Government Printing Office, 1970), 2:144; 5:368; 6:118.

17. William Conway Whittle, Sr., to Lewis Neale Whittle, 9 April 1859, William Conway Whittle, Sr., to Frances N. Lewis, 5 September 1859, in Lewis Neale Whittle Papers; Description of action at Anton Lizardo, off Mexico, written by William Conway Whittle, Jr., 8 December 1909, in Elizabeth Calvert Page Dabney Papers, Special Collections, Perry Library, Old Dominion University, Norfolk, Virginia, hereafter cited as Elizabeth Calvert Page Dabney Papers; Senate Executive Document No. 29, 36th Cong., 1st sess.

18. Lt. Robert Dabney Minor to Capt. William Conway Whittle, Sr., 23 March 1860, in Elizabeth Calvert Page Dabney Papers; Isaac Toucey to Midshipman William Conway Whittle, Jr., 19 April 1860, in the private papers of Mary Beverley Dabney, Norfolk, Virginia; John McIntosh Kell, *Recollections of a Naval Life, Including the Cruises of the Confederate States Steamers "Sumter" and "Alabama"* (Washington, D.C.: The Neale Company, 1901), 132.

19. Halstead, *Dewey,* 107, 144; copy of Whittle's service record, United States Navy, in William Conway Whittle, Jr. Papers, Kirn, Norfolk.

20. Service record of William Conway Whittle, Jr., Confederate States' Navy, in Stafford Whittle Family Papers, 1753–1960, Box 6, Folder 5; William S. Dudley, *Going South: U.S. Navy Officer Resignations & Dismissals on the Eve of the Civil War* (Washington, D.C.: Naval Historical Foundation, 1981), 43.

21. William Conway Whittle, Jr., "The Cruise of the C.S. Steamer Nashville," *Southern Historical Society Papers* 29 (1901):207–12; Bulloch, *Secret Service,* 1:117; *Frank Leslie's Illustrated Newspaper,* 12 April 1862; Stern, *Navy,* 73; *ORN,* ser. 1, 7:139; ser. 2, 2:603.

22. William Conway Whittle, Jr., "The Opening of the Lower Mississippi in 1862—A Reply to Admiral Porter," *Southern Historical Society Papers* 13 (1885):562, hereafter cited as Whittle, "Lower Mississippi"; Service record of William Conway Whittle, Jr., Confederate States' Navy, in Stafford Whittle Family Papers, 1753–1960; Scharf, *Confederate Navy,* 1:280–81, 300; *ORN,* ser. 1, 18:292–95.

23. Whittle, "Lower Mississippi," 564; *ORN,* ser. 1, 18:292–95.

24. Whittle, "Lower Mississippi," 568; Chew, Reminiscences, 17; *ORN,* ser. 1, 18:298–300; Service record of William Conway Whittle, Jr., Confederate States' Navy, in Stafford Whittle Family Papers, 1753–1960.

25. Service record of William Conway Whittle, Jr., Confederate States' Navy, in Stafford Whittle Family Papers, 1753–1960.

26. Maxine Turner, *Navy Gray: A Story of the Confederate Navy on the Chattahoochee and Apalachicola Rivers* (Tuscaloosa and London: University of Alabama Press, 1988), 53, 57, 63, hereafter cited as Turner, *Navy Gray.*

27. Ibid. 55–56; William C. Whittle, Jr. to Robert D. Minor, 7 September 1862, in Minor Family Papers, Virginia Historical Society, Richmond, hereafter cited as Minor Family Papers.

28. William C. Whittle, Jr. to Robert D. Minor, 30 September 1862, in Minor Family Papers.

29. William C. Whittle, Jr. to Robert D. Minor, 5 October 1862, ibid.

30. William C. Whittle, Jr. to Robert D. Minor, 7, 27 September, 13 October 1862, ibid.

31. William C. Whittle, Jr. to Robert D. Minor, 7, 23 September, 5, 13 October, 20 December 1862, ibid.

32. Turner, *Navy Gray,* 75, 78, 81–83; William C. Whittle, Jr. to Robert D. Minor, 20 December 1862, in Minor Family Papers.

33. Turner, *Navy Gray,* 98–99; Stephen R. Mallory to James D. Bulloch, 7 March 1863, *ORN,* ser. 2, 2:371.

34. Edward C. Anderson, *Confederate Foreign Agent: The European Diary of Major Edward C. Anderson,* ed. and with a prologue and an epilogue by W. Stanley Hoole (University, Ala.: Confederate Publishing Co., ca. 1976), 2 November 1861; Bulloch, *Secret Service,* 1:117–18; Bulloch to Mallory, 19 November 1861, Sinclair to North, 14 May 1863, Bulloch to Mallory, 9 July 1863, 29 August 1863, Slidell to Benjamin, 6 July 1863, in *ORN,* ser. 2, 2:106, 422, 455–57, 482–83; ser. 2, 3:834.

35. Mallory to Barron, 30 August 1863, in *ORN,* ser. 2, 2:485–86; 1863 Diary of William C. Whittle, Jr., 1–6 September 1863, in William C. Whittle, Jr. Papers, Kirn, Norfolk, hereafter cited as Whittle, 1863 Diary.

36. Whittle, 1863 Diary, 15, 17 September 1863.

37. Ibid., 12, 18 September 1863.

38. William C. Whittle, Sr., to Lewis Neale Whittle, 7, 21 December 1858, in Lewis Neale Whittle Papers.

39. Whittle, 1863 Diary, 30 September, 12, 13 October 1863.

40. Ibid., 26 October, 19 November 1863, and list of addresses at the end of the diary; William N. Still, Jr., ed., *Odyssey in Gray: A Diary of Confederate Service, 1863–1865,* by Douglas French Forrest (Richmond: Virginia State Library, 1979), 86, hereafter cited as Still, *Forrest Diary.*

41. Whittle, 1863 Diary, 19 November 1863; Still, *Forrest Diary,* 90.

42. John Grimball to John Berkley Grimball, July 6, 1864, in John Berkley Grimball Papers, in the Special Collections Department, William R. Perkins Library, Duke University, Durham, N.C., hereafter cited as Grimball Papers, Duke University.

43. Still, *Forrest Diary,* 193, 199; Diary of Captain Samuel Barron, 8, 12, 20, 21, 29 July, 2 August 1864, in *ORN,* ser. 2, 2:814–17.

44. Francis Thornton Chew, Journal, 1 August 1864, in Francis Thornton Chew Papers, Southern Historical Collection, University of North Carolina at Chapel Hill, hereafter cited as Chew, Journal.

45. Mallory to Bulloch, 18 July, 19 August 1864, in *ORN*, ser. 2, 2:687, 708.

46. Bulloch to Mallory, 19 August, 16 September 1864, in *ORN*, ser. 2, 2:713, 723–24.

47. Diary of Captain Samuel Barron, 5, 10 September 1864, in *ORN*, ser. 2, 2:818; Bulloch to Barron, 12 September 1864, in William Conway Whittle, Jr. Papers, Kirn, Norfolk; Chew, Journal, 1 November 1864.

48. Bulloch to Barron, 3 October 1864, William Conway Whittle, Jr. Papers, Kirn, Norfolk; William C. Whittle, Jr., "The Cruise of the Shenandoah," *Southern Historical Society Papers* 35 (1907):241–42, hereafter cited as Whittle, "Shenandoah Cruise."

49. Chew, Journal, 2 November 1864; Charles E. Lining, Journal kept on board the C.S. Str. "Shenandoah," 18 October 1864, Charles E. Lining Papers, Eleanor S. Brockenbrough Library, Museum of the Confederacy, Richmond, Virginia, hereafter cited as Lining, Journal; Thomas H. Dudley to William H. Seward, 6 October 1864, Senate, Committee on Foreign Relations, *Alabama Claims*, vol. 3, *Rebel Cruisers Claims Negotiations*, Senate Executive Document No. 11, vol. 4, 41st Cong., 1st sess. (Washington, D.C.: Government Printing Office, 1869), 316, hereafter cited as Alabama Claims.

50. *ORN*, ser. 1, 3:756; Waddell Notes on the *Shenandoah*, *ORN*, ser. 1, 3:795, hereafter cited as Waddell, Notes; Lining, Journal, 18 October 1864; Chew, Journal, 2 November 1864.

51. Lining, Journal, 19 October 1864; Testimony of John Wilson and John Hercus, Alabama Claims, 324–30; *Shenandoah* Log, *ORN*, ser. 1, 2:750–52.

52. Whittle, "Shenandoah Cruise," 244; Chew, Journal, 2 November 1864; Lining, Journal, 19 October 1864.

53. Chew, Reminiscences, 14, 16–18; Charles E. Lining, "Cruise of the Confederate Steamship 'Shenandoah,'" *Tennessee Historical Magazine* 8 (July 1924):103, hereafter cited as Lining, "Cruise"; John Thomson Mason, "Confederate Commerce Destroyers: IV, The Last of the Confederate Cruisers," *Century Magazine* 54, n.s. 34 (August 1898):603, hereafter cited as Mason, "Cruisers"; James D. Horan, ed., *C.S.S. Shenandoah: The Memoirs of Lieutenant Commanding James I. Waddell* (New York: Crown Publishers, 1960), 57–59, hereafter cited as Horan, *Waddell;* William Harwar Parker, *Recollections of a Naval Officer, 1861–1865* (New York: Charles Scribner's Sons, 1885), 117.

54. Chester G. Hearn, *Gray Raiders of the Sea: How Eight Confederate Warships Destroyed the Union's High Seas Commerce* (Camden, Maine: International Marine Publishing, ca. 1992), 271.

55. Lining, Journal, 18 October 1864; John Grimball, "The Cruise of the Shenandoah," *Southern Historical Society Papers* 25 (1897):117–18, hereafter cited as Grimball, "Shenandoah"; Horan, *Waddell,* 66.

56. Bulloch to Waddell, 5 October 1864, *ORN*, ser. 1, 3:749–55.

57. Herman Melville, *White-Jacket, or the World in a Man-of-War* (New York: Harper, 1850; reprint, Evanston and Chicago: Northwestern University and the Newberry Library, 1970), 24, hereafter cited as Melville, *White-Jacket.*

58. Lining, Journal, 18, 19, 20 October 1864; Mason, "Cruisers," 603; Chew, Journal, 2 November 1864; Waddell, Notes, *ORN*, ser. 1, 3:796, 798.

59. Whittle, Journal, 26 October, 2 November 1864; Lining, Journal, 23, 24, 25 October 1864; Waddell, Notes, *ORN*, ser. 1, 3:797–99.

60. Bulloch to Waddell, 5 October 1864, *ORN*, ser. 1, 3:754; Waddell, Notes, *ORN*, ser. 1, 3:798, 800.

61. Whittle, Journal, 29 October 1864; Lining, Journal, 29 October 1864; Chew, Journal, 29 October 1864.

62. Bulloch to Waddell, 5 October 1864, *ORN*, ser. 1, 3:753; Shipping Articles of the CSS *Shenandoah*, Eleanor S. Brockenbrough Library, Museum of the Confederacy, Richmond, Virginia, hereafter cited as Shipping Articles; List of prizes taken by the *Shenandoah*, *ORN*, ser. 1, 3:792; Lining, Journal, 5, 7 November 1864, 5 January, 20 February 1865; Waddell, Notes, *ORN*, ser. 1, 3:802, 809, 823; Chew Journal, 6 January, 2 April, 27 May 1865; Whittle, "Shenandoah Cruise," 257.

63. Ethel Trenholm Seabrook Nepveux, *George Alfred Trenholm: The Company That Went to War, 1861–1865* (Charleston, S.C.: Comprint, 1973), 22, 24; Lining, Journal, 5, 7, 10 November, 4 December 1864; Whittle, Journal, 5, 7, 10 November, 4, 5, 6 December 1864; Waddell, Notes, *ORN*, ser. 1, 3:801–2, 819.

64. Whittle, Journal, 5, 6, 24 December 1864, 2 April 1865; Waddell, Notes, *ORN*, ser. 1, 3:804; Lining, Journal, 7, 12, 30 December 1864, 11 April, 22 June 1865; Chew, Journal, 10 April, 27 May, 22, 26 June 1865; John Thomson Mason, 22 June 1865, Journal (4 vols.), John Thomson Mason Papers, Eleanor S. Brockenbrough Library, The Museum of the Confederacy, Richmond, Virginia, hereafter cited as Mason, Journal.

65. Tom Henderson Wells, *The Confederate Navy: A Study in Organization* (University: University of Alabama Press, 1971), 79–80, hereafter cited as Wells, *Navy*; William Still, "The Common Sailor, Part II: Confederate Tars," *Civil War Times, Illustrated* 24 (March 1985):36, hereafter cited as Still, "Confederate Tars"; Lining, Journal, 27 May, 22 June 1865; Whittle, Journal, 27 February 1865.

66. Shipping Articles; Whittle, "Shenandoah Cruise," 244; Testimony of John Williams, Alabama Claims, 416; Whittle, Journal, 7 November, 8 December 1864, 7, 8, 11 January 1865.

67. Affidavit and Testimony of John Williams, Alabama Claims, 415–16; William Blanchard to Sir Charles Darling, 15 February 1865, ibid., 423–25; William Blanchard to William H. Seward, 23 February 1865, ibid., 3:384–91; James G. Francis to James I. Waddell, 14 February 1865, *ORN*, ser. 1, 3:769; James I. Waddell to James G. Francis, 14 February 1865, *ORN*, ser. 1, 3:770–71.

68. C. J. Tyler to William Blanchard, 30 January 1865, Alabama Claims, 398, 421–22; Cyril Pearl, *Rebel Down Under: When the Shenandoah Shook Melbourne, 1865* (Melbourne: William Heinemann, 1970), 124–26, hereafter cited as Pearl, *Rebel Down Under;* James G. Francis to James I. Waddell, 15 February 1865, *ORN*, ser. 1, 3:772–73; Case of the Australian Government versus the CSS *Shenandoah*, 15 February 1865, *ORN*, ser. 1, 3:773–74; James I. Waddell to James G. Francis, 15 February 1865, James G. Francis to James I. Waddell, 16 February 1865, *ORN*, ser. 1, 3:774.

69. Mason, "Cruisers," 607; Grimball, "Shenandoah," 122; Whittle, "Shenandoah Cruise," 250; Whittle, Journal, 28 January 1865; Cornelius F. Hunt, *The Shenandoah, or the Last Confederate Cruiser* (New York: G. W. Carlton & Co.; London: S. Lawson

and Co., 1867; reprint, New York: W. Abbott, 1910), 113–15, hereafter cited as Hunt, *Last Cruiser;* Lining, Journal, 18 February 1865; Ralph W. Donnelly, *The Confederate States Marine Corps: The Rebel Leathernecks* (Shippensburg, Pa.: White Mane Publishing Company, 1989), 137; Waddell, Notes, *ORN,* ser. 1, 3:819; James E. Valle, *Rocks & Shoals: Order and Discipline in the Old Navy, 1800–1861* (Annapolis, Md.: Naval Institute Press, 1980), 22–23, hereafter cited as Valle, *Rocks & Shoals.*

70. Shipping Articles.

71. Still, "Confederate Tars," 18; Chew, Journal, 20 January 1865; Shipping Articles; Whittle, Journal, 13, 14 November 1864, 30 October 1865; Affidavit of William A. Temple, Alabama Claims, 489–90.

72. Bulloch, *Secret Service,* 2:153; Whittle, Journal 9, 12, November, 7 December 1864, 26 January, 13 April, 23, 28 June 1865; Waddell, Notes, *ORN,* ser. 1, 3:802–3, 809, 826, 829; Horan, *Waddell,* 195–98; Lining, Journal, 9, 12 November, 7 December 1864, 13 April, 28 June 1865.

73. Whittle, Journal, 29, 30 October, 5, 7, 12 November 1864; Lining, Journal, 29 October, 5 November 1864; Waddell, Notes, *ORN,* ser. 1, 3:801–2.

74. Whittle, Journal, 29, 30, 31 December 1864, 19, 26 January 1865; Lining, Journal, 29, 30 December 1864, 1, 6 January 1865; Waddell, Notes, *ORN,* ser. 1, 3:807, 809; Grimball, "Shenandoah," 122; Mason, "Cruisers," 606.

75. Whittle, Journal, 2, 8 December 1864, 19 January, 25 March 1865; Wells, *Navy,* 41.

76. Still, "Confederate Tars," 17, 37–38; Valle, *Rocks & Shoals,* 83, 185.

77. Whittle, Journal, 3, 4, 25 November 1865; James Iredell Waddell, 25 March 1865, Log of the CSS *Shenandoah,* microfilm copy, James Iredell Waddell Papers, 1864–1865, 2 vols., North Carolina Department of Archives, Raleigh, hereafter cited as Waddell, Shenandoah Log; Shipping Articles.

78. Whittle, Journal, 6, 14, 24, 25 November, 6 December 1864; Mason, Journal, 25 November 1864.

79. Valle, *Rocks & Shoals,* 85; William N. Still, "The Common Sailor, Part I: Yankee Blue Jackets," *Civil War Times, Illustrated* 24 (February 1985):35, hereafter cited as Still, "Blue Jackets"; Still, "Confederate Tars," 36; "Log of the Shenandoah," 27 October 1864, copy begun by Master Irvine S. Bulloch, microfilm copy from the Chicago Historical Society, Chicago, Illinois, hereafter cited as Bulloch, Shenandoah Log; Mason, Journal, 13 June, 27 August 1865; Chew, Journal, 12–19 November 1864; Whittle, Journal, 24 December 1865.

80. Bulloch, Shenandoah Log, 28, 29 January, 2, 6, 10 February 1865; Mason, Journal, 29 February, 10 October 1865; Hunt, *Last Cruiser,* 110–11.

81. Pearl, *Rebel Down Under,* 38–45; Lining, Journal, 31 January, 8, 10 February 1865; Hunt, *Last Cruiser,* 110–11.

82. Whittle, Journal, 27 February, 2 March 1865; Lining, Journal, 2 March 1865; Bulloch, Shenandoah Log, 15, 21, 25 March, 12, 24 April, 24 May 1865; Hunt, *Last Cruiser,* 134, 137–38.

83. Mason, Journal, 28 May 1865; Chew, Journal, 28 May 1865; Lining, Journal, 28 May 1865.

84. Whittle, Journal, 28 May 1865; Chew, Journal, 28 May 1865; Mason, Journal, 28 May 1865; Lining, Journal, 28, 29, 30, 31 May 1865; Hunt, *Last Cruiser*, 155.

85. Mason, Journal, 4, 22, 23, 28 June, 13 July 1865; Lining, Journal, 22, 23, 25, 26, 28 June 1865; Chew, Journal, 23, 25, 26, 28 June 1865.

86. Mason, Journal, 13 July, 10 October 1865; Lining, Journal, 22 February, 3, 17 August, 7, 8 September, 2, 29 October 1865; Whittle, Journal, 3 December 1864, 15 July 1865; Chew, Journal, 15 August, 13 October 1865; Mason, "Cruisers," 602.

87. Whittle, Journal, 4, 10, 27 November 1864, 14 April, 27 September, 8 October 1865; Mason, Journal, 21 October 1865.

88. Melville, *White-Jacket*, 24; Chew, Journal, 2 November 1864, 26 April 1865; Whittle, Journal, 18 January, 5 March, 19 April, 27 September, 30 October 1965; William Conway Whittle, Jr. Morning Order Book, 26, 27, 28 April 1865, in William Conway Whittle, Jr. Papers, Sargeant Room, Kirn Memorial Library, Norfolk, Virginia, hereafter cited as Whittle, Morning Order Book.

89. Whittle, Journal, 12, 13 January, 23 February, 21 July 1865; Whittle, Morning Order Book, 9, 19, 17, 25, 28 October 1865; Mason, Journal, 25 October 1865.

90. Whittle, Journal, 2 November 1864; Whittle, Morning Order Book, 3 March, 27, 28 July, 6 September 1865; Lining, Journal, 2 November 1864; Mason, Journal, 25 November 1864, 12 August, 10, 13 October 1865.

91. Chew, Journal, 14 July, 13, 30 October 1865; Whittle, Journal, 23 December 1864, 20 August 1865; Lining, Journal, 25 December 1864, 3 September 1865; Mason, Journal, 19 September, 1 October, 2 November 1865.

92. Lining, Journal, 4, 5, 23 November 1864, 10 January, 12 March, 29 April, 1, 16 May, 14 July, 8, 9 October 1865; Mason, Journal, 15 August, 9 October 1865; Whittle, Journal, 5 November 1864, 14 April, 14, 27 July 1865.

93. Lining, Journal, 26, 30 October 1865; Chew, Journal, 26, 27, 30, 31 October 1865; Mason, Journal, 27, 31 October 1865; Whittle, Morning Order Book, 30 October 1865; Whittle, Journal, 27 October 1865.

94. Lining, Journal 23 July 1865; Mason, Journal, 9 February 1865; Chew, Journal, 23 April 1865; Whittle, Journal, 30 October, 27 November 1864 and passim; Wells, *Navy*, 19.

95. Whittle, Journal, 6, 20, 27 November 1864, 8 January, 4, 25 June 1865; Lining, Journal, 17 November 1864, 5 August, 22 October 1865; Mason, Journal, 17 July 1865; Still, "Confederate Tars," 38.

96. Still, "Confederate Tars," 18–19; Chew, Journal, 13 March 1865; Lining, Journal, 19, 21 October 1865; Mason, Journal, 14 May, 1 June, 9 August 1865.

97. Chew, Journal, 18 September 1864, 10 March, 21 April 1865; Lining, Journal, 10 November 1864, 13, 15 July, 18, 21 October 1865; Whittle, Journal, 2 January 1865; Mason, Journal, 14 May 1865.

98. Lining, Journal, 10 November, 10 December 1864, 9, 11 May, 10, 29 June, 30 July, 15 September 1865; Chew, Journal, 19 September 1865; Mason, Journal, 24, 30 December 1864.

99. Chew, Journal, 12, 18, 23 May, 18 September 1965; Lining, Journal, 25 December 1864, 1 March, 20, 23 May, 22, 30 August, 23 September 1865; Whittle, Journal,

24 December 1864, 10 March 1865; Mason, Journal, 11 May, 27 August, 4, 25 October 1865.

100. Lining, Journal, 21, 22 December 1864, 3, 12, 20 January, 9 May, 15 June, 3 October 1865; Mason, Journal, 4 October 1865; Whittle, Journal, 11, 16 January 1865; Still, "Blue Jackets," 34.

101. Waddell, Notes, *ORN*, ser. 1, 3:796–97; Chew, Journal, 31 May, 12 June 1863, 22 April, 23 May, 19 June, 10 July 1865; Mason, Journal, 4, 8, 11 May, 1 June, 6, 9, 12, 15 August, 21, 27 October 1865; Lining, Journal, 6 May, 10, 24, 26, 30 July, 2, 6, 19 September 1865; Whittle, Journal, 23 April, 3 May 1865.

102. Lining, Journal, 11, 15 December 1864, 2, 3 May 1865; Chew, Journal, 23 May, 18 September 1865.

103. Lining, Journal, 8, 11 December 1864, 17 January, 16, 26 March 1865; Whittle, Journal, 27 November, 11 December 1864, 8 January, 23, 27 February, 11, 14, 17, 19, 26 March, 11, 18 June 1865; Chew, Journal, 13 March 1865; Mason, Journal, 18 March 1865.

104. Whittle, Morning Order Book, 27, 28 July 1865; Reminiscences and Journal of Francis Thornton Chew, Lieutenant, C.S.N., 3–22, Chew Papers; Martha Nevile Lumpkin, ed., *Minor, Scales, Cottrell, and Gray Families of Virginia, North Carolina, and Mississippi* (Clarksville, Tenn.: n.p., 1974), 47, hereafter cited as Lumpkin, *Scales.*

105. Chew, Journal, 1 August 1864; Lining, Journal, 13, 15 December 1864; Whittle, Journal, 18 March 1865.

106. Horan, *Waddell*, 58–59; Whittle, Journal, 15, 16 December 1864; Lining, Journal, 16 December 1864.

107. Whittle, Journal, 13, 16, 17 December 1864; Lining, Journal, 17, 18 December 1864.

108. Horan, *Waddell*, 22, 63–75; Jim Dan Hill, *Sea Dogs of the Sixties: Farragut and Seven Contemporaries* (New York: A. S. Barnes & Company, Inc., 1961), 227–29, hereafter cited as Hill, *Sea Dogs;* Flag Officer Samuel Barron to Lieutenant James I. Waddell, 5 September 1864, *ORN*, ser. 1, 3:749.

109. James D. Bulloch to Samuel Barron, 31 August 1864, in William C. Whittle, Jr. Papers, Kirn, Norfolk, Folder 7, #66; Bulloch, *Secret Service,* 2:145; Commander James D. Bulloch to Lieutenant James I. Waddell, 5 October 1864, *ORN*, ser. 1, 3:749–55; James D. Bulloch to Samuel Barron, 10, 12 September 1864, in William C. Whittle, Jr. Papers, Kirn, Norfolk, Folder 7, #72, #74.

110. Waddell, Notes, 796; Horan, *Waddell*, 96; Lining, Journal, 18 November, 16 December 1864.

111. Whittle, Journal, 13 December 1864.

112. Whittle, Journal, 23 December 1864; Chew, Journal, 6, 7 January 1865; Lining, Journal, 5 January 1865.

113. Chew, Journal, 8 January 1865.

114. Chew, Journal, 11 January 1865; Lining, Journal, 10 January 1865; Whittle, Journal, 10 January 1865.

115. Chew, Journal, 11, 25 January 1865.

116. Chew, Journal, 9 March, 16, 29, 31 May 1865.

117. Whittle, Journal, 25, 26, 27 February, 1 March 1865.

118. Whittle, Journal, 28 February 1865; 3, 15 March 1865.

119. Whittle, "Shenandoah Cruise," 253; Whittle, Journal, 22, 23 June 1865; Lining, Journal, 22 June 1865.

120. Waddell, Notes, 831; Horan, Waddell, 175; Lining, Journal, 2 August 1865; Mason, Journal, 3 August 1865.

121. George S. Shyrock to William C. Whittle, Sr., 8 March 1866, Journal of William C. Whittle, Sr., William Whittle Papers, 1753–1871; Lining, Journal, 2, 3 August 1865; Mason, Journal, 3 August 1865.

122. Whittle, Journal, 3 August 1865; Mason, Journal, 3 August 1865.

123. Whittle, Journal, 2, 30 August 1865; Lining, Journal, 6 October 1865.

124. Lining, Journal, 3, 26, 30 September, 3 October 1865; Mason, Journal, 28 September 1865.

125. Whittle, Journal, 3, 8, 10, 11, 25 October 1865; Lining, Journal, 10 October 1865.

126. Whittle, Journal, 10, 11, 12 October 1865; Lining, Journal, 10, 11, 12 October 1865.

127. Whittle, Journal, 31 October, 1, 2 November 1865.

128. Whittle, "Shenandoah Cruise," 256–57.

129. Orris A. Browne to William C. Whittle, 8 November 1893, in William Conway Whittle, Jr. Papers, Kirn, Norfolk; Whittle, "Shenandoah Cruise," 258; Lining, Journal, 8 November 1865.

130. William C. Whittle, Jr. to Commodore Samuel Barron, 13 April 1866, in the Barron Papers, Virginia Historical Society, Richmond, hereafter cited as Barron Papers.

131. Ibid.; William Conway Whittle, Sr., to Mrs. Frances M. Lewis, 7 July, 20 August, 1 October 1866, Conway Whittle Family Papers, Manuscripts Department, Earl Greg Swem Library, College of William and Mary, Williamsburg, Virginia, hereafter cited as Conway Whittle Family Papers.

132. "Case File of Applications from Former Confederates for Presidential pardon ("Amnesty Papers"), National Archives Microfilm Publication M1003, roll 71, frames 728–739; Records of the Adjutant General's Office, 1780s–1917, Record Group 94; William C. Whittle, Sr. to Mrs. Frances Lewis, 21 November 1866, in Conway Whittle Family Papers; William C. Whittle, Jr. to Robert Dabney Minor, 28 December 1868, Minor Family Papers.

133. William C. Whittle, Jr. to Robert Dabney Minor, 28 December 1868, 10 February 1869, Minor Family Papers.

134. Clipping, George S. Bernard Papers, Scrapbook, 1816–1890, 100, Rare Book, Manuscript and Special Collections Library, Duke University, Durham, North Carolina; Hunt, Last Cruiser, 268–69; Waddell Obituary, New York Times, 17 March 1886; William C. Whittle, Jr. to Robert Dabney Minor, 10 February 1869, Minor Family Papers.

135. Alexander Crosby Brown, Steam Packets of the Chesapeake: A History of the Old Bay Line Since 1840 (Cambridge, Md.: Cornell Maritime Press, 1961), 152–53;

Edward R. McKethan, "A History of the Bank and Trust Business in and near Norfolk, Virginia," unpublished thesis, Graduate School of Banking, Rutgers University, June 1947, 55-56.

136. *Proceedings of the Twenty-third Annual Meeting of the Grand Camp Confederate Veterans, Department of Virginia. Together with Orders of the Grand Commander Issued During the Past Year* (Richmond, Va.: Everett Wadday Co., Printers, 1911).

137. "The Cruise of the Shenandoah" [Obituary of John Thomson Mason, written by William C. Whittle and read by Dabney Scales], *Confederate Veteran* 12 (October 1904):489-90, hereafter cited as Mason Obituary.

138. "Obituary of Lieut. Commander D. M. Scales," *Confederate Veteran* 28 (November 1920):431, hereafter cited as Scales Obituary; John Grimball to Meta Morris Grimball, 1 September 1866, in Grimball Papers, Duke University.

139. John Grimball to Meta Morris Grimball, 1 September 1866, in Grimball Papers, Duke University; 20 January, 1 February 1867, John Berkley Grimball Diary, No. 15 (14 March 1865 to 15 May 1867), Southern Historical Collection, University of North Carolina Library, Chapel Hill; Yates Snowden, ed., *History of South Carolina*, 5 vols. (Chicago and New York: Lewis Publishing Company, 1920), 1:24-25.

140. Charleston *News & Courier,* Charleston, South Carolina, 2 March 1897, 6.

141. Alexandria *Gazette,* 15, 17 April 1888.

142. Mason Obituary; Orris Browne to William C. Whittle, 8 November 1893, in William Conway Whittle, Jr. Papers, Kirn, Norfolk.

143. Orris A. Browne to William C. Whittle, 8 November 1893, in William Conway Whittle, Jr. Papers, Kirn, Norfolk.

144. Scales Obituary; Unidentified clipping, Scrapbook, Grimball Family Papers, Southern Historical Collection, University of North Carolina Library, Chapel Hill; *The Virginian-Pilot and Norfolk Landmark,* 6 January 1920; *Norfolk Ledger-Dispatch,* 5 January 1920; Whittle, "Shenandoah Cruise," 258.

Prologue

1. Whittle, "Shenandoah Cruise," 235-45. This was published later as part of a pamphlet, William C. Whittle, *Cruises of the Confederate States Steamers "Shenandoah" and "Nashville"* (Norfolk, Va.: Privately printed, 1910), hereafter cited as Whittle, *Cruises of the Shenandoah and Nashville.* Lt. Whittle prepared this account first as an address to a meeting of the Stonewall Camp of the United Confederate Veterans, presented on 2 June 1897. Norfolk *Virginian,* 3 June 1897; "Address of William C. Whittle, Jr., (1897)," a typed copy furnished the editors by Professor William M. Dabney, University of New Mexico. Professor Dabney is the grandson of Lt. William C. Whittle.

2. Whittle failed to note that the sale of the ironclads Bulloch had under construction occurred just in time to provide the money to pay off the crew of the *Alabama* after she was sunk by the *Kearsarge,* with enough money remaining to purchase and outfit the *Sea King* and convert her to the *Shenandoah.* See Bulloch, *Secret Service,* 2:124-26.

3. Whittle closely parallels Bulloch's description in *Secret Service*, 126, and in James D. Bulloch to S. R. Mallory, 16 September 1864, *ORN*, ser. 2, 2:723. See also *Lloyds Register of British and Foreign Shipping; From 1st July 1864 to the 30th June 1865* (London: Cox and Wyman Printers, 1864).

4. One officer who embarked on the *Shenandoah*, Sidney Smith Lee, Jr., was ordered to Liverpool on 12 July 1864, before Bulloch knew he was likely to be able to obtain a cruiser. Other officers were ordered after Bulloch requested them on 27 August. Commodore Samuel Barron's diary shows that Engineers Matthew O'Brien and W. H. Codd and Sailmaker Henry Alcott were ordered to Liverpool on 4 September. On 10 September Barron listed all officers remaining in Europe, indicating with an "L" those designated for Liverpool, a total of six officers. On 14 September orders were given to Waddell, Whittle, and Grimball. The remainder of the complement seems to have been ordered to Liverpool on 30 September 1865. Midshipman Orris A. Browne woke Midshipman John T. Mason early in the morning of 1 October, and they proceeded immediately to Liverpool. "Diary from 1863 to 1865 of Captain S. Barron, C.S. Navy," in *ORN*, ser. 2, 2:814–19, hereafter cited as Barron Diary, *ORN*; James D. Bulloch to Samuel Barron, 27 August 1864, in William C. Whittle, Jr. Papers, Kirn, Norfolk; Francis Thornton Chew, Journal, 2 November 1864; John Thomson Mason, Journal, 5 October 1864.

5. Whittle left a blank space for this name in 1897 and 1907, but inserted Richard Wright's name when he republished the piece in 1910. When he wrote the speech in 1897 he probably used Bulloch's two-volume work published in Liverpool in 1883, as Bulloch also left out Wright's name. No copies of Bulloch's orders to Whittle have been found in the Whittle Papers. The volume of the *ORN* that included the complete letter from Bulloch to Whittle was not published until 1921, after Whittle's death. Whittle might not have had access to a copy of the orders when he wrote his speech but had access in 1910. Wright was the father-in-law of Charles K. Prioleau, of Fraser, Trenholm and Co. Perhaps Bulloch wished to protect Wright's identity in 1883; although he mentioned Charles K. Prioleau in his two-volume work, he never mentioned Wright. This is surprising since Wright was known to be the buyer of the *Sea King* by the middle of October 1864. See "Address of William C. Whittle, Jr." (1897); Whittle, "Shenandoah Cruise," 241; Whittle, *Cruises of the Shenandoah and Nashville*, 7; Bulloch, *Secret Service*, 2:133–34; *ORN*, ser. 2, 2:731–32; Thomas H. Dudley to William H. Seward, 18 October 1864, Alabama Claims, Serial 1396, 319–20.

6. This method was by now standard procedure with Bulloch. He first used it when he ordered Master John Low to take passage on the *Oreto*, when it proceeded to its rendezvous to become the *Florida*. Frank Lawrence Owsley, Jr., *The C.S.S. Florida: Her Building and Operations* (Philadelphia: University of Pennsylvania Press, 1965), 24.

7. Lt. Whittle kept either a journal of his voyage on the *Sea King* from London to Madeira or made extensive notes in the ledger in which he kept his *Shenandoah* journal. Ten sheets were cut out of the front of the ledger, just before the journal of the voyage of the *Shenandoah* begins. Writing is discernible on the stubs remaining in the volume. There are two plausible theories that would explain their removal.

Whittle may have included too much information about the cooperation of Captain Corbett and thus removed them before arrival at Liverpool in 1865. Or the sheets were removed to aid in making the changes to the *Sea King* to convert her into a cruiser; Whittle's orders instructed him to survey the ship and indicate what changes were necessary to convert her to a raider. Bulloch to William C. Whittle, [Jr.], 6 October 1864, *ORN*, ser. 2, 2:732.

8. John Grimball to John B. Grimball, letter begun at sea 23 December 1864, completed at Melbourne 25 January 1865, in Grimball Papers, Duke University.

9. Lt. Ramsay held an English certificate as well as a commission in the Confederate States Navy. James D. Bulloch to Samuel Barron, 15 September 1864, William Conway Whittle, Jr. Papers, Kirn, Norfolk; Bulloch, *Secret Service*, 2:135.

10. *ORN*, ser.1, 3:785.

11. The two engineers were John Hutchinson, acting second assistant engineer, and J. Ernest Maguffeney, acting third assistant engineer. The acting chief engineer, Matthew O'Brien, had been aboard the *Alabama*, as had Maguffeney, the latter under the name of Frank Cunan or Curran. O'Brien and William H. Codd were ordered, on 4 September 1864, to report to Bulloch at Liverpool. "Abstract Log of the Shenandoah," *ORN*, ser. 1, 3:785, hereafter cited as Abstract Log, *ORN*; Bulloch, *Secret Service*, 2:145; Barron Diary, *ORN*, ser. 2, 2:814–19; Arthur Sinclair, *Two Years Aboard the Alabama* (Boston: Lee and Shepherd, 1896; reprint, with notes and an introduction by William N. Still, Annapolis, Md.: Naval Institute Press, 1989), p. [293], hereafter cited as Sinclair, *Aboard the Alabama*. [The page number is in brackets because the text page numbers end with 288 and the index begins with page 299. There are no page numbers for the documents between. The document cited is "A General Muster Roll of the Officers, Petty Officers, Seamen, and Firemen of the Confederate States Steamer Alabama, from the day she was commissioned, Aug. 24, 1862, to the day she was sunk, June 19, 1864."—*Ed.*]

12. There were minor discrepancies in this number in the sources. Surgeon Charles Lining noted, "From a boat which came off from the 'Laurel' two more men and a carpenter shipped so that we have now twenty two men and twenty four officers." Lining's numbers were confirmed by Lt. Francis Thornton Chew. Whittle failed to note this last-minute addition to the crew except in the totals he listed on 26 October 1864. Irvine Bulloch's initial entry in the log showed twenty-three petty officers and men shipped. These discrepancies were cleared up by the Shipping Articles of the *Shenandoah*. The first twenty-two names on the articles enlisted on either 8 or 18 October 1865. The carpenter who came from the *Laurel* at the last minute was John Lynch, acting second carpenter. Lining, Journal, 19 October 1864; Chew, Journal, vol. 2, 2 November 1864; Abstract Log, *ORN*, ser. 1, 2:785; Bulloch, Shenandoah Log, 19 October 1864; Shipping Articles.

13. Whittle recorded the date and hour in sea time rather than civil time. The log of the *Shenandoah*, and Lining's Journal, indicate the actual date and hour was 6 P.M. 19 October 1864. The shift from the use of sea time to civil time on 8 November 1865 is noted in the abstract of the log of the *Shenandoah*. This notation appears in only

one of the manuscript copies of the log seen by the editors, that in the North Carolina State Archives; there is no note in the Bulloch, Grimball, or Mason copies. However, the Bulloch log in the Chicago Historical Society shows some evidence of changes in the dating of the early entries. Lining, Journal, 19 October 1864; Shenandoah Log, *ORN*, ser. 1, 3:786; Waddell, Shenandoah Log, 8 November 1864; Copy, Log of the Shenandoah [copied by] Lt. John Grimball, C.S. Navy, located in Charleston Library Society Collection, Charleston, South Carolina, microfiche, 19 October, 8 November 1864, hereafter cited as Grimball, Shenandoah Log; John Thomson Mason, "Log of the Shenandoah," John Thomson Papers, 1864–1865, in the Eleanor S. Brockenbrough Library, Museum of the Confederacy, Richmond, Virginia, 19 October, 8 November 1864, hereafter cited as Mason, Shenandoah Log; Bulloch, Shenandoah Log, 19, 20, 21, 28, 31 October, 8 November 1864. Navigators kept the log in sea time when they left port; upon returning to port, the log shifted back to civil time. Sea time was twelve hours ahead of civil time. The use of this practice dates to as early as Spanish voyages in the sixteenth century. For historical background on the use of nautical time see D. W. Waters, *The Art of Navigation in Elizabethan and Early Stuart Times* (New Haven, Conn.: Yale University Press, 1958), 76, 203, 579. For the continuation of its use into the twentieth century, see T. S. Lecky, *Wrinkles in Practical Navigation,* 18th ed., revised and enlarged by William Allingham (London: George Philip & Son, Ltd., 1917), 741–42.

14. The ordnance may have been mounted, but with the exception of the two twelve-pound signal guns previously installed on the *Sea King,* no guns could be fired. Lt. Whittle failed to mention that the gun tackles had not been put on board the vessel. They would have to capture the required tackle, even though adequate rope was available. Waddell, Notes, *ORN,* ser. 1, 3:798.

15. Bulloch, in his instructions to Lt. Waddell, stated, "I have stipulated with the ostensible owner that you will make no prizes until Captain Corbett has had time to reach England and cancel the register, for which purpose you should allow thirty days." Waddell violated these instructions; the *Shenandoah* stopped and seized the *Alina* on 29 October. Chew stated that Captain Waddell at first refused to capture any American ships until six weeks had passed, in order for Corbett to have time to cancel the registration of the *Sea King.* Waddell, in his notes, expressed considerable apprehension about his inability to use his guns. The need for gun tackle or the need for additional crew may have caused him to ignore the instructions. Bulloch, *Secret Service,* 2:140; Waddell, Shenandoah Log, 29 October 1864; Abstract Log, *ORN,* ser. 1, 3:752; Chew, Journal, 2 November 1864, 26; Waddell, Notes, *ORN,* ser. 1, 3:798–800.

Chapter 1

1. Whittle's figures are correct. He included the captain in the officers and acknowledged the three additional men who came from the *Laurel* at the last minute. See Prologue, note 12, this volume.

2. Whittle was well aware of the situation of the *Rappahannock;* he had been

in contact with the ship when he was aide to Flag Officer Samuel Barron. Also five of the officers of the *Shenandoah* had been aboard the *Rappahannock* on 16 May 1864; they were J. F. Minor, Cornelius Hunt, and Lodge Colton, all Masters Mates, Wm. H. Codd, Chief Engineer, and John Guy, Gunner. See List of Officers & Crew of the C.S. Steamer, "Rappahannock" enclosed in a letter from Lt. Charles M. Fauntleroy to Commodore Samuel Barron, 15 May 1864, William Conway Whittle, Jr. Papers, Kirn, Norfolk. Numerous letters in this collection indicate the fate that might have befallen the *Shenandoah* had she entered any port to await a crew. One wonders about the advice given Waddell by Lt. John F. Ramsay, captain of the *Laurel,* since he also had been aboard the *Rappahannock.*

3. The man shipped was Herman Wicker. Shipping Articles.

4. These men were Peter Raymond, Louis Rowe, Charles Behnche, John Blanking, John Wilson, and Baner Johnson. Shipping Articles.

5. George Silvester and another fireman, Thomas Jackson, were the only deserters at Melbourne from the original twenty-two men enlisted when the *Shenandoah* was commissioned on 19 October 1865. Shipping Articles.

6. John Davey, William West, George R. Bracket, George Flood, Walter Madden, and John Williams shipped for six months. Shipping Articles.

7. The cook was John Williams, who gave Whittle much trouble on the voyage to Melbourne. Once in the harbor at Melbourne, Williams left the *Shenandoah,* went to the United States Consul, William Blanchard, and helped precipitate the crisis over "Charley," allegedly recruited in violation of British neutrality. "Sworn statement by John Williams, February 10, 1865," Alabama Claims, Serial 1396, 415. Consul Blanchard's attempts to gather enough evidence to force Australian authorities to act against the *Shenandoah* are found in ibid., 384–444.

8. The wardroom steward's name was William Bruce. Shipping Articles.

9. Whittle's fears were borne out. Thomas Adamson, Jr., United States Consul at Pernambuco, Brazil, did learn of the activities of the *Shenandoah,* but not until the *Kate Prince,* with the second group of released prisoners aboard, reached Pernambuco on 29 November 1864. Adamson notified Charles Francis Adams on 30 November 1864. Adams wrote to Secretary of State Seward on 22 December 1864. Thomas Adamson, Jr., to Charles Francis Adams, 30 November 1864, and Adams to William H. Seward, 22 December 1864, Alabama Claims, Serial 1396, 332–33.

10. These three men were John H. Pitts, James Ford, and Walter Way. Shipping Articles.

11. The word "manaverling" or "manavilin" is listed in the *Oxford English Dictionary* (hereafter *OED*) with the earliest usage as 1865. The word seems to have originated in the South Seas. It means "small matters," "odds and ends," or "articles supplementary to the ordinary fare." This would fit the usage of Lt. Whittle. Lt. Chew also used the term to describe the action of the boatswain in taking a "straw hat which he had 'marnaviled,' the polite expression on board for stealing or a promiscuous laying hold of things belonging to a prize ship." *OED* (1989), 9:296; Chew, Journal, 5–12 November 1864. See also Rex Clements, *Manavilins: A Muster of Sea-songs,*

as distinguished from Shanties, written for the most part by seamen, and sung on board ship during the closing years of the Age of Sail (London: Heath, Cranton, Limited, 1928), 17.

Chapter 2

1. The seaman's name was Alphonso Robson. Shipping Articles.

2. Lee had crossed the equator and become a shellback during his years in the merchant marine. Bulloch, *Secret Service,* 2:145–46.

3. Lt. Whittle most likely picked up the tobacco habit at the Naval Academy at Annapolis. See Todorich, *Academy,* 108–9.

4. The log notes that Hall, 2nd Mate, was triced up for "pumping ship on deck"— in other words, urinating over the side of the ship. Waddell, Shenandoah Log, 27 November 1864; Eric Partridge, *A Dictionary of Slang and Unconventional English* (New York: Macmillan Co., 1956), 667.

5. The "sea food" Whittle described fits the description of "krill."

6. Whittle's speculation that the seamen placed ashore at Tristan da Cunha might be there for a year before being rescued proved inaccurate. Commander C. R. P. Rodgers of the USS *Iroquois* touched at the island on 28 December 1864 and removed the castaways to Cape Town. Commander Rodgers was at that point only three weeks behind the *Shenandoah,* but he had no specific orders to hunt for her. C. R. P. Rodgers to Gideon Welles, 9 January 1865, *ORN,* ser. 1, 3:403–4.

Chapter 3

1. This unusual incident was also reported by Lining and Cornelius Hunt, although Hunt placed it in the Pacific Ocean, rather than in the Indian Ocean. Lining, Journal, 25 December 1864; John Grimball, to John B. Grimball, letter begun at sea 23 December 1864 completed at Melbourne 25 January 1865, in Grimball Papers, Duke University; Hunt, *Last Cruiser,* 147.

2. The men shipped from the *Delphine* were Wm. E. Strom, Chas. Henning, Peter Jorennsin, A. Tidman, Otto Swartz, and John Hoagland. Shipping Articles.

3. The wardroom cook made "two splendid buns with beautiful Confed. flags upon them." Chew, Journal, 1 January 1865.

4. Lt. Chew noted in his journal that he had been made Master in place of Bulloch but wondered why the Captain had done this. Whittle's entry offers a clear explanation. Chew, Journal, 11 January 1865.

5. Dr. Lining gave the name as *Sancho Panza.* Lining, Journal, 17 January 1865.

6. Whittle's fears were well founded. The *Shenandoah* took no more prizes until she reached Ponape on 1 April 1865. Captain Waddell noted that he suspected the whalers had been warned and did not venture into the New Zealand whaling grounds. Chew indicated that head winds prevented the ship from going to New Zealand. "Having lost so much time the Capt. gave up the idea of cruising off the coast of New Zealand & stood up to the N*d;* through the passage between New Caledonia and the

Fiji islands, following the Whaling fleet and hoping to overtake some of them." Waddell, Notes, *ORN*, ser. 1, 3:814; Chew, Journal, 12 March 1865.

Chapter 4

1. The departure of this mail vessel from Melbourne rather quickly informed United States forces of the location of the *Shenandoah*. Commander C. R. P. Rodgers of the USS *Iroquois* wrote to Secretary of the Navy Gideon Welles, from Point de Galle, Ceylon, that he had learned from Australian newspapers and from the mail steamer that the *Shenandoah* had arrived in Melbourne on 25 January and was still there when the mail ship departed on 26 January. The knowledge would have aided Rodgers but little, had he had orders to chase her; the *Shenandoah* left Melbourne the same day the Commander wrote to the Secretary of the Navy. C. R. P. Rodgers to Gideon Welles, 18 February 1965, *ORN*, ser. 1, 3:431.

2. On this particular Saturday the *Shenandoah* was "besieged with boats containing visitors anxious to gratify their curiosity by a personal inspection." Melbourne *Age*, 30 January 1865, quoted in Ernest Scott, "The Shenandoah Incident, 1865," *The Victorian Historical Magazine* 11 (September 1926):68. The *Argus* reported that 7,024 persons traveled from Melbourne to Sandridge on that Saturday to visit the *Shenandoah*. Pearl, *Rebel Down Under*, 57.

3. Waddell reported that eighteen men were induced to desert at Melbourne. The shipping articles show a "D" after the names of twenty men. One of these was George Silvester, who gave Whittle considerable trouble, and the other was Thomas Jackson, both firemen. It is possible these two were "encouraged" to desert, leaving the others to be induced to desert by Blanchard. This might account for the discrepancy in the figures. Waddell, Notes, *ORN*, ser. 1, 3:811; Shipping Articles.

4. Whittle did visit Mr. Weymouth. He and Dr. Charles Lining went ashore on 8 February 1865, met Mr. Weymouth, and the three of them took the train to South Yarra, a suburb of Melbourne. Whittle and Lining dined with Mr. Weymouth and his son, John. The ladies of the household had eaten earlier and merely remained in the dining room to engage in conversation. Whittle, who seems to have left the *Shenandoah* only two or three times during the stay in Melbourne, chose this excursion to step out of character. The Dr. noted that " 'Whittle,' much to my surprise, got exceedingly tight, neither knowing what he was doing, or where he was going, so that I had a devil of a time taking care of him. *Walked him around* until it was nearly time for the cars to start & thus got him to the ship safely." Lining said that only Bulloch, who returned with them, realized that the Executive Officer had drunk too much. Lining, Journal, 8 February 1865.

5. Whittle, "Shenandoah Cruise," 249–51.

6. The man sought by the authorities was "Charley," whose presence was noted by the United States Consul William Blanchard, after several seamen who left the *Shenandoah* informed him of stowaways on board. "Charley" was discovered by the officers of the *Shenandoah*, after the Australian authorities had asked for permission to search the ship and been refused. John Williams, the black sailor who shipped

as a cook from the *D. Godfrey,* was one of the former crewmen of the *Shenandoah* who swore affidavits that "Charley" and several more stowaways were on board the Confederate cruiser. Another was William Madden. Alabama Claims, Serial 1396, 384–442.

7. Waddell reported that eighteen men were induced to desert. Waddell, Notes, *ORN,* ser. 1, 3:811.

8. The collier that coaled the *Shenandoah* was the *John Fraser,* which had been sent out from Liverpool expressly for that purpose, according to one source. The *John Fraser* was a Charleston, S.C., ship, transferred to British registry, which belonged to Fraser, Trenholm, and Co. Waddell, in his notes, indicated that the *John Fraser* appeared by chance in Melbourne with the exact type of coal needed. Considering the care with which James D. Bulloch sent the Confederate raiders to sea, it is more likely that he ordered coal ships to possible ports of call for the *Shenandoah.* Chew, Journal, 12 March 1865, Melbourne; Lining, Journal, 17 February 1865; Waddell, "Shenandoah Log," 17 February 1865; "Affidavit of William A. Temple, 6 December 1865," Alabama Claims, Serial 1396, 481; Nepveaux, *George Alfred Trenholm,* 24, 26, 56; Waddell, Notes, *ORN,* ser. 1, 3:812.

9. Whittle noted the names of all of these men in the back of his Morning Order book, with the exception of Blacker, who was to become the Captain's clerk and was listed among the officers. William Conway Whittle, Jr. Papers, Kirn, Norfolk.

10. According to David M. Sullivan, who has done considerable research on Confederate Marines, George P. Canning was an aide-de-camp to General (Bishop) Polk. David M. Sullivan to the editors, 18 February 1989.

Chapter 5

1. Among the forty-two stowaways from Melbourne was J. C. Blacker, who held a master's licence from the British government. Waddell appointed him Captain's clerk. Blacker was reported as having left the *Saxonia* on 17 February 1865, with his nautical instruments and his steward. His steward, "a black boy," was then seen on the *Shenandoah.* Constable James Witcher's police report on Blacker also indicated that he "was a first-class pilot for the Australian, India, and China Seas." *ORN,* ser. 1, 3:785; "Report of Constable James Witcher . . . Williamstown Water-police Station, February 21, 1865," U.S. Congress, House, Committee on Foreign Affairs, *Geneva Arbitration, British Case and Evidence,* House Executive Documents, vol. 14, no. 282, 42d Cong., 2d sess (Washington, D.C.: Government Printing Office, 1872), Serial 1517, 816–17.

2. Captain Waddell, promenading with Lt. Chew, during Chew's forenoon watch, told the lieutenant "he was chasing the N. Z. fleet since he had arrived too late to catch them in N. Z." Waddell told Chew he planned to go after the Northern Whaling fleet after checking on whalers in the mid-Pacific. Chew, Journal, 14 March 1865.

3. Lt. Chew described this incident, indicating that "the 1st Lieut. with the assistance of some of the men rushed out nearly up to their waists in water, passed a line around [the 12 pounder] and secured it, thus disposing of quite a terrible cus-

tomer." Chew, Journal, 12 March 1865. Chew's entry begun on 12 March covered activities in Melbourne as well as later dates.

4. Whittle quoted a British Navy song popular when Britain's major enemy was France, "How Little Do the Landsmen Know." See Charles Dibden, *Songs, Naval and National; of the Late Charles Dibden; with a memoir and Addenda.* Collected and arranged by Thomas Dibden . . . with Characteristic Sketches by George Cruikshank (London: John Murray, 1841), 311.

5. George Flood was confined during the afternoon watch on 14 March "for fighting & drunkenness." The following day Flood was reduced in rank to seaman and James Spring rated Captain of the Hold. Waddell, Shenandoah Log, 14, 15 March 1865.

6. Twenty-two men signed for six months, six of whom deserted in Melbourne leaving sixteen aboard the *Shenandoah.* Lt. Whittle failed to note that some of the men shipped on 8 October 1864; times for these eight men ended on 8 April. Shipping Articles.

7. Waddell, Shenandoah Log, 21 March 1865.

8. Ibid., 25 March 1865.

9. Ibid., 27 March 1865.

10. John Bockstoce described this ship as "the little Hawaiian trading schooner *Pfiel,* a vessel that frequently spent its summers in the Arctic, trading whiskey for furs and ivory, and its winters in the Pacific, trading for tortoise shell." Lining gave the name as "Pefils," and the log listed the ship as the *Pelin.* Cornelius E. Hunt gave the name of this vessel as the *P. Fiert.* John Bockstoce, *Whales, Ice and Men: The History of Whaling in the Western Arctic* (Seattle and London: University of Washington Press, in association with the New Bedford Whaling Museum, Massachusetts, 1986), 110, hereafter cited as Bockstoce, *Whales, Ice and Men;* Lining, Journal, 29 March 1865; Abstract Log, *ORN,* ser. 1, 3:788; Waddell, Shenandoah Log, 29 March 1865; Hunt, *Last Cruiser,* 119.

Chapter 6

1. Lt. Chew had a bracelet tattooed on his wrist. Chew, Journal, 5 April 1865.

2. Whittle failed to note in his journal that John A. Park, Joseph Stevenson, and James Welch shipped on 1, 2, and 3 April, respectively. Benedicto Espagñol and Civio De la Case were shipped on 4 April. A total of ten men shipped at Ponape. Shipping Articles.

3. "Triced up Marlow (W.R.C.) and Jas. Ore for quarrelling and neglect of duty." Waddell, Shenandoah Log, 12 April 1865.

4. Lt. Grimball went off the watch bill on 12 April and returned to it on 19 April. Whittle's concern for Lt. Grimball arose from the fact that they were classmates at Annapolis. Waddell, Shenandoah Log, 12–19 April 1865.

5. Checking the shipping articles indicated that John W. Jones, David Marshall, Michael Moran, Thomas Hall, and John Griffiths shipped on 18 October 1864 for six months. The articles show Marshall, Moran, Griffiths, and Jones reshipped on 18 April

1865 for twelve months. Whittle's journal entry of 8 May 1865 noted that "Davey & West Capts of Tops, Jones (Qr. M.) and Griffiths (Cox) four of the best men I ever saw . . . reship[ped] upon condition that they would be discharged at the first European port we got to." Of the five who shipped for six months on 8 October, only Thomas Hall is unaccounted for on the shipping articles in the chronological order. A note next to Hall's name in the first column of the shipping articles indicated he reshipped for twelve months on 18 April 1865. Reshipping dates were backdated for Griffiths and Jones. Shipping Articles; Whittle, Journal, 8 May 1865.

6. John Davey, William West, and George Flood shipped on 7 November 1864. Shipping Articles.

7. Those men who had not reshipped on 7 May were John W. Jones, William Crawford, Michael Reid, William Simpson, Henry Fox, William Warren, John Griffiths, Peter Raymond, Louis Rowe, John Davey, William West, and George Flood. Shipping Articles.

8. Waddell called this storm a typhoon. Waddell, Notes, *ORN,* ser. 1, 3:822.

9. Captain Waddell again referred to this storm as a typhoon. Ibid.

10. Lt. Chew, noting the colder weather, remarked "No stoves are used on a Man-of-War except that for cooking; there is a stove on this ship, however, which was used before we bought her; it has not yet been put up, and I fear the Capt. will not allow it to be done. Think of four hours on a wet deck, the wind strong and cutting, after which no warm place to go to; you enter your quarters, and there find it also cold and desolate." Chew, Journal, 18 May 1865.

Chapter 7

1. Although not mentioned by Whittle, 20 May 1865 marked the day a stove was put into the ward room. Lining noted in his journal, "This evening got up the stove in the wardroom, & we spent our first comfortable evening." Chew wrote, "What a difference in every respect. Dry warm quarters; one can read or write with some care and comfort." The Captain said he "was without a stove . . . [until] the *Abigail* supplied the requisition." Whether the Captain had a stove in his cabin is not entirely clear, as Lining noted on 3 June, "Captain in the wardroom most of the day to get the benefit of the stove." Lining, Journal, 20 May, 3 June 1865; Chew, Journal, 23 May 1865; Waddell, Notes, *ORN,* ser.1, 3:823.

2. Lt. Chew stated they took off some provisions and twenty barrels of liquor. He noted the whiskey "was all over the ship, so we found it impossible to prevent our men from getting it, and one was so drunk he had to be sent on board our own ship. While in the boat he jumped overboard. The water was below the freezing point and the cold bath did him much good. Had to lash him in the boat." The sailor who fell into the water and had to be lashed in the boat was Swanton. Chew, Journal, 27, 28 May 1865; Lining, Journal, 27 May 1865.

3. The names of the officers were not given by Lt. Whittle, but John Lynch, 2nd Carpenter, and 1st Assistant Engineer W. H. Codd, who was suspended from duty on 30 May, were the likely individuals. There are other possibilities as to the identities of

the officers. On the following day Lt. Scales was relieved from duty for bringing liquor aboard for personal use, and the 2nd carpenter, John Lynch, was put in irons for being drunk again. This incident prompted an order from the captain to the effect that no materials could be removed from a prize without going through the 1st lieutenant and the paymaster. Lining remarked, "so all 'menavelines' are stopped." Lining, Journal, 27, 28, 29 May 1865; Abstract Log, *ORN,* ser. 1, 3:775; Waddell, Shenandoah Log, 30 May 1865.

4. Lt. Chew, who took Lt. Scales's watch, protested that the Captain "was making a *convenience* of him" by having him replace various officers. As a result Chew was placed back on the watch bill by the captain, in regular rotation. Chew, Journal, 29, 31 May 1865.

5. Whittle did not mention it, but the liquor incident continued to have repercussions. Blacker, said the captain, was ordered out of the cabin to steerage because he had kept part of a keg of whiskey in his room, and denied that it was there. Blacker stated the captain wanted him to "spy" on the officers in the wardroom and he refused. Also the "Boatswain's Mate [was] broken and disrated." Lining, Journal, 30 May 1865.

6. The steamer *Lelia,* a new blockade runner, sank off Liverpool on 14 January 1865. The ship carried six passengers bound for Bermuda; among them was Captain Arthur Sinclair. Also drowned was "Gunner P.C. [Thomas C.] Cuddy, late of the *Alabama.*" Whittle did not give the source of his information about his uncle, but since it was mentioned soon after the taking of the *Abigail* it is likely he read it in a newspaper taken from that ship. He had mentioned earlier, on 21 April, that the last news received was from California of the date 27 January; information on Arthur Sinclair's death was not likely to have come from that source. As the *Abigail* had recently been in Yokohama, it could have been a newspaper from one of the English colonies rather than a paper from the United States. Lining noted 31 May, "Reading newspapers etc. are our only occupation." *The Times* (London), 16, 18, 28 January, 2 February 1865; Samuel Barron to Stephen R. Mallory, 20 January 1865, *ORN,* ser. 2, 2:789–90; Lining, Journal, 31 May 1865.

7. Cornelius Hunt wrote that he made friends with some of the captured sailors and obtained information for the captain about whale ships in the Bering Sea. When Thomas Manning shipped aboard the *Shenandoah* he piloted the ship to the area where the whalers should be. Hunt, *Last Cruiser,* 161–63.

8. Considering Whittle's frequent references to God and his regular reading of services in the *Book of Common Prayer,* this reference to not being a "Christian" seems unusual. What Whittle referred to was the fact that he had never been confirmed in the Protestant Episcopal Church. He was confirmed by his uncle, The Right Reverend Francis McNeece Whittle, Bishop of the Diocese of Virginia, on 14 April 1870, in St. John's Episcopal Church in Portsmouth, Virginia. William C. Whittle, Jr., to Robert D. Minor, 25 April 1870 in Minor Family Papers, Virginia Historical Society, Richmond; Parish Register No. 1, 1821–1884, Trinity Episcopal Church, Portsmouth, Virginia. A note in the parish register indicated Whittle was confirmed at St. John's because he could not be present at night at Trinity.

9. Lt. Chew noted that they took off provisions, "beef, pork sugar, coffee, potatoes & about 1000 gallons of fresh water." Chew, Journal, 22 June 1865.

10. Captain Frederick A. Barker of the *Robert Towns* hailed the *Shenandoah,* which identified herself as the Russian ship *Petropavlovski.* Barker had been in Australia when the cruiser was in Melbourne and became suspicious. He went into the ice and warned as many whalers as he could find. Had he not warned the whaling fleet, greater destruction might have occurred. Bockstoce, *Whales, Ice and Men,* 113.

11. *Book of Common Prayer,* Psalm 37, v. 25. Lt. Whittle quoted this passage correctly here. His frequent use of the quotation in later entries allowed minor errors to creep in, but they have not been noted.

12. This action was necessary due to the press of prisoners, but an untoward result several days later was that a warning was sent to the remainder of the whaling fleet when the *Abigail's* captain, Ebenezer Nye, his first mate, and several men took two whale boats and rowed into the ice. Bockstoce, *Whales, Ice and Men,* 113, 116.

13. There was a fourth vessel. The New Bedford bark, *William Gifford,* was warped to the French whaler *Gustave* of Havre. Both were painted gray and probably appeared as one ship. The French and Hawaiian vessels moved off to warn the whaling fleet; the *William Gifford* escaped to the south. Ibid., 116.

14. Waddell said the chase lasted three hours; Lt. Chew said two hours. The log showed the *Shenandoah* began the chase at 5 P.M., fired a rifled gun at the chase at 5:55, and at 7 P.M. was "Lying to near prize." There is no inconsistency in the records here, except in regard to Waddell's recollection. Chew measured the time from the beginning of the chase, Whittle from the firing of the gun. Waddell, Notes, *ORN,* ser. 1, 3:826; Chew, Journal, 22 June 1865; Waddell, Shenandoah Log, 22 June 1865.

15. When the *Shenandoah* was out of sight of the *Milo,* Captain Ebenezer Nye, the master of the *Abigail,* his first mate and some of his men seized two whale boats and rowed to warn the whaling fleet at Cape Bering. On 25 June Captain Nye warned the *Mercury* of New Bedford; immediately the *Mercury* and three other whalers moved westward to escape the danger. Bockstoce, *Whales, Ice and Men,* 116–17.

16. The log noted these sightings, indicating only the nationality of the ships. Bockstoce believes they could have been the *Victoria* and the *Winslow.* Waddell, Shenandoah Log, 25 June 1965; Abstract Log, *ORN,* ser. 1, 3:790; Bockstoce, *Whales, Ice and Men,* 117.

17. Waddell, in his notes on the cruise, said that one of the captains of the vessels taken in the Bering Straits was the brother of Thomas S. Manning. Whittle's list of the vessels taken, with the name of the captain included, has no Manning. The only instances of duplication of last names were those of Josh L. Macumber and Jno. A. Macumber, captains, respectively, of the *Martha 2nd* and the *Hillman,* both captured on 28 June. As this meeting of brothers is the occasion for a Waddell diatribe against Yankee materialism, his story is somewhat suspect. Waddell, Notes, *ORN,* ser. 1, 3:829.

18. Noted as the *Benjamin Cummings* in Bockstoce, *Whales, Ice and Men,* 117.

19. Lt. Chew indicated they took 9,000 gallons of fresh water from the *Isabella.* Chew, Journal, 25 June 1865.

20. Kedge—a light anchor used to warp a vessel; in other words, to attach a line to the kedge and move the vessel by hauling on that line.

Chapter 8

1. Whittle estimated the time of arrival rather accurately. The *Milo* arrived in San Francisco on 20 July 1865, three days after his entry. For some reason several of the messages to Washington announcing this arrival were marked as received on 18 August 1865. Pursuit of the *Shenandoah* by U.S. vessels was generally directed toward the Arctic. *ORN*, ser. 1, 3:569, 576–77, 588–89.

2. Henderson Island was a reported navigational hazard in the vicinity of Alijos Rocks off the coast of Mexico. Although the Alijos Rocks existed, ships searching for Henderson and other reported islands in this area failed to find them. United States Hydrographic Office, Bureau of Navigation Publication No. 56, *The West Coast of Mexico, from the Boundary Line Between the United States and Mexico to Cape Corrientes, including the Gulf of California* (Washington, D.C.: Government Printing Office, 1880), 50–51.

3. Whittle's comment about crossing the equator east of 115— W in order to clear the Tahiti group of islands indicated a course to Cape Horn. Lining noted that the captain was persuaded to change course for Australia on 2 August, then changed his mind overnight. Although some of the crew petitioned Waddell to take the ship to Australia, according to Mason the Captain replied, "I shall take the ship into the *nearest* English port and all I have to ask of you men, is to stand by me to the last." Mason reported that Waddell's speech was greeted by cries of support, although they wanted to "know . . . which is . . . 'the nearest English port.'" Chew's and Hunt's accounts agree with those of Lining and Mason. Lining, Journal, 2, 3, 4 August 1865; Mason, Journal 4, 5 August 1865; Chew, Journal, 6, 13 August 1865; Hunt, *Last Cruiser,* 222–23.

4. Whittle's note that this was Lt. Chew's birthday was erroneous; the correct date was 24 September 1865. It is difficult to explain this error. For almost a month his entries were rather sparse. He was upset by the news that the Confederacy had fallen and was extremely worried about his family. Surgeon Lining on 5 October expressed concern about Whittle's distress. It is possible that Lt. Whittle wrote some of the entries after 2 August 1865, later than the actual date of the events, but probably while still aboard the vessel. Chew, Journal, 24 September 1865; Lining, Journal, 5 October 1865.

5. Cornelius Hunt related that the *Shenandoah* raced another ship and, when it pulled away, exchanged signals with her and found her to be a sister ship built by the same firm that had built the *Sea King*. Hunt is probably wrong about the exchange of signals, since Waddell did not want the ship's identity or location revealed, but could be correct about the origin of the other ship. Hunt, *Last Cruiser,* 225–26.

6. Lt. Whittle failed to record that the captain's decision to add more sail resulted in an accident. As Mason related it, "the foreroyal yard rope parted & the yard came down by the run as far as the topmast-rigging where the parral caught in the cross-

trees & enabled the men to secure it." The parral was damaged and a rope parral substituted. Two men were injured. Mason, Journal, 15 September 1865.

7. Lt. Whittle evidently left out a word or simply in haste composed an obscure sentence. The sentence is printed exactly as written.

Chapter 9

1. The petition published in the *ORN* listed only 71 names. If the names of the officers who supported Waddell's decision are counted, the total comes to 76. *ORN*, ser, 1, 3:782–83.

2. After Waddell took the ship around Cape Horn, two petitions from officers requested the Captain to steer for Cape Town. Two more, from officers and crew, supported continuing to a European port. Lt. Chew, after a heated council of the lieutenants had backed the captain, asked the captain to state specifically where they were going. His indefinite reply prompted the following comment in Chew's journal: "Ah! it seems indecision continues the reign begun at the Desertas in Oct. of last year." Horan, *Waddell*, 179; *ORN*, ser. 1, 3:779–83; Hunt, *Last Cruiser*, 222–23; Chew, Journal, 29 September 1865.

3. No evidence has been uncovered to indicate that this duel between McNulty and Whittle took place. The incident seems to have been forgotten in the anxiety preceding the release of the officers and crew by the British. Mason went into considerable detail on the possibility of a duel. Lining also wrote an extended account of the incident. Neither Chew nor Hunt included the incident in their accounts. Captain Waddell's Memoirs also failed to mention it. According to Mason he learned of it by accident, as Whittle, McNulty, Lee, and Scales kept knowledge of the challenge very close. Mason, Journal, 12, 13 October 1865; Lining, Journal, 11, 12 October 1865.

4. Lt. Chew devoted nearly two pages of his journal to describing his "letting everything fly," including a comment made by the captain that he had heard of it but had never seen it before. But he did not mention that the executive officer had come on deck. Chew, Journal, 16 October 1865.

5. The captain's account of this incident was first related in his notes on the voyage. Waddell later stated that he had been told this ship was the *Saranac*, under Captain Walke. Waddell, Notes, *ORN*, ser.1, 3:833–34; Horan, *Waddell*, 181.

6. Dr. Lining remarked: "William Bill, a native of Maui . . . died. . . . Poor fellow! he had been suffering from Venerial for a long time & was covered with ulcers all about the throat a[nd] chest. It must have attacked his internal organs as well, as he had all the symptoms of sub acute inflammation of the brain & chest. I had very little hope that he would live." Lining, Journal, 26 October 1865.

7. The captain read the burial service from the *Book of Common Prayer*. Surgeon Lining thought the ceremony "very badly managed." For some reason Mason said the first lieutenant read the service. It is possible that Whittle read a portion of it. Lining, Journal, 27 October 1865; Chew, Journal, 27 October 1865; Mason, Journal, 27 October 1865.

8. Dr. Lining noted that Sgt. Canning died at 5:45 P.M. "His disease was 'Phthisis'

brought on by a gun shot wound through the right lung, which he said, was received at the battle of 'Shiloh' while he was serving on Gen'l Polk's staff—There is something in the history of this man that none of us know. . . . In fact we know nothing about him. And now after having overhauled all his things nothing can be found which will give a clue to where any of his people are, or who he has been." Midshipman Mason had promised to take care of Canning's possessions and see that his friends and relatives received them. But no address was found in his notebook or anywhere among his papers. Upon arrival in Liverpool, Mason tried to contact Canning's wife, supposedly in St. Germain, and relatives. He was unsuccessful, advertisements turning up some strange letters and characters. One of the last entries in Mason's journal, however, indicated a letter had arrived from a man claiming to be Canning's brother. Unfortunately Mason's journal ends shortly after that with no further information given about Canning. Hunt also indicated letters were sent to Paris to try locate Canning's wife. Lining, Journal, 30 October 1865; Mason, Journal, 30, 31 October, 12, 14, 17, 22 November 1865; Hunt, *Last Cruiser,* 235–37.

9. Lining noted that he was due $547.19 but got $77.06. "It reverses the old saying of more days more money, for now it is more days less money." Lining, Journal, 3 November 1865.

10. The officers and crew received their pay. Lt. Grimball noted at the end of the copy he made of the log of the *Shenandoah,* "The Confederate agent Capt. J. D. Bulloch has saved our pay for us." Lt. Grimball later wrote his father that he had received £300 before leaving England. Grimball, Shenandoah Log, note following entry of 5 November 1865; John Grimball to John B. Grimball, 22 February 1866, in Grimball Papers, Duke University.

Epilogue

1. Whittle, "Shenandoah Cruise," 256–57.

2. Lining noted that when the pilot hailed the ship and asked her name, Bulloch, officer of the deck, answered, "Araminta" to prevent their arrival from being reported by the pilot boat before they anchored. "Whittle thought [this] very disgraceful." Chew recorded the incident but said they told the pilot the *Shenandoah* "was the 'Armenian,' 92 days from Calcutta." The discrepancy between these two sources is puzzling. Lloyd's listed the names of both ships. We are inclined to accept Lining's account since he seems to have been writing daily journal entries and specifically stated he was present when the pilot came aboard. Chew, on the other hand, began his entry on 4 November 1865, mentioned 5 November in the entry, and carried it up to 6 November and beyond. He certainly wrote much of the entry later than 6 November 1865. Yet he specifically said the ship was "92 days from Calcutta"; Lloyds listed the *Armenian* as being from Calcutta. The length of the ship was nearer to *Shenandoah's* length. The *Araminta* was nearly 100 feet shorter. Without further evidence, resolution of this problem seems impossible. What is clear, however, is that the *Shenandoah* continued its subterfuge to the very last. Hunt's version of the boarding of the pilot is mostly fiction. Lining, Journal, 6 November 1865; Chew, Journal, entry beginning

with 4 November 1865 [p. 241]; *Lloyds Register of British and Foreign Shipping; from 1st July 1865 to the 30th June 1866* (London: Cox and Wyman Printers, 1865), nos. 827 and 926; Hunt, *Last Cruiser,* 241.

3. The word "unprecedentedly" was misspelled in the (1907) *SHSP* edition. It had been spelled correctly in the speech given in 1897 and in the 1910 publication. Whittle, "Shenandoah Cruise," 257; Whittle, *Cruises of the Shenandoah and Nashville,* 22; "Address of William C. Whittle, Jr., (1897)," typed copy furnished by Professor William M. Dabney, University of New Mexico.

Bibliographical Essay

This study is primarily based upon original sources. During the Civil War more individuals participated in the armies than in the navies, and manuscript sources of the naval participants in the war are less numerous than those of army participants. Yet naval officers often kept excellent personal journals; where they exist they offer invaluable information about naval warfare and shipboard life.

One of the best of the naval accounts is the journal kept by William Conway Whittle, Jr., while he was executive officer of the CSS *Shenandoah*. The journal, which is in the Eleanor S. Brockenbrough Library of the Museum of the Confederacy in Richmond, Virginia, must be supplemented with material from other manuscript and printed sources, many of which are also in the museum's library. When the Whittle family donated this journal to the museum, it joined two other journals kept on board the *Shenandoah*. The most informative of these is that of Surgeon Charles Edward Lining. Many of the surgeon's comments on the health and mental condition of the officers and crew of the *Shenandoah* reveal the tensions and clashes that occurred on the voyage.

The third journal available at the Museum of the Confederacy is in the papers of John Thomson Mason. Mason had a close connection with Whittle; Mason, Whittle, Sidney Smith Lee, Jr., and Orris A. Browne, all officers on the *Shenandoah*, migrated to Argentina in January 1866. Mason and Browne returned to Virginia in 1867 and Whittle in 1868, probably accompanied by Lee. The son of Major Issac S. Rowland, who died in the Mexican war, Mason's name was legally changed at the request of his maternal grandfather. James I. Waddell, captain of the *Shenandoah*, required Midshipmen Mason and

Browne to keep journals which he wished to see from time to time. Mason kept a private journal, which he concealed from the captain. Although kept intermittently, with long passages in which he brought events up to the current day, Mason's journal records many important incidents of the *Shenandoah*'s cruise and comments about the men aboard it.

Other papers in the Brockenbrough Library were useful to this project, especially the "Shipping Articles of the C.S.S. Shenandoah," which helped clarify many names and dates in the Whittle journal. The papers of Thomas Rowland, brother of John Thomson Mason, helped with family connections. Many of the photographs of the officers are from the Museum of the Confederacy.

Francis Thornton Chew also kept a journal aboard the *Shenandoah*. It is in the Chew Papers in the Southern Historical Collection, at the University of North Carolina, Chapel Hill. Also among these papers is an unfinished autobiography by Chew detailing life at Annapolis and his experiences in the Confederate navy prior to being ordered to Europe. Lieutenant Chew chronicled his experiences in learning to sail, for he admitted he had little experience on the high seas prior to embarking on the *Shenandoah*. Since much of the shipboard life at sea was new to him, he recorded details about events and life on the ship not found in other sources. It suffers from the same difficulty as found in Mason's journal: Chew's entries are not always current.

Papers of the Whittle family, other than William C. Whittle's journal, are in various archives or private collections. In Norfolk two Whittle granddaughters retained papers. The Elizabeth Calvert Page Dabney Papers are in the Manuscripts Department, Perry Library, Old Dominion University. Mary Beverley Dabney retained family papers still in a private collection. A grandson, Professor William M. Dabney at the University of New Mexico, furnished copies of several documents in his possession. The William C. Whittle, Jr. Papers in the Sargeant Room, Kirn Memorial Library, Norfolk, contain letters from James D. Bulloch to Samuel Barron regarding the purchase of the *Sea King* and the selection of officers for the *Shenandoah* in 1864, an 1863 diary kept by Whittle, and his Morning Order Book from the *Shenandoah*. The Lewis Neale Whittle Papers in the Southern Historical Collection at the University of North Carolina at Chapel Hill contain letters from William C. Whittle, Jr. when he was on the CSS *Chattahooche* in Georgia as well as other family letters. The journal of William C. Whittle, Sr. and other papers are in the Stafford Gorman Whittle Papers, in the Manuscripts Department, Corcoran Library, University of Virginia, Charlottesville. The Conway Whittle Family Papers, in the Manuscripts Department, the Earl Greg Swem Library in Williamsburg, Virginia, contain numerous letters from William C. Whittle,

Sr., to relatives, especially his cousin, Mrs. Frances Whittle Lewis. Also at William and Mary are the Whittle-Greene Family Papers containing family letters and the sixty-volume diary kept by Chloe Whittle Greene, Conway Whittle's daughter.

Letters of John Grimball to his father, in the John Berkley Grimball Papers at Duke University, Durham, North Carolina, were helpful. Grimball kept a journal on the ship, for he copied portions of it in letters to his father. Supplementing these letters were the John Berkley Grimball Diary, the Grimball Family Papers, and the Meta Morris Grimball Diary in the Southern Historical Collection at the University of North Carolina. The Virginia Historical Society, in Richmond, holds the Minor Family Papers, the Thom Family Papers, the Barron Family Papers, and the John Kirkwood Mitchell Papers, all of which contain some correspondence from or about William C. Whittle, Jr. The Barron Papers, for instance, contain a long informative letter from Whittle, in Argentina, to Barron. Some Barron Papers are at William and Mary. Waddell Family Papers at the North Carolina Department of Archives and History, Raleigh, were helpful.

The logs of the Shenandoah deserve special mention. They are found at the Chicago Historical Society, the Museum of the Confederacy, the Charleston Library Association, and the North Carolina State Archives. Looking at these logs benefitted the authors since some contained additional information not included elsewhere. Irvine S. Bulloch began the log located in the Chicago Historical Society, for he signed each entry when he was watch officer, whereas "(Signed)" is placed before the name of the other watch officer's entries. He stopped signing entries on 11 November 1864 when he was removed from the watch bill to devote full time as navigator or pilot. Other officers then kept this log, for the writing changes from time to time. After 2 August 1865 only summaries were entered, and entries stopped entirely on 23 October. This volume also contained loose sheets listing farm supplies probably purchased when the four officers bought a farm in Argentina. The names of Whittle, Smith Lee, Orris Browne, and John T. Mason are found on the fly leaf of the volume. The Chicago Historical Society microfilmed this log in 1977. John Grimball copied the log while the Shenandoah sailed back to Liverpool, England, and added manuscript notes at the end. This log, owned by the Charleston Library Society, was published in microfiche in Spartanburg, South Carolina, by The Reprint Company, 1981. The log kept by John Thomson Mason is in the Museum of the Confederacy. An abstract of the log was published in volume 3 of the *Official Records of the Union and Confederate Navies*. The only manuscript log that has in it the shift from sea time to civil time noted in the abstract is in the James Iredell Waddell Papers at the North Carolina State Archives in Raleigh. This indicates that either this log, or another copy, was used in the preparation of that abstract. The North Carolina Department of Archives and History microfilmed this log.

Public Documents

Of the numbers of United States government publications on the Civil War, the main source for this work was Department of the Navy, *Official Records of the Union and Confederate Navies in the War of the Rebellion* (Washington, D.C.: U.S. Government Printing Office, 1894–1927), thirty volumes. The first three volumes cover the cruisers and efforts to capture them. Volume 3 contains the material on the *Shenandoah:* the abstract of the log, the notes of the captain of the *Shenandoah,* James Iredell Waddell, orders, and correspondence concerning the expedition. Another published collection that aided the research were the documents usually referred to collectively as the "Alabama Claims," published by the U.S. Congress, Senate Committee on Foreign Relations, in *Alabama Claims,* Senate Doc. No. 11, 41st Cong., 1st sess. (Washington, D.C.: U.S. Government Printing Office, 1869). Other material on the cruisers was published by the U.S. Congress, House Committee of Foreign Affairs, in *Geneva Arbitration, British Case and Evidence,* House Exec. Doc. No. 282, 42d Cong., 2d Sess. (Washington, D.C.: U.S. Government Printing Office, 1872). Other useful Federal publications were Department of the Navy, Naval History Division, compilers, *Civil War Naval Chronology, 1861–1865* (Washington, D.C.: U.S. Government Printing Office, 1971), and Department of the Navy, Office of Naval Records and Library. *Register of Officers of the Confederate States Navy: 1861–1865.* The War Department's major collection of documents on the Civil War, *War of the Rebellion: A Compilation of the Official Records of the Union and Confederate Armies,* 130 volumes (Washington, D.C.: U.S. Government Printing Office, 1880–1901), was referred to in this study only a few times, mostly in connection with the exchange of prisoners of war.

Published Memoirs, Diaries, and Correspondence

The published material bearing on the voyage of the *Shenandoah* is rather extensive. The absolutely indispensable publication is James Dunwody Bulloch's two-volume work, *The Secret Service of the Confederate States in Europe, or How the Confederate Cruisers were Equipped* (Liverpool, 1883; reprinted, with a new introduction by Philip Van Doren Stern, New York and London: Thomas Yoseloff, 1959). Bulloch successfully sent out the *Alabama,* the *Florida* and the *Shenandoah* as cruisers, as well as several blockade runners. He also negotiated for the building of ironclads but had limited success. Several of the officers of the *Shenandoah* published accounts of the voyage. The earliest of these, Cornelius F. Hunt, *The Shenandoah; or the Last Confederate Cruiser* (New York: G. W. Carlton & Co, and London: S. Lawson and Co., 1867), was reprinted in 1910 by W. Abbott in New York. One must use Hunt with care as many incidents mentioned, while they occurred, did not happen at the time or place where Hunt says they did. There are also some descriptions of events that seem to be fictional; they do not agree with contemporaneous journal accounts. James I. Waddell's memoirs were published in part as notes in volume 3 of the official records. The full document was published as *C.S.S. Shenandoah: The Memoirs of Lieutenant James I. Waddell, C.S.N.*, edited with an introduction by James David Horan (New York: Crown Publishers, 1960).

William C. Whittle, Jr. wrote several articles that were printed in the *Southern Historical Society Papers* (SHSP). The first of these was "The Opening of the Lower Mississippi in 1862—A Reply to Admiral Porter," *SHSP* 13 (1885):560–72. He was in demand as a speaker and on 3 June 1897 gave a speech on the *Shenandoah* to the Stonewall Camp of the United Confederate Veterans. This was published as "The Cruise of the Shenandoah," in *SHSP* 35 (1907):235–58. Whittle's experiences on the *Nashville* were printed as "The Cruise of the C.S. Steamer Nashville," in *SHSP* 29 (1901):207–12. Whittle combined these accounts in *Cruises of the Confederate States Steamers "Shenandoah" and "Nashville,"* privately printed in Norfolk, Virginia, in 1910. Portions of Whittle's account of the *Shenandoah*'s adventures are included in this work to cover periods removed from the original manuscript or not included in the journal. Other articles on the *Shenandoah* in the *Southern Historical Society Papers* were John Grimball, "The Cruise of the Shenandoah," *SHSP* 25 (1897):116–26, and James Riley, "The Shenandoah" [Account told to Riley by Dr. F. J. McNulty of Boston], *SHSP* 21 (1893):165–76.

Some officers published accounts in other periodicals. Dabney Minor Scales wrote a short article, "The Cruise of the Shenandoah," for *The Confederate Veteran* 12 (1904):489–90, which also contained an obituary of John Thomson Mason written by Whittle. Mason wrote the last article in a series on Confederate raiders for *Century Magazine*, "Confederate Commerce Destroyers: IV, The Last of the Confederate Cruisers," *Century Magazine* 54, n.s. 34 (August 1898):600–610. Surgeon Charles E. Lining's account "Cruise of the Confederate Steamship 'Shenandoah,'" was posthumously published by the *Tennessee Historical Magazine* 8 (July 1924):102–11.

Another helpful published source was Douglas French Forrest's *Odyssey in Gray: A Diary of Confederate Service, 1863–1865*, edited by William N. Still, Jr. (Richmond: Virginia State Library, 1979). Forrest's entries when he was in Paris, France, described what life was like for the Confederate naval personnel living there. Also helpful in setting the scene in Europe was Edward C. Anderson, *Confederate Foreign Agent: The European Diary of Major Edward C. Anderson,* edited with prologue and epilogue by W. Stanley Hoole (University, Ala.: Confederate Publishing Company, 1976). John McIntosh Kell, *Recollections of a Naval Life, Including the Cruises of the Confederate States Steamers "Sumter" and "Alabama"* (Washington, D.C.: The Neale Company, 1901), included information on Confederate practices in seizing Union ships and information on crewmen who later served on the *Shenandoah.* Arthur Sinclair, Whittle's cousin, also included information on men who served on both the *Alabama* and the *Shenandoah* in his *Two Years Aboard the Alabama* (Boston: Lee and Shepherd, 1896; reprinted, with notes and introduction by William N. Still, Annapolis, Md.: Naval Institute Press, 1989).

Secondary Sources

Several secondary works aided the editors in writing the introduction and explanatory endnotes. William S. Dudley, *Going South: U.S. Navy Officer Resignations & Dismissals on the Eve of the Civil War* (Washington, D.C.: Naval Historical Foundation, 1981) contained information on when various naval officers left the Union navy and joined the Confederate navy. Two accounts of the *Shenandoah*'s cruise were published in the 1940s. Stanley F. Horn, *Gallant Rebel: The Fabulous Cruise of the C.S.S. Shenandoah* (New Brunswick, N.J.: Rutgers University Press, 1947), is a straightforward narrative of the journey. Murray Morgan, *Dixie Raider: The Saga of the C.S.S. Shenandoah* (New York: E. P. Dutton, Inc., 1948), was based in part on the accounts of the ships the *Shenandoah* captured and offers a different perspective. A work of great assistance was John Bockstoce, *Whales, Ice and Men: The History of Whaling in the Western Arctic* (Seattle and London: University of Washington Press, in association with the New Bedford Whaling Museum, 1986), which greatly facilitated identifying the various ships captured in the Arctic. George W. Dalzell, *The Flight from the Flag: The Continuing Effect of the Civil War upon the American Carrying Trade* (Chapel Hill: University of North Carolina Press, 1940), discusses the impact of raiders like the *Shenandoah.*

Several works supplemented the primary sources on Whittle's early life and his four years at Annapolis. Peter Karsten, *The Naval Aristocracy: The Golden Age of Annapolis and the Emergence of Modern American Navalism* (New York: The Free Press, 1972), places the Whittle family in that aristocracy. Charles Todorich, *The Spirited Years: A History of the Antebellum Naval Academy* (Annapolis, Md.: Naval Institute Press, 1984), gives an excellent account of the life of the midshipmen and their academic preparation. Another good account is Edward Chauncey Marshall, *History of the United States Na-*

val Academy (New York: D. Van Nostrand, 1962). Murat Halstead, *Life and Achievements of Admiral Dewey from Montpelier to Manila* (Chicago: Our Possessions Publishing Company, 1899), although clearly a biography cashing in on Dewey's exploits in Manila Bay, contained informative documents relating to the lives of midshipmen in Dewey and Whittle's class at Annapolis.

A number of secondary works helped place the exploits of the *Shenandoah* in the context of the larger Civil War. An indispensable older work was John Thomas Scharf, *History of the Confederate States Navy* (New York: Rogers & Sherwood, 1887), primarily for the factual information and the biographical material it contained. A shorter well-written work is *The Confederate Navy: The Ships, Men and Organization, 1861–65* (Annapolis, Md.: Naval Institute Press and Conway Maritime Press, 1997), edited by William N. Still, Jr., with articles by William S. Dudley, Robert M. Browning, et al. Frank J. Merli, *Great Britain and the Confederate Navy, 1861–1865* (Bloomington: Indiana University Press, 1970), covers naval and diplomatic activity during the Civil War. Warren F. Spencer, in *The Confederate Navy in Europe* (Tuscaloosa: University of Alabama Press, 1983), expands that with extensive coverage of the *Shenandoah*. Philip Van Doren Stern, in *The Confederate Navy: A Pictorial History* (New York: Doubleday & Company, 1962), devotes a chapter to the *Shenandoah*, including naval architectural drawings of the ship, and he covered diplomacy of the conflict in *When the Guns Roared: World Aspects of the American Civil War* (Garden City, N.Y.: Doubleday & Co., 1965). Maxine Turner, *Navy Gray: A Story of the Confederate Navy on the Chattahoochee and Apalachicola Rivers* (Tuscaloosa and London: University of Alabama Press, 1988), treats a little-known bit of naval activity in which Whittle served. The visit of the *Shenandoah* to Melbourne is well documented in Cyril Pearl, *Rebel Down Under: When the Shenandoah Shook Melbourne, 1865* (Melbourne: William Heinemann, 1970). A more recent work by Raimondo Luraghi, *A History of the Confederate Navy* (Annapolis, Md.: Naval Institute Press, 1996), gives a modern European insight to the naval Civil War.

Several works we consulted were valuable in explaining the daily activity of sailing and navigating the ship, disciplining the crew, and understanding the lines of governmental control. James E. Valle, *Rocks & Shoals: Order and Discipline in the Old Navy, 1800–1861* (Annapolis, Md.: Naval Institute Press, 1980), dealt with questions of discipline. D. W. Waters, *The Art of Navigation in Elizabethan and Early Stuart Times* (New Haven, Conn.: Yale University Press, 1958), cleared up questions of archaic navigation practices. On navigation questions we also consulted T. S. Lecky, *Wrinkles in Practical Navigation* (London: George Philip & Son, Ltd., 1917). Herman Melville, in his autobiographical novel, *White Jacket, or the World in a Man-of-War* (New York: Harper, 1850; reprint, Evanston and Chicago: Northwestern University and the Newberry Library, 1970), gives vivid descriptions of life aboard a nineteenth-century man-of-war. Tom Henderson Wells, *The Confederate Navy: A Study in Organization* (University, Ala.: University of Alabama Press, 1971), deals with the difficulties the Confederate naval authorities confronted. For questions concerning rigging, sails, equipment, and general seamanship we consulted John Harland, *Seamanship in the Age of Sail: An Account of the Shiphandling of the Sailing Man-of-War 1600–1860* (Annapolis, Md.: Naval Institute Press, 1984, 1992). An extremely handy and informative book on technical aspects of sailing ships is *The Lore of Sail* by William Avery Baker, Sam Svensson, and Rolf Scheen (New York: Facts on File, 1983). It will be especially useful for readers unfamiliar with nineteenth-century sailing ships.

Only a few periodical articles were of much assistance in this work. Two articles by William N. Still, Jr., in *Civil War Times, Illustrated,* were the most important. Still covered the daily lives of the seamen in "The Common Sailor, Part I: Yankee Bluejackets" (24 [February 1985]:24–39) and "The Common Sailor, Part II: Confederate Tars" (24 [March 1985)]:12–19). Richard S. West, "The Superintendents of the Naval Academy," *Proceedings of the United States Naval Institute* 72 (April 1946):60–61, gives information on the education of midshipmen at Annapolis. Ernest Scott, "The Shenandoah Incident, 1865," *The Victorian Historical Magazine* 11 (September 1926):55–75, explained events in Melbourne. Biographical information on James Dunwody Bulloch was obtained from William P. Roberts, "James Dunwoody [*sic*] Bulloch and the Confederate Navy," *North Carolina Historical Review* 24 (July 1947):315–66. A good article on Waddell and the *Shenandoah* is George W. Groh, "Last of the Rebel Raiders," *American Heritage* 10 (December 1958):48–51.

Index

Abigail, 24, 154, 160, 167

Adams, Charles Francis, 41, 213

Adelaide, 67–68, 129

Alabama, CSS, 2, 10–13, 213

alcohol, 18, 119, 154, 176

Alcott, Henry, 27

Alina, 16, 55–56, 65, 145

Amphitrite Strait, 152, 159, 161

Amsterdam Island, 99

Amukta Island, 177

Anchorage, the, 9

Anna Jane, 20, 65

Annapolis, Maryland, 3

Apalachicola, Florida, 8

Arctic Circle, crossed, 171

Articles of War, 30

Ascension Island (Ponape), 3, 19, 38, 130, 136–141, 178

Aspinwall (Colon, Panama), 5

Atlanta, CSS, 14

Baker, George O., 215

Ballarat, Australia, 24

Baltimore, Maryland, 42, 43

Baracouta, 39, 42, 182, 192

Barron, Samuel, 9, 11–12, 109

Benjamin, Judah P., 9

Behring (Bering) Sea, 161

Bermuda, 9

Bill, William, 29, 207

Blacker, J. C., 19, 136, 200–202

Blake, George S., 5

Blanchard, William, 18

Bombay, 109

Borunsky Island, 162

Brandywine, USS, 70

Brooke, John Mercer, 47

Brooklyn, New York, 42

Brown, W. C., 12, 48

Browne, Orris Applethwait, 14, 23, 28, 41–43, 66, 102, 136

Browne, Dr. Peter, 41

Brunswick, 170

Buenos Ayres, Argentina, 41, 68

Bulloch, Irvine S., 14, 29, 37, 55, 56, 61, 79, 82, 83, 102, 103, 119, 212

Bulloch, James Dunwody, 1, 11, 12, 46, 48, 49

Buchanan, Virginia, 9, 39,

Burnside, Ambrose, 6

Calais, France, 51

Canning, George P., 208

Cape Alevina, 158

Cape Clear, 209, 210

Cape Horn, 39, 192, 193

Cape Narvin, 165

Cape Town, 39, 196

Cape Verde Islands, 204, 205
capturing the crew, 18
Carter, Robert R., 11, 47, 48
Catherine, 169
Chagulak Island, 174
Challenge to duel, 200–202
Charleston, fall of, 38
Charleston, 43,
"Charley," 18–19
Charter Oak, 61
Chattahooche, CSS, 7, 8
Chew, Francis Thornton, 2, 11, 12,
    34, 37, 43, 72, 90–93, 95, 102,
    136, 188
Coaling, 113
Colon, Panama, 5
Confederate raiders, 46–47
Confederate States Navy, 46
Congress, 170
Copper Island, 163
Corbett, Peter Suther, 12, 13, 49, 51, 56
Cornubia, 9
Covington, 170
Cunningham's self-reefing topsails,
    59, 78
Cyane, CSS, 14

D. Godfrey, 63–65
Dale, USS, 3
Darling, Sir Charles H., 109
David Brown, 107
Davies, Mary Ann, 3
Davies, William, 3
Davis, Jefferson, 38
Deaths, William Bill, 207; George F.
    Canning, 208
Decatur, USS, 3
Delphine, 18, 19, 98, 101
Desertas, 49, 52
Desertion, 110, 113
Dewey, George, 4
Dia del Mario, 81
Diego Ramererz Rock, 192
Diomede Island, 170
Discipline, 21–23, 26
Donegal, HMS, 40–41, 212
Drummond Island, 127–128
Duncan, Johnson K., 7

Earl of Clarendon, 41
Edward, 2, 82
Edward Carey, 136, 139
Eldridge, Captain, 215
engines, 27
England, 52
Erlanger, Emile, 10
Euphrates, 166

Falkland Islands, 195
Farragut, David G., 6
Fauntleroy, Charles M., 11
Favorite, 170
Florida, CSS, 2, 72, 108
Ford, Marcellus, 8
Foreign Enlistment Act, 112
Forrest, Douglas French, 10
Forrest, French, Sr., 8
Fox, Gustavus Vasa, 6
free black sailors, 20
friction among officers, 34
Fronkonronskey, 152
Funchal, Madeira 12, 49

Games, 32, 102–103, 104
General Pike, 20, 169
General Williams, 168
Georgian Islands and Shag Rock, 193
Gilman, Samuel J., 20, 61–63
Gipsey, 169
Goldsborough, Louis Malesherbes, 4
Grimball, John, 2, 10, 12, 14, 43, 44, 59,
    62, 72, 87, 88, 99, 103, 104, 106, 108,
    124, 125, 136, 141, 142, 157, 181, 196

Halifax, Nova Scotia, 9
Hall, Thomas, 23
Hallett, H. W., 65
Harvest, 136, 215, 140
Harwood, George, 25
Hector, 136, 139
Henderson Island, 180
Hillman, 170
Hunt, Cornelius, 25, 55, 56, 81, 169

Illnesses on *Shenandoah,* 27–30, 62, 79,
    102, 124, 125, 141, 176, 180, 220
Inspection (Sunday morning), 30

Isaac Howland, 170
Isabella, 169

James Maury, 20, 170
Jireh Swift, 167, 168
Johnston, Albert Sidney, 206
Jones, Catesby ap Roger, 7
Juarez, Benito, 5

Kamchatska, 152, 154, 159
Kate Prince, 20, 67
Kell, John McIntosh, 5, 10
King of Ponape. *See* Nananierikie

Laird rams, 11
Landis, CSS, 7
Laurel, 12, 49, 50, 51
Lee, Robert E., 38, 166
Lee, Sidney Smith, Jr., 14, 41–43, 73, 90,
    119, 129, 136, 181, 196, 201
Lincoln, Abraham, 38, 108, 120, 182
Lining, Charles Edward, 2, 10, 14, 16, 43,
    52, 59, 69, 81, 103, 104, 109, 111, 189,
    201, 202
Liverpool, 36, 39, 40, 209, 210
livestock, 3
Lizzie M. Stacey, 70
Louisiana, CSS, 6, 7
Lynch, John, 24, 25, 154

Madeira, 36, 49, 204
Maffit, John Newland, 5
magazine, construction of, 94, com-
    pleted, 106
Mallory, Stephen J., 23
manaverlings, 66
Manning, Thomas S., 160, 169
Martha (2), 170
Mason, John Thomson, 2, 23, 26, 28,
    41–43, 56, 61, 136
Maury, Matthew Fontaine, 47
McAskill Island, 131
McNulty, Frederick, 40, 73, 102, 104, 127,
    197, 200–204, 202, 209
Mecklenburg County, Virginia, 3
Melbourne, Australia, ix, 20, 107, 108,
    112, 178
Mexico, 43

Milo, 167, 178
Minor, John F., 23, 35, 82, 83, 136
Minor, Robert Dabney, 5, 7, 42
Missouri, 43
Mitchell, John K., 7
Mogul, 55
morale, 34
Mugguffeney, Ernest, (Frank Curran or
    Cunan), 25
Murdaugh, William R., 4, 12

Nananierikie (King of Ponape), 137
Nashville, CSS, 5, 6, 208
Nassau, 170
Naval Academy, United States, 3–5, 13, 43
New Orleans, Battle of (1815), 101
New Orleans, fall of, 6–7
New Orleans, CSS, 14
New York City, 43
Nichols, Mrs. William G., 105, 109
Nichols, William G., 98
Nile, 20, 170
Nimrod, (British ship), 104
Nimrod, 169
Norfolk, Virginia, 3
Norfolk and Western Railroad, 42
North, James H., 10
Nye, Ebenezer, 24, 154, 160

O'Brien, Matthew, 14, 27, 77, 81, 105, 119
Officers of CSS *Shenandoah,* 50. *See also
    names of individuals*
Ohio, USS, 3
Okhotsk, Sea of, 38, 152
Old Bay Line, 42
Olski, Island, 158
Onekotan Island, 152
O'Shea, John, 29, 60, 94

Pacific Mail Line, 42
Page, John, 41
Page, Thomas Jefferson, 41
Palmetto State, CSS, 14
pardons, 41, 42
Patrick Henry, CSS, 14
Pattie, 64, 69, 74, 78, 87, 96, 98, 99, 104,
    109, 123, 124, 126, 161, 164, 177, 184,
    186, 188, 191, 197, 204, 205, 208

Paynter, J. C., 212
Pearl, 136, 215
Pegram, Robert B., 6
Pelin, 130
Pendergrast, Mr., 68–69
piracy, 41, 196
Point de Galle, Ceylon, 55
Ponape. *See Ascension Island*
Pontchartrain, CSS, 14
Porter, David Dixon, 7
Preble, USS, 5
prize court, 16
provisions, 17, 25
punishments of crew members, 60, 76,
    77, 80, 81, 86, 87, 93, 95, 96, 100, 101,
    103, 106, 115, 119, 123, 126, 127, 154,
    169, 177, 180, 189, 190, 200

Raymond, Peter, 23, 28
Ramsey, John F., 12, 13, 39, 51
Rappahannock, CSS, 10, 13, 51, 54
Re-enlistments of crew, 123
Repairs to ship, 86–87, 104–105, 110, 112,
    114–115, 121, 185
Rest and recreation, 31
Richmond, Virginia, 38
Robertson, Moses, 109
Rosario, Argentina, 41, 42
Rowe, Lewis, 23, 28
Royal Saxon, 65

Sailing, 26
St. Jona's Island, 154, 155
St. Lawrence Island, 168
St. Paul's Island, 99–100
San Francisco, 38, 39, 178
San Jacinto, USS, 6
Saratoga, USS, 5
Savannah, 38
Savannah, CSS, 14
Savannah, USS, 5
Scales, Dabney Minor, 12, 14, 29, 43, 77,
    79, 90, 95, 119, 124, 127, 136, 146, 157,
    196, 201
Schrinsky Island, 161, 162
Sea King, 11, 12, 13, 48, 49, 51, 101, 212
Sea of Okhotsk, 38, 152

sea time, 65
Shenandoah, CSS, ix, 2, 13, 15, 39, 51–
    53, 183
Siberia, 154
Sidney, Australia, 166
Sinclair, Arthur, 3, 9, 24, 111, 160
Sinclair, Elizabeth Beverley, 3
Sinclair, George Terry, 3, 10
Sinclair, William, 3, 10
Smith, William Breedlove, 14
Sophia Thornton, 167
Southern Historical Society Papers, 52
Soutter, James T., 10
"Splice the main brace," 23
Spence, James, 70
Spence, Louisa, 10
Staples, Everett, 20, 56, 58, 65, 98
Stern, Philip Van Doren, 1
storms, 120
stowaways, 113, 114
Stribling, Cornelius K., 4
Strong's Island (Onalan), 130–131
Sultan of Zanzibar, 214
Susan, 66–67
Susan Abigail, 167
Swanton, William, 25
Sydney, Australia, 39

Tahiti, 183
Tausk Bay, 155, 158
Trent affair, 5–6
Tristan d'Acunha, 20, 80, 82, 84
Tropic of Capricorn, 198
Tuscarora, USS, 6
Tuskar Light House, 212
Tuxpan, Mexico, 3

United Confederate Veterans, 42, 43, 45
United States Navy, 46
University of Virginia, 43

Victoria, Australia, 24
Virginia Bank and Trust Company, 42
Virginia Military Institute, 47

Waddell, James Iredell, 12, 13, 34, 36–42,
    44, 47, 51, 52, 119, 175

wardroom, 38
War of 1812, 45
Washington, D.C., 43
Washington, George, 3, 115
water, fresh, 25
Waverley, 70
Waymouth (Weynouth?), Mr., 24, 111
W. Burton, CSS, 7
Welles, Gideon, 6
West Australian, 192
Whittle family, 3, 115, 182, 198
Whittle, Conway, 3, 4
Whittle, Fortescue, 3
Whittle, James, 3
Whittle, John Samuel, 3
Whittle, Stafford, 9

Whittle, William Conway, Jr., ix, 3, 4, 16,
    41, 44, 52; education, 3–5, Waddell's
    interference, 37; fears for family after
    Appomatox, 39; challenged to duel by
    McNulty, 40; clashes with Waddell,
    89–90, 90–93, 94–95, 102, 116–118,
    124, 127, 155
Whittle, William Conway, Sr., 3, 6, 42,
    109, 187
Wilkes, Charles, 6
William C. Nye, 169
William Thompson, 166, 167
Williams, James P., 68
Williams, John, 18, 23, 86, 101, 103, 106
Wilmington, North Carolina, 38, 160
Wright, Richard, 11, 12, 48, 49